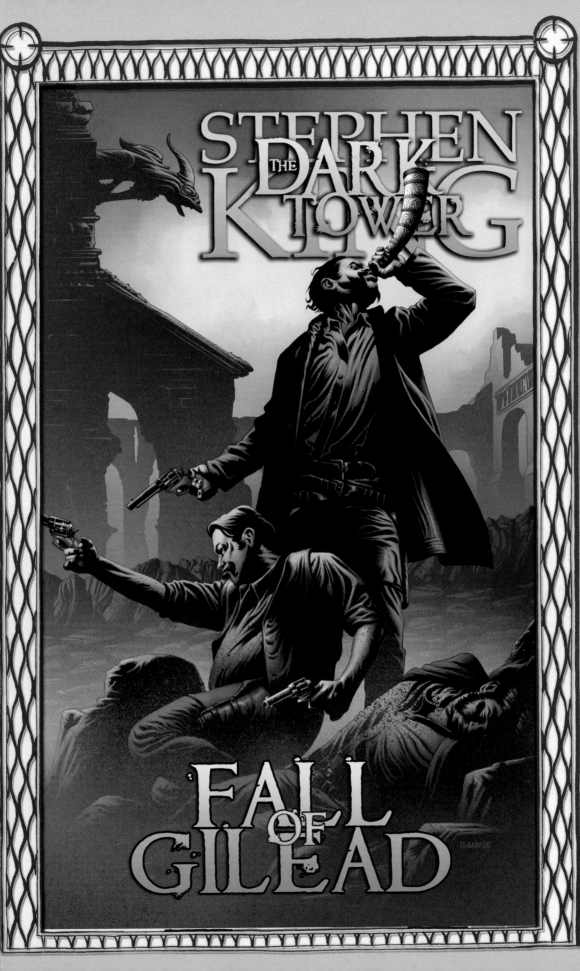

STEPHEN KING

THE DARK TOWER

FALL OF GILEAD

STEPHEN KING

THE DARK TOWER

FALL OF GILEAD

CREATIVE DIRECTOR AND EXECUTIVE DIRECTOR
STEPHEN KING

THE SORCERER
PLOT AND SCRIPT
ROBIN FURTH

ART
RICHARD ISANOVE

LETTERING
CHRIS ELIOPOULOS

FALL OF GILEAD
PLOTTING AND CONSULTATION
ROBIN FURTH

SCRIPT
PETER DAVID

ART
RICHARD ISANOVE

COLOR ASSISTS
DEAN WHITE

LETTERING
CHRIS ELIOPOULOS

ASSISTANT EDITOR
MICHAEL HORWITZ

EDITORS
RALPH MACCHIO & LAUREN SANKOVITCH

COVER ART
RICHARD ISANOVE

COLLECTION EDITOR
MARK D. BEAZLEY

ASSISTANT EDITORS
JOHN DENNING AND ALEX STARBUCK

EDITOR, SPECIAL PROJECTS
JENNIFER GRÜNWALD

SENIOR EDITOR, SPECIAL PROJECTS
JEFF YOUNGQUIST

SENIOR VICE PRESIDENT OF SALES
DAVID GABRIEL

SENIOR VICE PRESIDENT OF STRATEGIC DEVELOPMENT
RUWAN JAYATILLEKE

BOOK DESIGN
SPRING HOTELING AND PATRICK McGRATH

EDITOR IN CHIEF
JOE QUESADA

PUBLISHER
DAN BUCKLEY

SPECIAL THANKS TO CHUCK VERRILL, MARSHA DEFILIPPO,
RALPH VICINANZA, BARBARA ANN McINTYRE, BRIAN STARK,
JIM NAUSEDAS, JIM McCANN, ARUNE SINGH, CHRIS ALLO,
JEFF SUTER, JOHN BARBER & JIM CALAFIORE

FOR MORE INFORMATION ON DARK TOWER COMICS, VISIT MARVEL.COM/DARKTOWER.
TO FIND MARVEL COMICS AT A LOCAL COMIC SHOP, CALL 1-888-COMICBOOK.

DARK TOWER: FALL OF GILEAD. Contains material originally published in magazine form as DARK TOWER: FALL OF GILEAD and DARK TOWER: THE SORCERER. First printing 2010. ISBN# 978-0-7851-2951-6. Published by MARVEL PUBLISHING, INC., a subsidiary of MARVEL ENTERTAINMENT, INC. OFFICE OF PUBLICATION: 417 5th Avenue, New York, NY 10016. © 2009 and 2010 Stephen King. All rights reserved. $24.99 per copy in the U.S. (GST #R127032852); Canadian Agreement #40668537. All characters featured in this issue and the distinctive names and likenesses thereof, and all related indicia are trademarks of Stephen King. No similarity between any of the names, characters, persons, and/or institutions in this magazine with those of any living or dead person or institution is intended, and any such similarity which may exist is purely coincidental. **Printed in the U.S.A.** ALAN FINE, EVP - Office Of The Chief Executive Marvel Entertainment, Inc. & CMO Marvel Characters B.V.; DAN BUCKLEY, Chief Executive Officer and Publisher - Print, Animation & Digital Media; JIM SOKOLOWSKI, Chief Operating Officer; DAVID GABRIEL, SVP of Publishing Sales & Circulation; DAVID BOGART, SVP of Business Affairs & Talent Management; MICHAEL PASCIULLO, VP Merchandising & Communications; JIM O'KEEFE, VP of Operations & Logistics; DAN CARR, Executive Director of Publishing Technology; JUSTIN F. GABRIE, Director of Publishing & Editorial Operations; SUSAN CRESPI, Editorial Operations Manager; ALEX MORALES, Publishing Operations Manager; STAN LEE, Chairman Emeritus. For information regarding advertising in Marvel Comics or on Marvel.com, please contact Mitch Dane, Advertising Director, at mdane@marvel.com. For Marvel subscription inquiries, please call 800-217-9158. **Manufactured between 11/23/09 and 12/26/09 by R.R. DONNELLEY, INC., SALEM, VA, USA.**

10 9 8 7 6 5 4 3 2 1

INTRODUCTION

Considering the title of this volume, I don't suppose I'd be giving away any secrets by stating the barony of Gilead falls to the forces of the Good Man, John Farson. Despite the best efforts of Steven Deschain and his son Roland, they fail.

Mid-World may not be our own reality, but the inhabitants of both realms know stunning success and dismal failure. And each has their singular figures that rise above the rest with their gargantuan goals and desires. The Dark Tower novels are about one man's blind obsession with reaching a tower that is the fulcrum of existence. Yet the stories are also about the descent of a line to its final member: The familial line of the House of Eld. From Arthur, who practically willed Gilead into existence and is distant ancestor of Steven, to Roland, youngest man to ever become a gunslinger. Roland has enormous, backbreaking responsibilities and tragedies thrust upon him at such a young age. He is barely a teen when the siren song of the Tower calls to him. Then, Roland was agonizingly unable to save the life of the one woman he loved, Susan Delgado, from being burned at the stake in Hambry. Later, he kills his own mother, accidentally, when still at a tender age. And he becomes the last of his line in charge of the defenses of his besieged city only days later. What an unbearable burden for any youth.

Yet all these hardships are only the prelude for what awaits him post Gilead. I think with this hardcover collection the Constant Reader should pause and reflect on the nature of the protagonist Stephen King has so brilliantly conceived. What manner of man could not be broken by all that has happened to him in the space of but a few years? Are these tests or trials some higher power

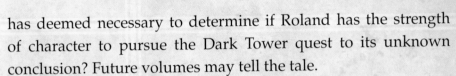

has deemed necessary to determine if Roland has the strength of character to pursue the Dark Tower quest to its unknown conclusion? Future volumes may tell the tale.

But at this juncture, with the Crimson King active and ascendant, and the Beams of the Dark Tower faltering, we've bet the farm on a very flawed gunslinger. Reality's actual survival as we know it is on his still slender shoulders.

He failed to save Gilead from the forces of the Good Man. Very troubling. Is this merely a misstep or an ominous portent of things to come? Roland Deschain is a fascinating character rich with potential and contradiction. His journey toward the ultimate truth of existence is one of the more compelling in popular literature. We continue the fleshing out process on the pages that follow.

Enjoy

Ralph Macchio

Ralph Macchio

In a world that has moved on...

Earning the title of Gunslinger at the unheard-of age of fourteen, young Roland Deschain quickly became a target for his father's enemies, namely John Farson, and was forced to flee his home of Gilead or face death.

Accompanied by his ka-tet mates, Cuthbert and Alain, Roland journeyed to the seaside town of Hambry and fell in love with Susan Delgado. When Susan was killed by the townspeople, who were revealed to be under the control of Farson and his evil master, the Crimson King, the boys fled with their lives and Farson's greatest prize: the sphere known as Maerlyn's Grapefruit.

Roland and his ka-tet returned home to Gilead after he barely survived his first nearly-fatal experience with the sphere's evil power. Still under the mentally destructive influence of the sphere, Roland kept it hidden from his father Steven until his ka-tet forced him to reveal it. Wisely, Steven locked it away so it could harm no one.

As Gilead prepared for the festive celebration of its newly titled Gunslingers, Roland's mother prepared to repent for her adulterous sins with the sorcerer Marten. Seemingly out of nowhere, Marten appeared and lured Gabrielle into the sinful assassination of her husband Steven with the help of Farson's spy. Distrusting of his returned mother, Roland left the festivities to find the sphere stolen away into her chambers. The sphere drew him into a hallucination which provoked him into fatally shooting Gabrielle.

Behind these tragic events there has been one constant: the sorcerer Marten. What was his part in the vile deeds that have transpired and, moreover, what were his motivations?

STEPHEN KING

THE DARK TOWER

THE SORCERER

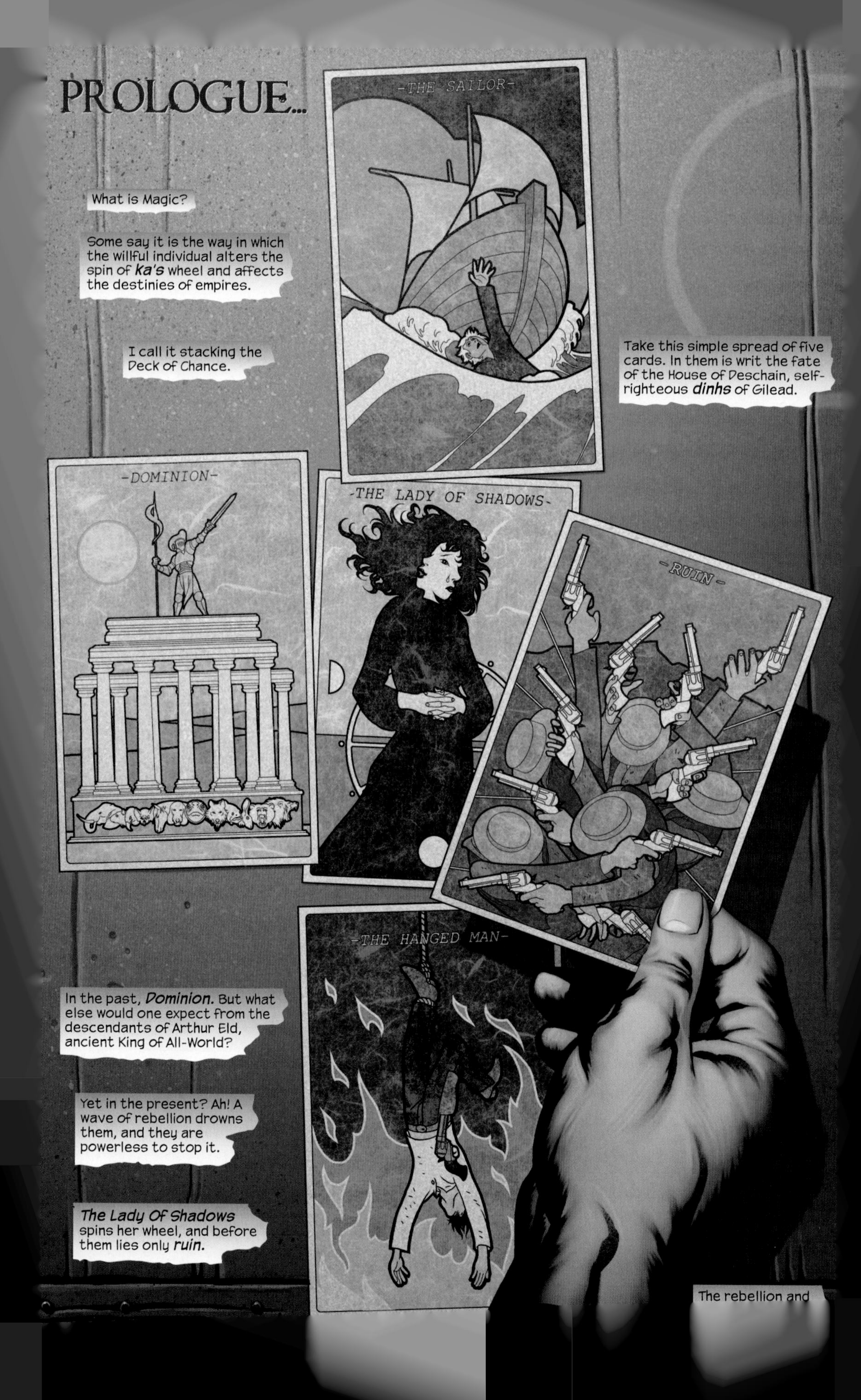
PROLOGUE...
-THE SAILOR-
What is Magic?
Some say it is the way in which the willful individual alters the spin of *ka's* wheel and affects the destinies of empires.
I call it stacking the Deck of Chance.
Take this simple spread of five cards. In them is writ the fate of the House of Deschain, self-righteous *dinhs* of Gilead.
-DOMINION-
-THE LADY OF SHADOWS-
-RUIN-
-THE HANGED MAN-
In the past, *Dominion.* But what else would one expect from the descendants of Arthur Eld, ancient King of All-World?
Yet in the present? Ah! A wave of rebellion drowns them, and they are powerless to stop it.
The Lady Of Shadows spins her wheel, and before them lies only *ruin.*
The rebellion and

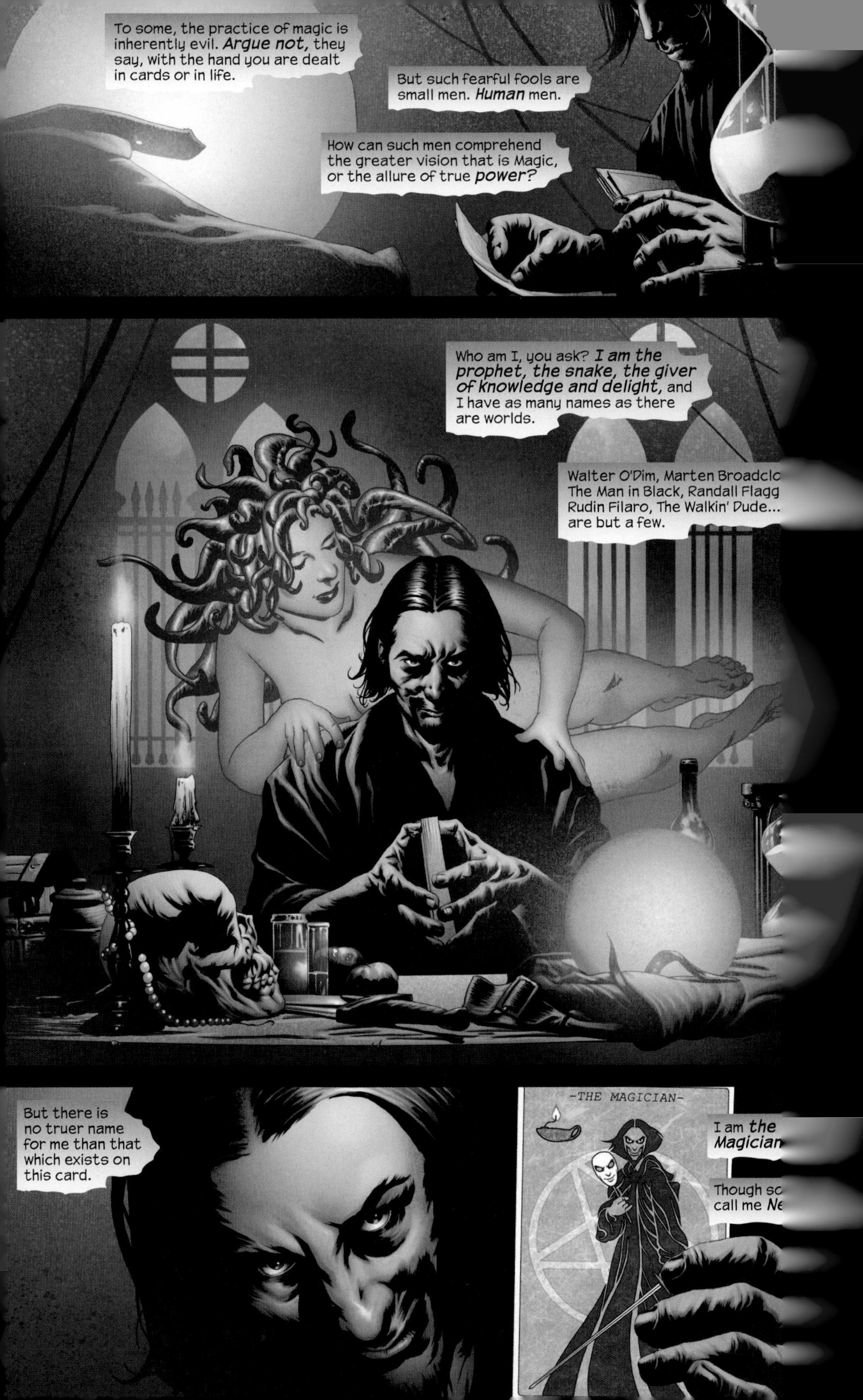
To some, the practice of magic is inherently evil. *Argue not,* they say, with the hand you are dealt in cards or in life.
But such fearful fools are small men. *Human* men.
How can such men comprehend the greater vision that is Magic, or the allure of true *power?*
Who am I, you ask? *I am the prophet, the snake, the giver of knowledge and delight,* and I have as many names as there are worlds.
Walter O'Dim, Marten Broadclo
The Man in Black, Randall Flagg
Rudin Filaro, The Walkin' Dude...
are but a few.
But there is no truer name for me than that which exists on this card.
-THE MAGICIAN-
I am *the*
Though
call me

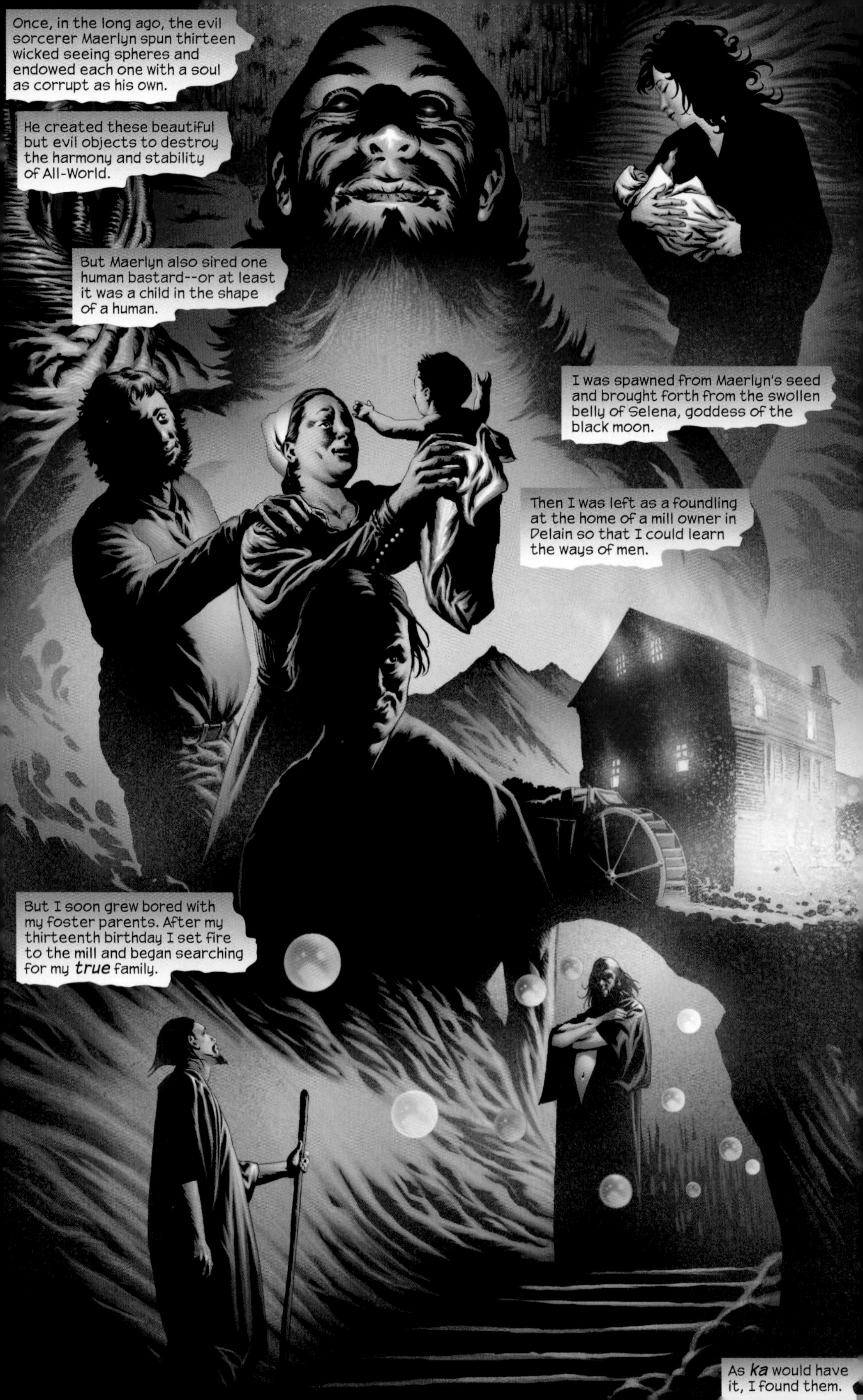
Once, in the long ago, the evil sorcerer Maerlyn spun thirteen wicked seeing spheres and endowed each one with a soul as corrupt as his own.
He created these beautiful but evil objects to destroy the harmony and stability of All-World.
But Maerlyn also sired one human bastard--or at least it was a child in the shape of a human.
I was spawned from Maerlyn's seed and brought forth from the swollen belly of Selena, goddess of the black moon.
Then I was left as a foundling at the home of a mill owner in Delain so that I could learn the ways of men.
But I soon grew bored with my foster parents. After my thirteenth birthday I set fire to the mill and began searching for my *true* family.
As *ka* would have it, I found them.

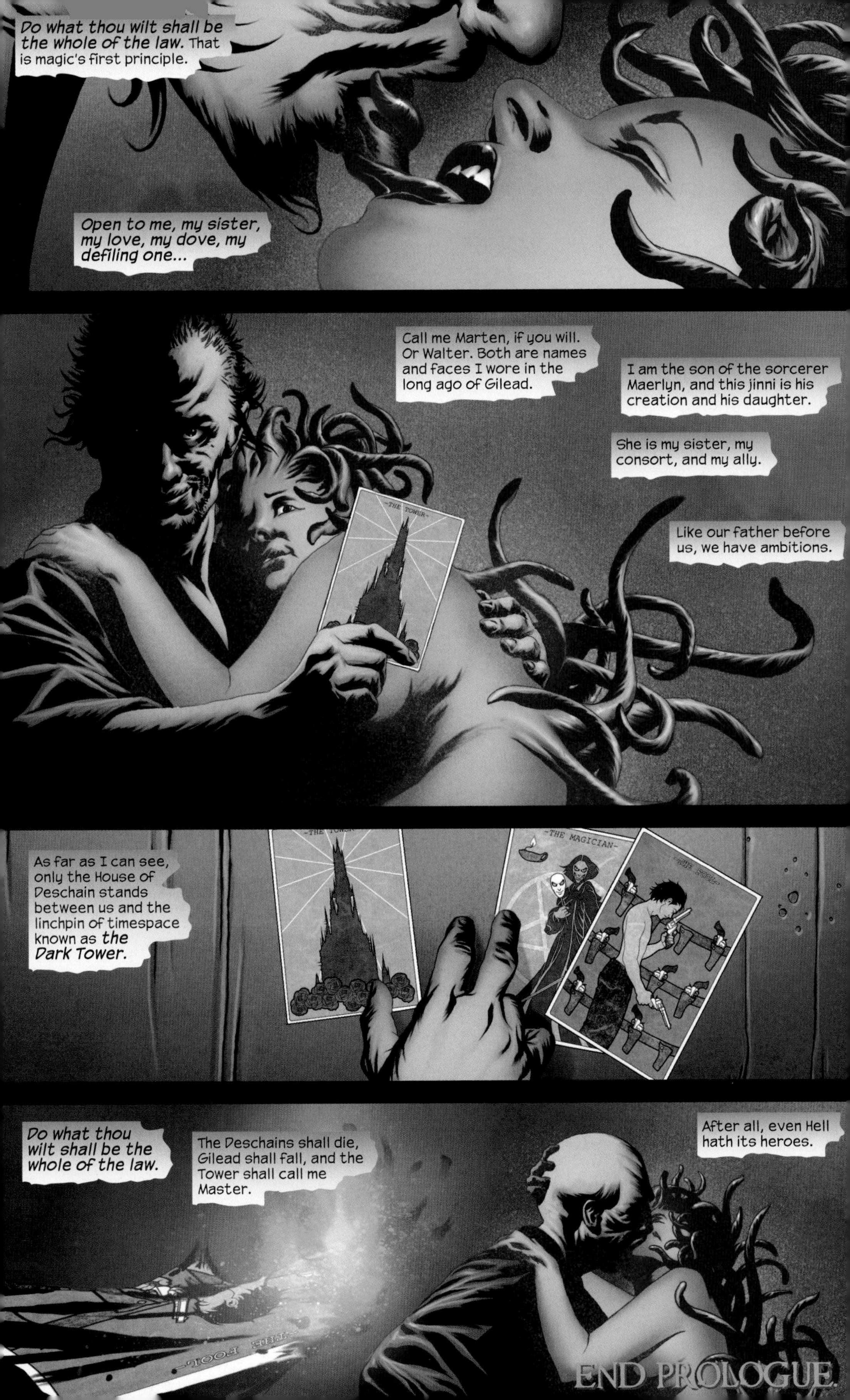

Do what thou wilt shall be the whole of the law. That is magic's first principle.
Open to me, my sister, my love, my dove, my defiling one...
Call me Marten, if you will. Or Walter. Both are names and faces I wore in the long ago of Gilead.
I am the son of the sorcerer Maerlyn, and this jinni is his creation and his daughter.
She is my sister, my consort, and my ally.
Like our father before us, we have ambitions.
-THE TOWER-
As far as I can see, only the House of Deschain stands between us and the linchpin of timespace known as the Dark Tower.
-THE MAGICIAN-
Do what thou wilt shall be the whole of the law.
The Deschains shall die, Gilead shall fall, and the Tower shall call me Master.
After all, even Hell hath its heroes.
END PROLOGUE.

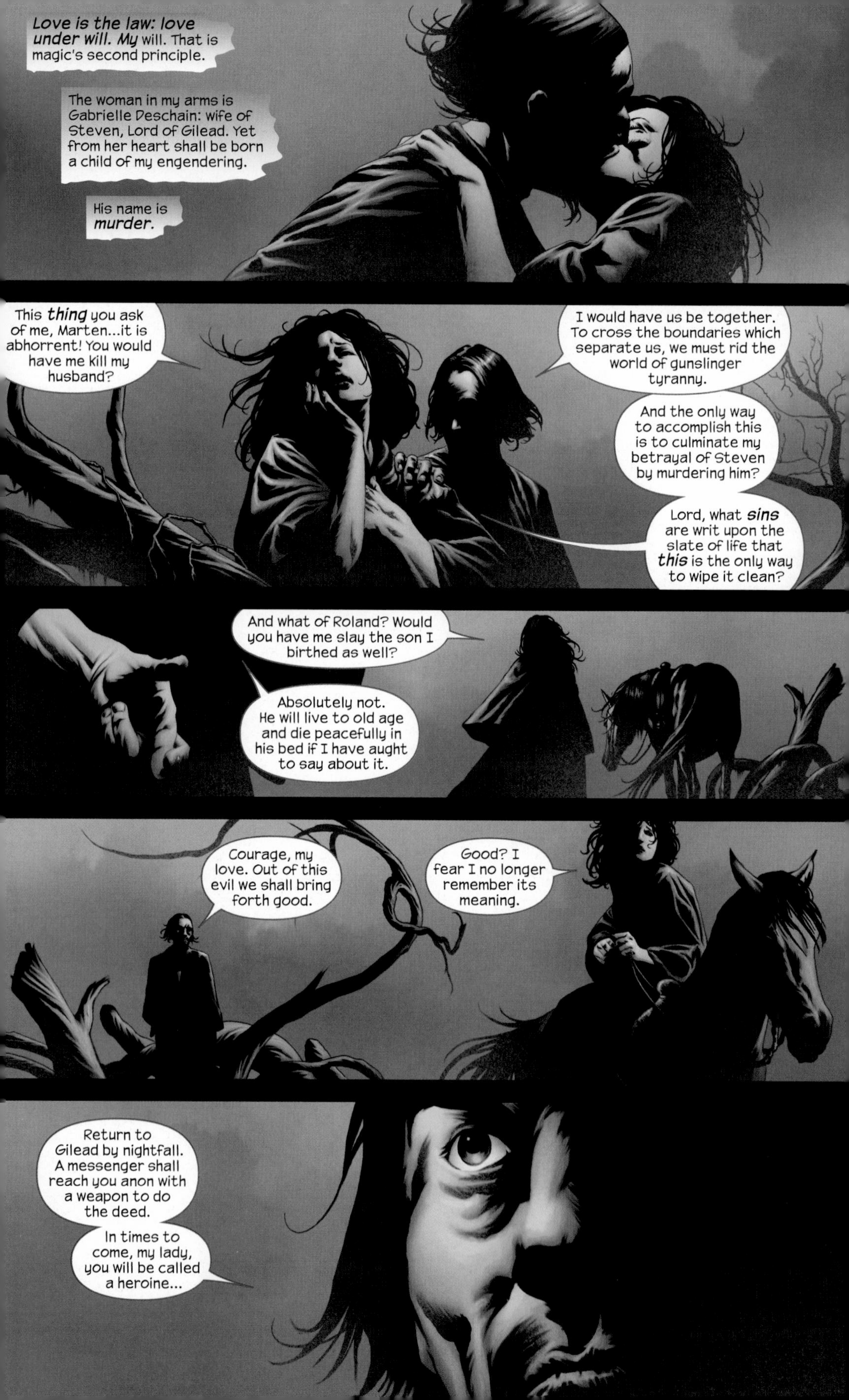
Love is the law: love under will. My will. That is magic's second principle.
The woman in my arms is Gabrielle Deschain: wife of Steven, Lord of Gilead. Yet from her heart shall be born a child of my engendering.
His name is murder.
This thing you ask of me, Marten...it is abhorrent! You would have me kill my husband?
I would have us be together. To cross the boundaries which separate us, we must rid the world of gunslinger tyranny.
And the only way to accomplish this is to culminate my betrayal of Steven by murdering him?
Lord, what sins are writ upon the slate of life that this is the only way to wipe it clean?
And what of Roland? Would you have me slay the son I birthed as well?
Absolutely not. He will live to old age and die peacefully in his bed if I have aught to say about it.
Courage, my love. Out of this evil we shall bring forth good.
Good? I fear I no longer remember its meaning.
Return to Gilead by nightfall. A messenger shall reach you anon with a weapon to do the deed.
In times to come, my lady, you will be called a heroine...

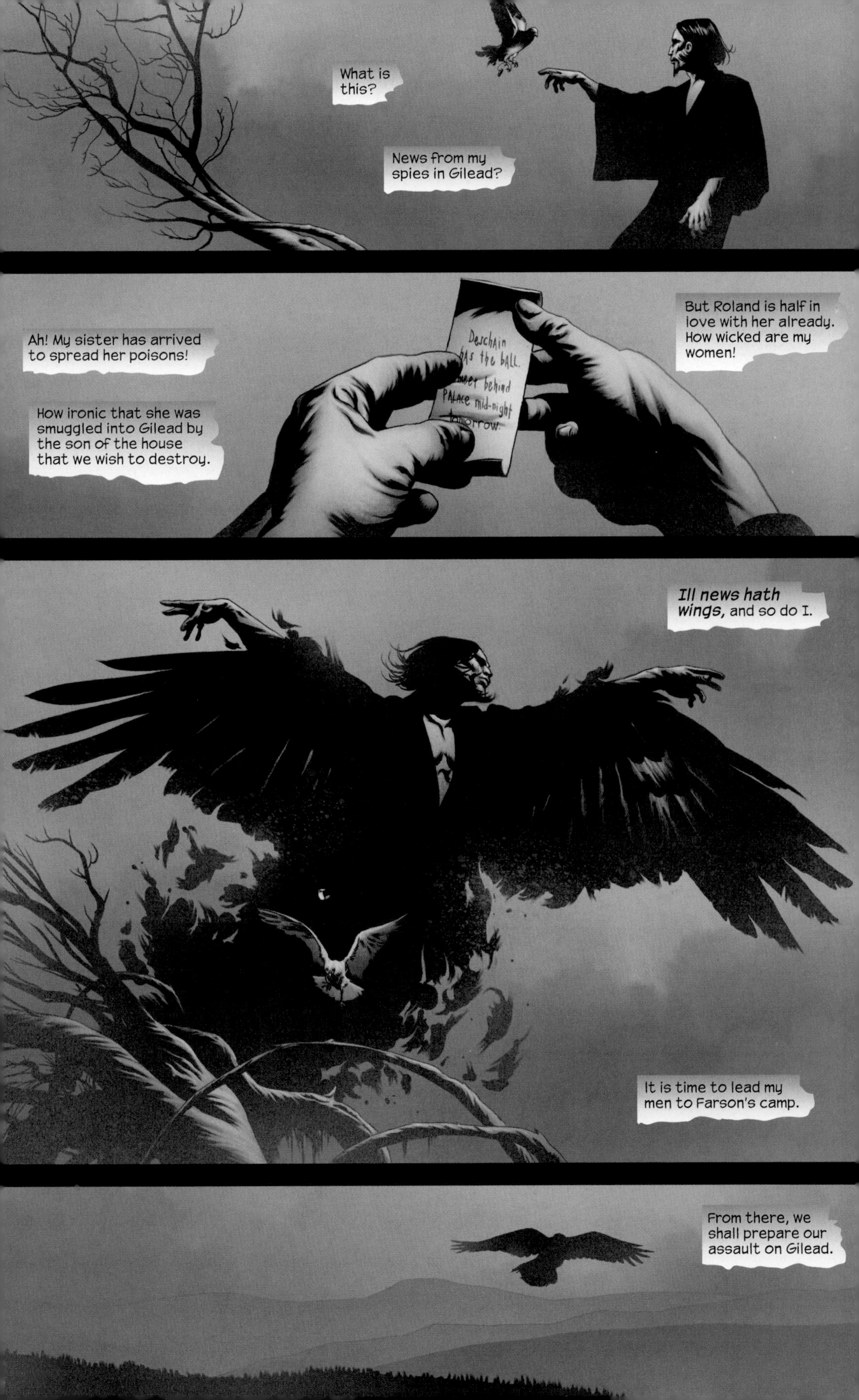
What is this?
News from my spies in Gilead?
Ah! My sister has arrived to spread her poisons!
How ironic that she was smuggled into Gilead by the son of the house that we wish to destroy.
But Roland is half in love with her already. How wicked are my women!
Ill news hath wings, and so do I.
It is time to lead my men to Farson's camp.
From there, we shall prepare our assault on Gilead.

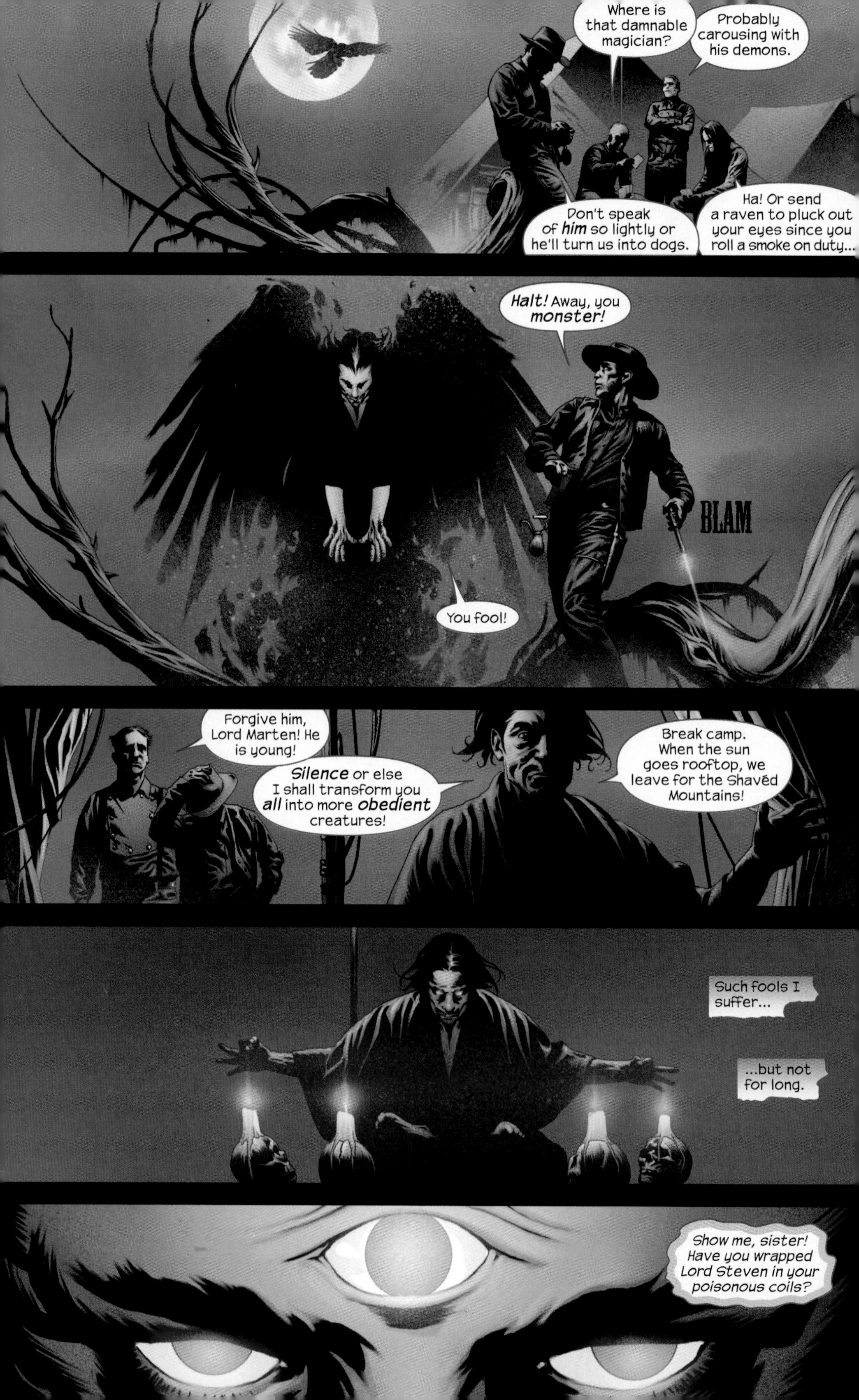

Where is that damnable magician?
Probably carousing with his demons.
Don't speak of *him* so lightly or he'll turn us into dogs.
Ha! Or send a raven to pluck out your eyes since you roll a smoke on duty...
Halt! Away, you *monster!*
BLAM
You fool!
Forgive him, Lord Marten! He is young!
Silence or else I shall transform you *all* into more *obedient* creatures!
Break camp. When the sun goes rooftop, we leave for the Shavéd Mountains!
Such fools I suffer...
...but not for long.
Show me, sister! Have you wrapped Lord Steven in your poisonous coils?

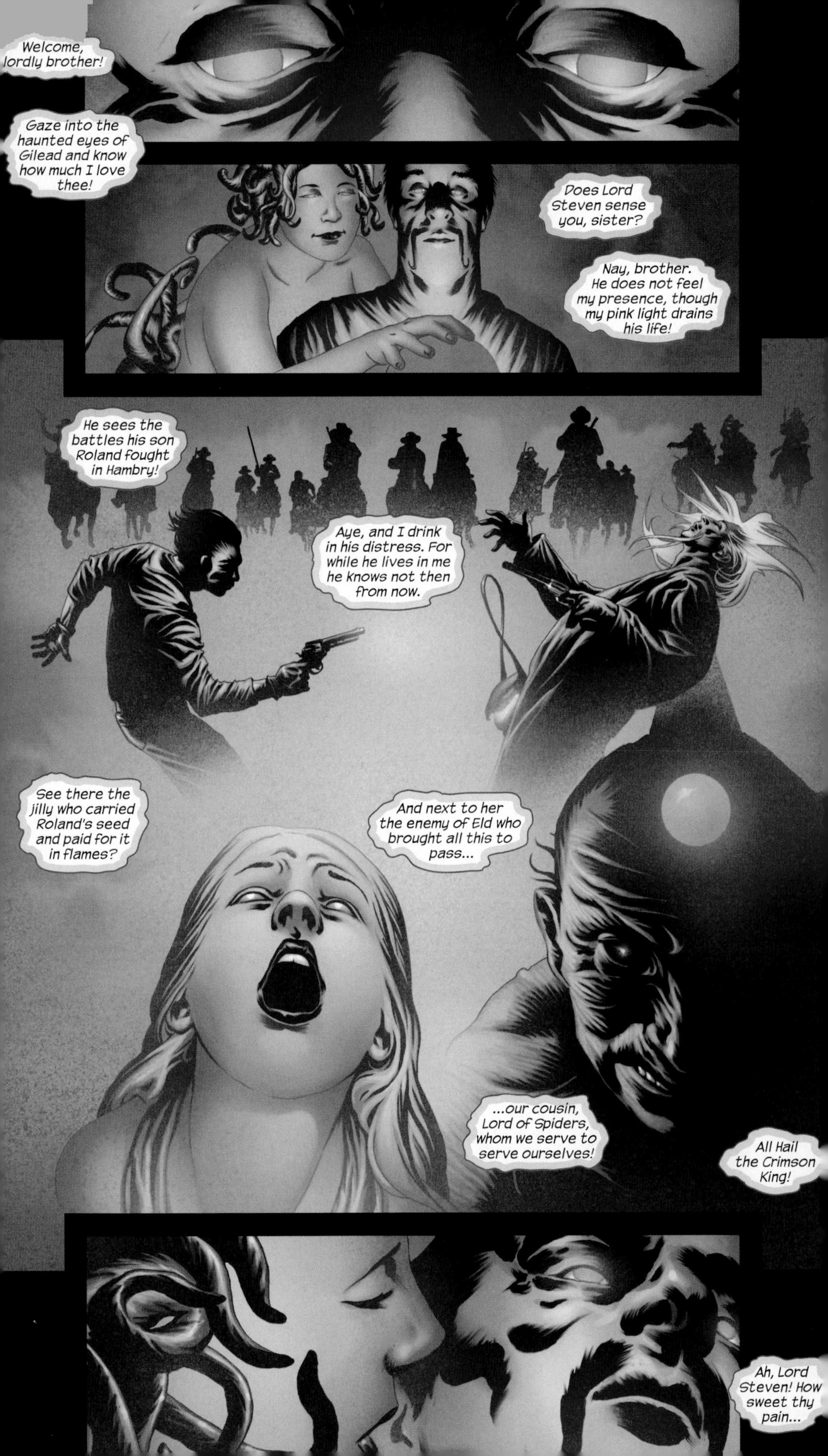

Welcome, lordly brother!
Gaze into the haunted eyes of Gilead and know how much I love thee!
Does Lord Steven sense you, sister?
Nay, brother. He does not feel my presence, though my pink light drains his life!
He sees the battles his son Roland fought in Hambry!
Aye, and I drink in his distress. For while he lives in me he knows not then from now.
See there the jilly who carried Roland's seed and paid for it in flames?
And next to her the enemy of Eld who brought all this to pass...
...our cousin, Lord of Spiders, whom we serve to serve ourselves!
All Hail the Crimson King!
Ah, Lord Steven! How sweet thy pain...

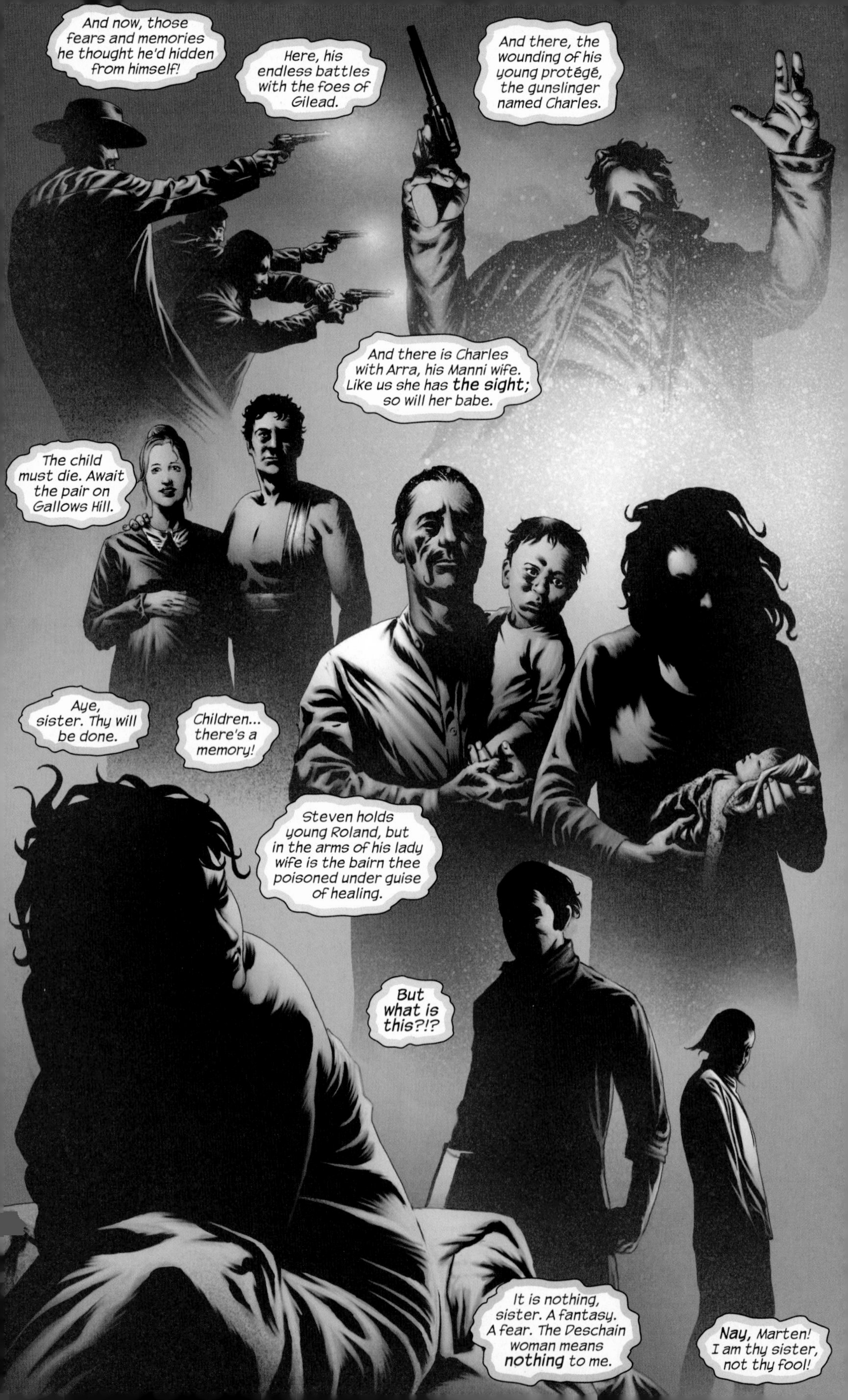

And now, those fears and memories he thought he'd hidden from himself!
Here, his endless battles with the foes of Gilead.
And there, the wounding of his young protégé, the gunslinger named Charles.
And there is Charles with Arra, his Manni wife. Like us she has **the sight;** so will her babe.
The child must die. Await the pair on Gallows Hill.
Aye, sister. Thy will be done.
Children... there's a memory!
Steven holds young Roland, but in the arms of his lady wife is the bairn thee poisoned under guise of healing.
But what is this?!?
It is nothing, sister. A fantasy. A fear. The Deschain woman means **nothing** to me.
Nay, Marten! I am thy sister, not thy fool!

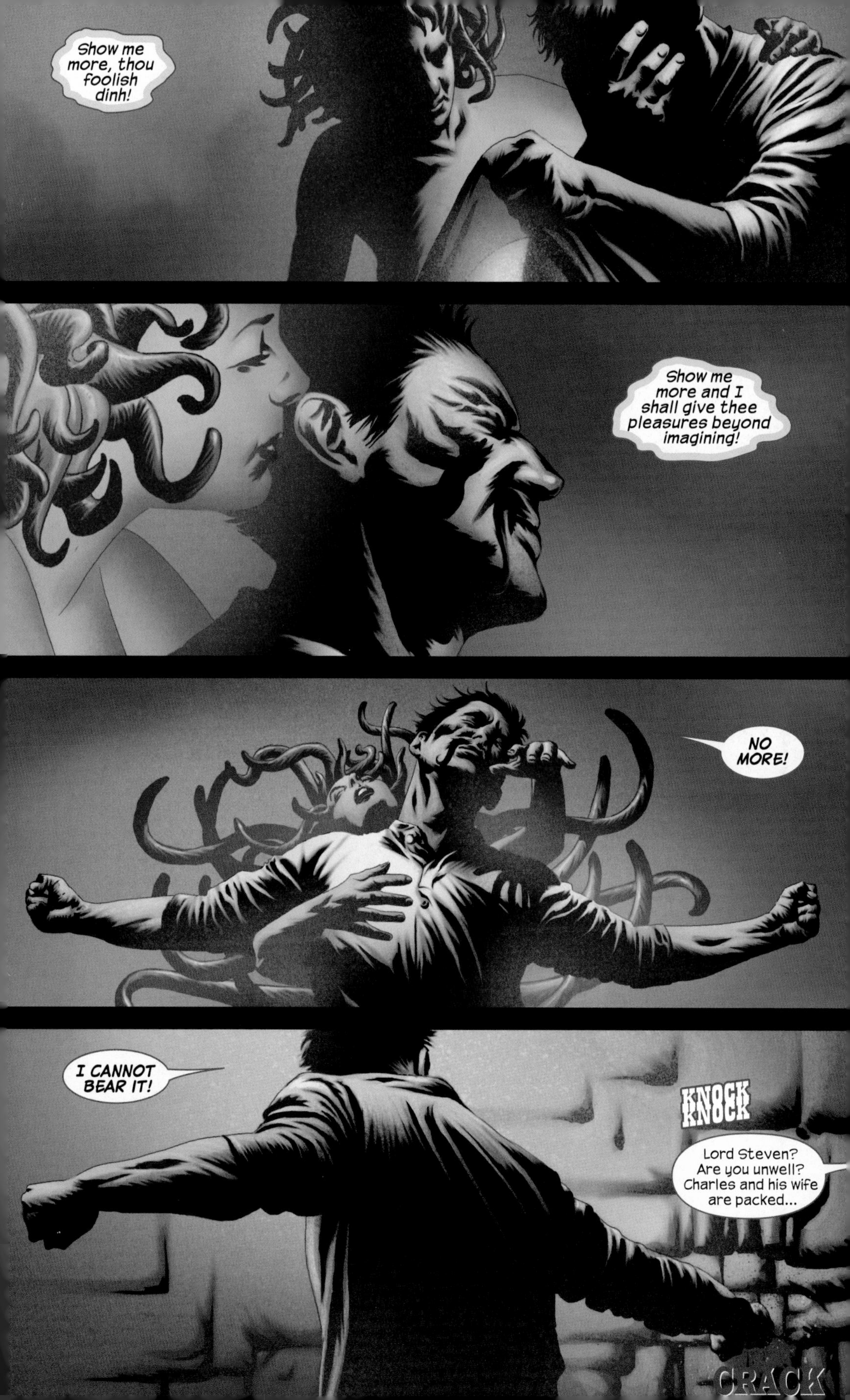
Show me more, thou foolish dinh!
Show me more and I shall give thee pleasures beyond imagining!
NO MORE!
I CANNOT BEAR IT!
KNOCK KNOCK
Lord Steven? Are you unwell? Charles and his wife are packed...
CRACK

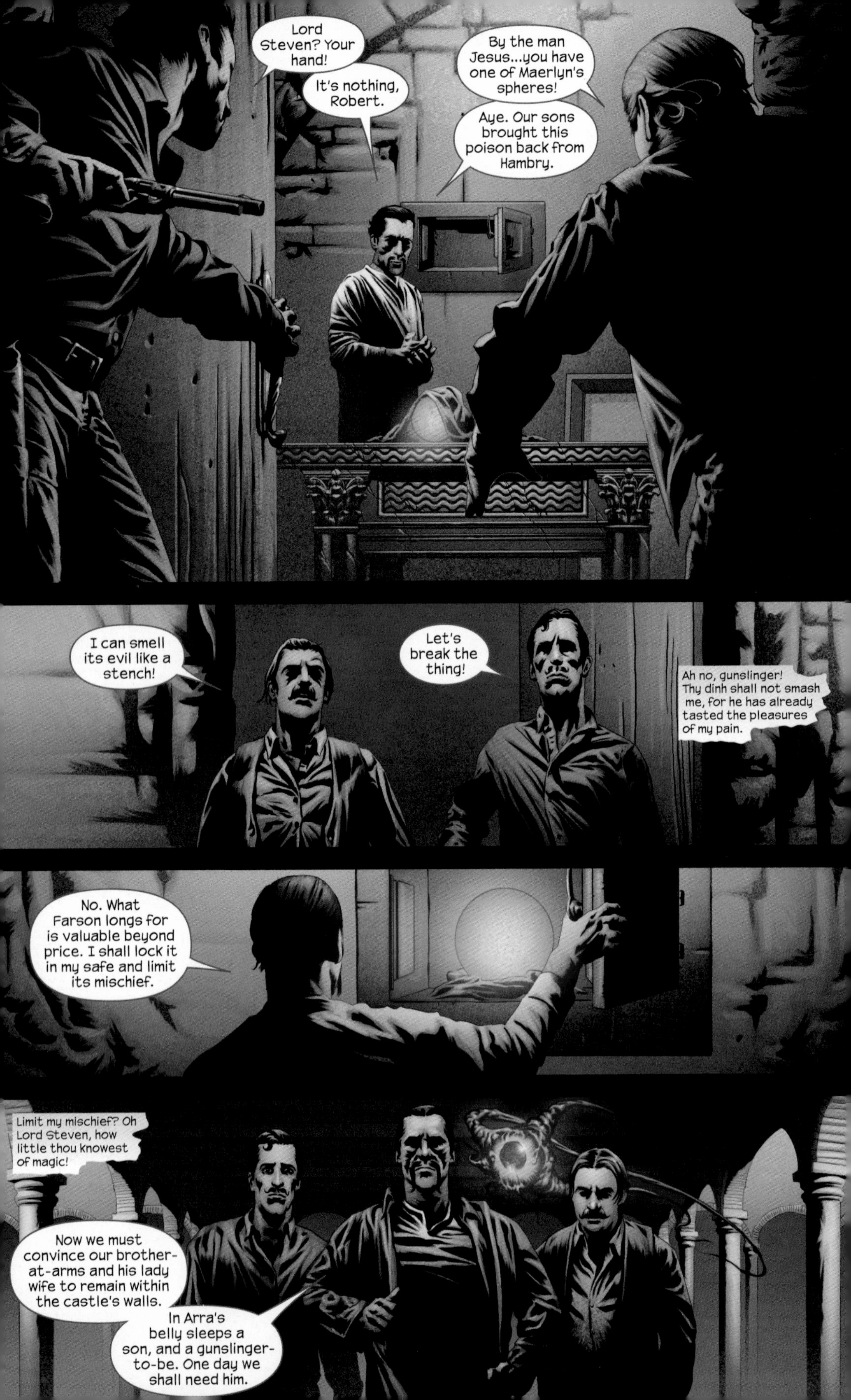
Lord Steven? Your hand!
It's nothing, Robert.
By the man Jesus...you have one of Maerlyn's spheres!
Aye. Our sons brought this poison back from Hambry.
I can smell its evil like a stench!
Let's break the thing!
Ah no, gunslinger! Thy dinh shall not smash me, for he has already tasted the pleasures of my pain.
No. What Farson longs for is valuable beyond price. I shall lock it in my safe and limit its mischief.
Limit my mischief? Oh Lord Steven, how little thou knowest of magic!
Now we must convince our brother-at-arms and his lady wife to remain within the castle's walls.
In Arra's belly sleeps a son, and a gunslinger-to-be. One day we shall need him.

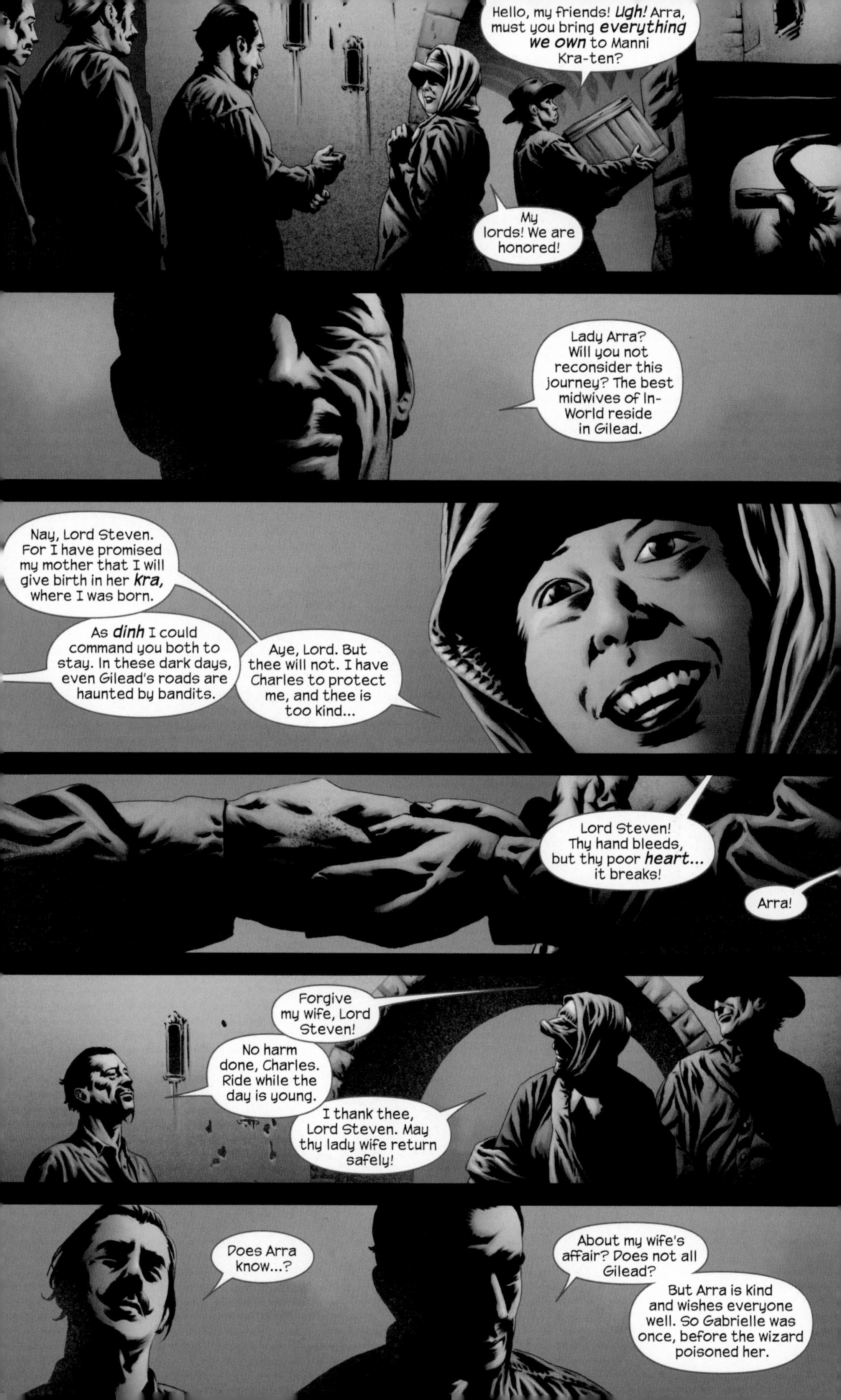

Hello, my friends! Ugh! Arra, must you bring everything we own to Manni Kra-ten?
My lords! We are honored!
Lady Arra? Will you not reconsider this journey? The best midwives of In-World reside in Gilead.
Nay, Lord Steven. For I have promised my mother that I will give birth in her kra, where I was born.
As dinh I could command you both to stay. In these dark days, even Gilead's roads are haunted by bandits.
Aye, Lord. But thee will not. I have Charles to protect me, and thee is too kind...
Lord Steven! Thy hand bleeds, but thy poor heart... it breaks!
Arra!
Forgive my wife, Lord Steven!
No harm done, Charles. Ride while the day is young.
I thank thee, Lord Steven. May thy lady wife return safely!
Does Arra know...?
About my wife's affair? Does not all Gilead?
But Arra is kind and wishes everyone well. So Gabrielle was once, before the wizard poisoned her.

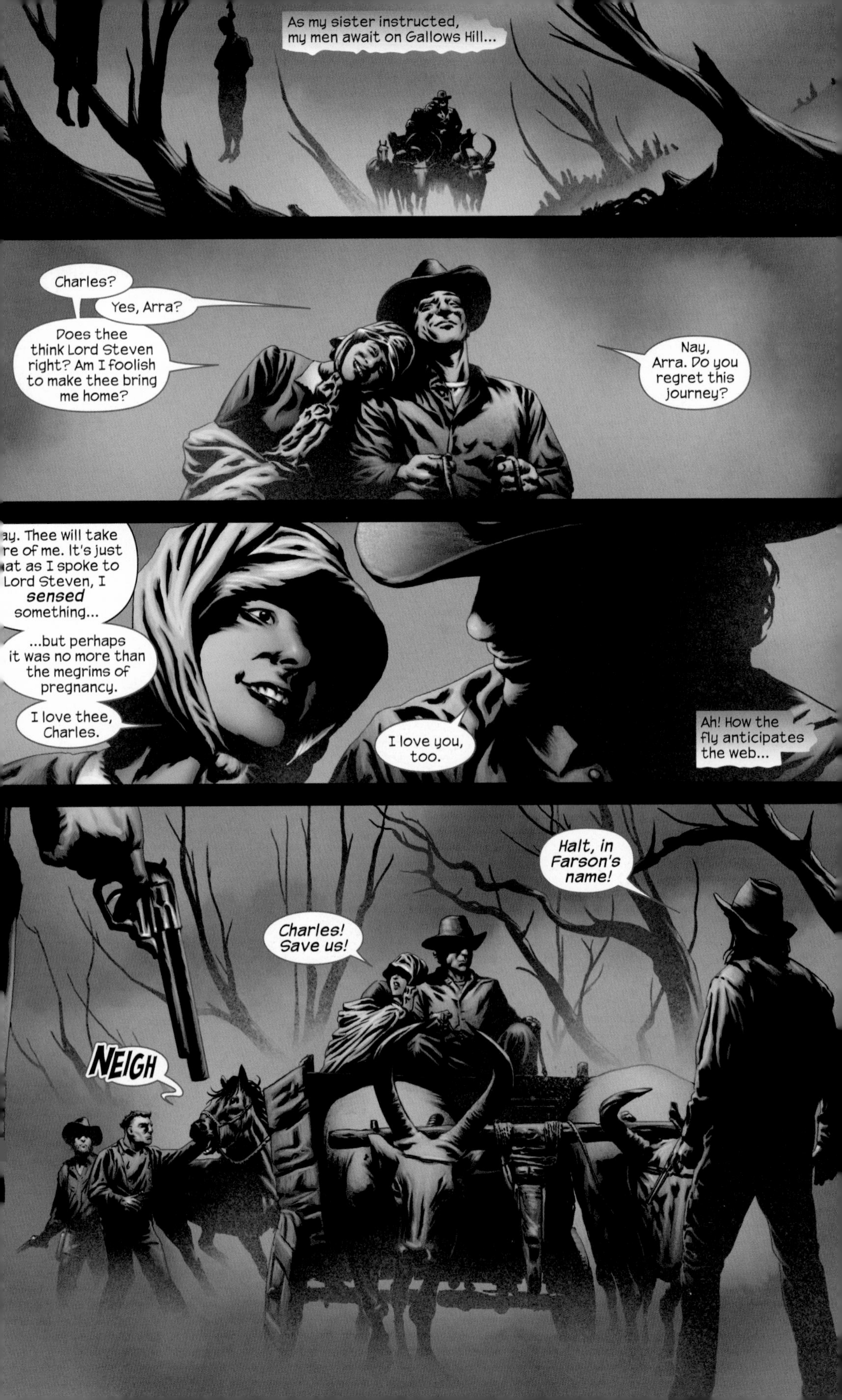
As my sister instructed, my men await on Gallows Hill...
Charles?
Yes, Arra?
Does thee think Lord Steven right? Am I foolish to make thee bring me home?
Nay, Arra. Do you regret this journey?
ay. Thee will take re of me. It's just at as I spoke to Lord Steven, I *sensed* something...
...but perhaps it was no more than the megrims of pregnancy.
I love thee, Charles.
I love you, too.
Ah! How the fly anticipates the web...
Halt, in Farson's name!
Charles! Save us!
NEIGH

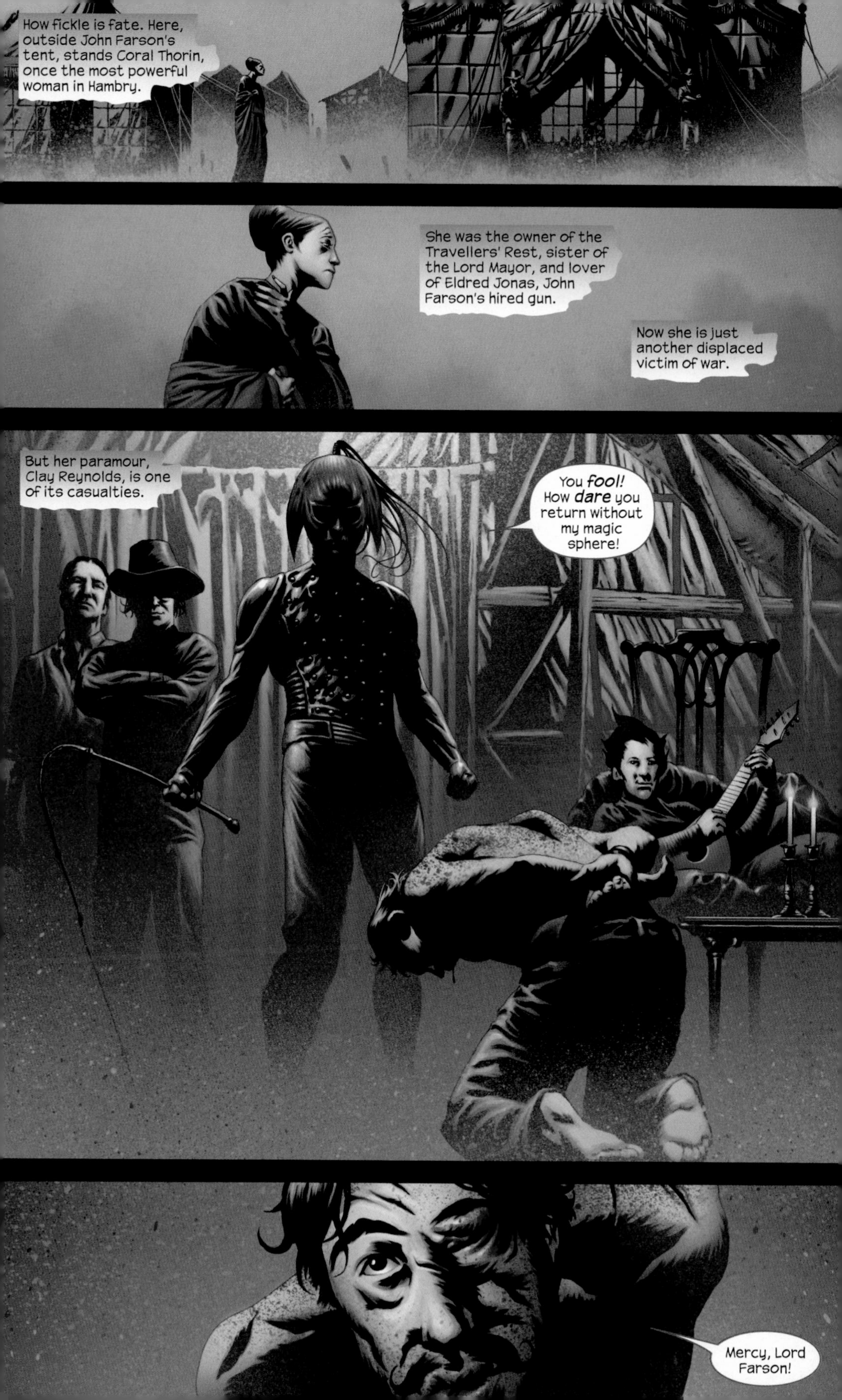
How fickle is fate. Here, outside John Farson's tent, stands Coral Thorin, once the most powerful woman in Hambry.
She was the owner of the Travellers' Rest, sister of the Lord Mayor, and lover of Eldred Jonas, John Farson's hired gun.
Now she is just another displaced victim of war.
But her paramour, Clay Reynolds, is one of its casualties.
You *fool!* How *dare* you return without my magic sphere!
Mercy, Lord Farson!

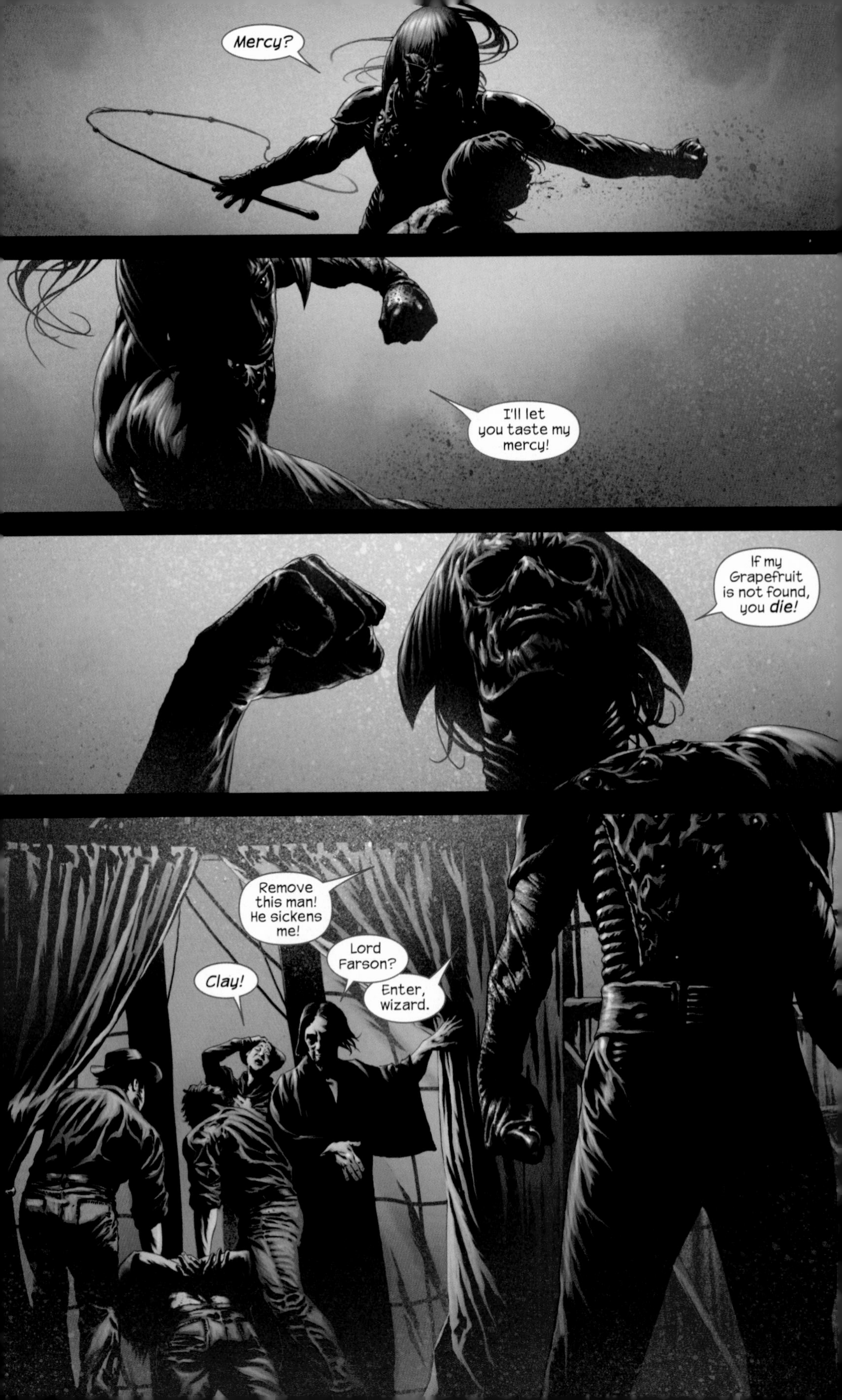
Mercy?
I'll let you taste my mercy!
If my Grapefruit is not found, you *die!*
Remove this man! He sickens me!
Lord Farson?
Clay!
Enter, wizard.

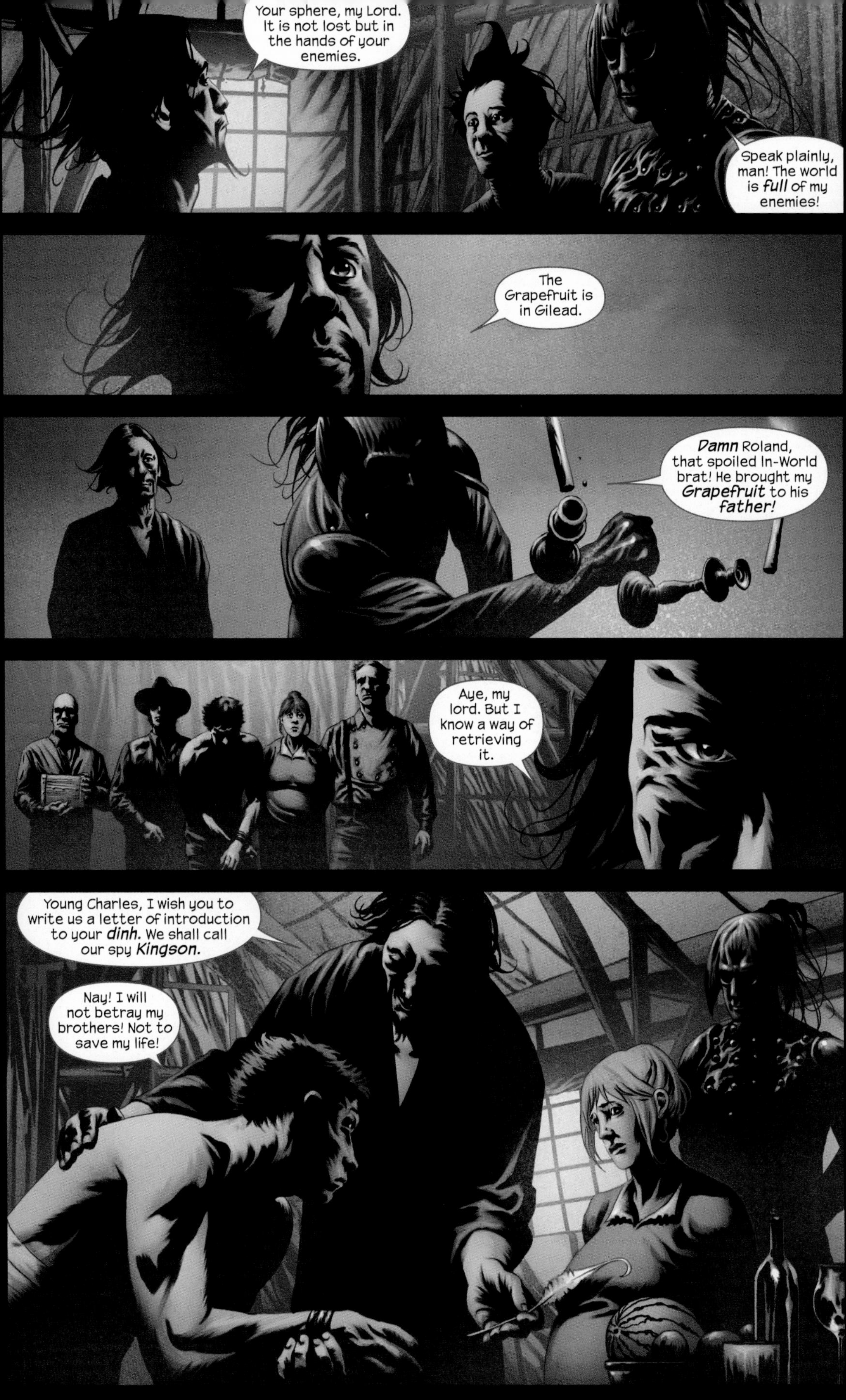

Your sphere, my Lord. It is not lost but in the hands of your enemies.
Speak plainly, man! The world is *full* of my enemies!
The Grapefruit is in Gilead.
Damn Roland, that spoiled In-World brat! He brought my *Grapefruit* to his *father!*
Aye, my lord. But I know a way of retrieving it.
Young Charles, I wish you to write us a letter of introduction to your *dinh.* We shall call our spy *Kingson.*
Nay! I will not betray my brothers! Not to save my life!

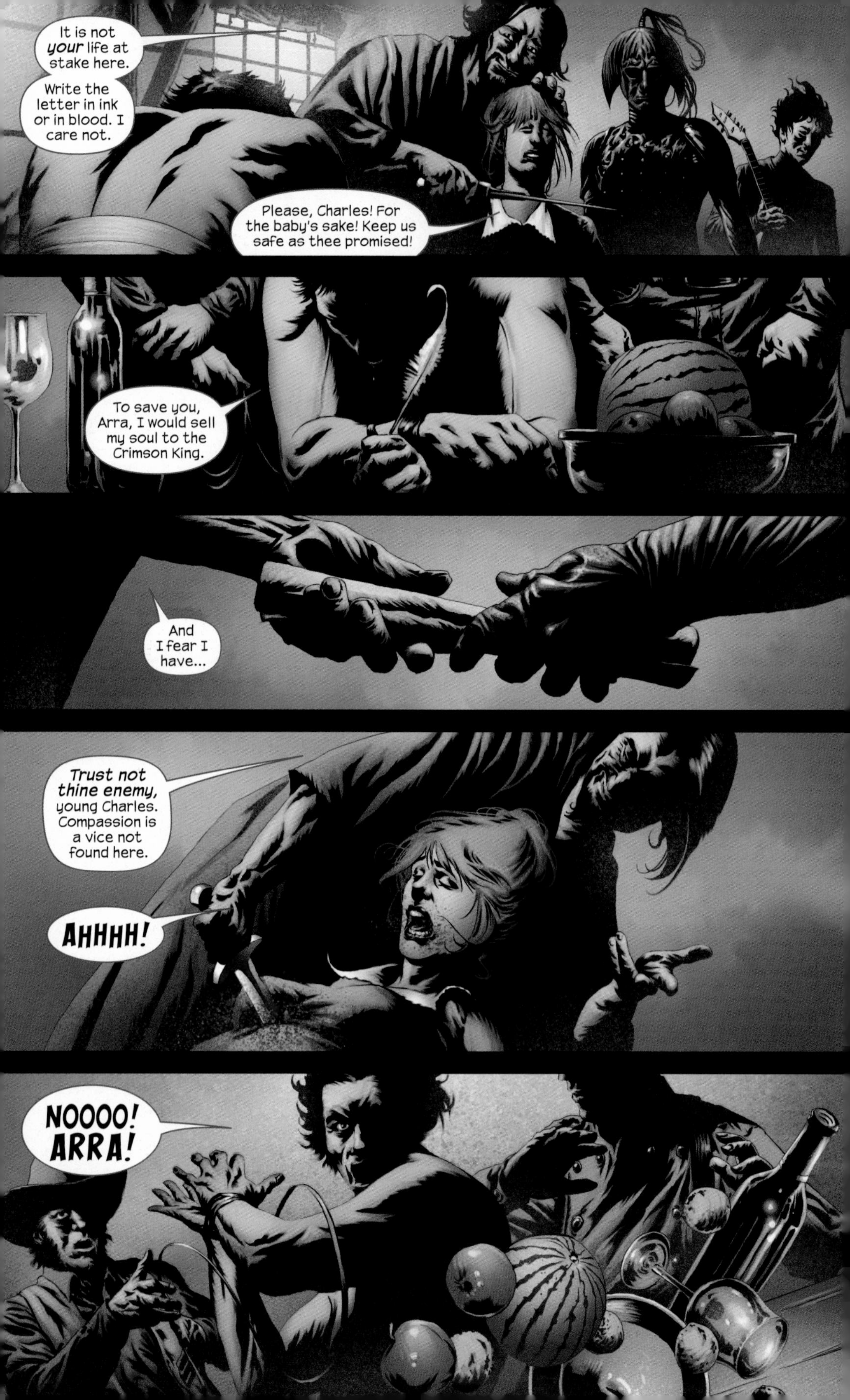
It is not *your* life at stake here.
Write the letter in ink or in blood. I care not.
Please, Charles! For the baby's sake! Keep us safe as thee promised!
To save you, Arra, I would sell my soul to the Crimson King.
And I fear I have...
Trust not thine enemy, young Charles. Compassion is a vice not found here.
AHHHH!
NOOOO! ARRA!

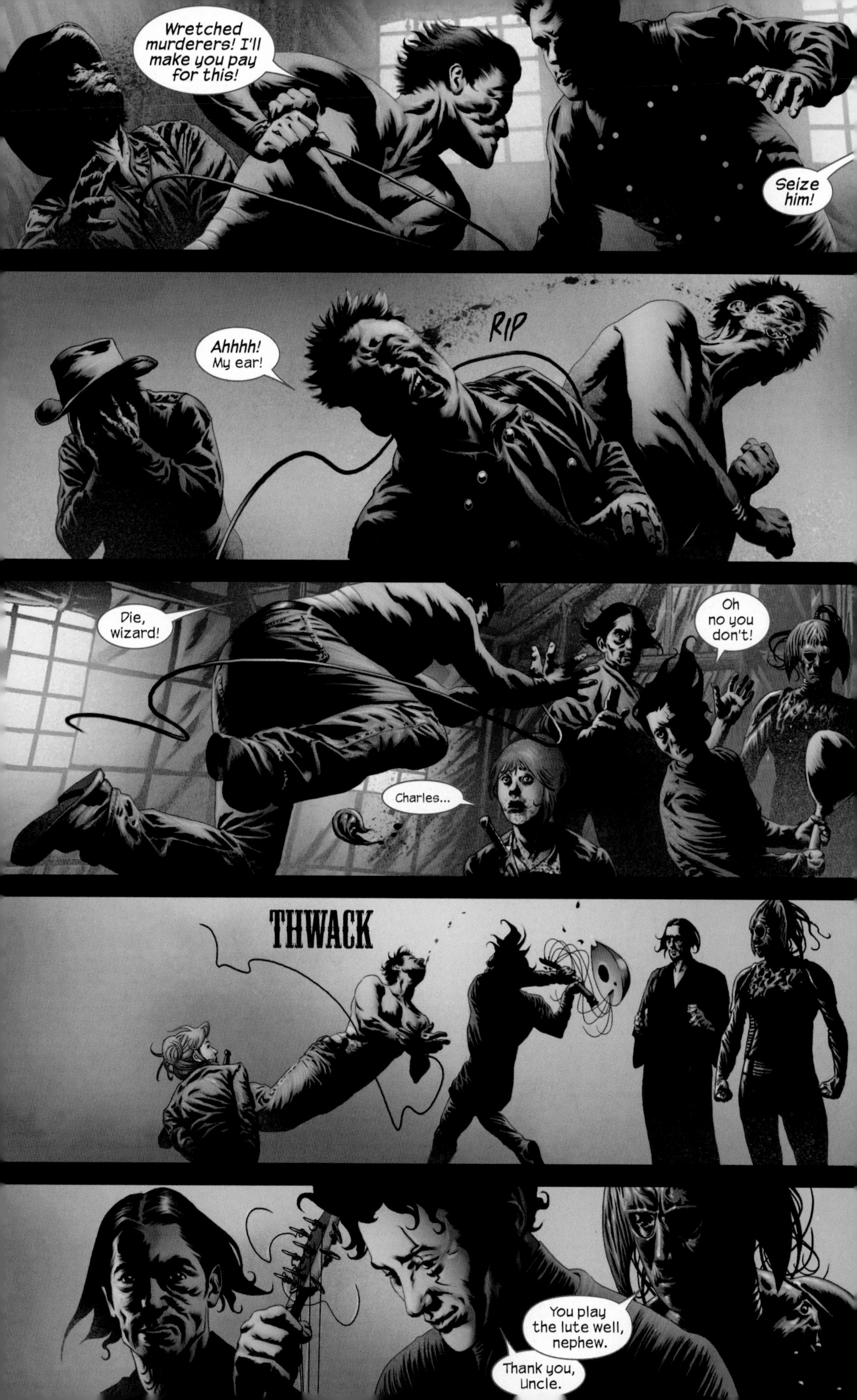
Wretched murderers! I'll make you pay for this!
Seize him!
Ahhhh! My ear!
RIP
Die, wizard!
Oh no you don't!
Charles...
THWACK
You play the lute well, nephew.
Thank you, Uncle.

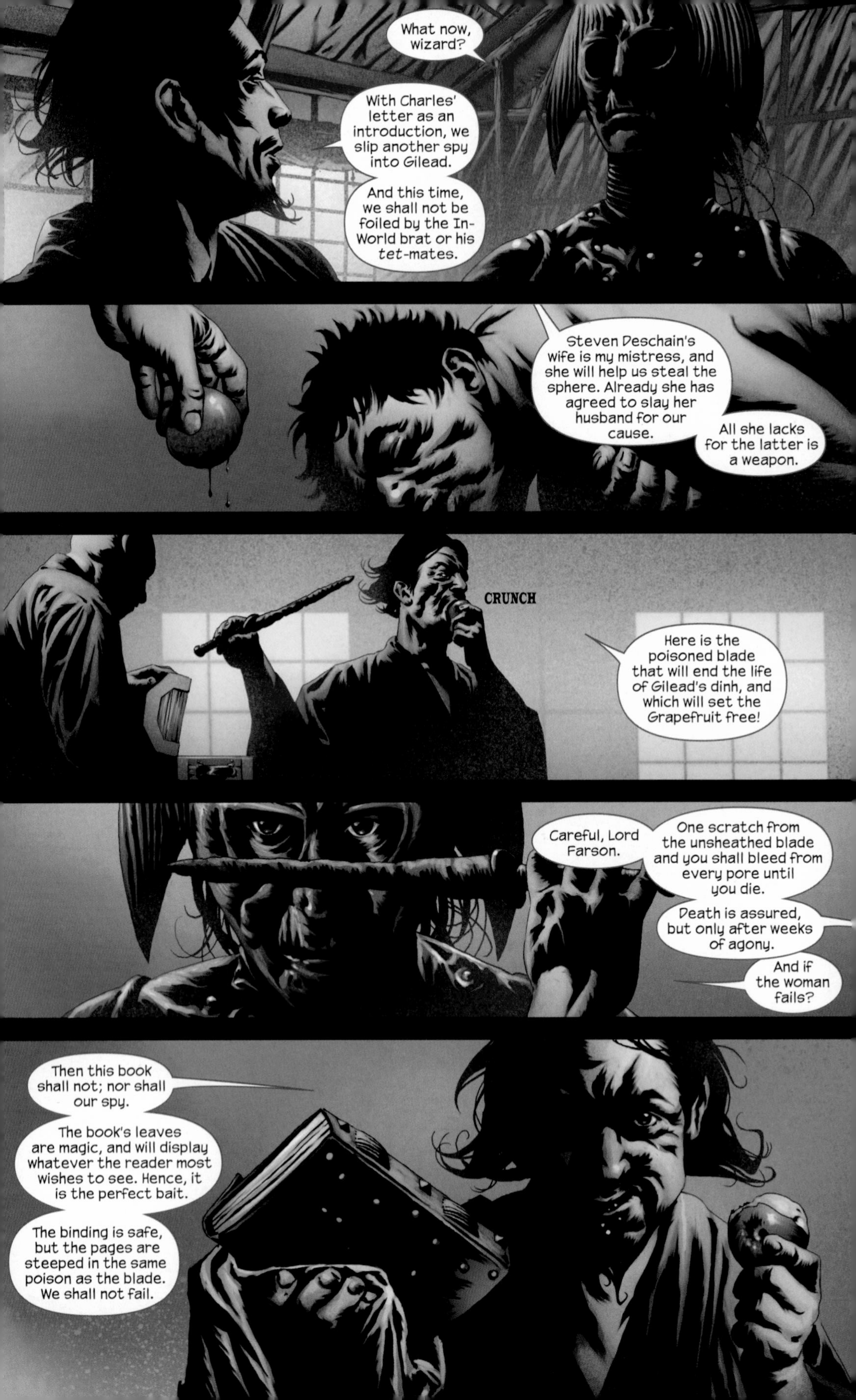
What now, wizard?
With Charles' letter as an introduction, we slip another spy into Gilead.
And this time, we shall not be foiled by the In-World brat or his *tet*-mates.
Steven Deschain's wife is my mistress, and she will help us steal the sphere. Already she has agreed to slay her husband for our cause.
All she lacks for the latter is a weapon.
CRUNCH
Here is the poisoned blade that will end the life of Gilead's dinh, and which will set the Grapefruit free!
Careful, Lord Farson.
One scratch from the unsheathed blade and you shall bleed from every pore until you die.
Death is assured, but only after weeks of agony.
And if the woman fails?
Then this book shall not; nor shall our spy.
The book's leaves are magic, and will display whatever the reader most wishes to see. Hence, it is the perfect bait.
The binding is safe, but the pages are steeped in the same poison as the blade. We shall not fail.

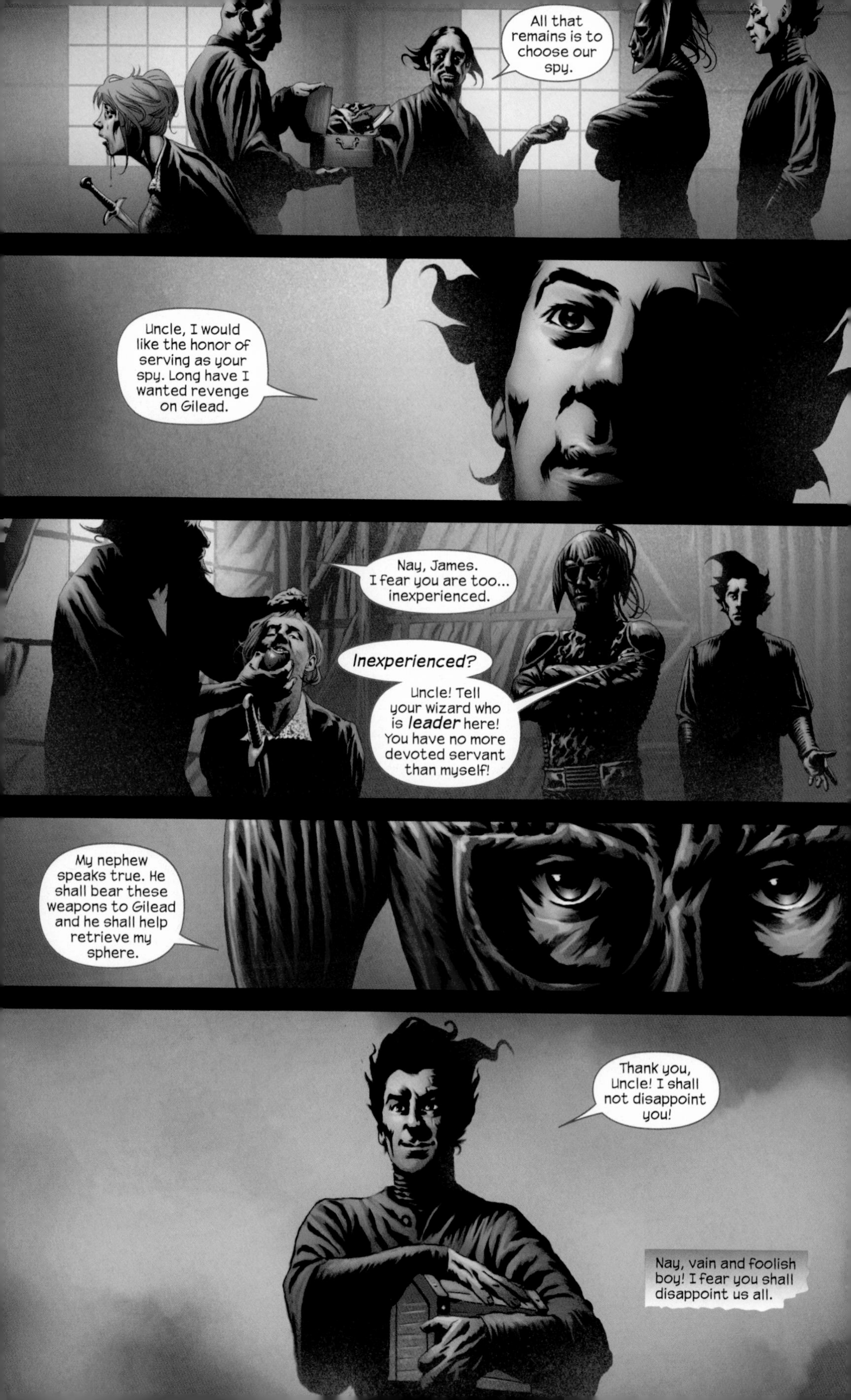
All that remains is to choose our spy.
Uncle, I would like the honor of serving as your spy. Long have I wanted revenge on Gilead.
Nay, James. I fear you are too... inexperienced.
Inexperienced?
Uncle! Tell your wizard who is *leader* here! You have no more devoted servant than myself!
My nephew speaks true. He shall bear these weapons to Gilead and he shall help retrieve my sphere.
Thank you, Uncle! I shall not disappoint you!
Nay, vain and foolish boy! I fear you shall disappoint us all.

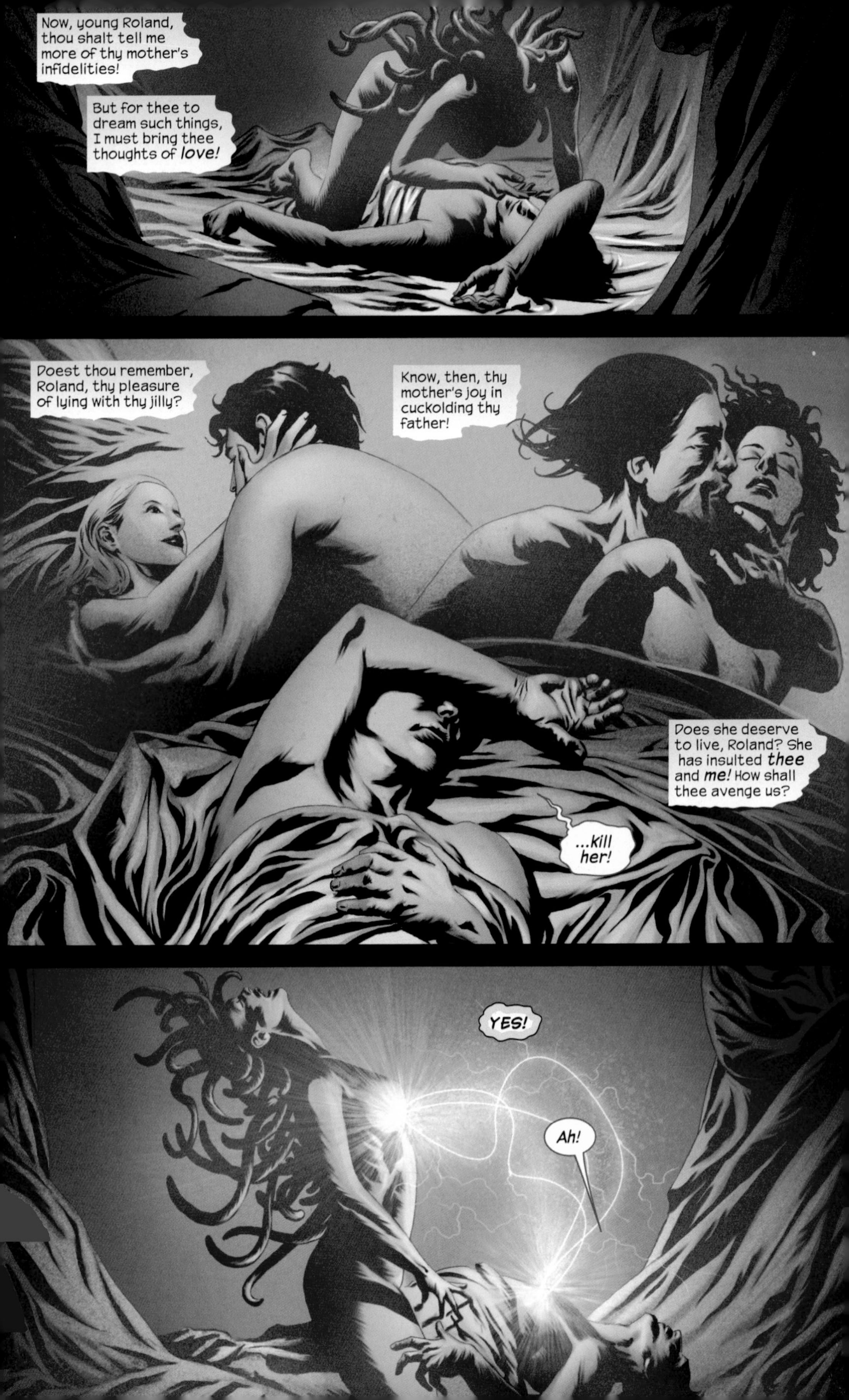
Now, young Roland, thou shalt tell me more of thy mother's infidelities!
But for thee to dream such things, I must bring thee thoughts of *love!*
Doest thou remember, Roland, thy pleasure of lying with thy jilly?
Know, then, thy mother's joy in cuckolding thy father!
Does she deserve to live, Roland? She has insulted *thee* and *me!* How shall thee avenge us?
...kill her!
YES!
Ah!

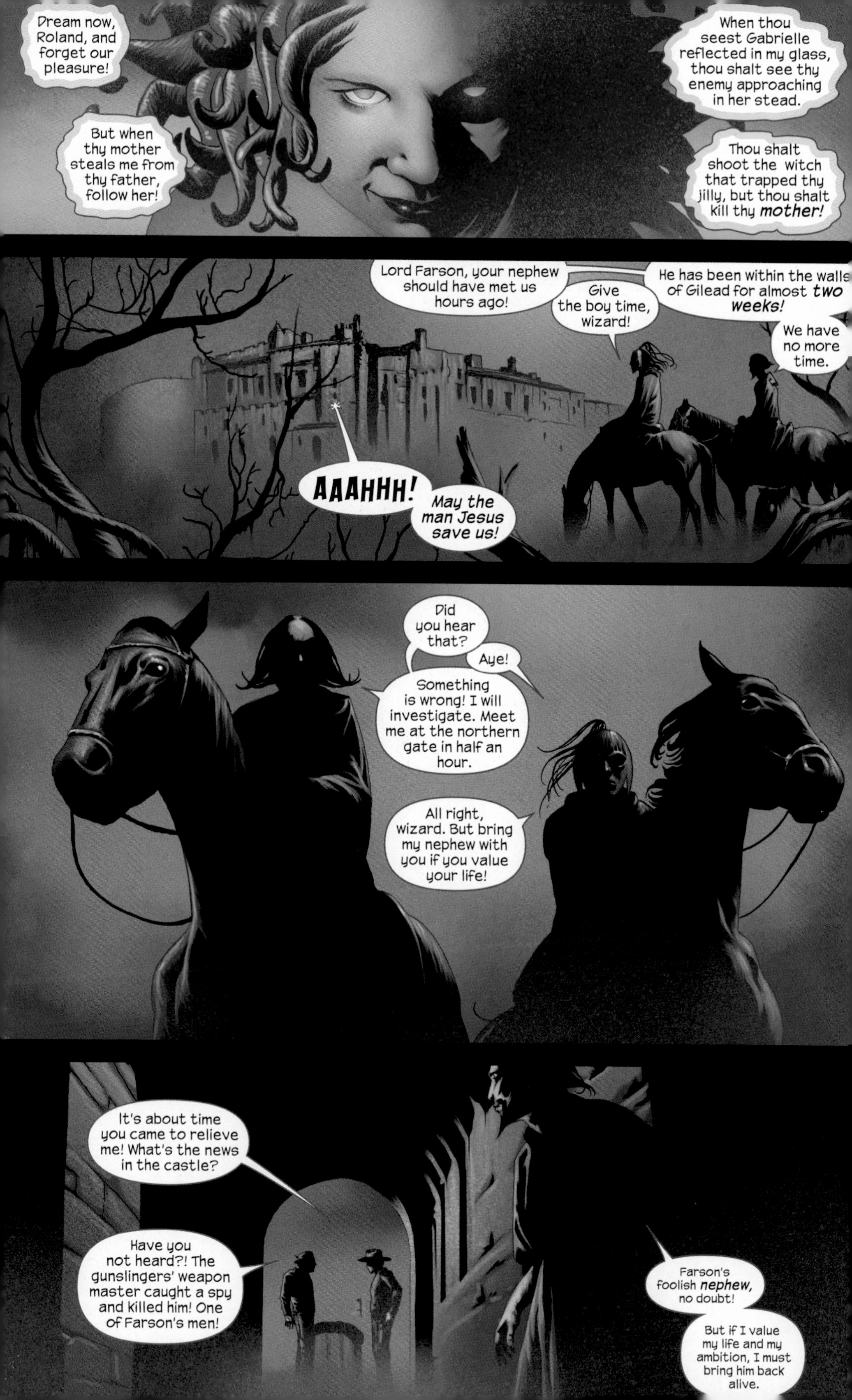
Dream now, Roland, and forget our pleasure!
But when thy mother steals me from thy father, follow her!
When thou seest Gabrielle reflected in my glass, thou shalt see thy enemy approaching in her stead.
Thou shalt shoot the witch that trapped thy jilly, but thou shalt kill thy *mother!*
Lord Farson, your nephew should have met us hours ago!
Give the boy time, wizard!
He has been within the walls of Gilead for almost *two weeks!*
We have no more time.
AAAHHH!
May the man Jesus save us!
Did you hear that?
Aye!
Something is wrong! I will investigate. Meet me at the northern gate in half an hour.
All right, wizard. But bring my nephew with you if you value your life!
It's about time you came to relieve me! What's the news in the castle?
Have you not heard?! The gunslingers' weapon master caught a spy and killed him! One of Farson's men!
Farson's foolish *nephew,* no doubt!
But if I value my life and my ambition, I must bring him back alive.

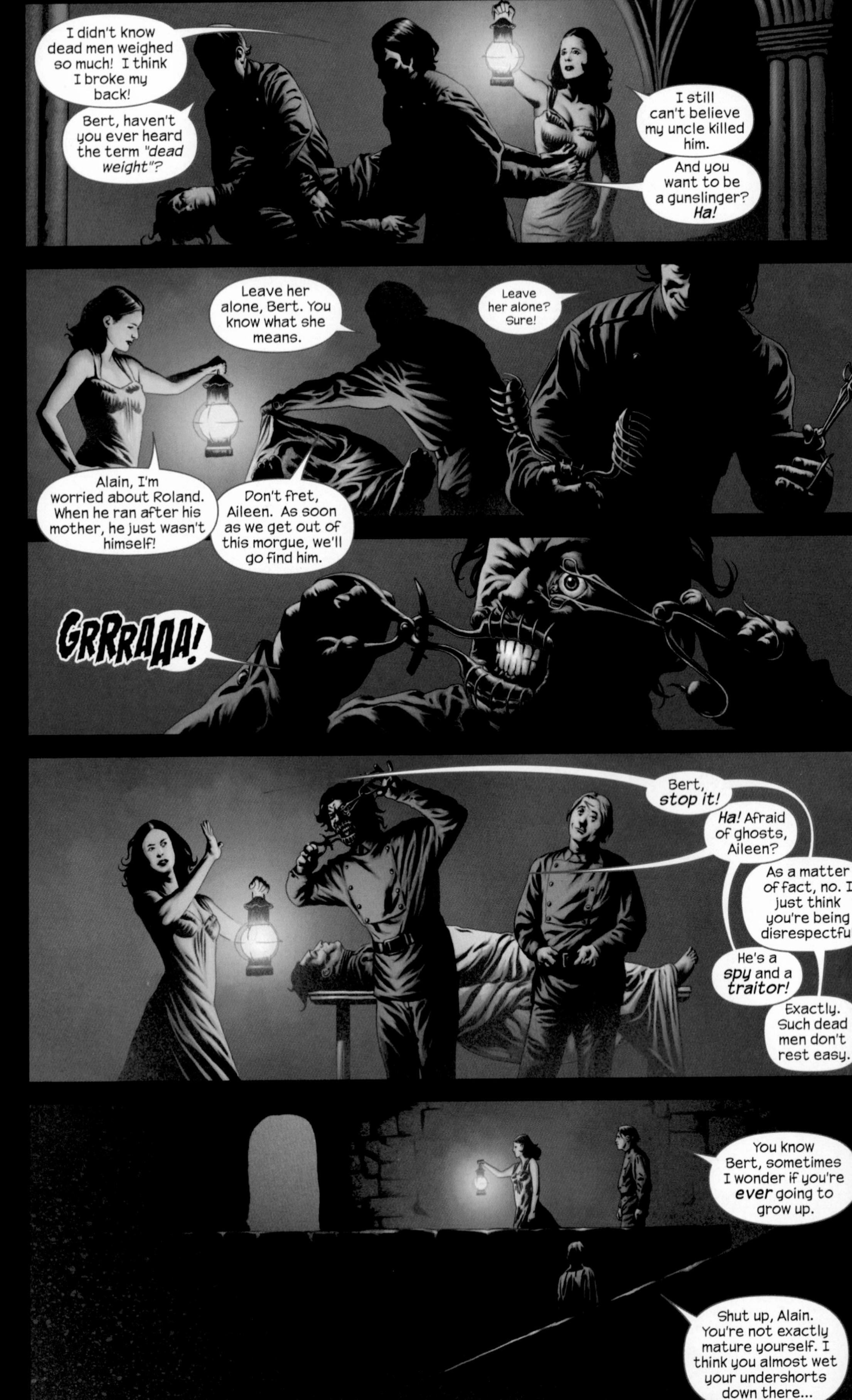
I didn't know dead men weighed so much! I think I broke my back!
Bert, haven't you ever heard the term "dead weight"?
I still can't believe my uncle killed him.
And you want to be a gunslinger? Ha!
Leave her alone, Bert. You know what she means.
Leave her alone? Sure!
Alain, I'm worried about Roland. When he ran after his mother, he just wasn't himself!
Don't fret, Aileen. As soon as we get out of this morgue, we'll go find him.
GRRRAAA!
Bert, stop it!
Ha! Afraid of ghosts, Aileen?
As a matter of fact, no. I just think you're being disrespectfu
He's a spy and a traitor!
Exactly. Such dead men don't rest easy.
You know Bert, sometimes I wonder if you're ever going to grow up.
Shut up, Alain. You're not exactly mature yourself. I think you almost wet your undershorts down there...

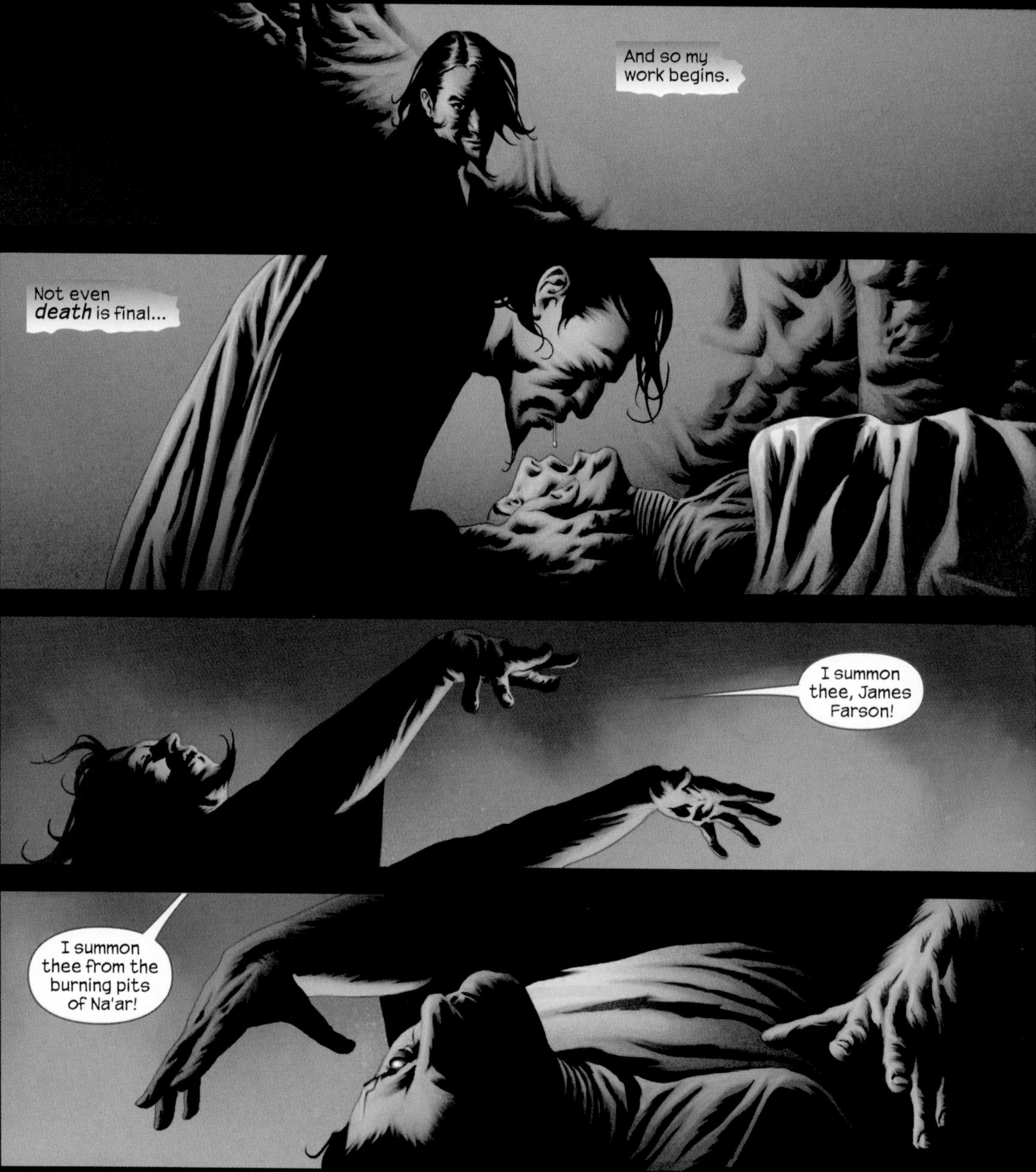
And so my work begins.
Not even *death* is final...
I summon thee, James Farson!
I summon thee from the burning pits of Na'ar!

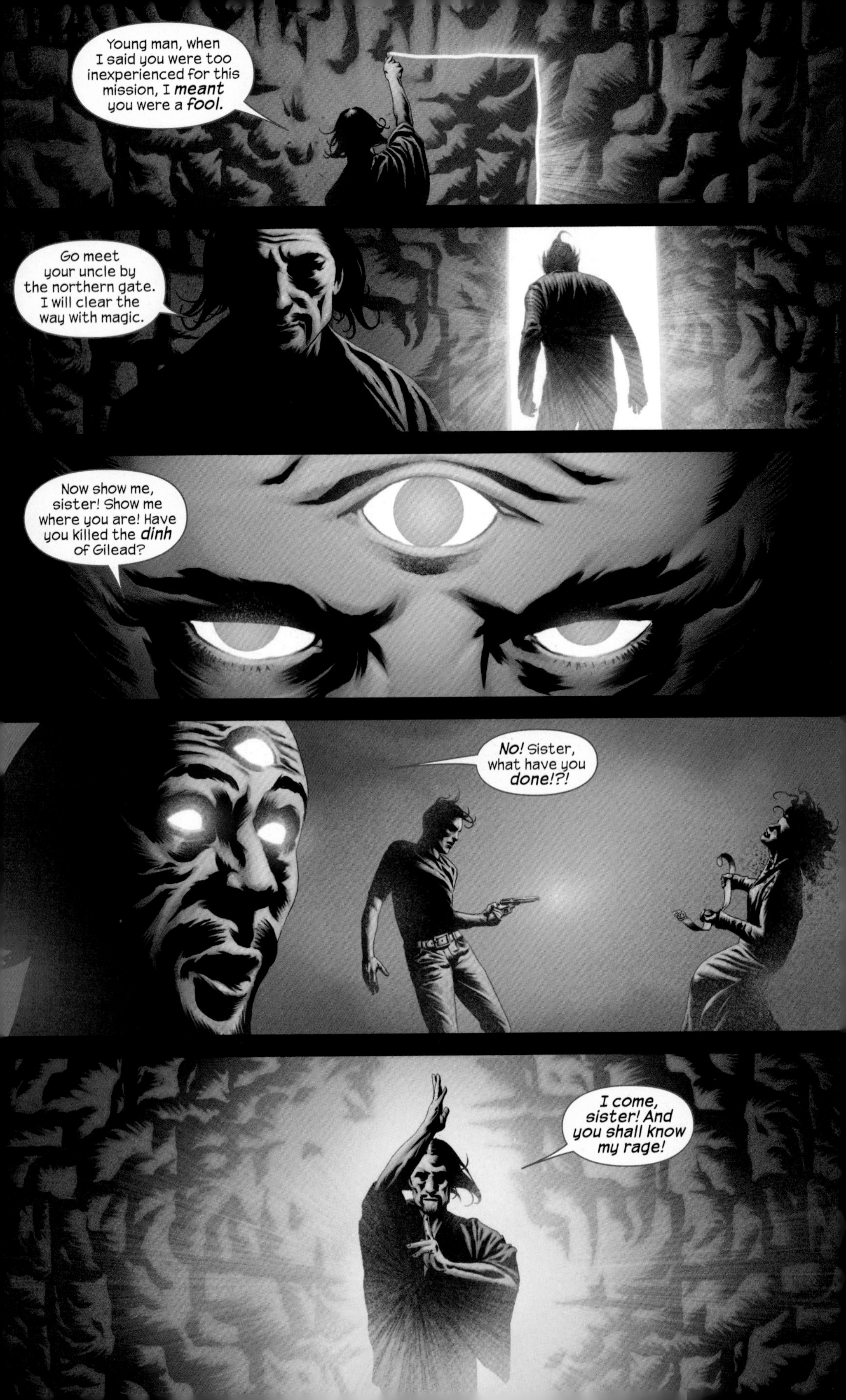
Young man, when I said you were too inexperienced for this mission, I *meant* you were a *fool.*
Go meet your uncle by the northern gate. I will clear the way with magic.
Now show me, sister! Show me where you are! Have you killed the *dinh* of Gilead?
No! Sister, what have you *done!?!*
I come, sister! And you shall know my rage!

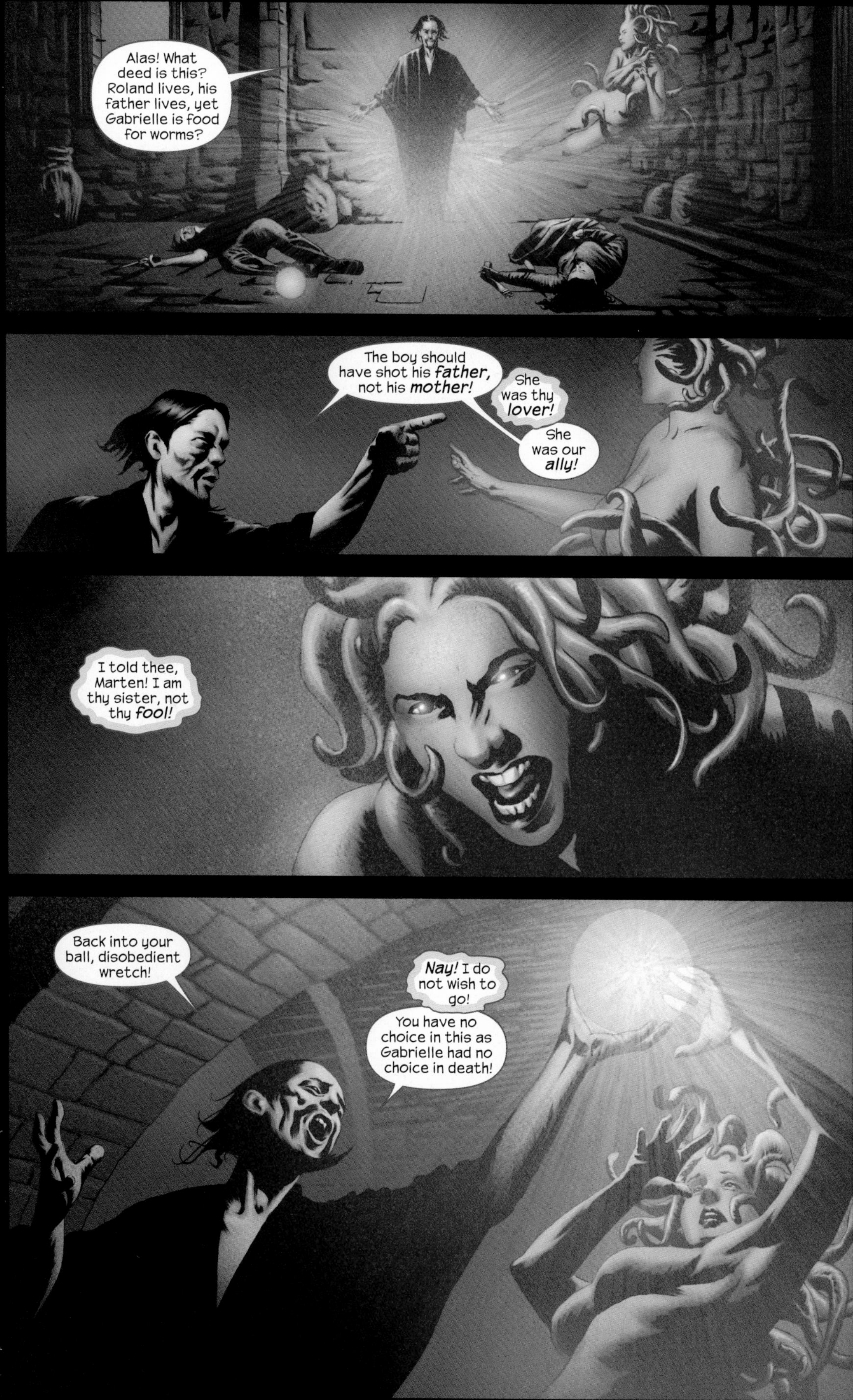
Alas! What deed is this? Roland lives, his father lives, yet Gabrielle is food for worms?
The boy should have shot his *father*, not his *mother*!
She was thy *lover*!
She was our *ally*!
I told thee, Marten! I am thy sister, not thy *fool*!
Back into your ball, disobedient wretch!
Nay! I do not wish to go!
You have no choice in this as Gabrielle had no choice in death!

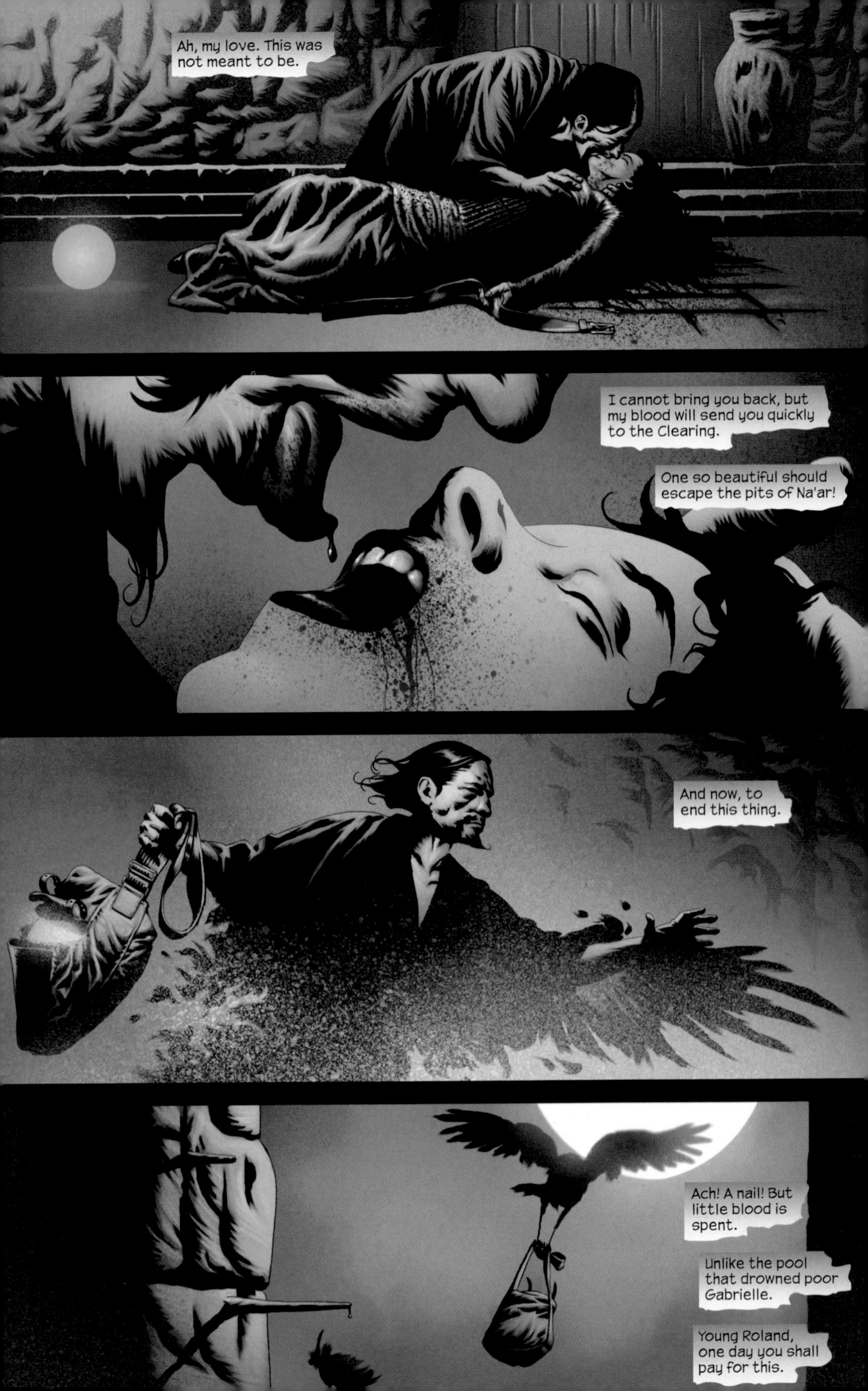
Ah, my love. This was not meant to be.
I cannot bring you back, but my blood will send you quickly to the Clearing.
One so beautiful should escape the pits of Na'ar!
And now, to end this thing.
Ach! A nail! But little blood is spent.
Unlike the pool that drowned poor Gabrielle.
Young Roland, one day you shall pay for this.

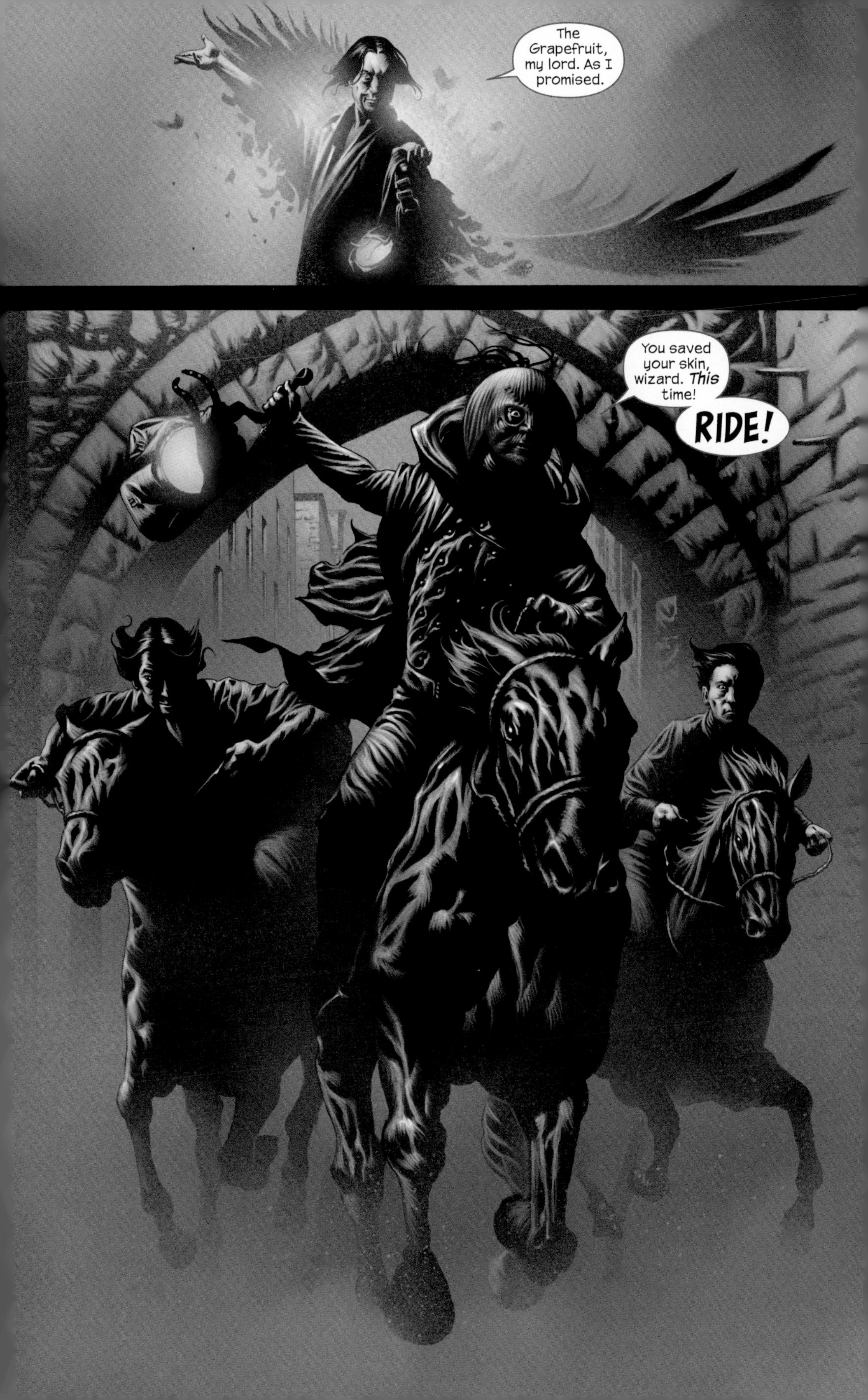
The Grapefruit, my lord. As I promised.
You saved your skin, wizard. *This* time!
RIDE!

STEPHEN KING

THE DARK TOWER

FALL OF GILEAD

CHAPTER ONE

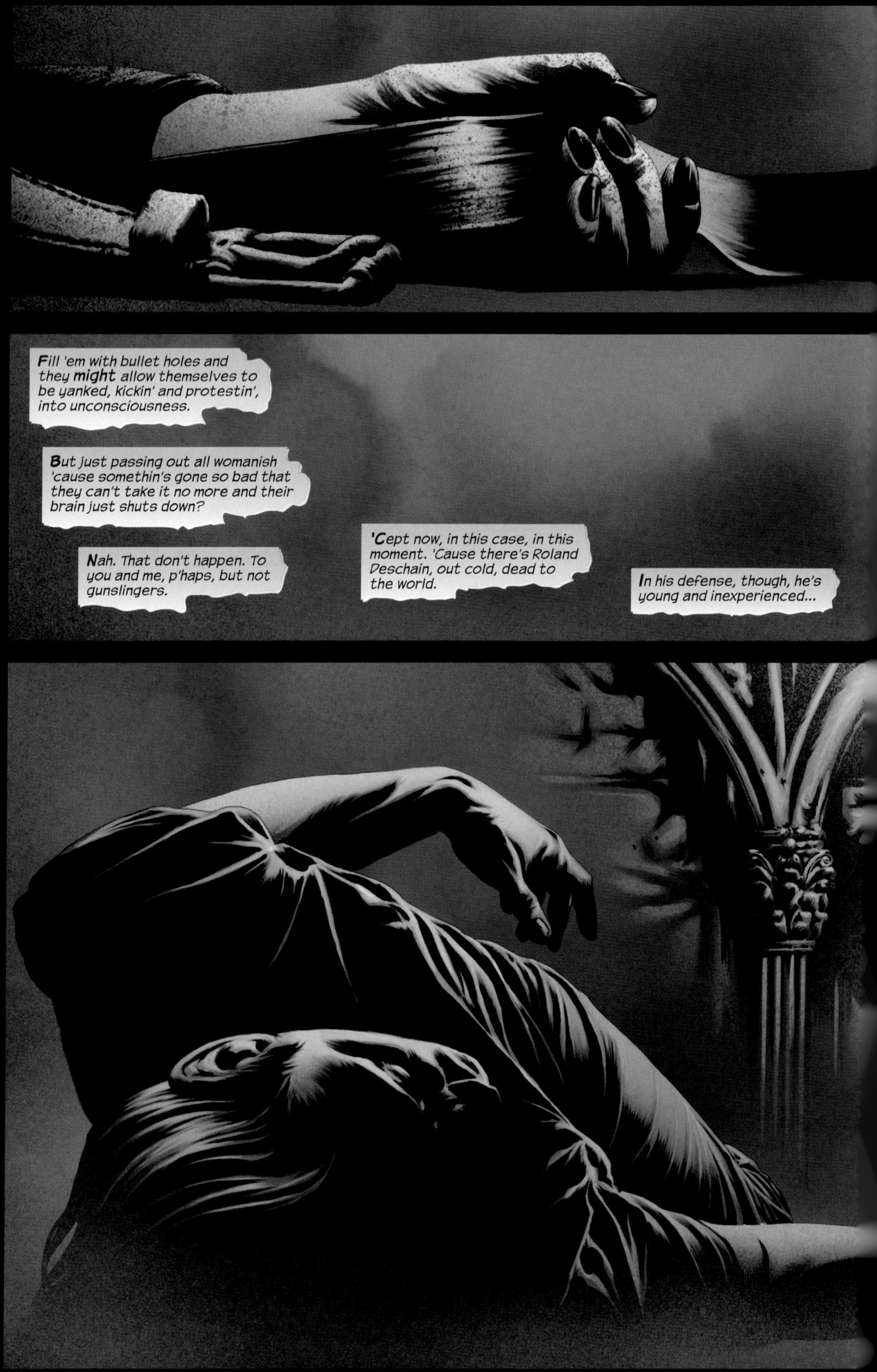
Fill 'em with bullet holes and they might allow themselves to be yanked, kickin' and protestin', into unconsciousness.
But just passing out all womanish 'cause somethin's gone so bad that they can't take it no more and their brain just shuts down?
Nah. That don't happen. To you and me, p'haps, but not gunslingers.
'Cept now, in this case, in this moment. 'Cause there's Roland Deschain, out cold, dead to the world.
In his defense, though, he's young and inexperienced...

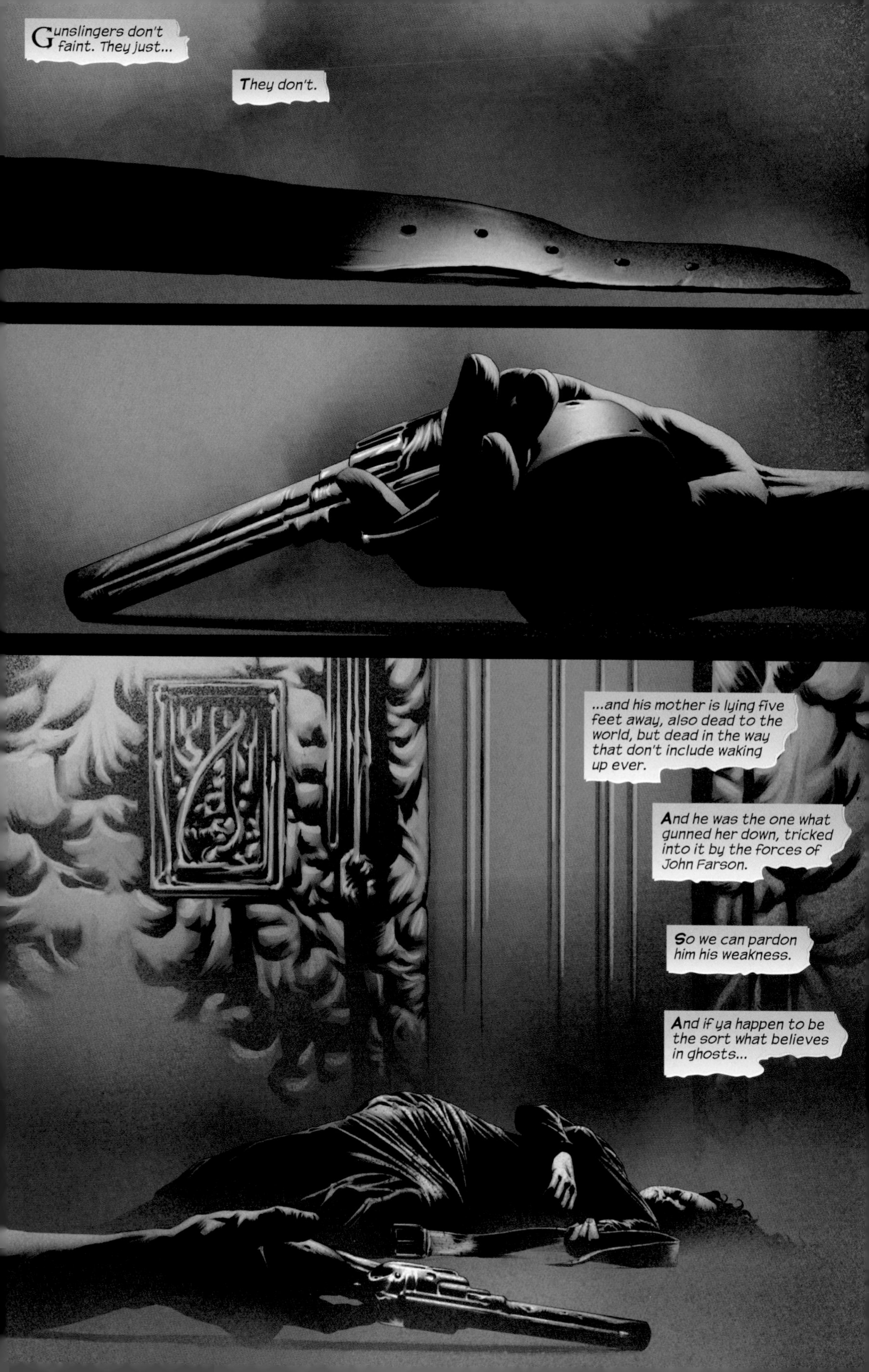
Gunslingers don't faint. They just...
They don't.
...and his mother is lying five feet away, also dead to the world, but dead in the way that don't include waking up ever.
And he was the one what gunned her down, tricked into it by the forces of John Farson.
So we can pardon him his weakness.
And if ya happen to be the sort what believes in ghosts...

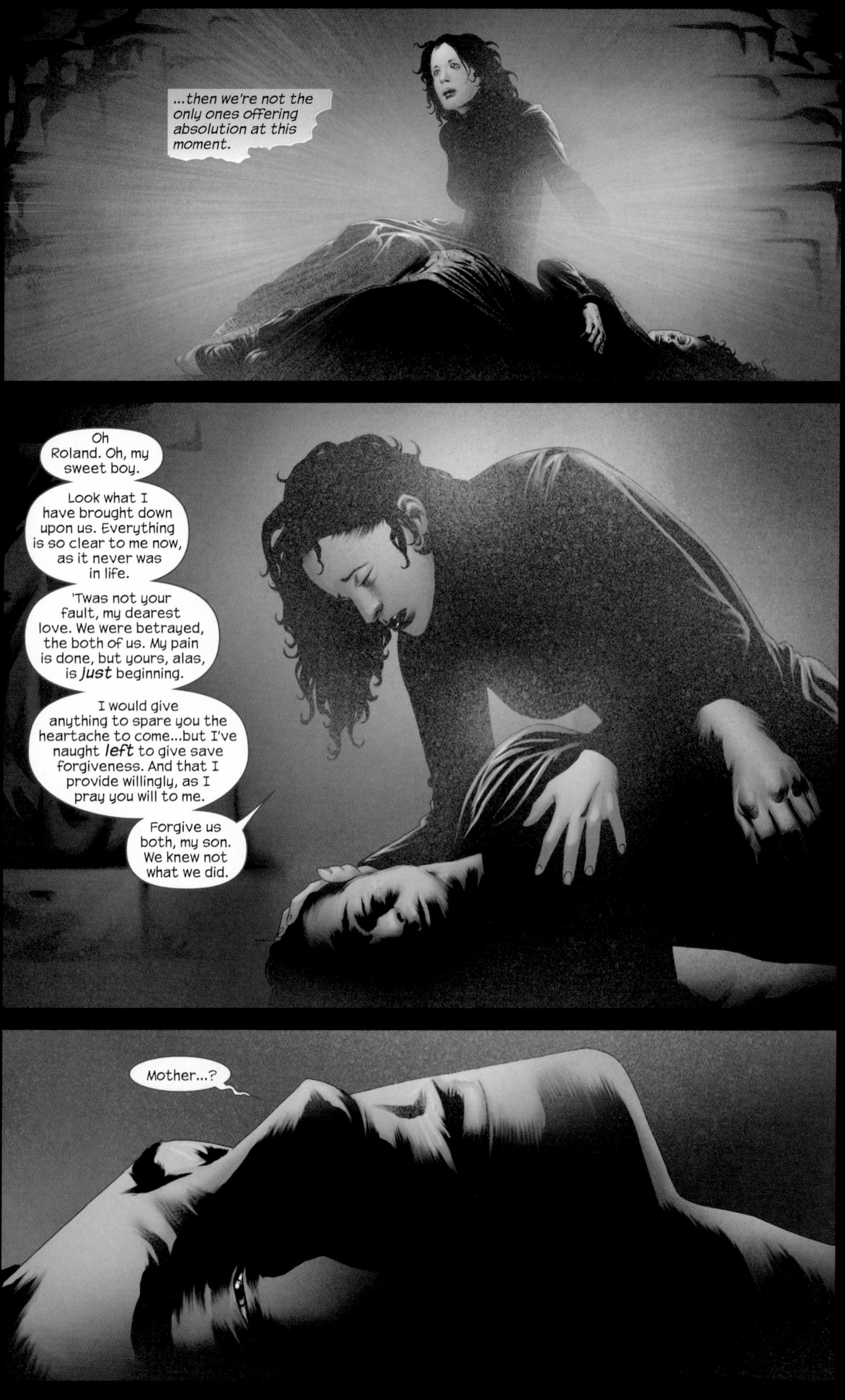
...then we're not the only ones offering absolution at this moment.
Oh Roland. Oh, my sweet boy.
Look what I have brought down upon us. Everything is so clear to me now, as it never was in life.
'Twas not your fault, my dearest love. We were betrayed, the both of us. My pain is done, but yours, alas, is *just* beginning.
I would give anything to spare you the heartache to come...but I've naught *left* to give save forgiveness. And that I provide willingly, as I pray you will to me.
Forgive us both, my son. We knew not what we did.
Mother...?

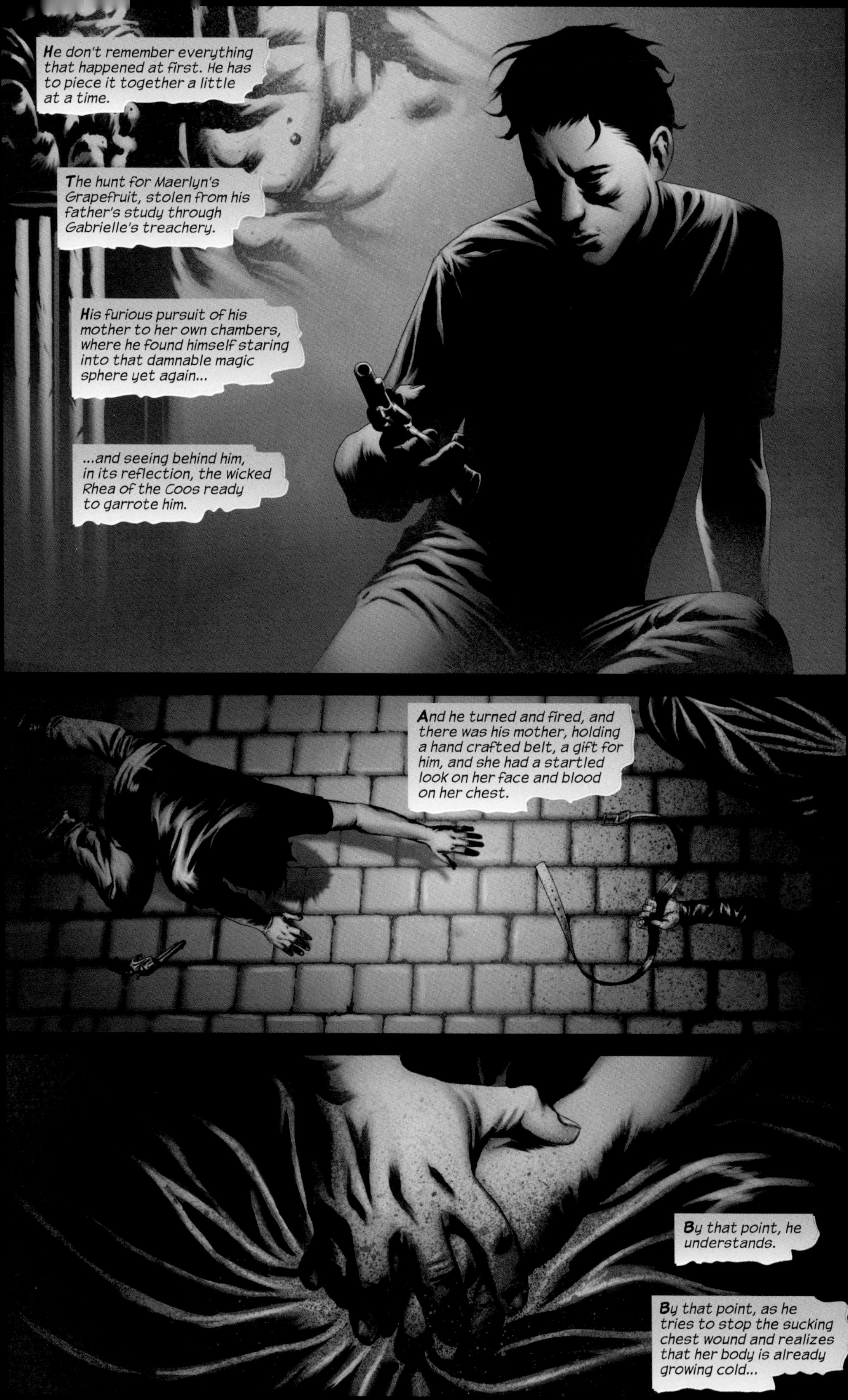
He don't remember everything that happened at first. He has to piece it together a little at a time.
The hunt for Maerlyn's Grapefruit, stolen from his father's study through Gabrielle's treachery.
His furious pursuit of his mother to her own chambers, where he found himself staring into that damnable magic sphere yet again...
...and seeing behind him, in its reflection, the wicked Rhea of the Coos ready to garrote him.
And he turned and fired, and there was his mother, holding a hand crafted belt, a gift for him, and she had a startled look on her face and blood on her chest.
By that point, he understands.
By that point, as he tries to stop the sucking chest wound and realizes that her body is already growing cold...

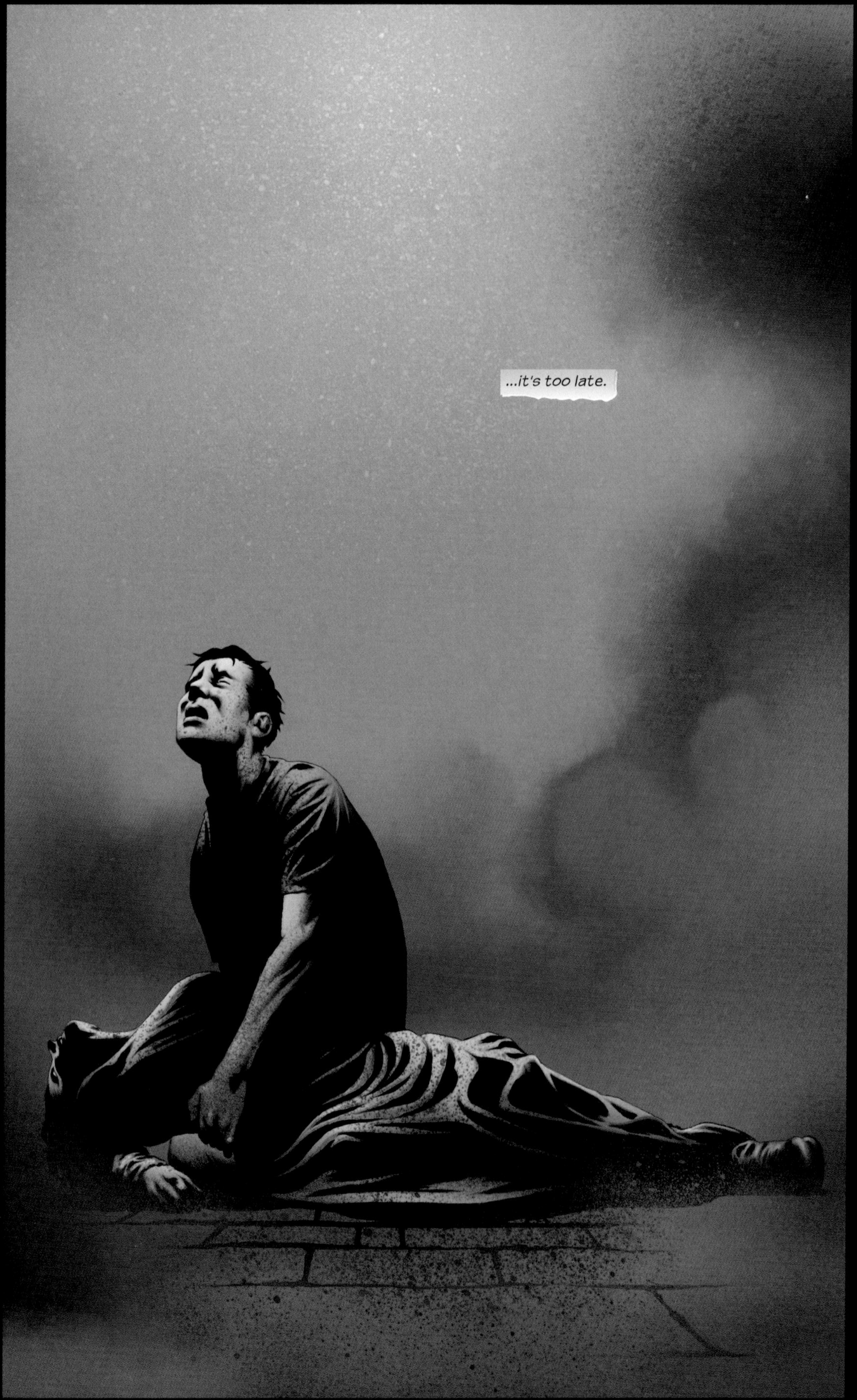
...it's too late.

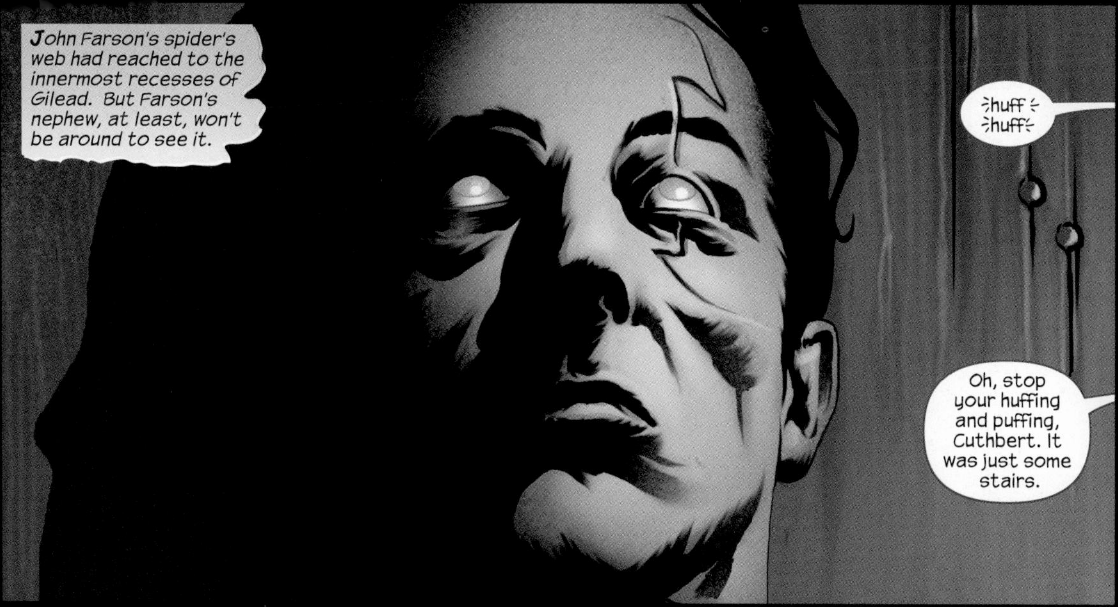
John Farson's spider's web had reached to the innermost recesses of Gilead. But Farson's nephew, at least, won't be around to see it.
huff huff
Oh, stop your huffing and puffing, Cuthbert. It was just some stairs.

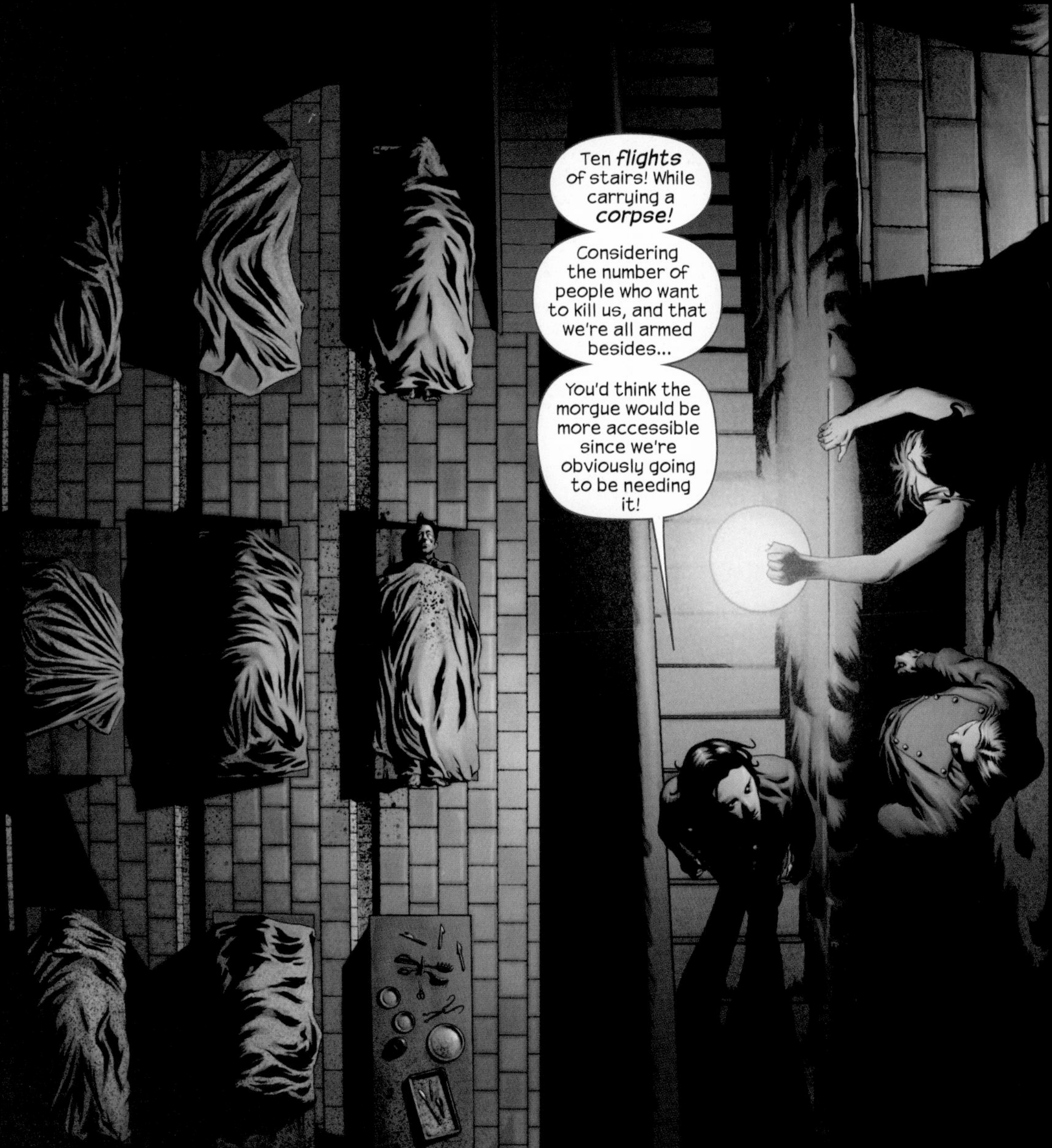
Ten flights of stairs! While carrying a corpse!
Considering the number of people who want to kill us, and that we're all armed besides...
You'd think the morgue would be more accessible since we're obviously going to be needing it!

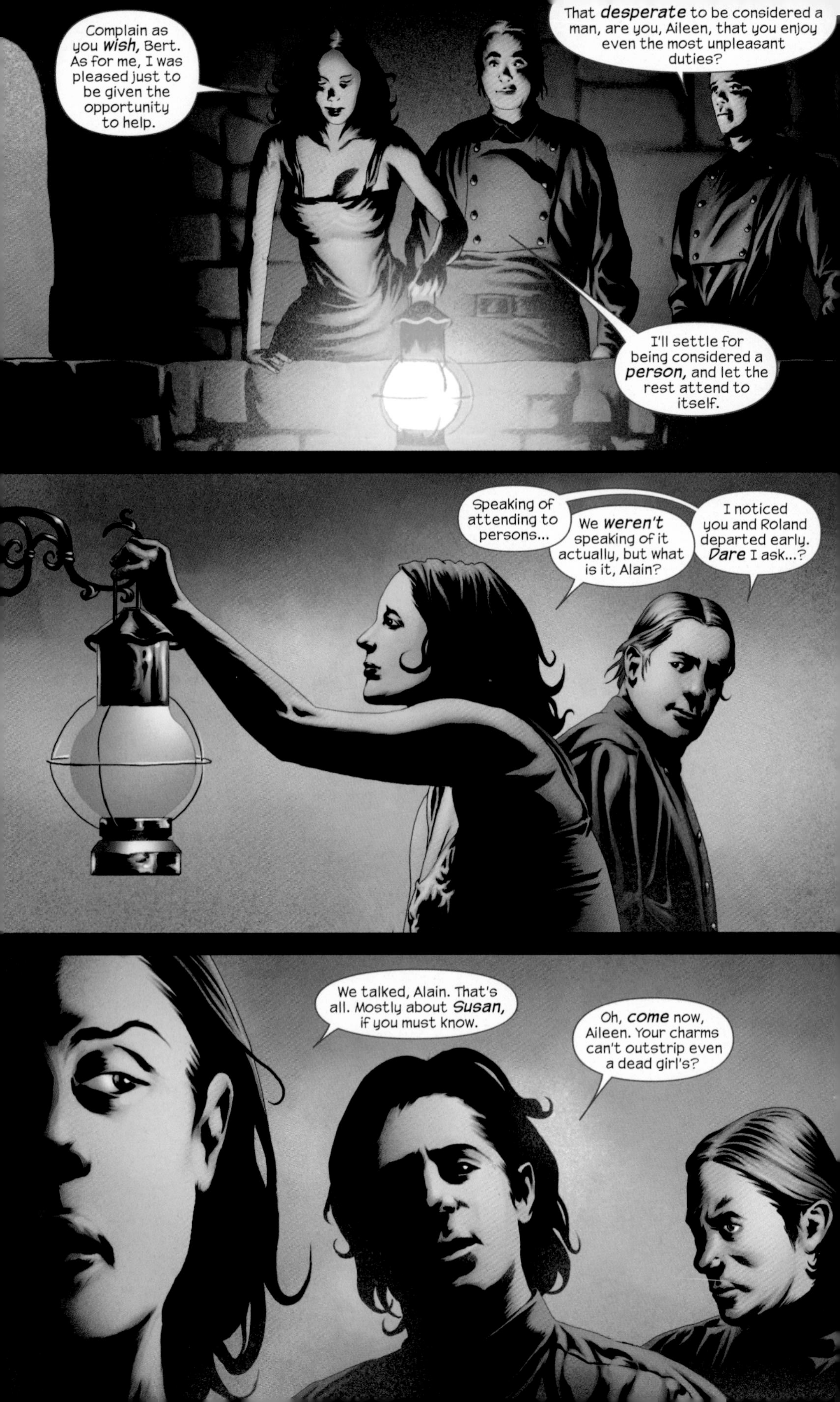
Complain as you *wish,* Bert. As for me, I was pleased just to be given the opportunity to help.
That *desperate* to be considered a man, are you, Aileen, that you enjoy even the most unpleasant duties?
I'll settle for being considered a *person,* and let the rest attend to itself.
Speaking of attending to persons...
We *weren't* speaking of it actually, but what is it, Alain?
I noticed you and Roland departed early. *Dare* I ask...?
We talked, Alain. That's all. Mostly about *Susan,* if you must know.
Oh, *come* now, Aileen. Your charms can't outstrip even a dead girl's?

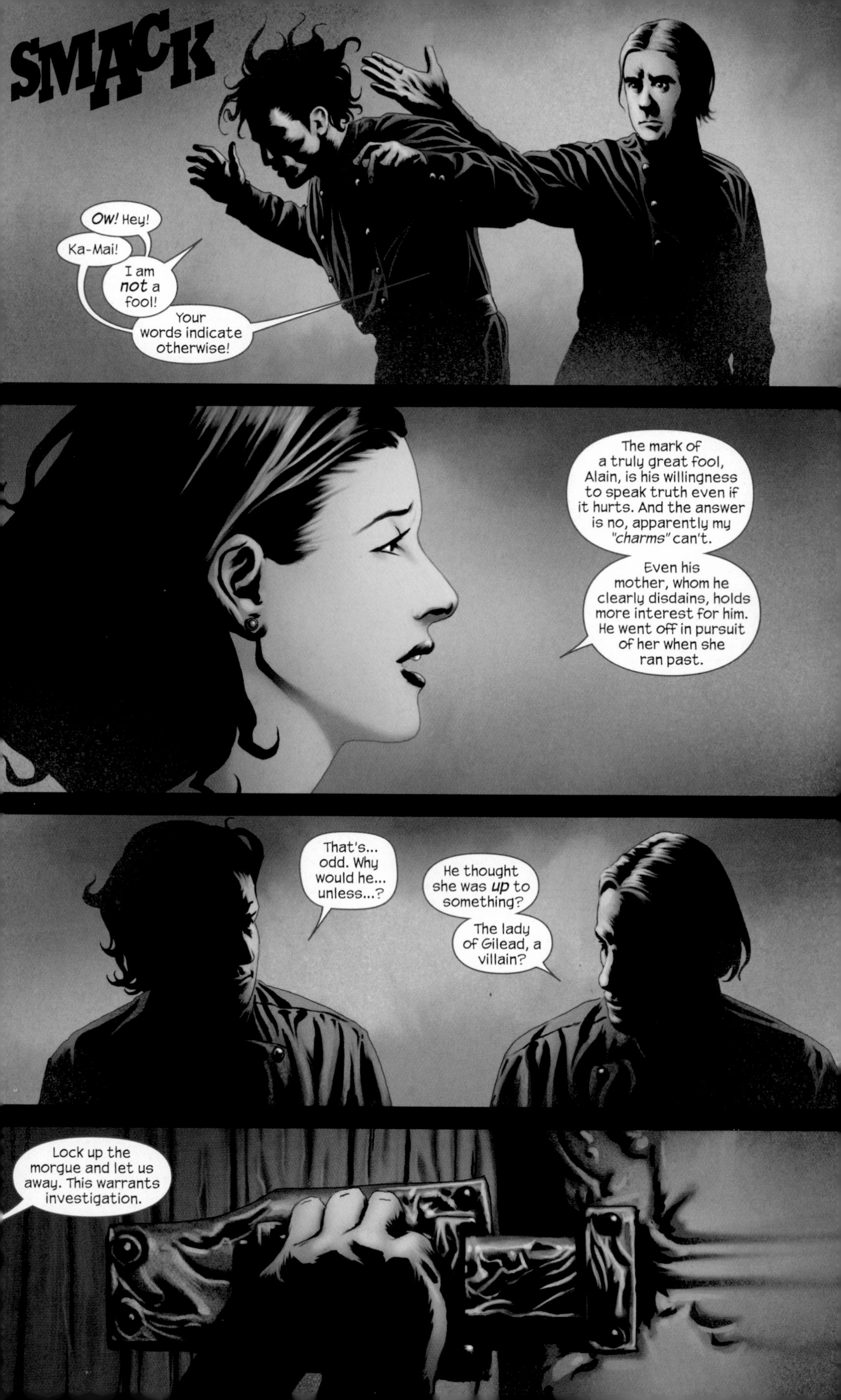
SMACK
OW! Hey!
Ka-Mai!
I am not a fool!
Your words indicate otherwise!
The mark of a truly great fool, Alain, is his willingness to speak truth even if it hurts. And the answer is no, apparently my "charms" can't.
Even his mother, whom he clearly disdains, holds more interest for him. He went off in pursuit of her when she ran past.
That's... odd. Why would he... unless...?
He thought she was up to something?
The lady of Gilead, a villain?
Lock up the morgue and let us away. This warrants investigation.

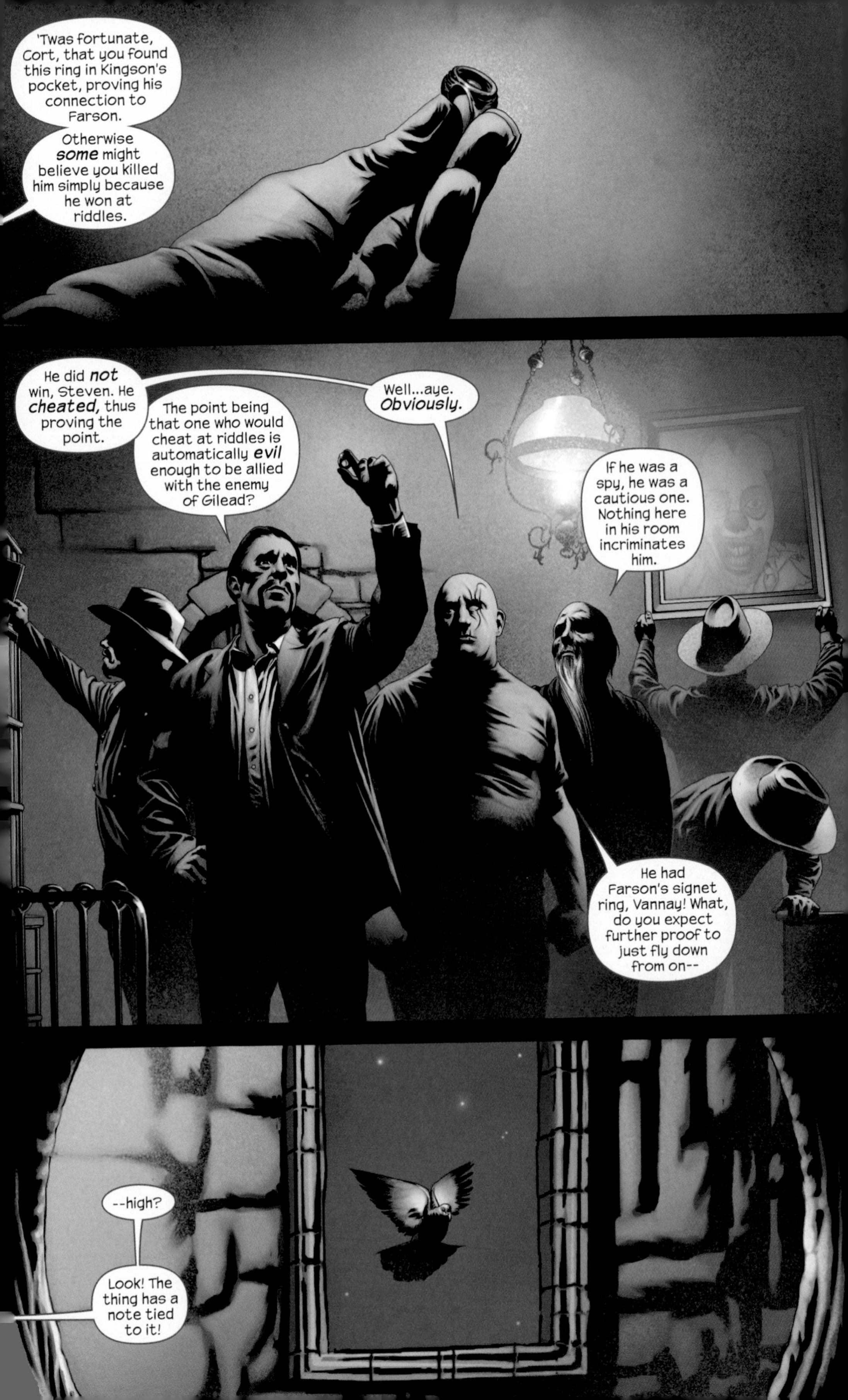

'Twas fortunate, Cort, that you found this ring in Kingson's pocket, proving his connection to Farson.
Otherwise *some* might believe you killed him simply because he won at riddles.
He did *not* win, Steven. He *cheated,* thus proving the point.
Well...aye. *Obviously.*
The point being that one who would cheat at riddles is automatically *evil* enough to be allied with the enemy of Gilead?
If he was a spy, he was a cautious one. Nothing here in his room incriminates him.
He had Farson's signet ring, Vannay! What, do you expect further proof to just fly down from on--
--high?
Look! The thing has a note tied to it!

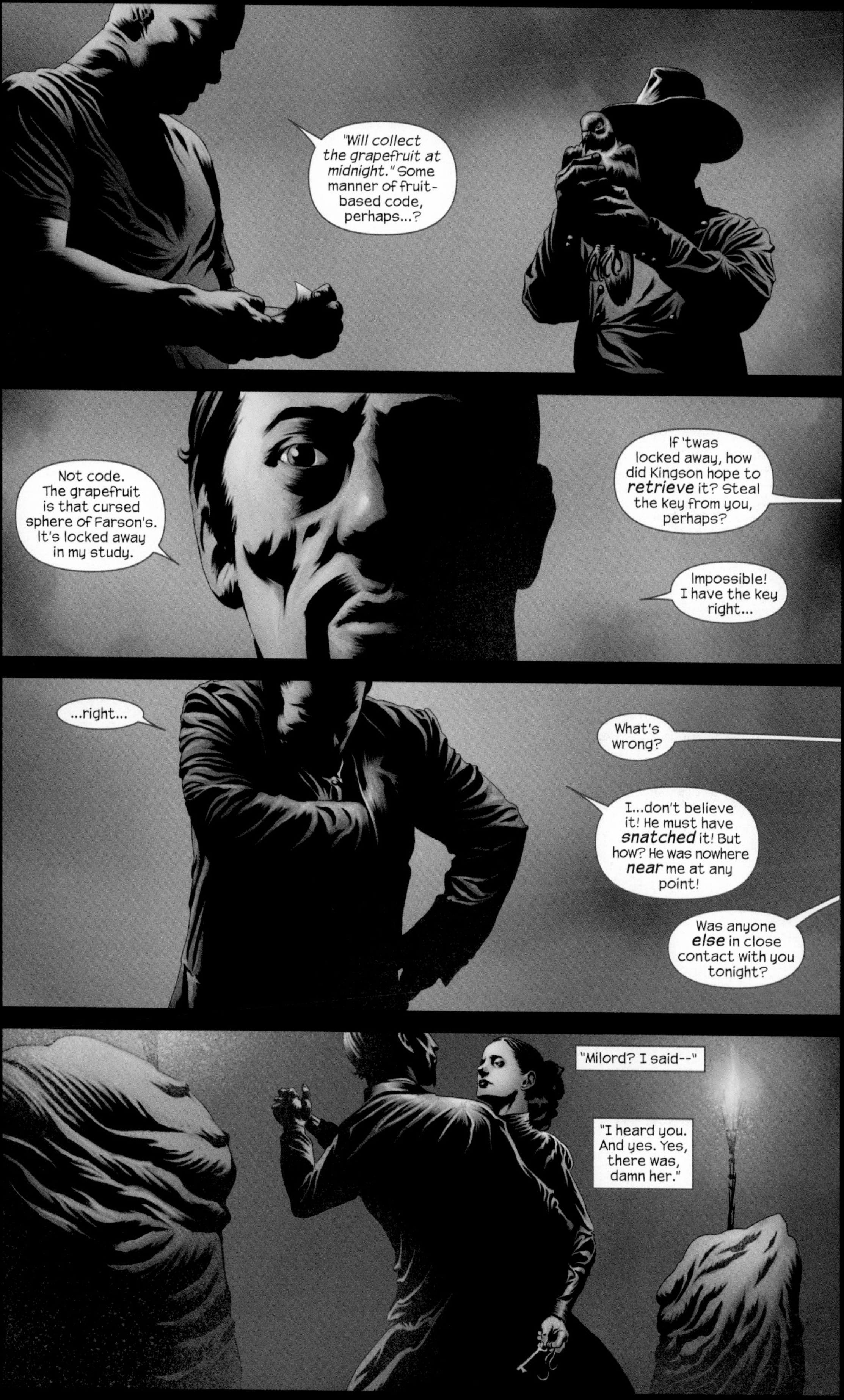
"Will collect the grapefruit at midnight." Some manner of fruit-based code, perhaps...?
Not code. The grapefruit is that cursed sphere of Farson's. It's locked away in my study.
If 'twas locked away, how did Kingson hope to retrieve it? Steal the key from you, perhaps?
Impossible! I have the key right...
...right...
What's wrong?
I...don't believe it! He must have snatched it! But how? He was nowhere near me at any point!
Was anyone else in close contact with you tonight?
"Milord? I said--"
"I heard you. And yes. Yes, there was, damn her."

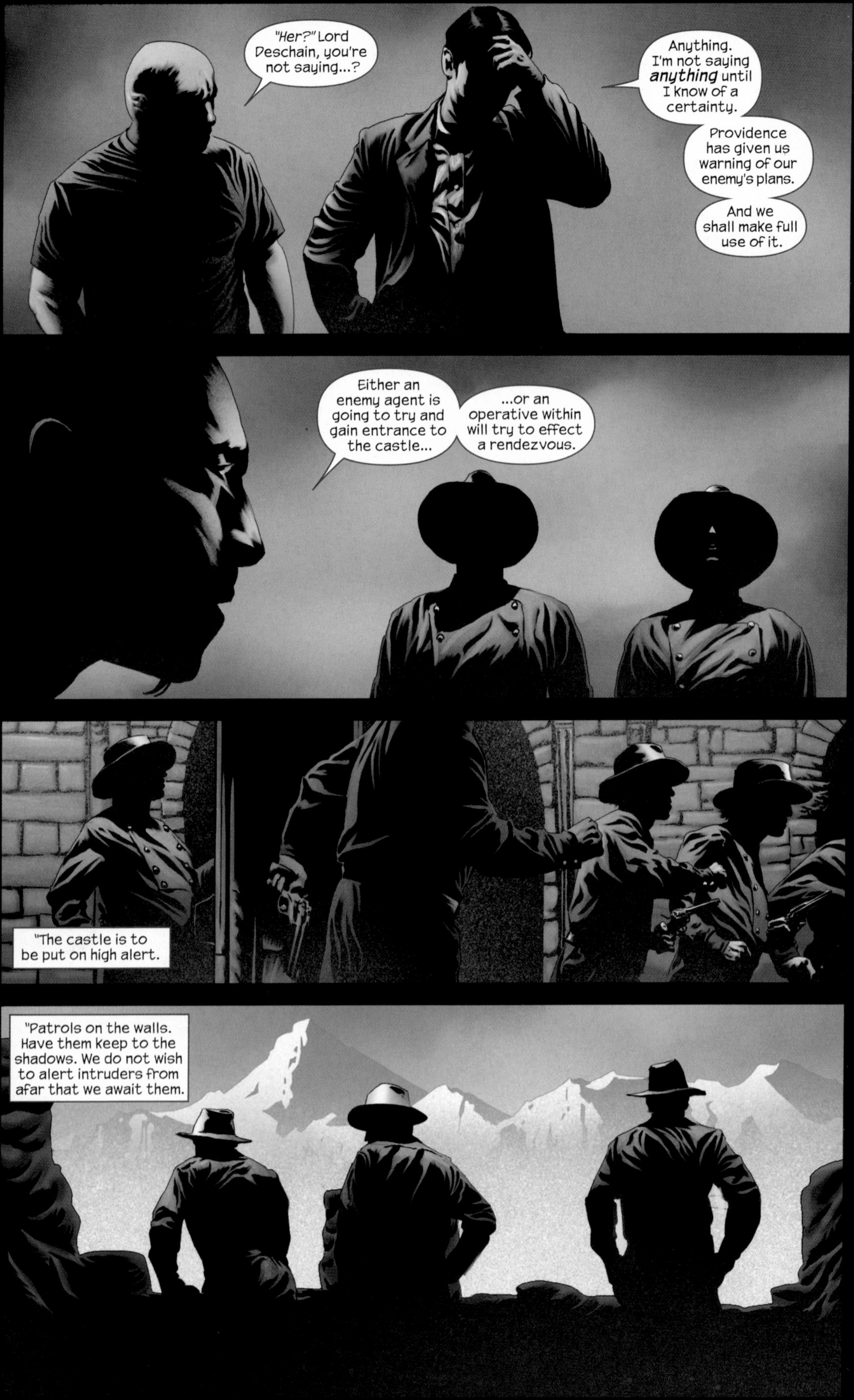
"Her?" Lord Deschain, you're not saying...?
Anything. I'm not saying anything until I know of a certainty.
Providence has given us warning of our enemy's plans.
And we shall make full use of it.
Either an enemy agent is going to try and gain entrance to the castle...
...or an operative within will try to effect a rendezvous.
"The castle is to be put on high alert.
"Patrols on the walls. Have them keep to the shadows. We do not wish to alert intruders from afar that we await them.

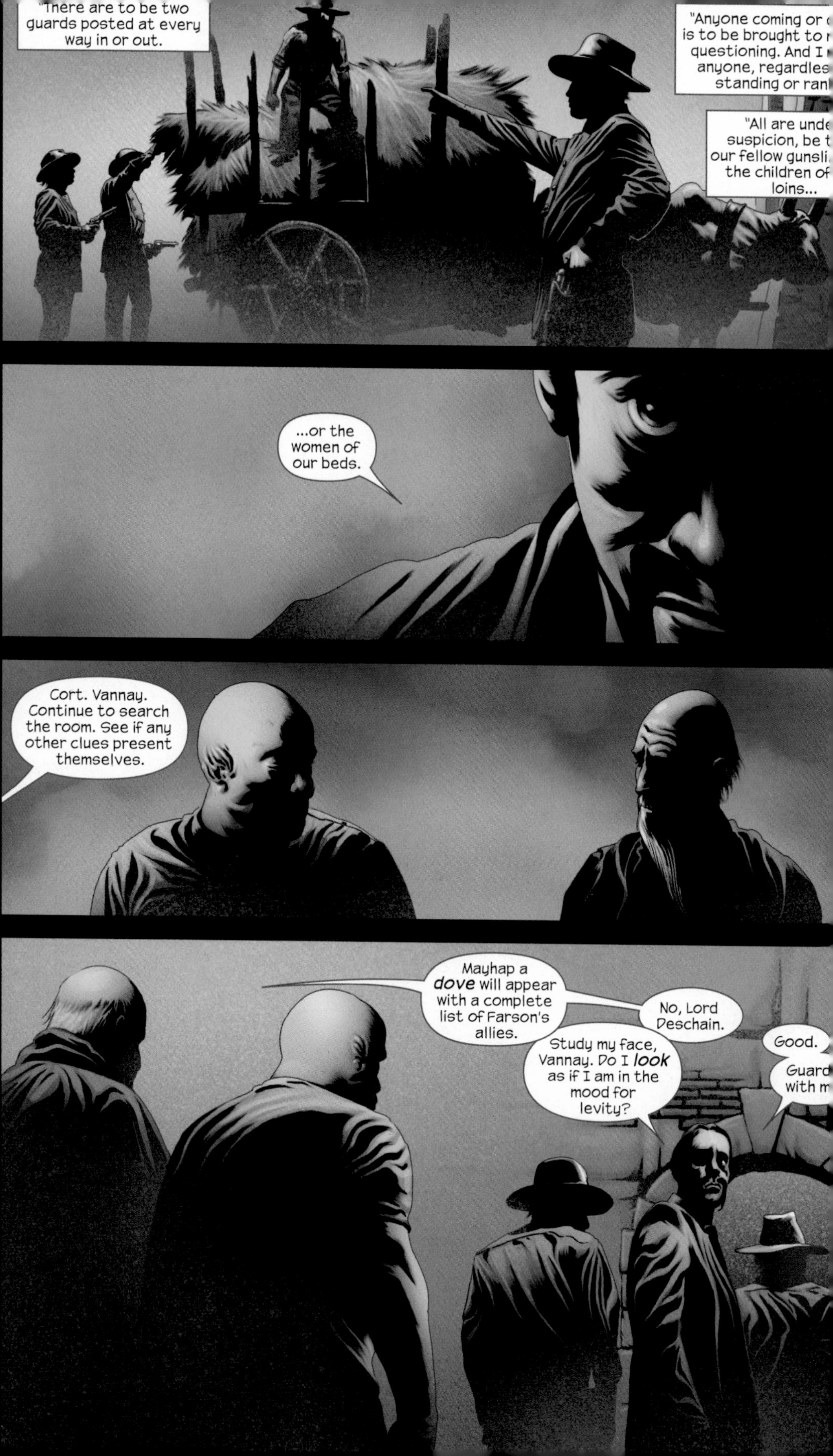
"There are to be two guards posted at every way in or out.
"Anyone coming or is to be brought to questioning. And I anyone, regardless standing or
"All are under suspicion, be our fellow the children of loins...
...or the women of our beds.
Cort. Vannay. Continue to search the room. See if any other clues present themselves.
Mayhap a *dove* will appear with a complete list of Farson's allies.
No, Lord Deschain.
Study my face, Vannay. Do I *look* as if I am in the mood for levity?
Good.
Guard with

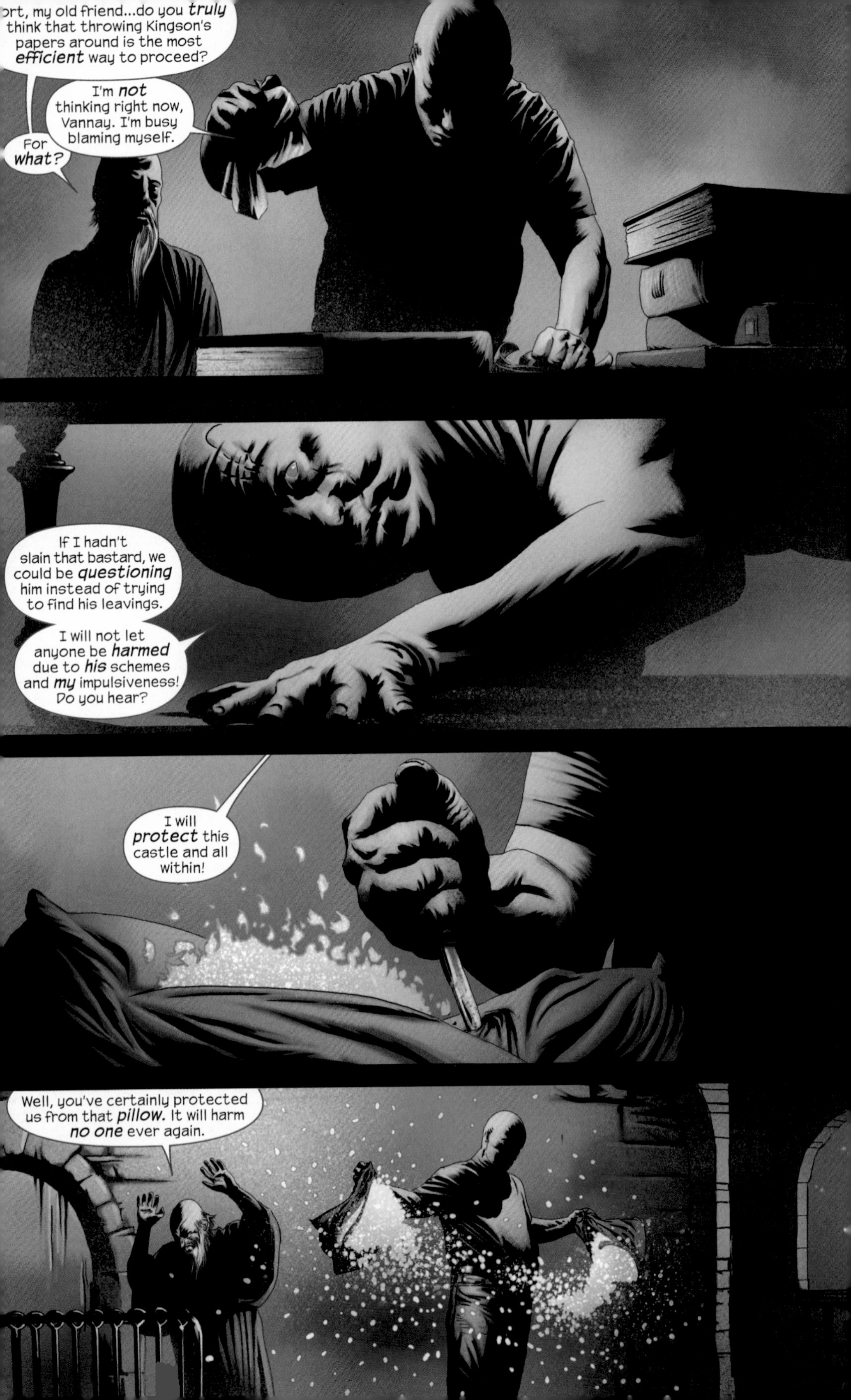
rt, my old friend...do you *truly* think that throwing Kingson's papers around is the most *efficient* way to proceed?
I'm *not* thinking right now, Vannay. I'm busy blaming myself.
For *what?*
If I hadn't slain that bastard, we could be *questioning* him instead of trying to find his leavings.
I will not let anyone be *harmed* due to *his* schemes and *my* impulsiveness! Do you hear?
I will *protect* this castle and all within!
Well, you've certainly protected us from that *pillow.* It will harm *no one* ever again.

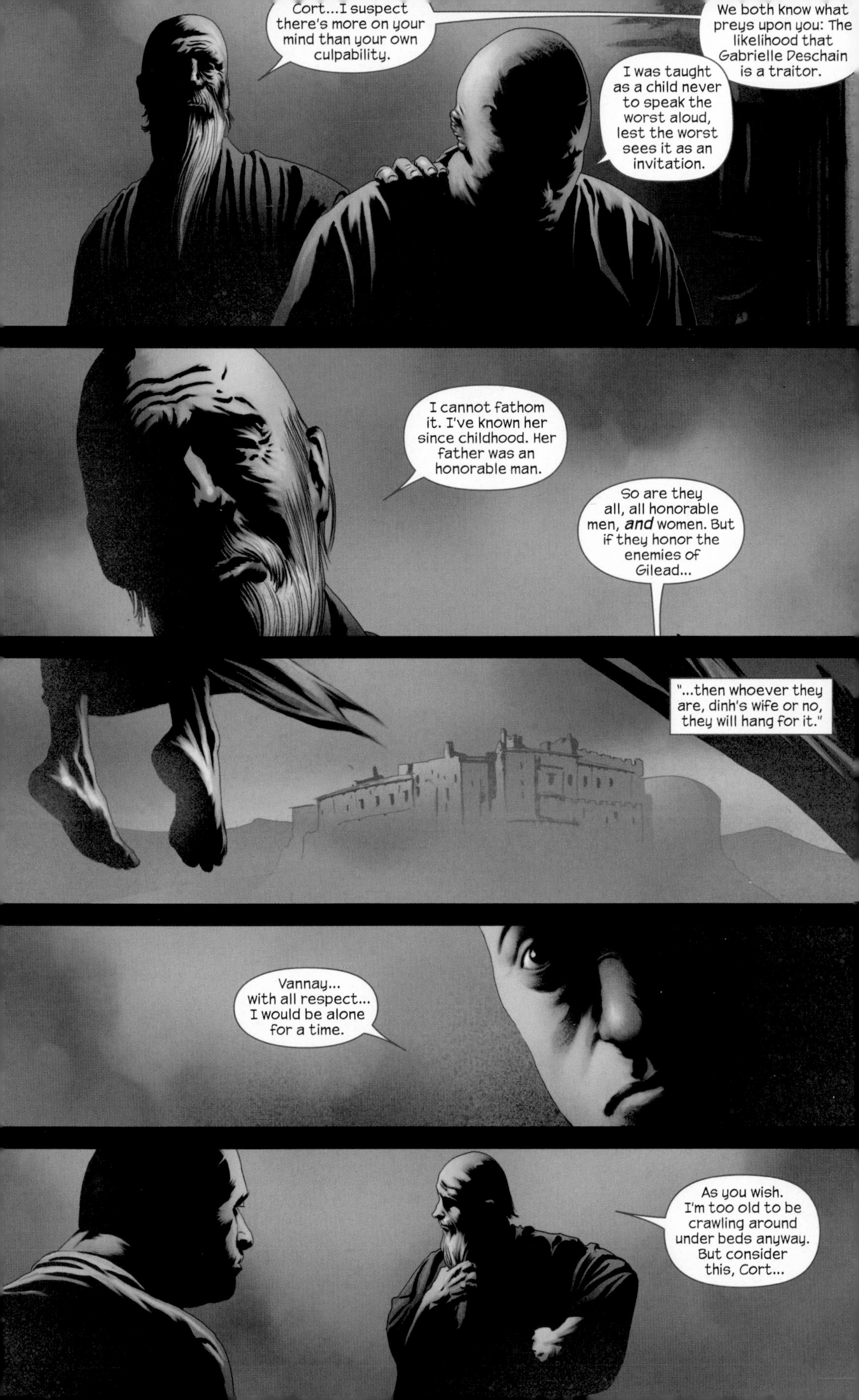
Cort...I suspect there's more on your mind than your own culpability.
We both know what preys upon you: The likelihood that Gabrielle Deschain is a traitor.
I was taught as a child never to speak the worst aloud, lest the worst sees it as an invitation.
I cannot fathom it. I've known her since childhood. Her father was an honorable man.
So are they all, all honorable men, *and* women. But if they honor the enemies of Gilead...
"...then whoever they are, dinh's wife or no, they will hang for it."
Vannay... with all respect... I would be alone for a time.
As you wish. I'm too old to be crawling around under beds anyway. But consider this, Cort...

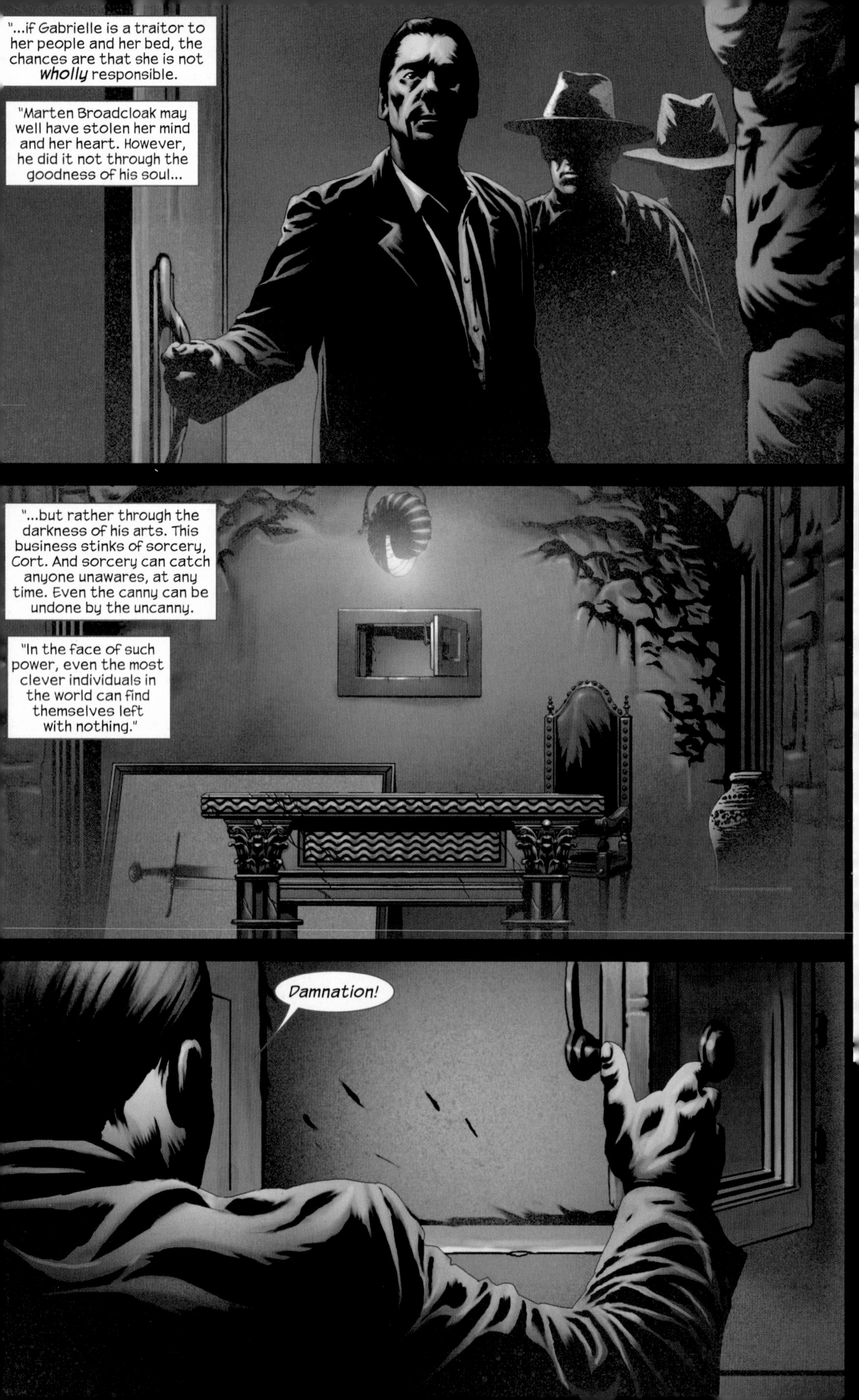
"...if Gabrielle is a traitor to her people and her bed, the chances are that she is not *wholly* responsible.
"Marten Broadcloak may well have stolen her mind and her heart. However, he did it not through the goodness of his soul...
"...but rather through the darkness of his arts. This business stinks of sorcery, Cort. And sorcery can catch anyone unawares, at any time. Even the canny can be undone by the uncanny.
"In the face of such power, even the most clever individuals in the world can find themselves left with nothing."
Damnation!

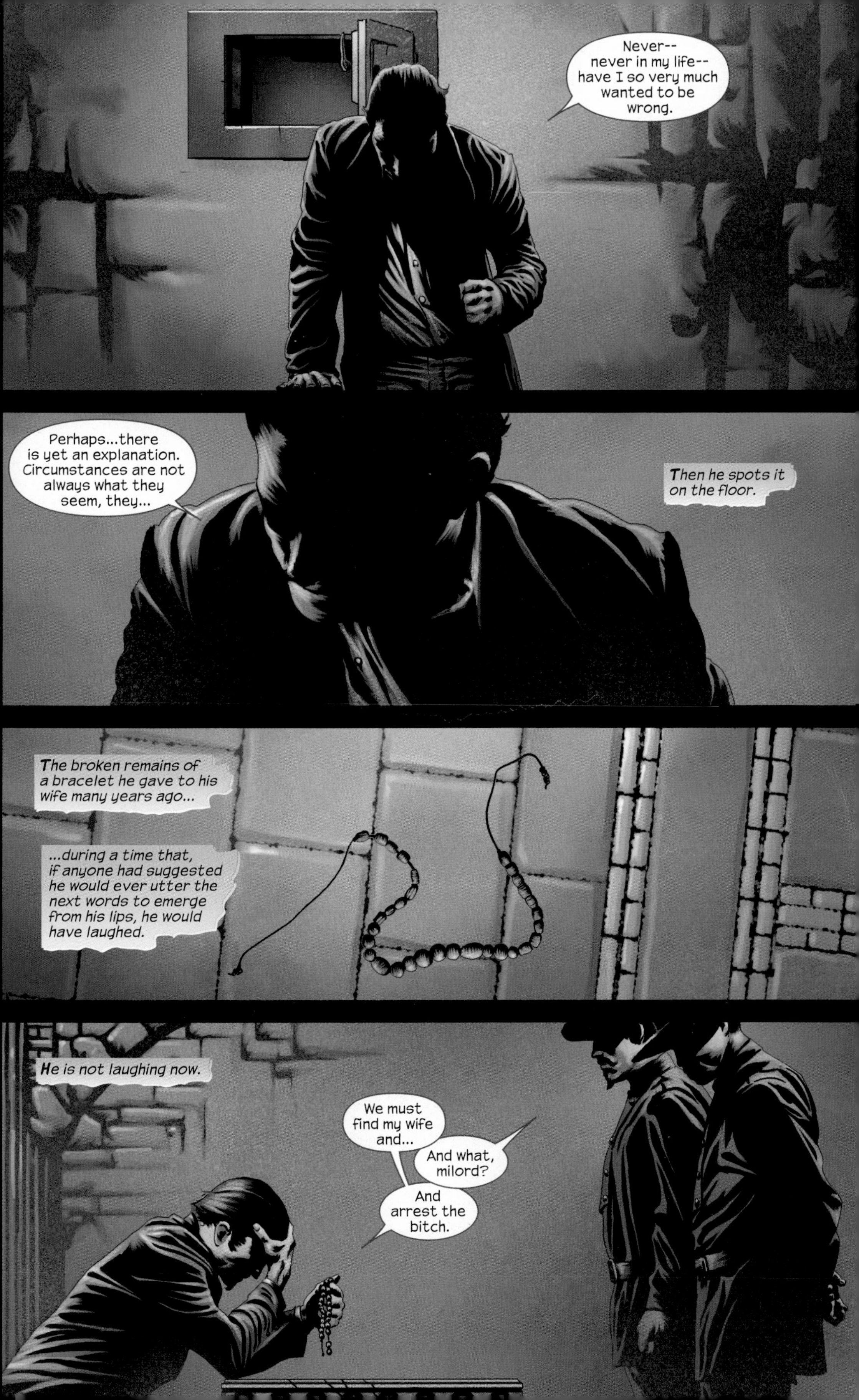
Never-- never in my life-- have I so very much wanted to be wrong.
Perhaps...there is yet an explanation. Circumstances are not always what they seem, they...
Then he spots it on the floor.
The broken remains of a bracelet he gave to his wife many years ago...
...during a time that, if anyone had suggested he would ever utter the next words to emerge from his lips, he would have laughed.
He is not laughing now.
We must find my wife and...
And what, milord?
And arrest the bitch.

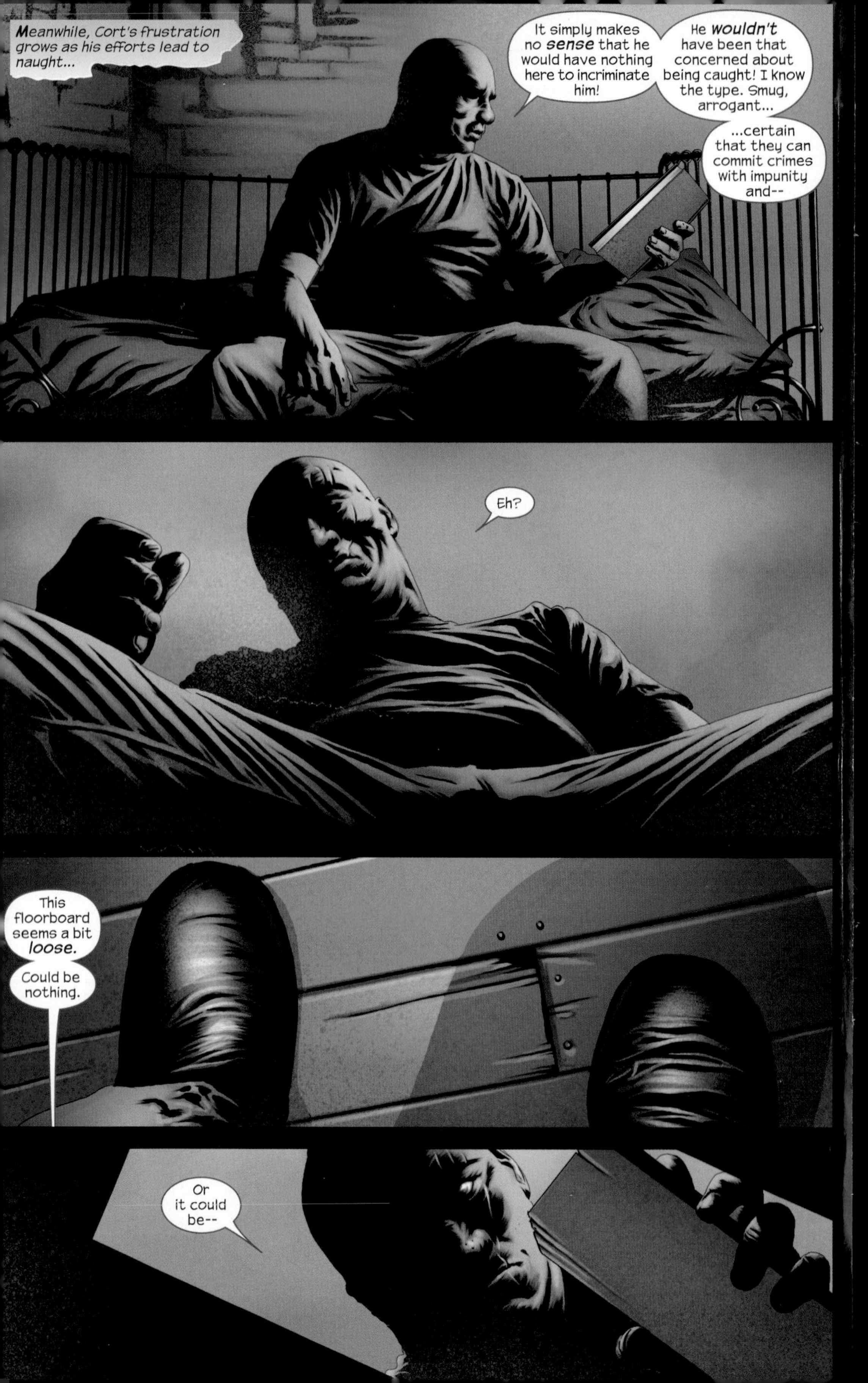

Meanwhile, Cort's frustration grows as his efforts lead to naught...
It simply makes no sense that he would have nothing here to incriminate him!
He wouldn't have been that concerned about being caught! I know the type. Smug, arrogant...
...certain that they can commit crimes with impunity and--
Eh?
This floorboard seems a bit loose.
Could be nothing.
Or it could be--

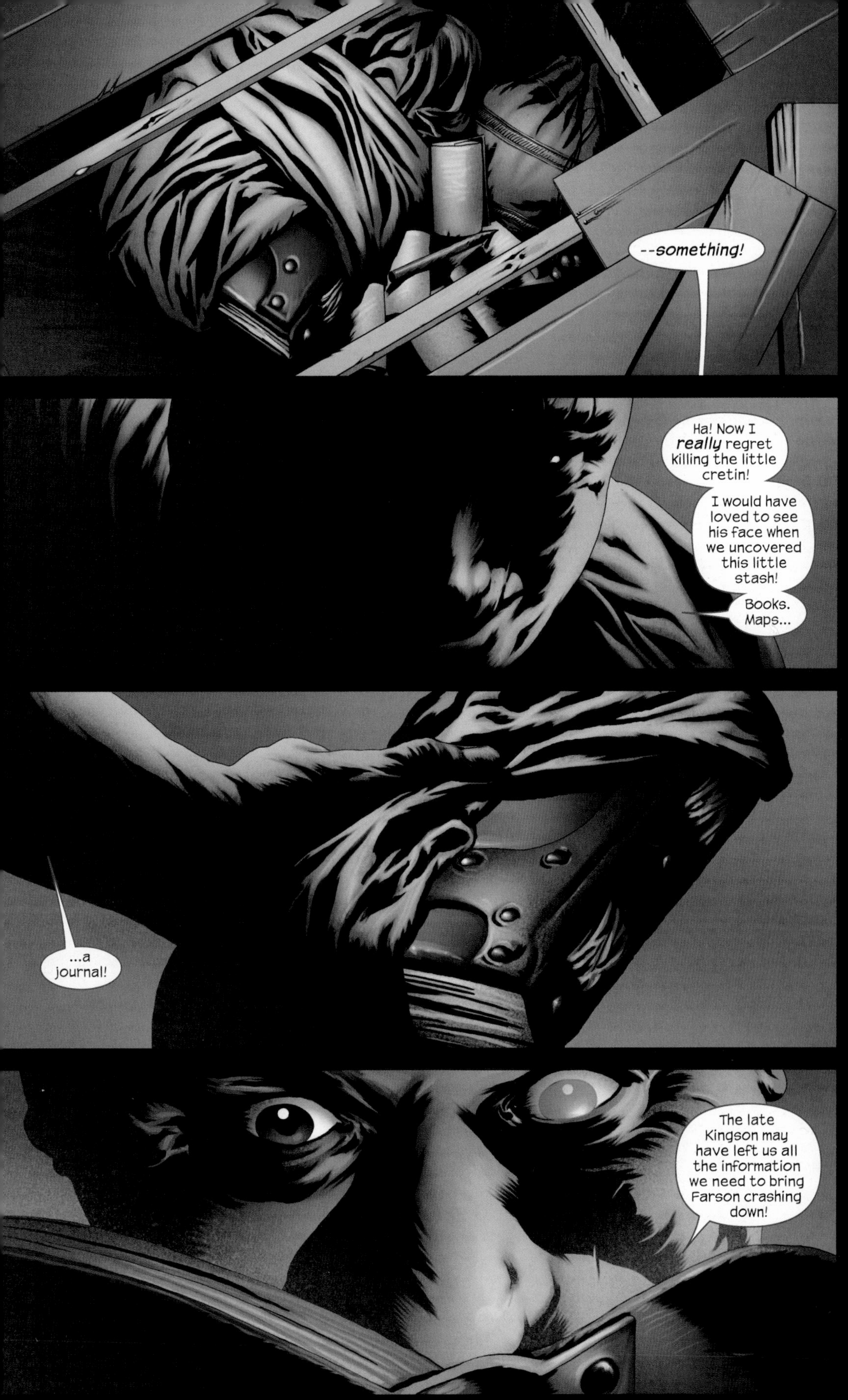
--something!
Ha! Now I really regret killing the little cretin!
I would have loved to see his face when we uncovered this little stash!
Books. Maps...
...a journal!
The late Kingson may have left us all the information we need to bring Farson crashing down!

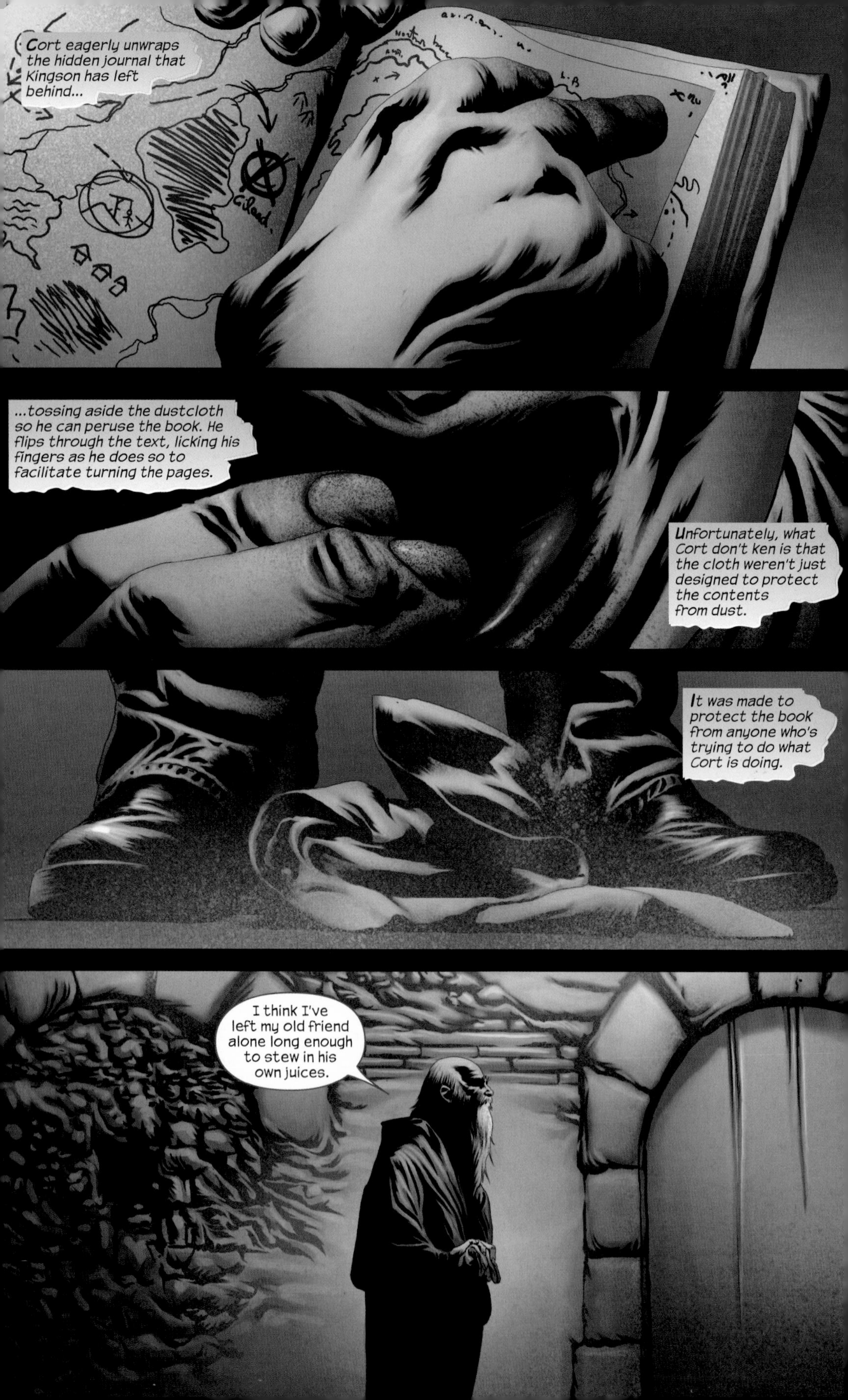
Cort eagerly unwraps the hidden journal that Kingson has left behind...
...tossing aside the dustcloth so he can peruse the book. He flips through the text, licking his fingers as he does so to facilitate turning the pages.
Unfortunately, what Cort don't ken is that the cloth weren't just designed to protect the contents from dust.
It was made to protect the book from anyone who's trying to do what Cort is doing.
I think I've left my old friend alone long enough to stew in his own juices.

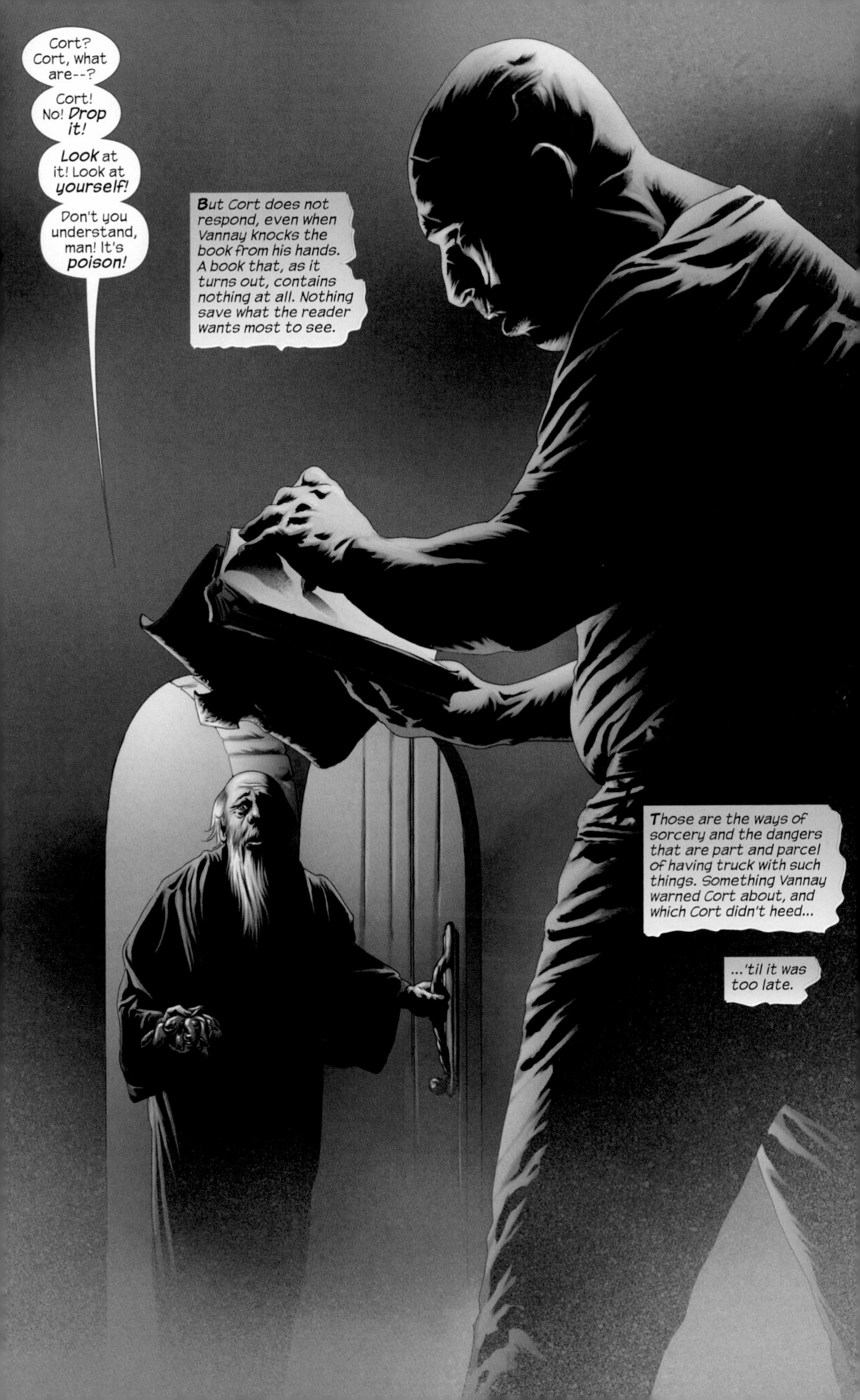
Cort? Cort, what are--?
Cort! No! *Drop it!*
Look at it! Look at *yourself!*
Don't you understand, man! It's *poison!*
But Cort does not respond, even when Vannay knocks the book from his hands. A book that, as it turns out, contains nothing at all. Nothing save what the reader wants most to see.
Those are the ways of sorcery and the dangers that are part and parcel of having truck with such things. Something Vannay warned Cort about, and which Cort didn't heed...
...'til it was too late.

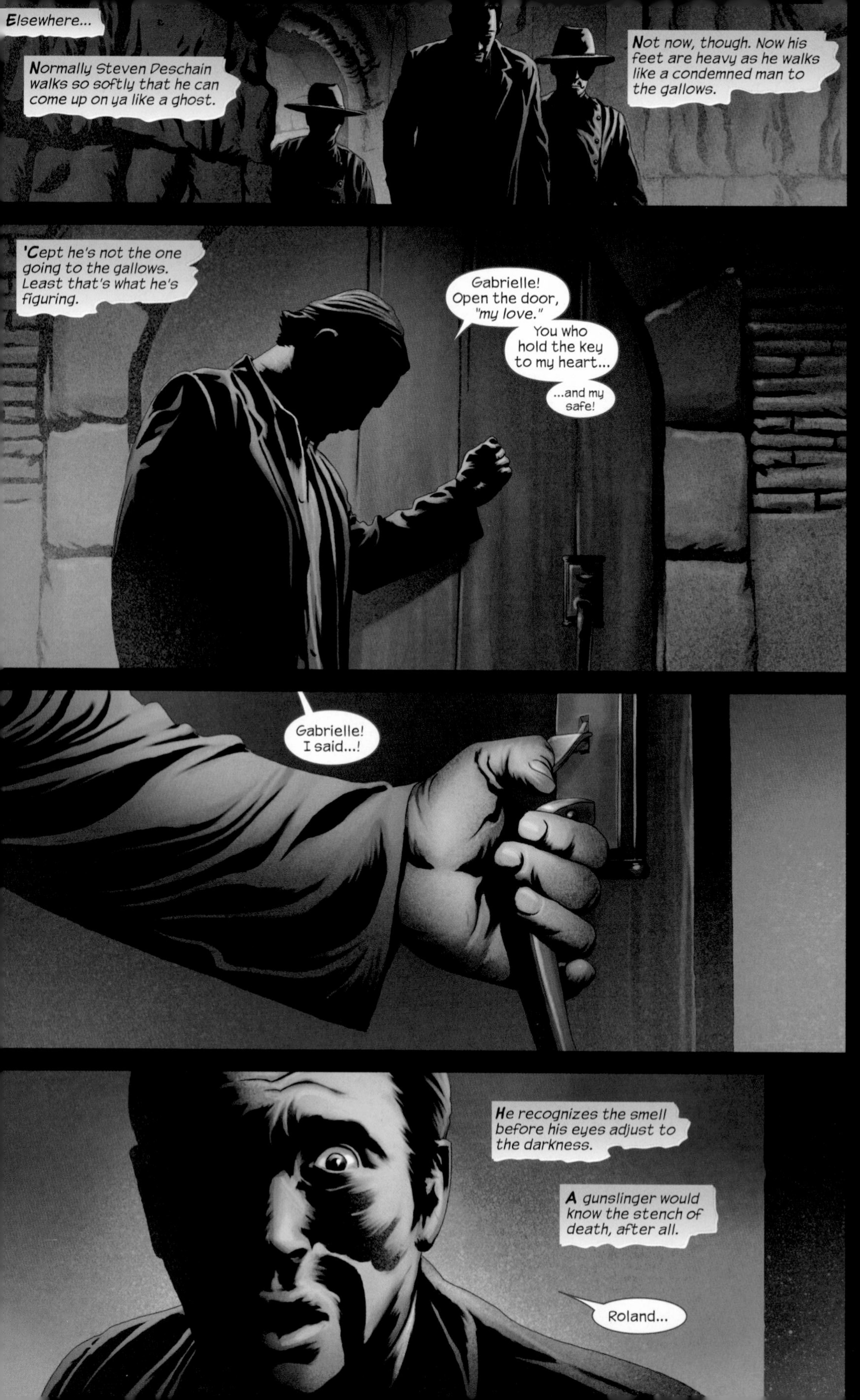
Elsewhere...
Normally Steven Deschain walks so softly that he can come up on ya like a ghost.
Not now, though. Now his feet are heavy as he walks like a condemned man to the gallows.
'Cept he's not the one going to the gallows. Least that's what he's figuring.
Gabrielle! Open the door, "my love."
You who hold the key to my heart...
...and my safe!
Gabrielle! I said...!
He recognizes the smell before his eyes adjust to the darkness.
A gunslinger would know the stench of death, after all.
Roland...

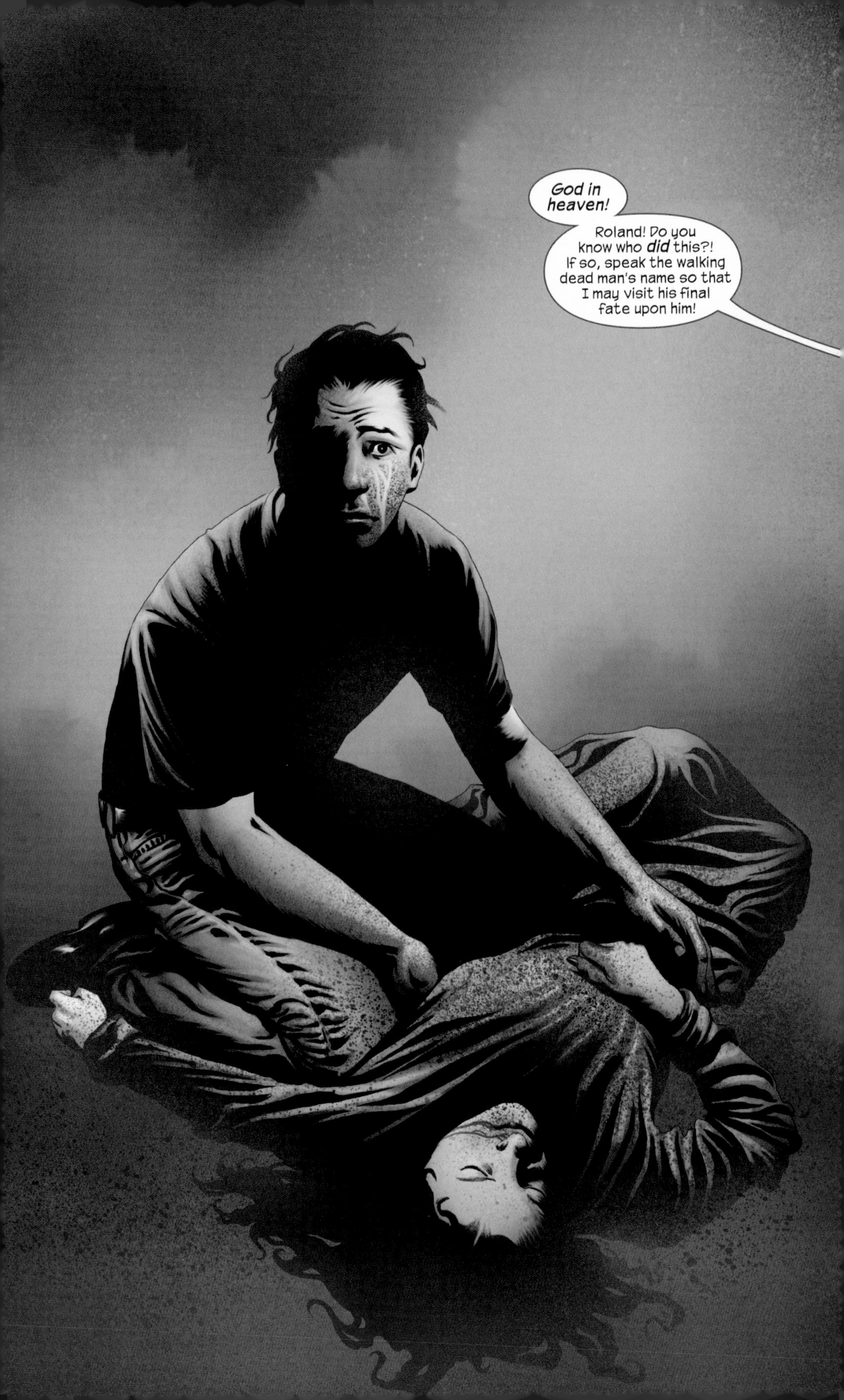
God in heaven!
Roland! Do you know who *did* this?! If so, speak the walking dead man's name so that I may visit his final fate upon him!

STEPHEN KING

THE DARK TOWER

FALL OF GILEAD

CHAPTER TWO

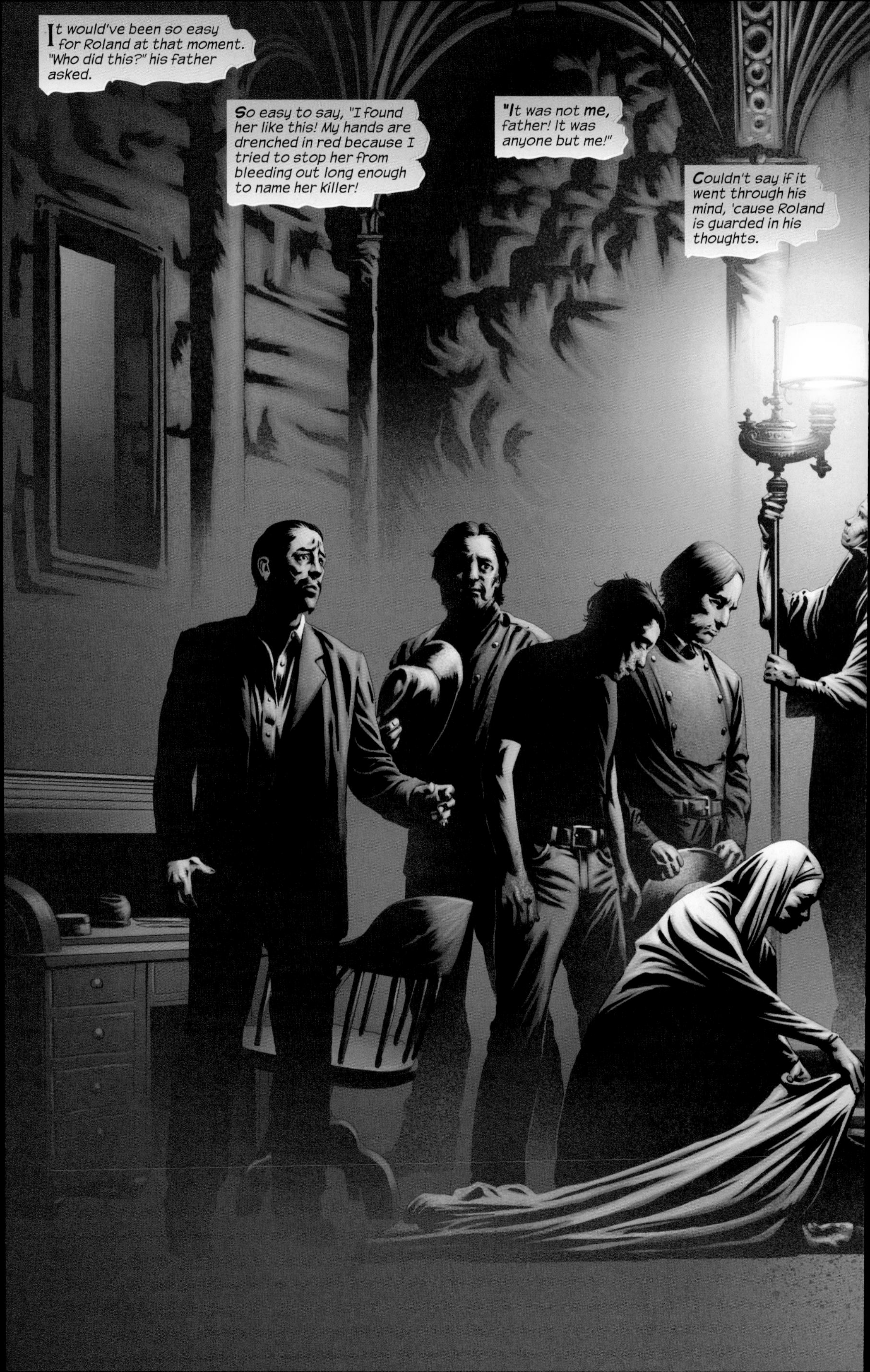
It would've been so easy for Roland at that moment. "Who did this?" his father asked.
So easy to say, "I found her like this! My hands are drenched in red because I tried to stop her from bleeding out long enough to name her killer!
"It was not me, father! It was anyone but me!"
Couldn't say if it went through his mind, 'cause Roland is guarded in his thoughts.

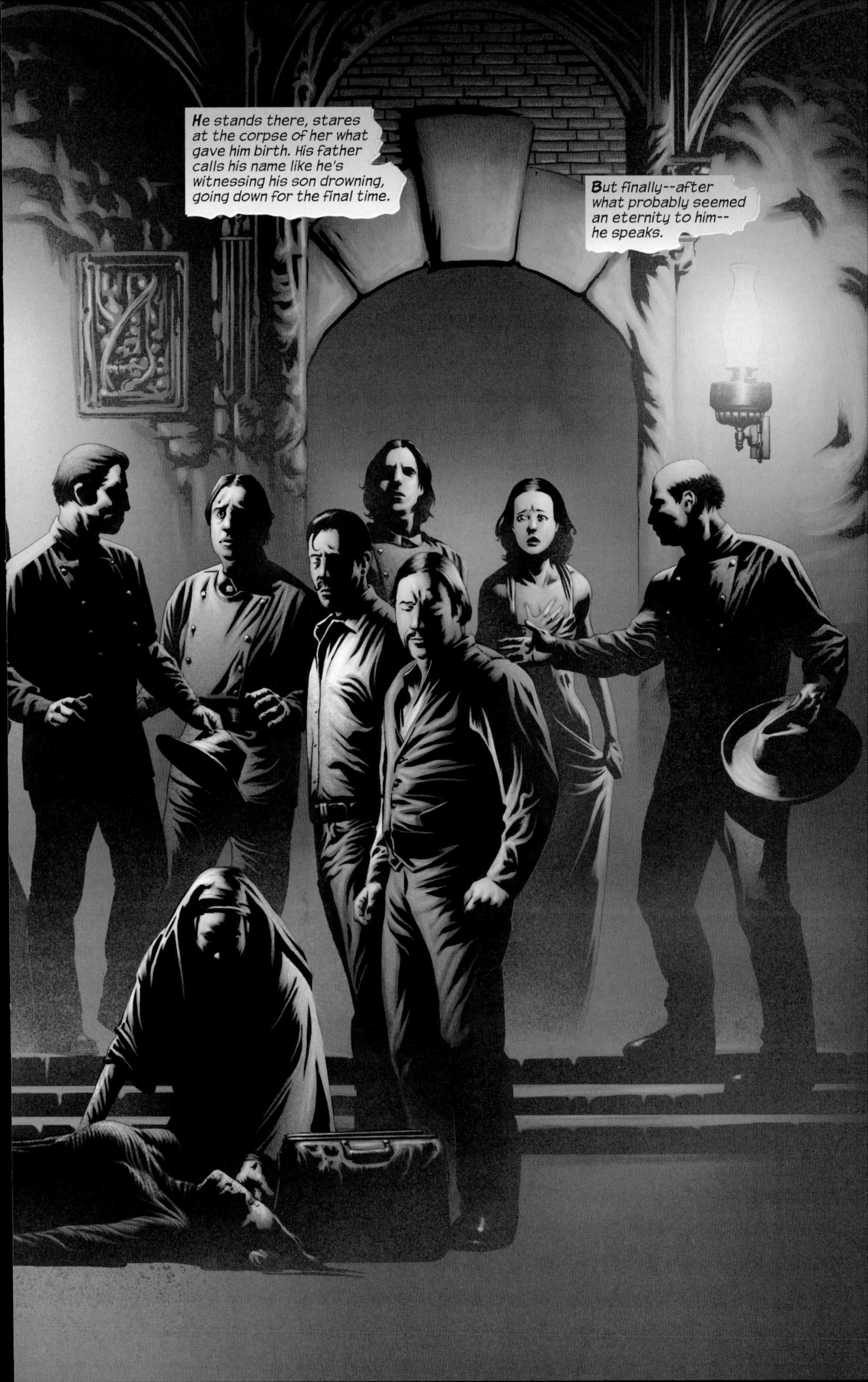
He stands there, stares at the corpse of her what gave him birth. His father calls his name like he's witnessing his son drowning, going down for the final time.
But finally--after what probably seemed an eternity to him--he speaks.

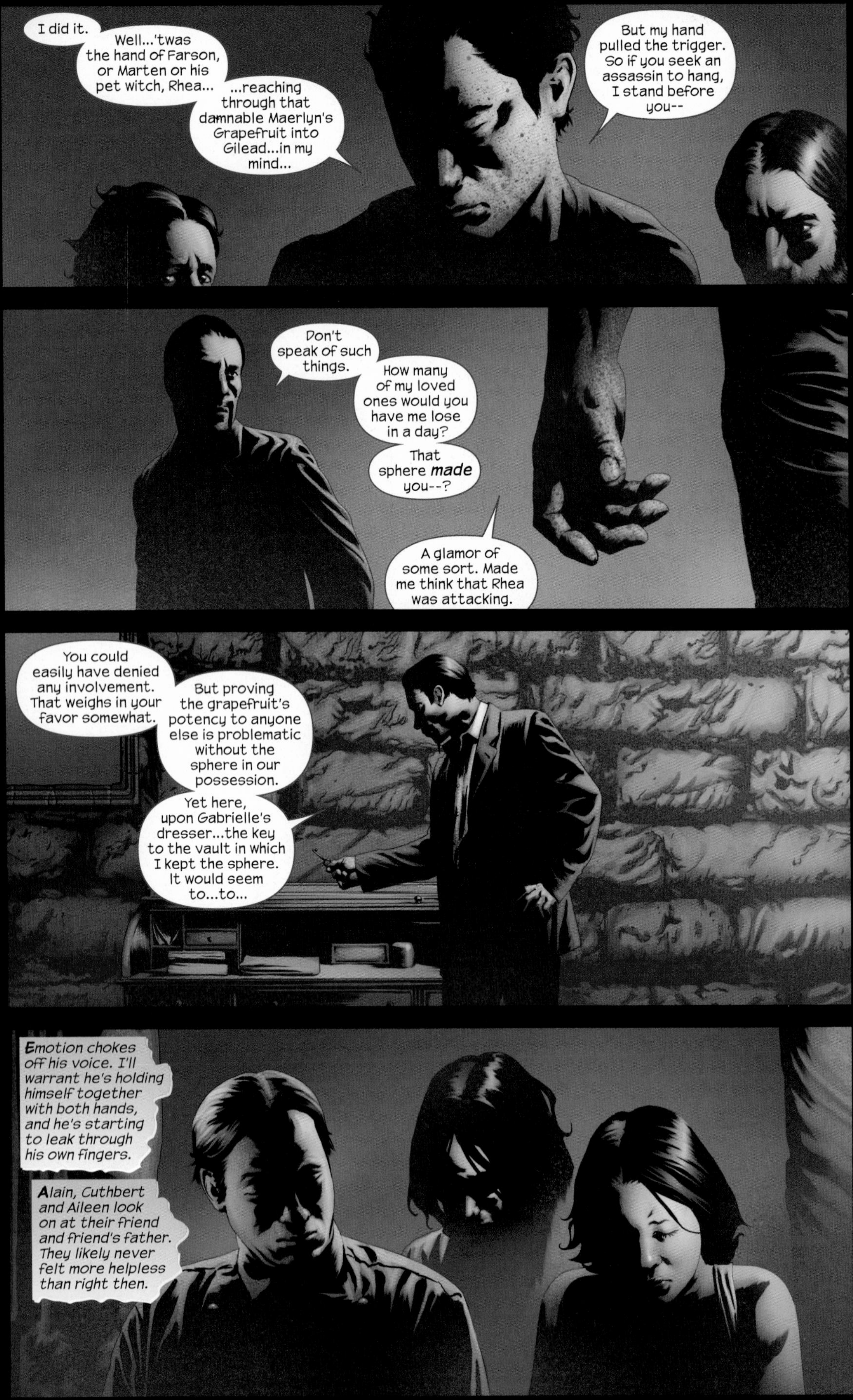
I did it.
Well...'twas the hand of Farson, or Marten or his pet witch, Rhea...
...reaching through that damnable Maerlyn's Grapefruit into Gilead...in my mind...
But my hand pulled the trigger. So if you seek an assassin to hang, I stand before you--
Don't speak of such things.
How many of my loved ones would you have me lose in a day?
That sphere *made* you--?
A glamor of some sort. Made me think that Rhea was attacking.
You could easily have denied any involvement. That weighs in your favor somewhat.
But proving the grapefruit's potency to anyone else is problematic without the sphere in our possession.
Yet here, upon Gabrielle's dresser...the key to the vault in which I kept the sphere. It would seem to...to...
Emotion chokes off his voice. I'll warrant he's holding himself together with both hands, and he's starting to leak through his own fingers.
Alain, Cuthbert and Aileen look on at their friend and friend's father. They likely never felt more helpless than right then.

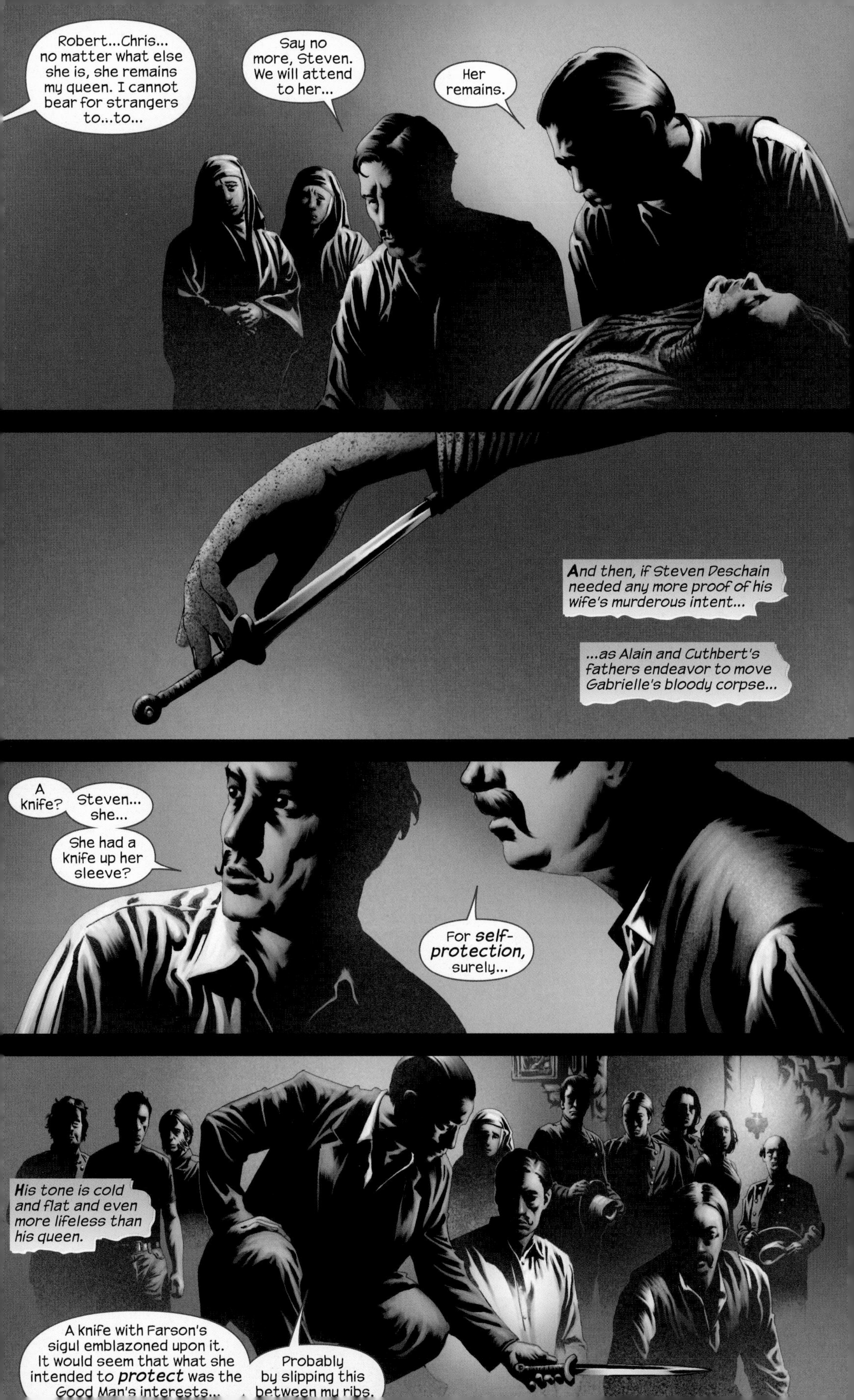

Robert...Chris... no matter what else she is, she remains my queen. I cannot bear for strangers to...to...
Say no more, Steven. We will attend to her...
Her remains.
And then, if Steven Deschain needed any more proof of his wife's murderous intent...
...as Alain and Cuthbert's fathers endeavor to move Gabrielle's bloody corpse...
A knife?
Steven... she...
She had a knife up her sleeve?
For self-protection, surely...
His tone is cold and flat and even more lifeless than his queen.
A knife with Farson's sigul emblazoned upon it. It would seem that what she intended to protect was the Good Man's interests...
Probably by slipping this between my ribs.

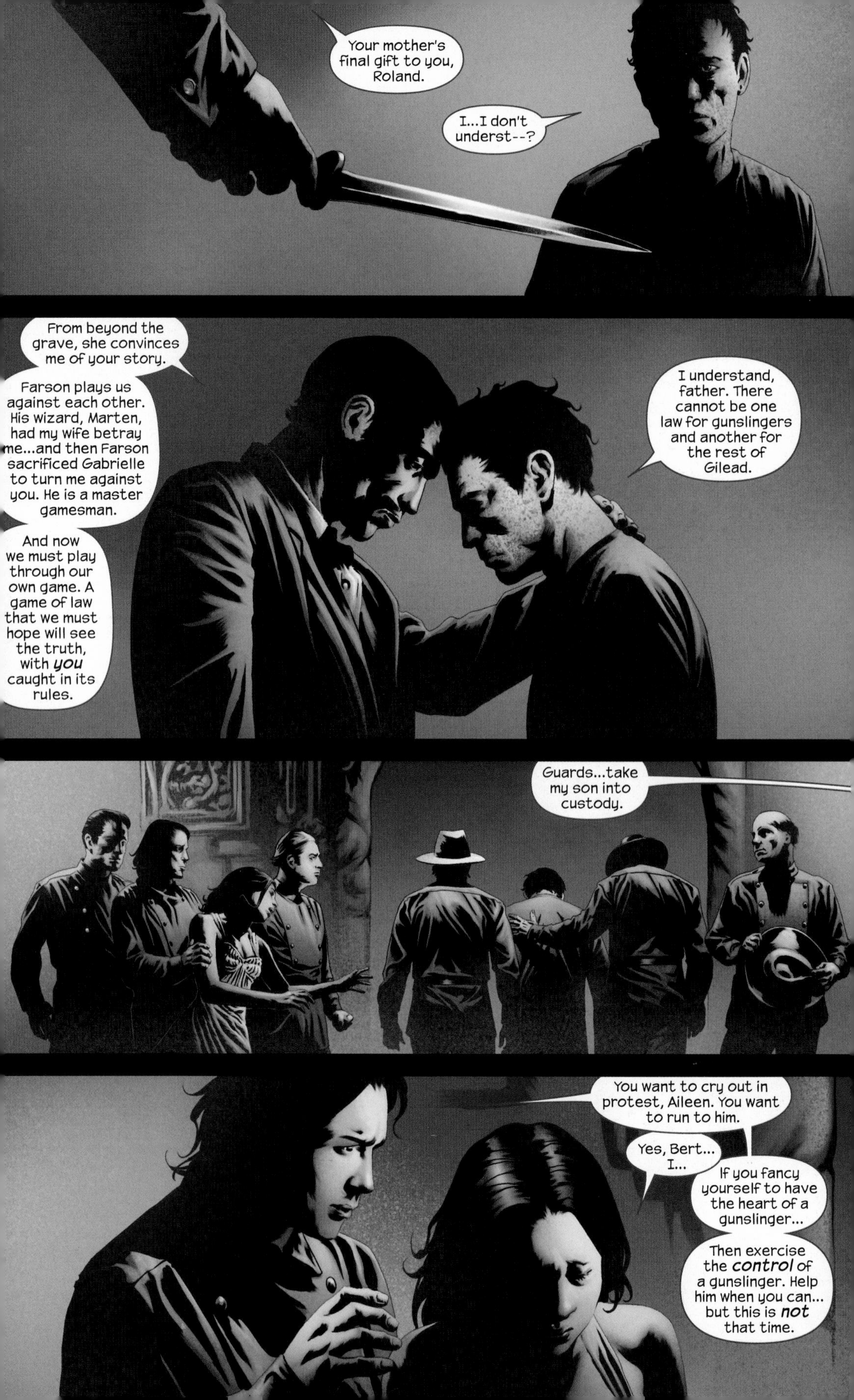

Your mother's final gift to you, Roland.
I...I don't underst--?
From beyond the grave, she convinces me of your story.
Farson plays us against each other. His wizard, Marten, had my wife betray me...and then Farson sacrificed Gabrielle to turn me against you. He is a master gamesman.
And now we must play through our own game. A game of law that we must hope will see the truth, with *you* caught in its rules.
I understand, father. There cannot be one law for gunslingers and another for the rest of Gilead.
Guards...take my son into custody.
You want to cry out in protest, Aileen. You want to run to him.
Yes, Bert... I...
If you fancy yourself to have the heart of a gunslinger...
Then exercise the *control* of a gunslinger. Help him when you can... but this is *not* that time.

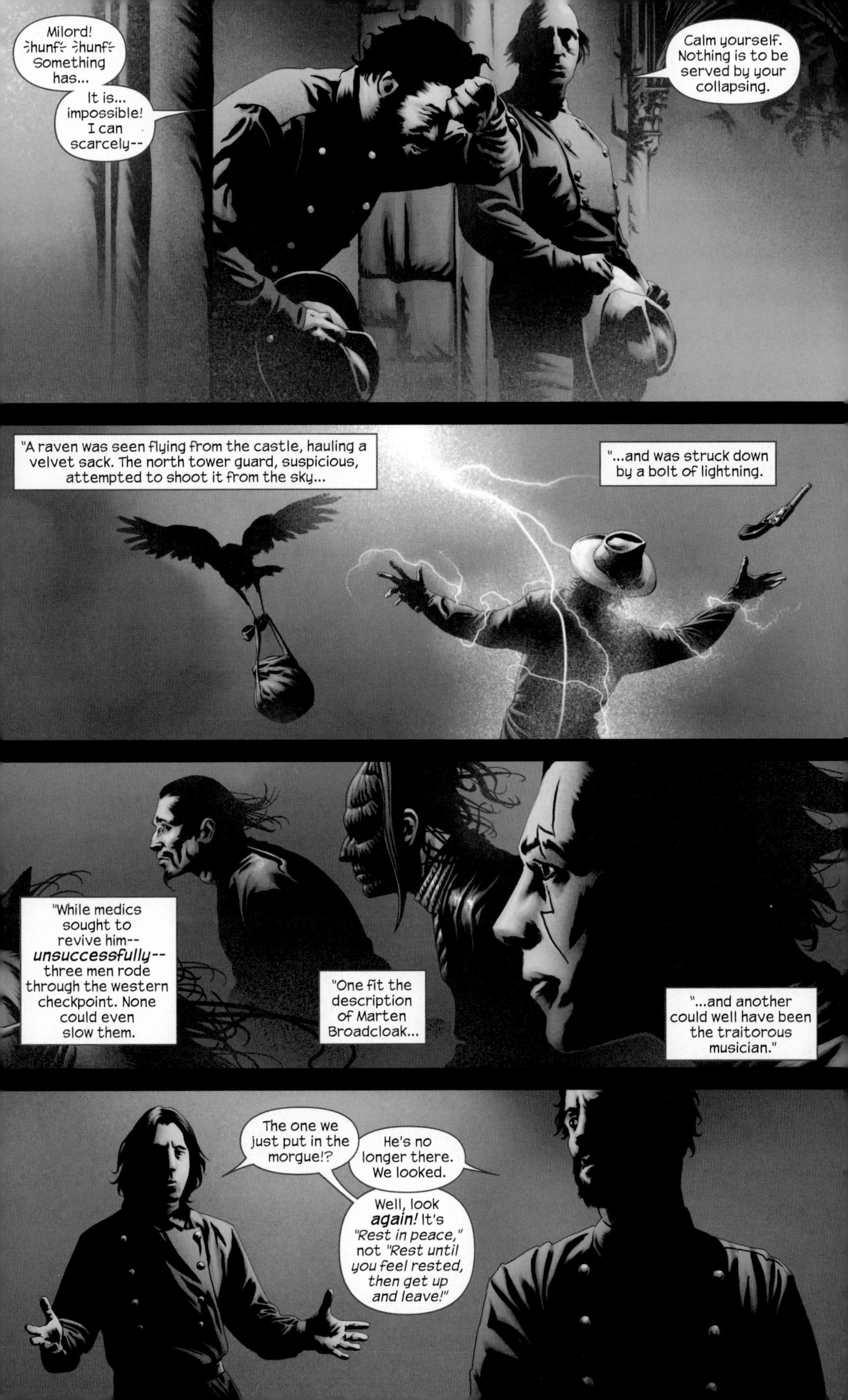
Milord! ~hunf~ ~hunf~ Something has...
It is... impossible! I can scarcely--
Calm yourself. Nothing is to be served by your collapsing.
"A raven was seen flying from the castle, hauling a velvet sack. The north tower guard, suspicious, attempted to shoot it from the sky...
"...and was struck down by a bolt of lightning.
"While medics sought to revive him--*unsuccessfully*--three men rode through the western checkpoint. None could even slow them.
"One fit the description of Marten Broadcloak...
"...and another could well have been the traitorous musician."
The one we just put in the morgue!?
He's no longer there. We looked.
Well, look *again!* It's *"Rest in peace,"* not *"Rest until you feel rested, then get up and leave!"*

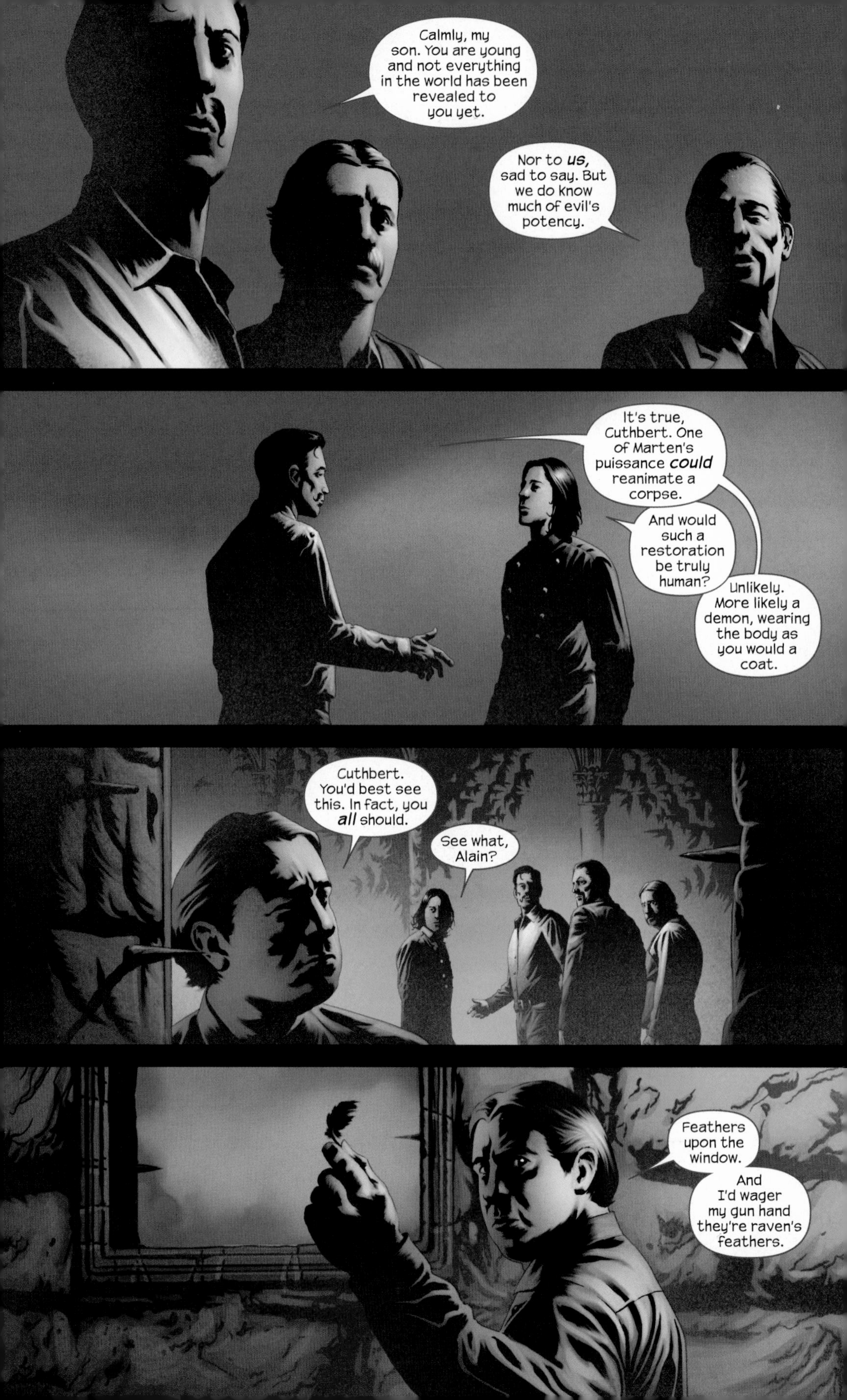
Calmly, my son. You are young and not everything in the world has been revealed to you yet.
Nor to us, sad to say. But we do know much of evil's potency.
It's true, Cuthbert. One of Marten's puissance could reanimate a corpse.
And would such a restoration be truly human?
Unlikely. More likely a demon, wearing the body as you would a coat.
Cuthbert. You'd best see this. In fact, you all should.
See what, Alain?
Feathers upon the window.
And I'd wager my gun hand they're raven's feathers.

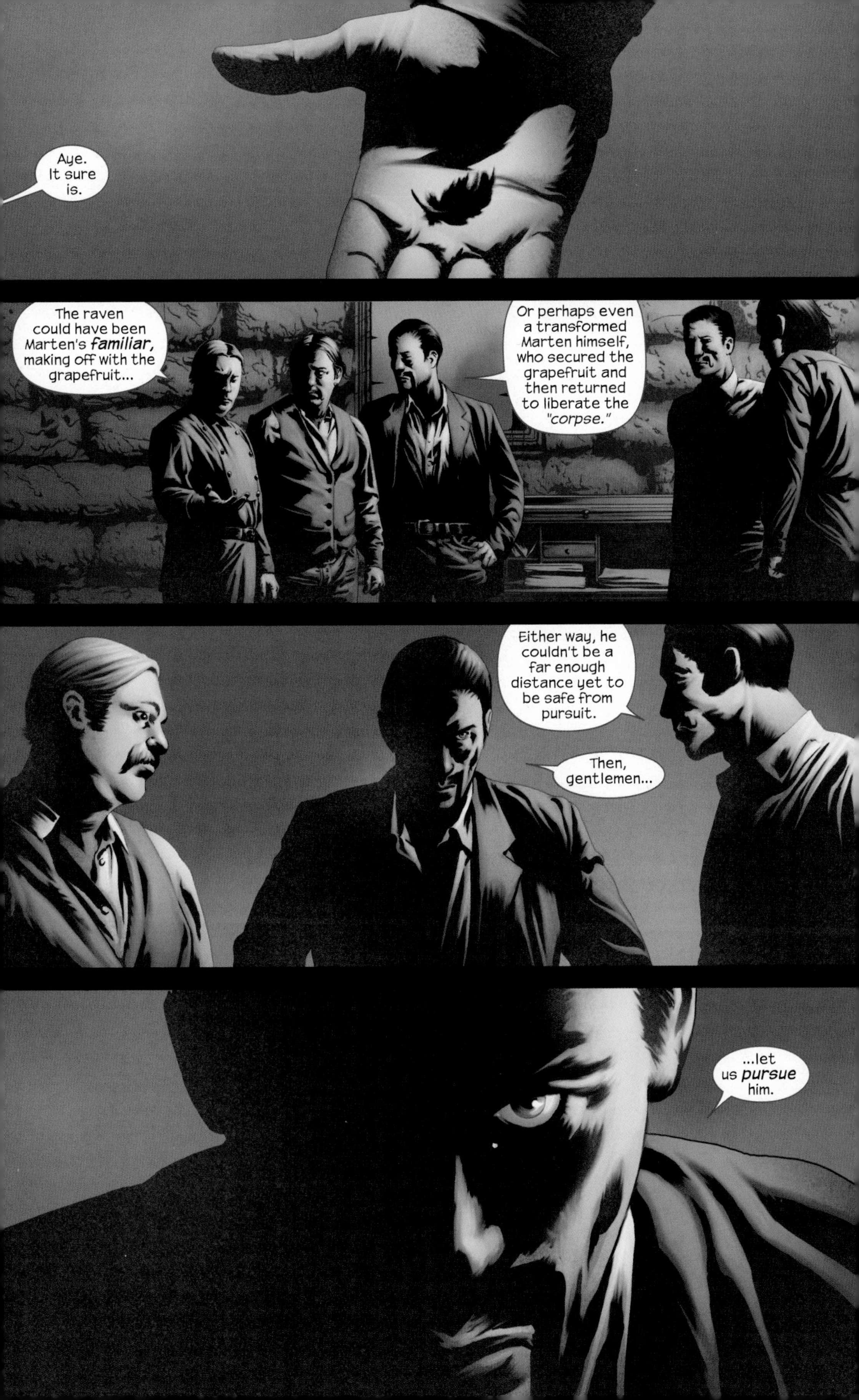
Aye. It sure is.
The raven could have been Marten's *familiar,* making off with the grapefruit...
Or perhaps even a transformed Marten himself, who secured the grapefruit and then returned to liberate the "*corpse.*"
Either way, he couldn't be a far enough distance yet to be safe from pursuit.
Then, gentlemen...
...let us *pursue* him.

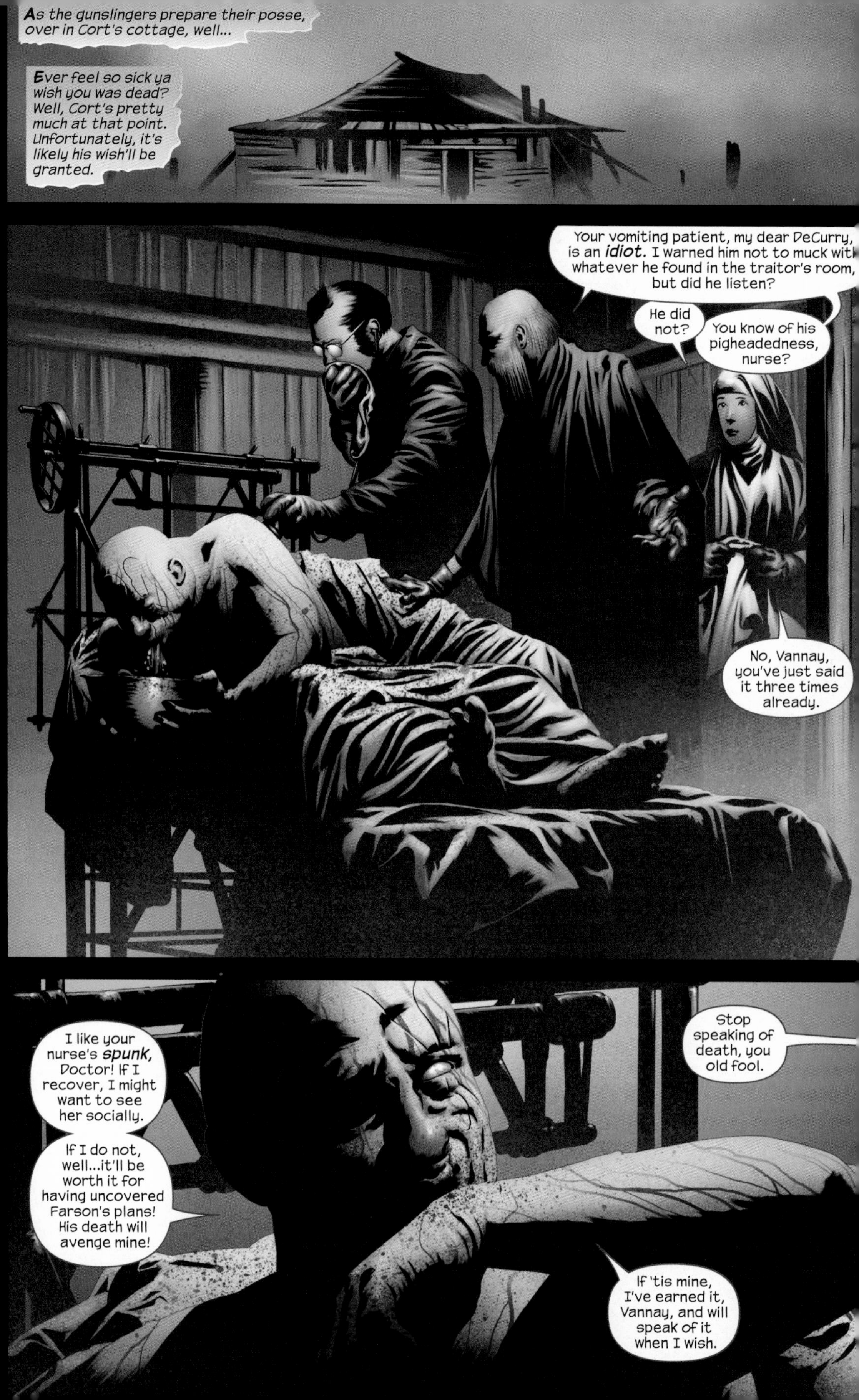
As the gunslingers prepare their posse, over in Cort's cottage, well...
Ever feel so sick ya wish you was dead? Well, Cort's pretty much at that point. Unfortunately, it's likely his wish'll be granted.
Your vomiting patient, my dear DeCurry, is an *idiot.* I warned him not to muck with whatever he found in the traitor's room, but did he listen?
He did not?
You know of his pigheadedness, nurse?
No, Vannay, you've just said it three times already.
I like your nurse's **spunk,** Doctor! If I recover, I might want to see her socially.
If I do not, well...it'll be worth it for having uncovered Farson's plans! His death will avenge mine!
Stop speaking of death, you old fool.
If 'tis mine, I've earned it, Vannay, and will speak of it when I wish.

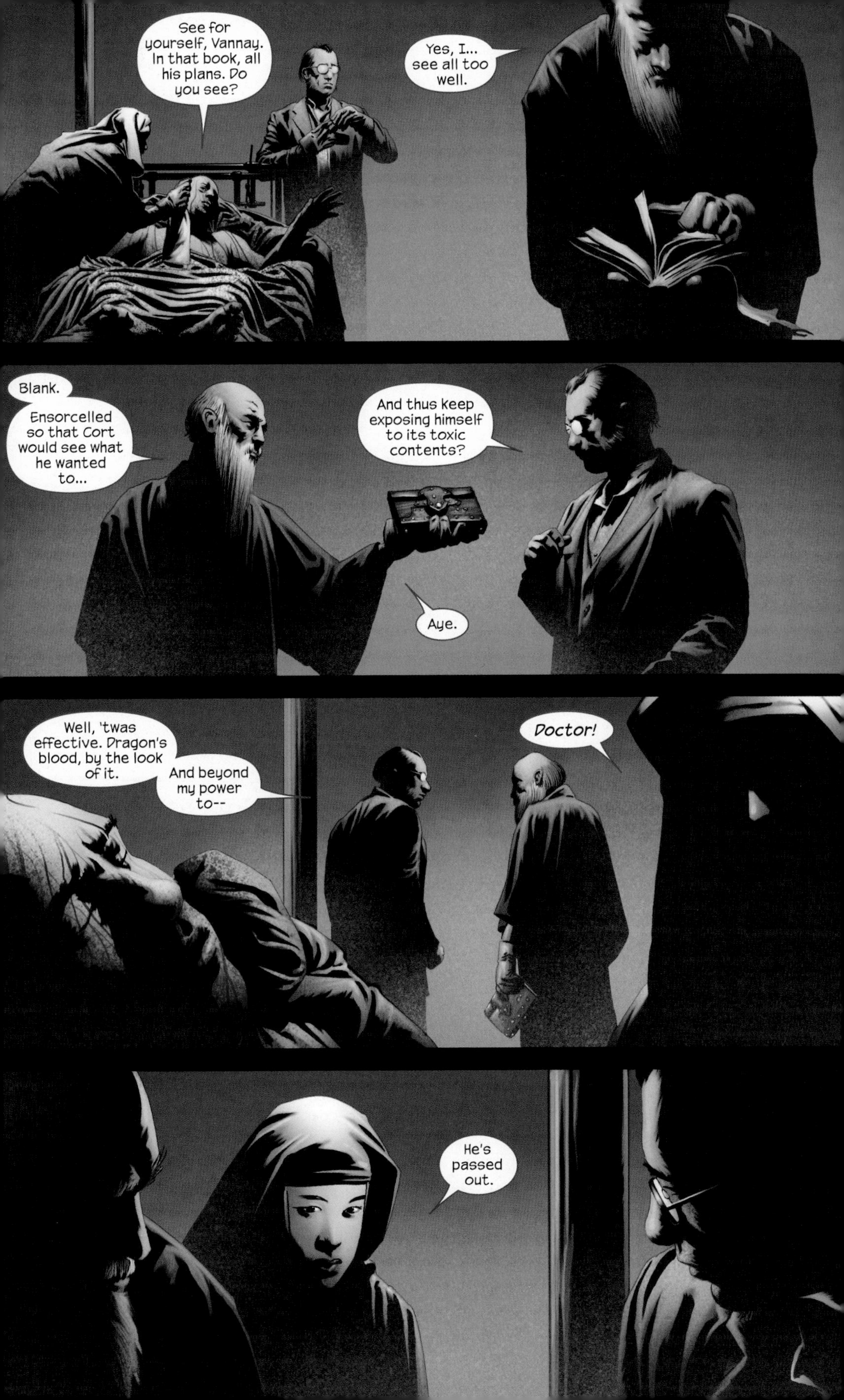
See for yourself, Vannay. In that book, all his plans. Do you see?
Yes, I... see all too well.
Blank.
Ensorcelled so that Cort would see what he wanted to...
And thus keep exposing himself to its toxic contents?
Aye.
Well, 'twas effective. Dragon's blood, by the look of it.
And beyond my power to--
Doctor!
He's passed out.

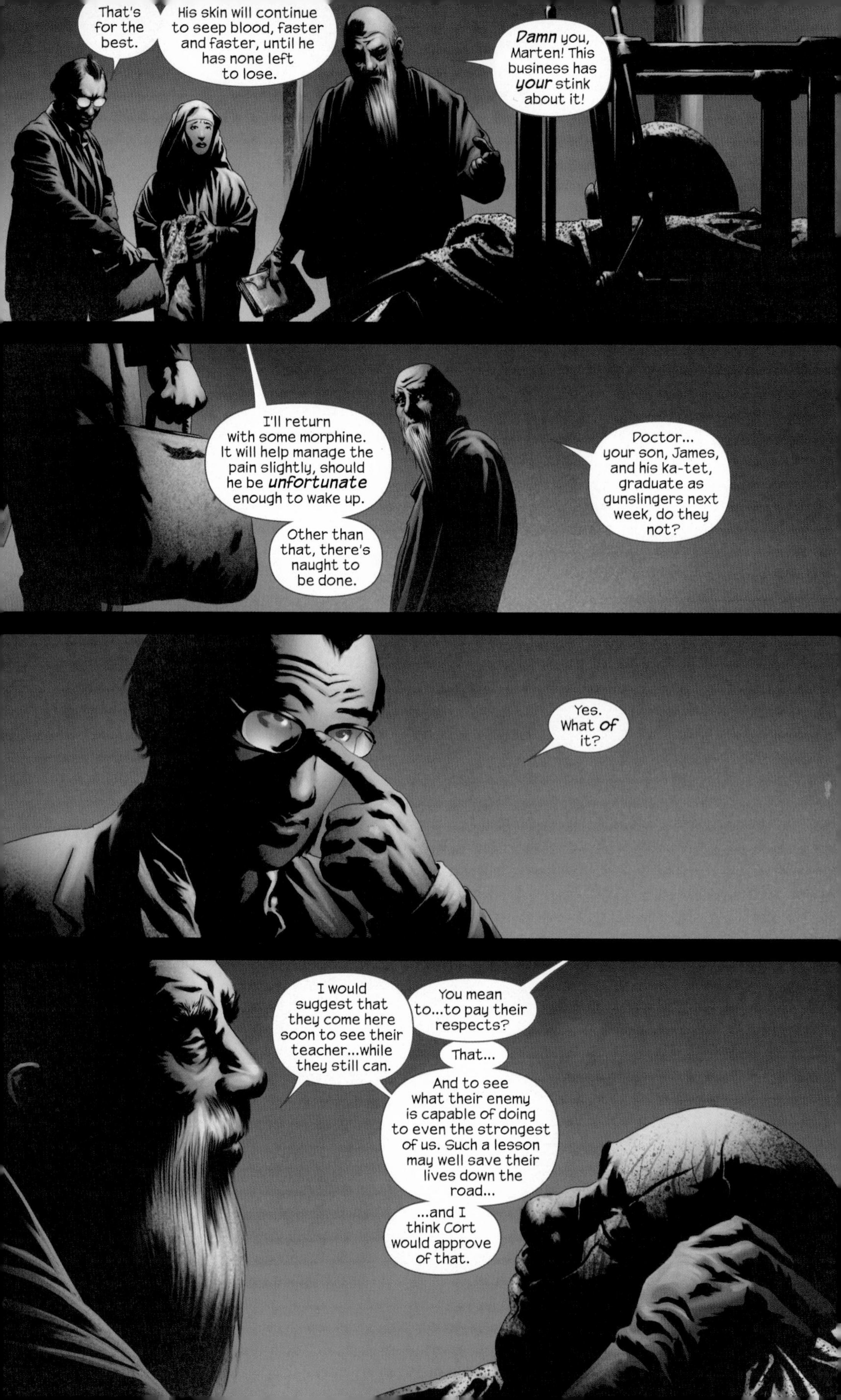
That's for the best.
His skin will continue to seep blood, faster and faster, until he has none left to lose.
Damn you, Marten! This business has *your* stink about it!
I'll return with some morphine. It will help manage the pain slightly, should he be *unfortunate* enough to wake up.
Other than that, there's naught to be done.
Doctor... your son, James, and his ka-tet, graduate as gunslingers next week, do they not?
Yes. What *of* it?
I would suggest that they come here soon to see their teacher...while they still can.
You mean to...to pay their respects?
That...
And to see what their enemy is capable of doing to even the strongest of us. Such a lesson may well save their lives down the road...
...and I think Cort would approve of that.

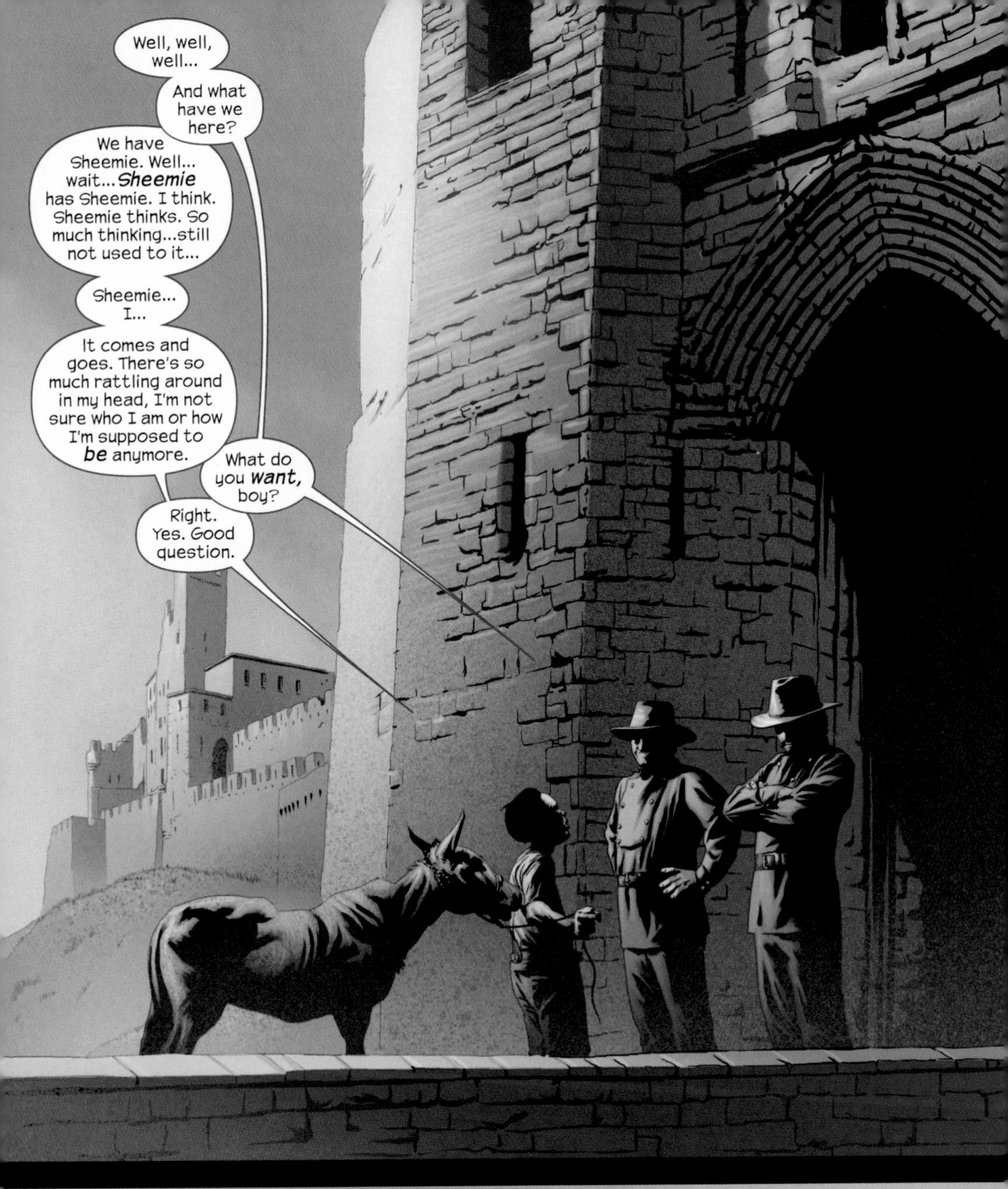
Well, well, well...
And what have we here?
We have Sheemie. Well... wait... *Sheemie* has Sheemie. I think. Sheemie thinks. So much thinking...still not used to it...
Sheemie... I...
It comes and goes. There's so much rattling around in my head, I'm not sure who I am or how I'm supposed to *be* anymore.
What do you *want,* boy?
Right. Yes. Good question.

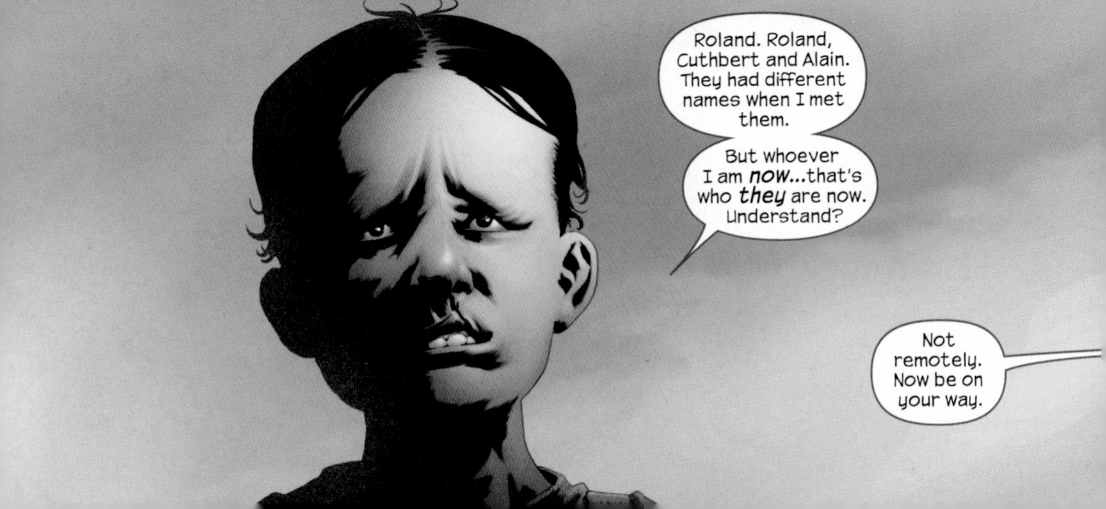
Roland. Roland, Cuthbert and Alain. They had different names when I met them.
But whoever I am *now*...that's who *they* are now. Understand?
Not remotely. Now be on your way.

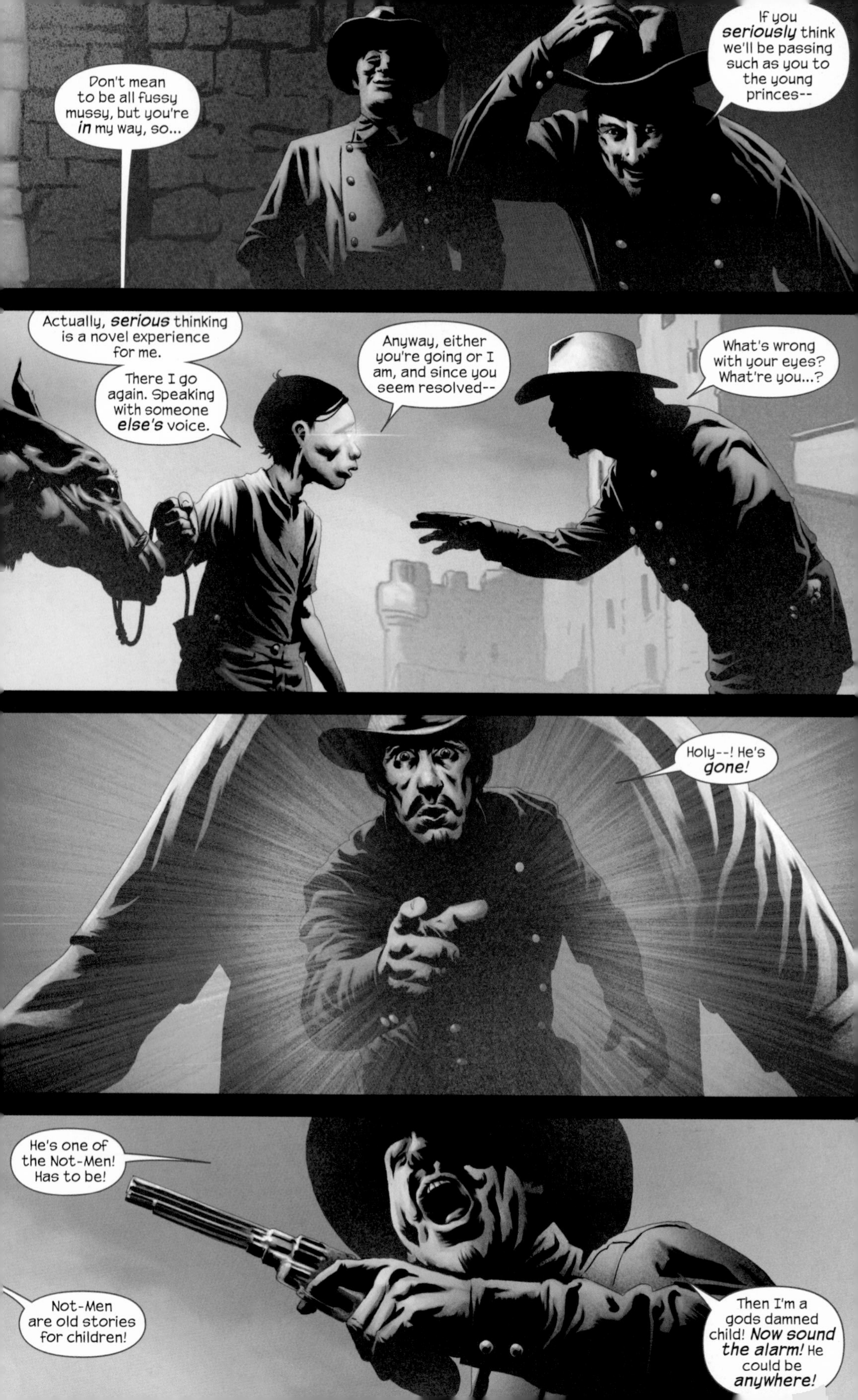
Don't mean to be all fussy mussy, but you're *in* my way, so...
If you *seriously* think we'll be passing such as you to the young princes--
Actually, *serious* thinking is a novel experience for me.
There I go again. Speaking with someone *else's* voice.
Anyway, either you're going or I am, and since you seem resolved--
What's wrong with your eyes? What're you...?
Holy--! He's *gone!*
He's one of the Not-Men! Has to be!
Not-Men are old stories for children!
Then I'm a gods damned child! *Now sound the alarm!* He could be *anywhere!*

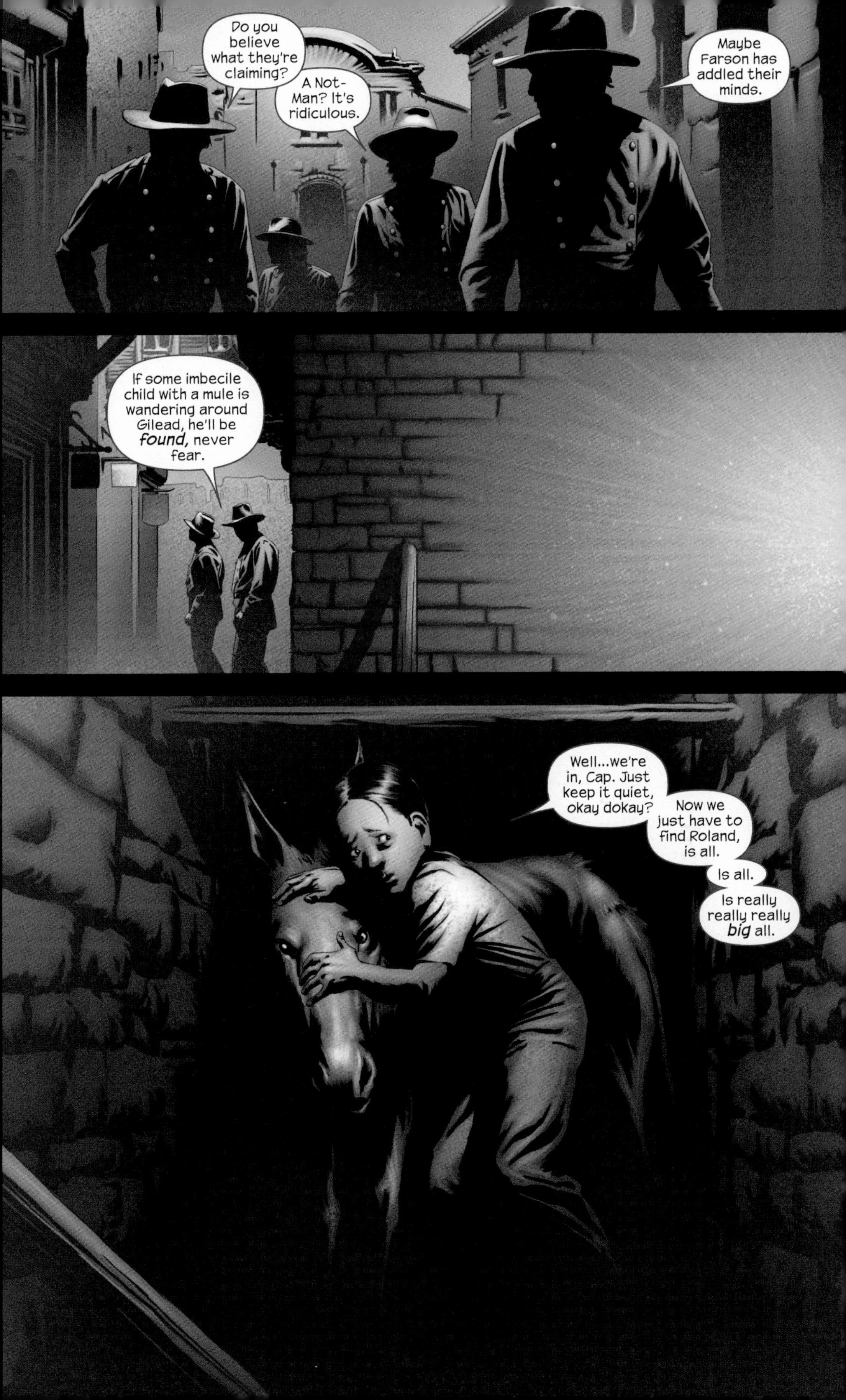

Do you believe what they're claiming?
A Not-Man? It's ridiculous.
Maybe Farson has addled their minds.
If some imbecile child with a mule is wandering around Gilead, he'll be *found,* never fear.
Well...we're in, Cap. Just keep it quiet, okay dokay?
Now we just have to find Roland, is all.
Is all.
Is really really really *big* all.

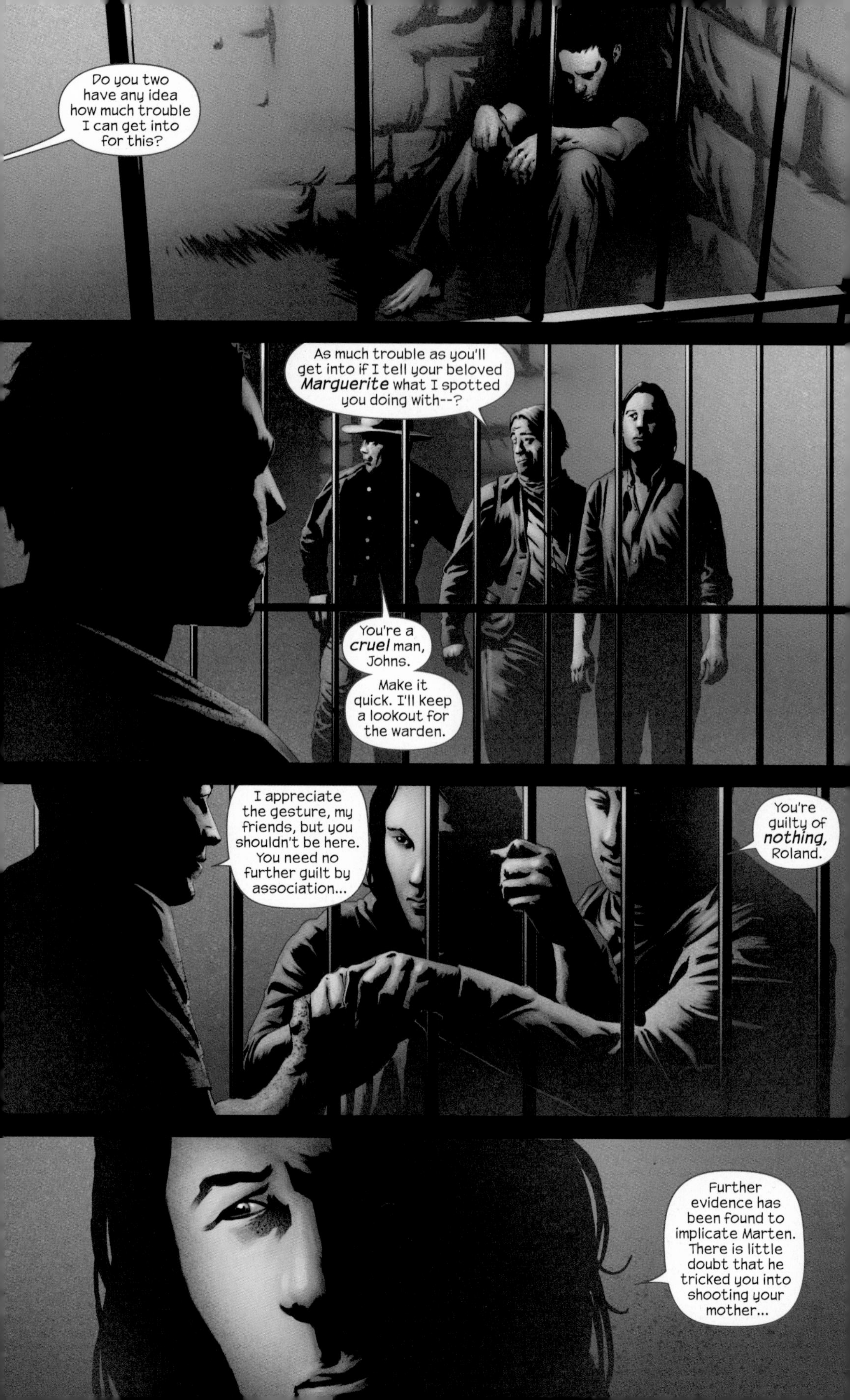
Do you two have any idea how much trouble I can get into for this?
As much trouble as you'll get into if I tell your beloved *Marguerite* what I spotted you doing with--?
You're a *cruel* man, Johns.
Make it quick. I'll keep a lookout for the warden.
I appreciate the gesture, my friends, but you shouldn't be here. You need no further guilt by association...
You're guilty of *nothing,* Roland.
Further evidence has been found to implicate Marten. There is little doubt that he tricked you into shooting your mother...

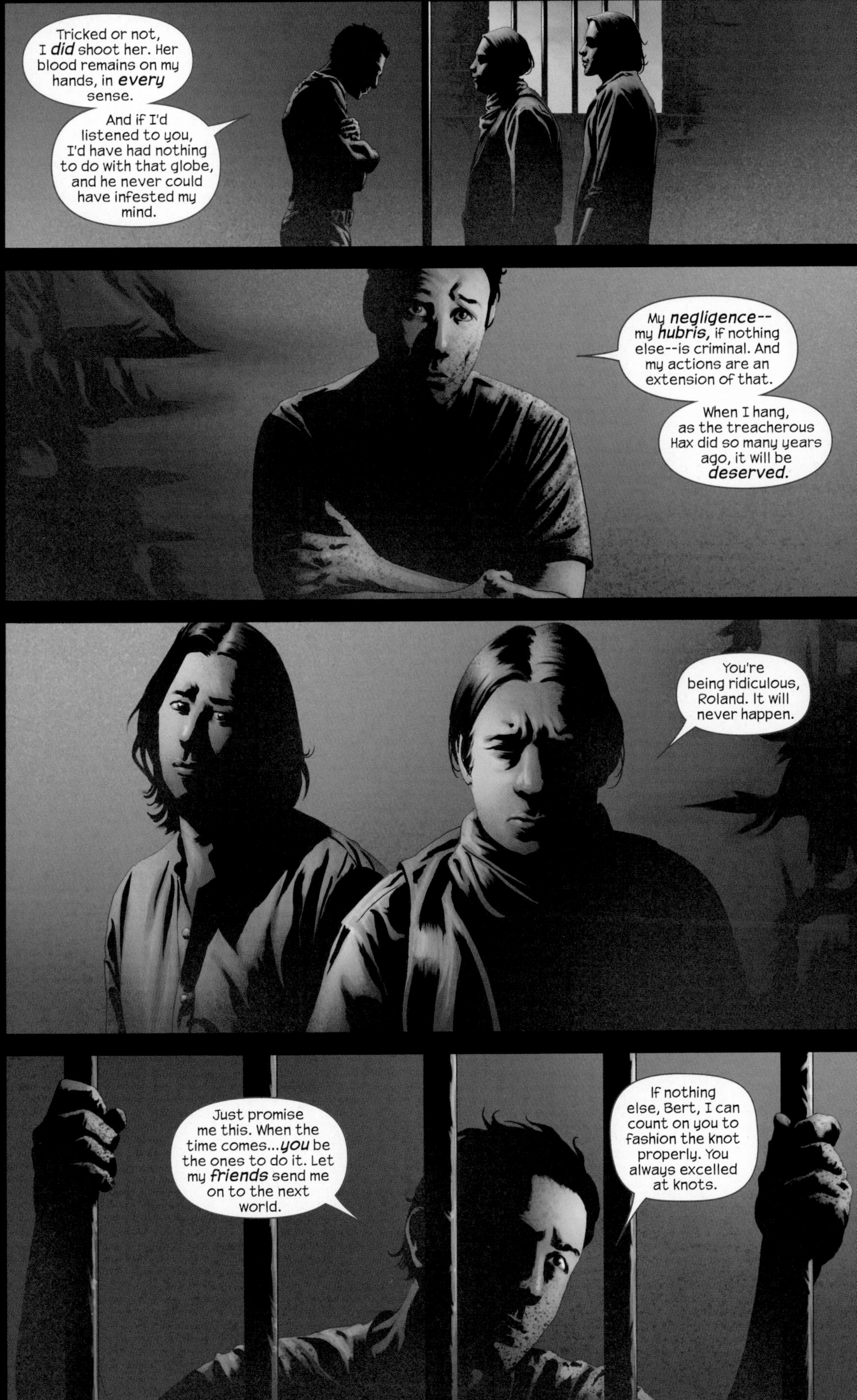
Tricked or not, I did shoot her. Her blood remains on my hands, in every sense.
And if I'd listened to you, I'd have had nothing to do with that globe, and he never could have infested my mind.
My negligence--my hubris, if nothing else--is criminal. And my actions are an extension of that.
When I hang, as the treacherous Hax did so many years ago, it will be deserved.
You're being ridiculous, Roland. It will never happen.
Just promise me this. When the time comes...you be the ones to do it. Let my friends send me on to the next world.
If nothing else, Bert, I can count on you to fashion the knot properly. You always excelled at knots.

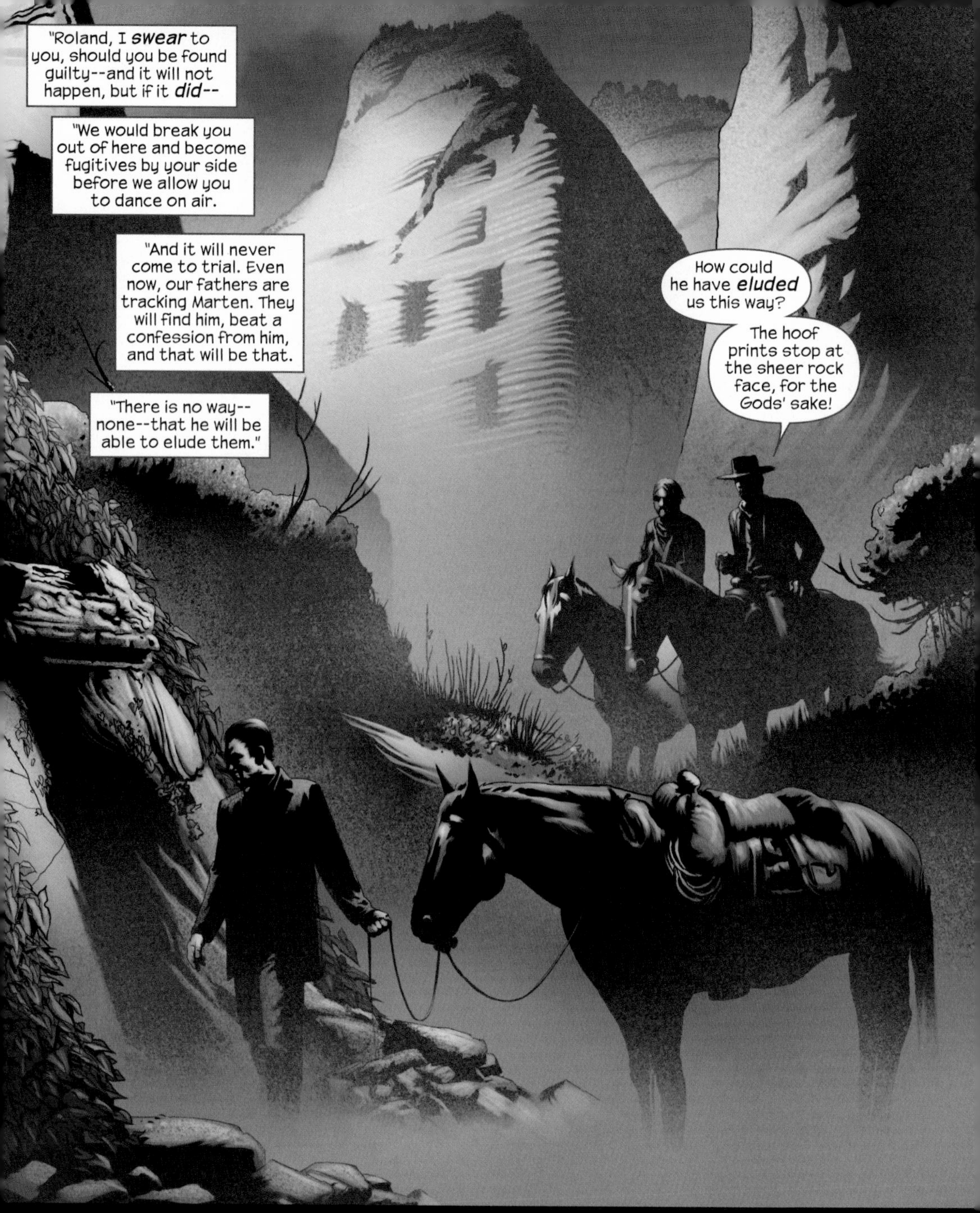
"Roland, I swear to you, should you be found guilty--and it will not happen, but if it did--
"We would break you out of here and become fugitives by your side before we allow you to dance on air.
"And it will never come to trial. Even now, our fathers are tracking Marten. They will find him, beat a confession from him, and that will be that.
"There is no way--none--that he will be able to elude them."
How could he have eluded us this way?
The hoof prints stop at the sheer rock face, for the Gods' sake!

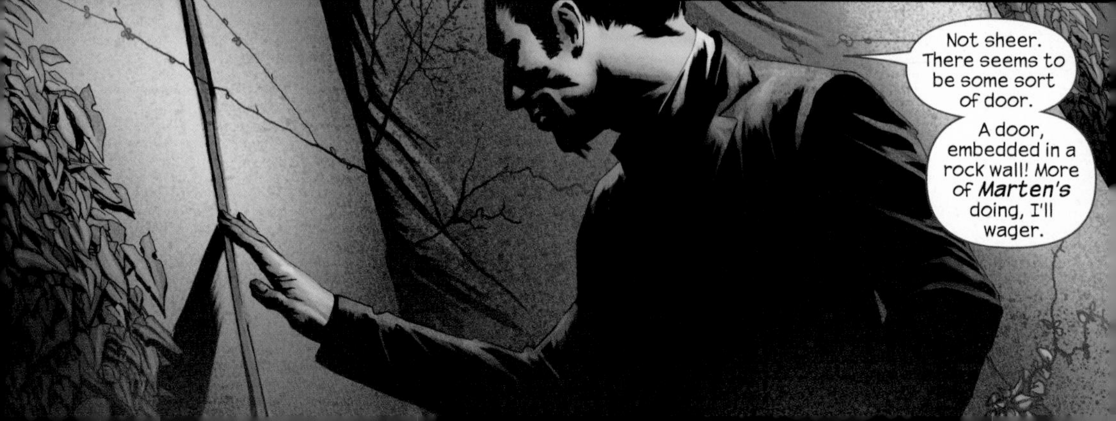
Not sheer. There seems to be some sort of door.
A door, embedded in a rock wall! More of Marten's doing, I'll wager.

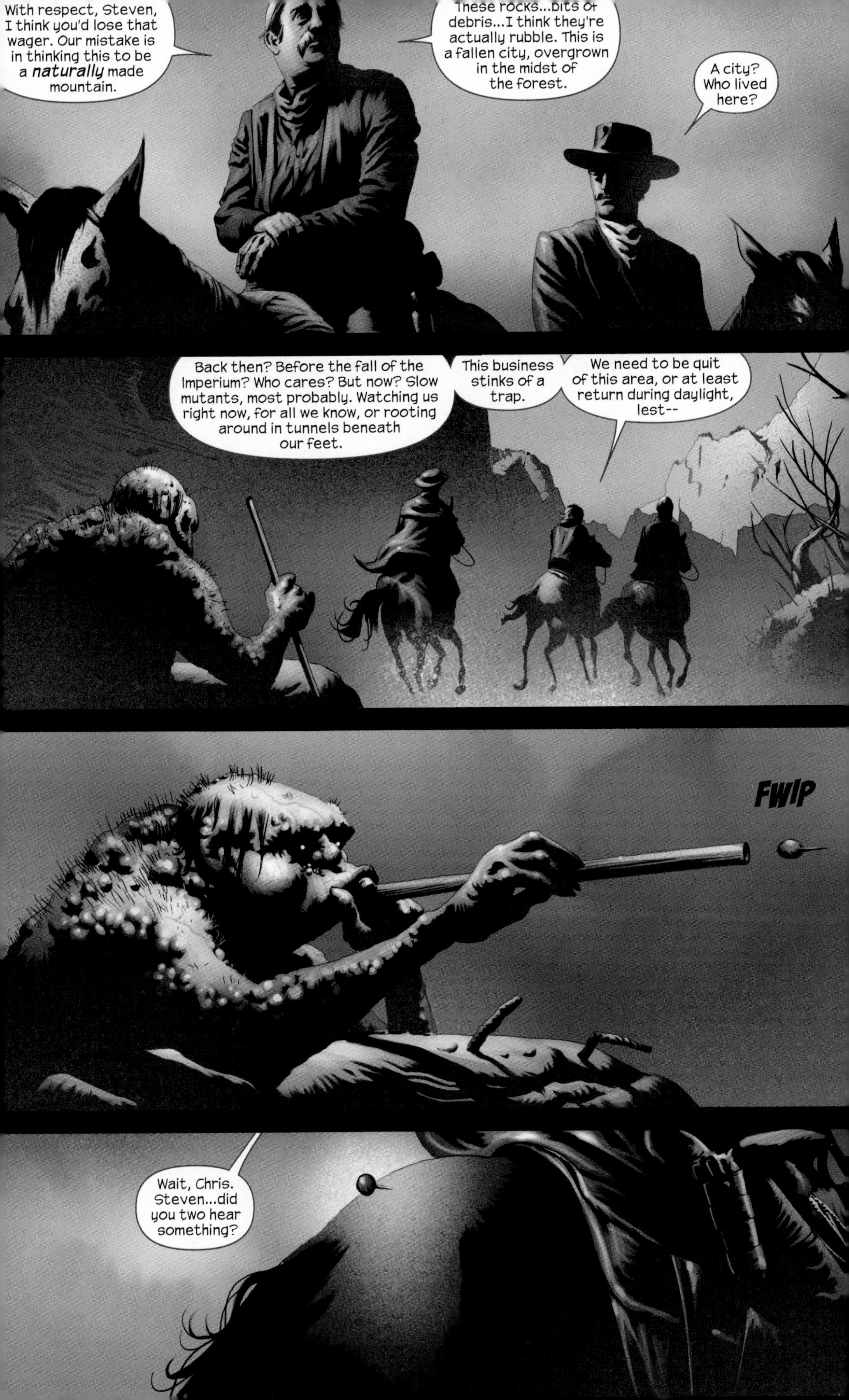
With respect, Steven, I think you'd lose that wager. Our mistake is in thinking this to be a *naturally* made mountain.
These rocks...bits of debris...I think they're actually rubble. This is a fallen city, overgrown in the midst of the forest.
A city? Who lived here?
Back then? Before the fall of the Imperium? Who cares? But now? Slow mutants, most probably. Watching us right now, for all we know, or rooting around in tunnels beneath our feet.
This business stinks of a trap.
We need to be quit of this area, or at least return during daylight, lest--
FWIP
Wait, Chris. Steven...did you two hear something?

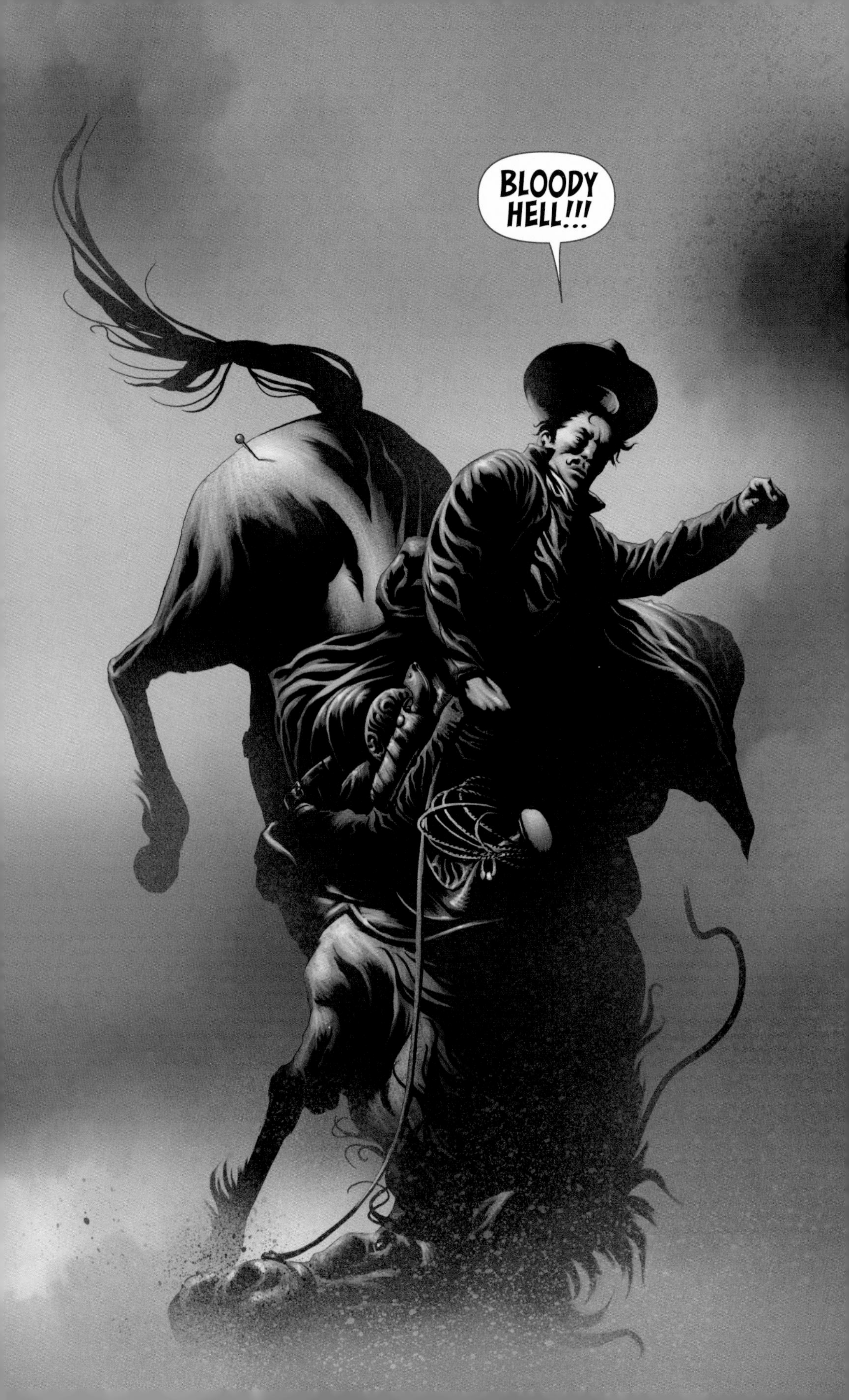
BLOODY HELL!!!

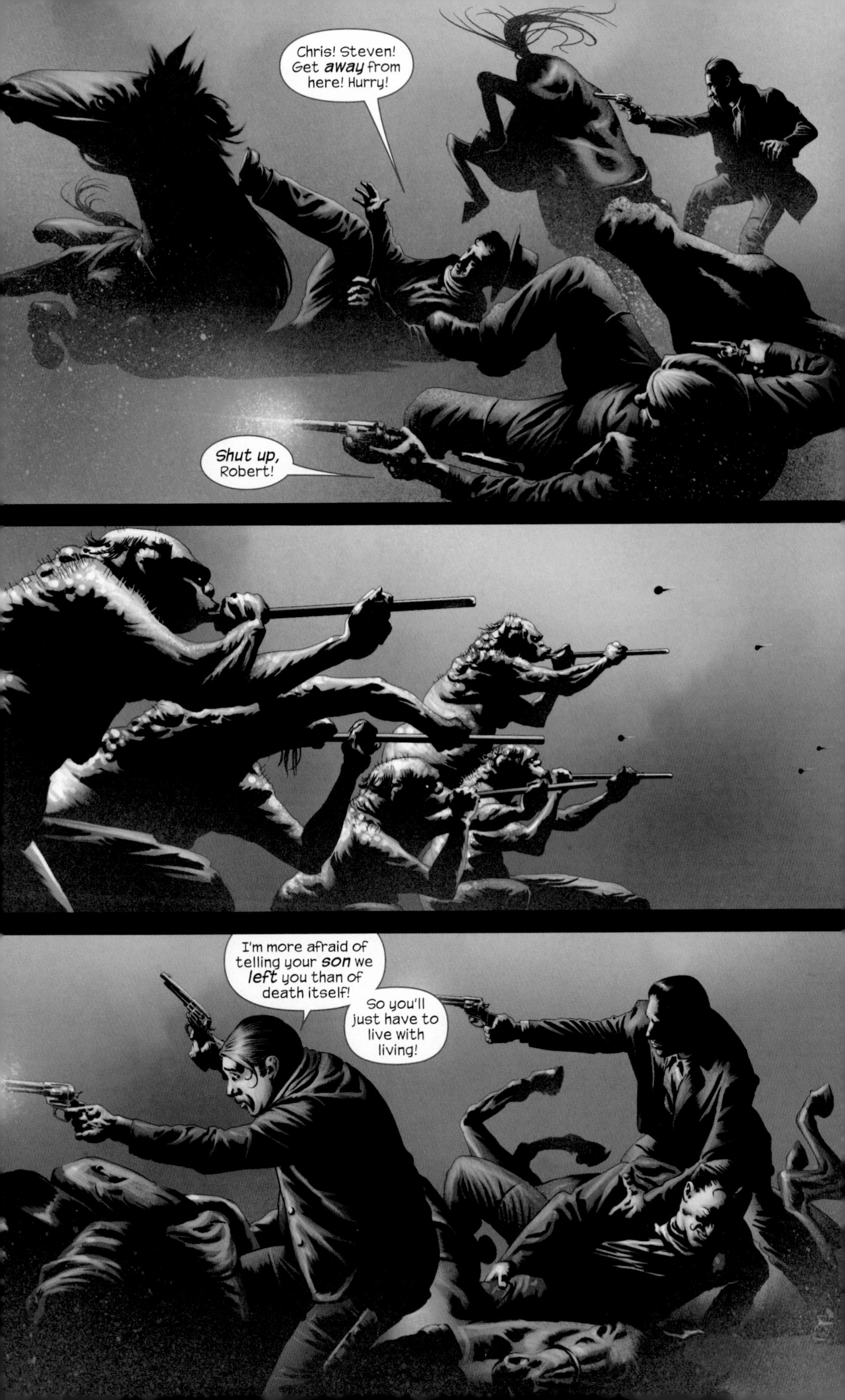
Chris! Steven! Get away from here! Hurry!
Shut up, Robert!
I'm more afraid of telling your son we left you than of death itself!
So you'll just have to live with living!

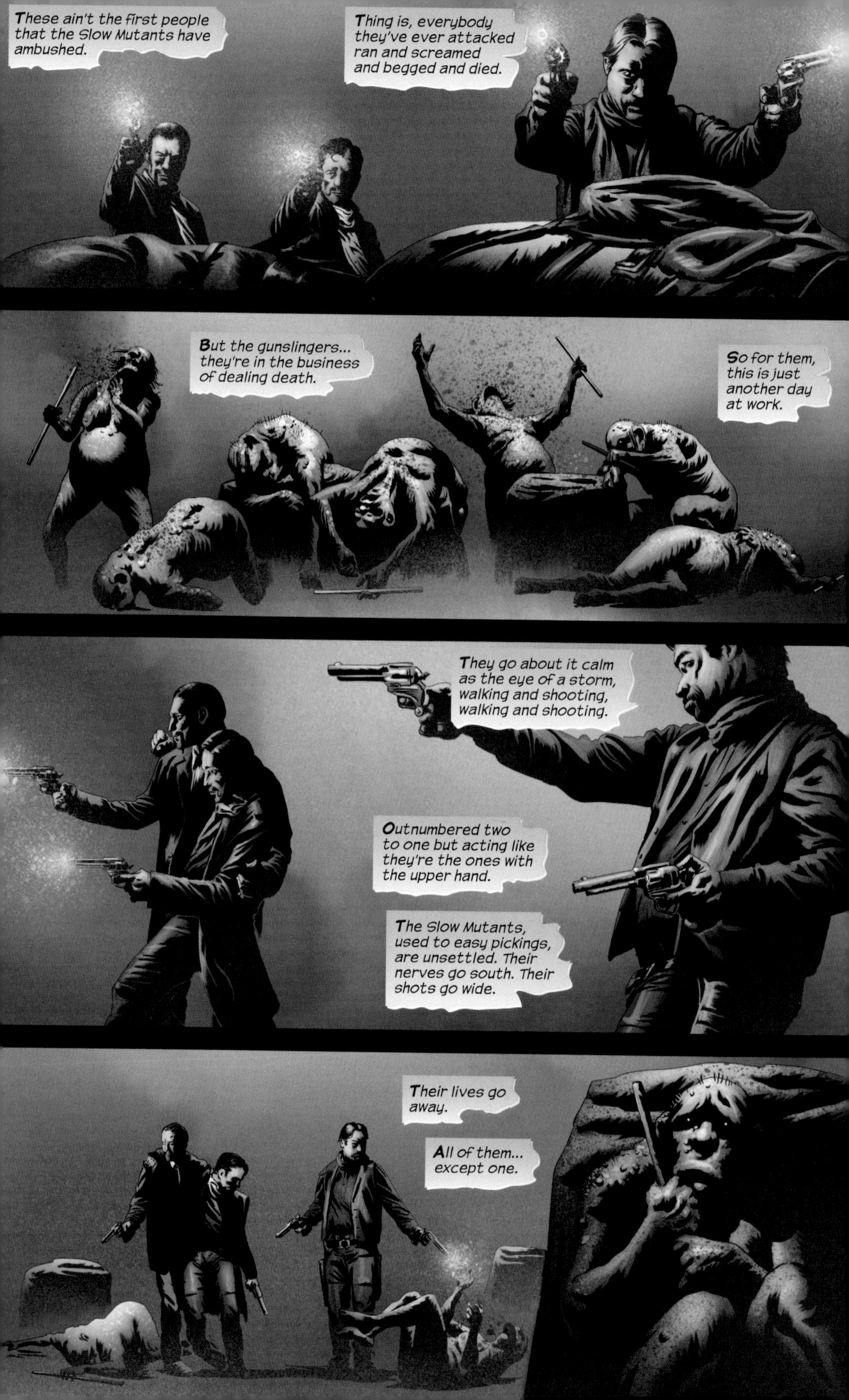
These ain't the first people that the Slow Mutants have ambushed.
Thing is, everybody they've ever attacked ran and screamed and begged and died.
But the gunslingers... they're in the business of dealing death.
So for them, this is just another day at work.
They go about it calm as the eye of a storm, walking and shooting, walking and shooting.
Outnumbered two to one but acting like they're the ones with the upper hand.
The Slow Mutants, used to easy pickings, are unsettled. Their nerves go south. Their shots go wide.
Their lives go away.
All of them... except one.

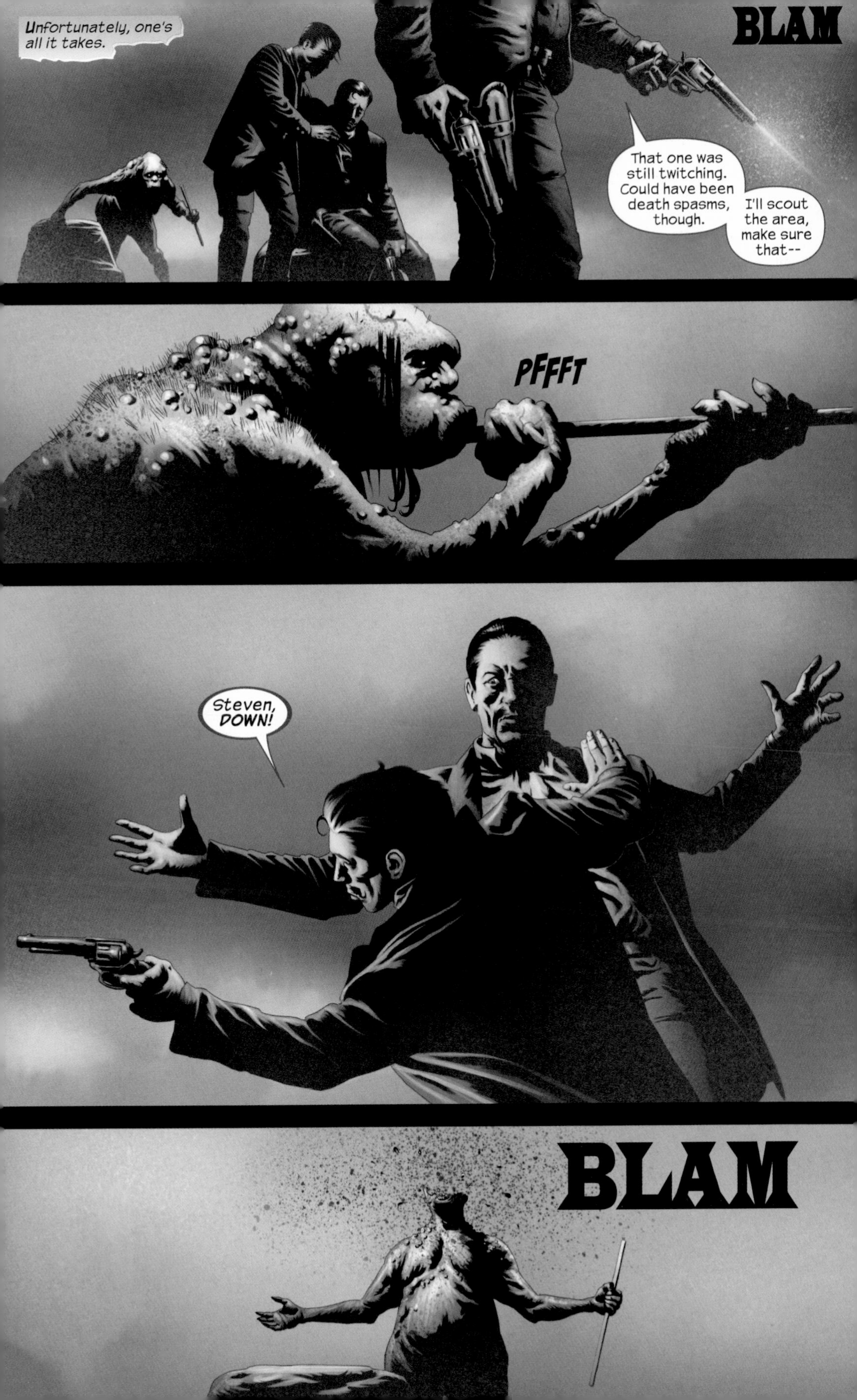
Unfortunately, one's all it takes.
BLAM
That one was still twitching. Could have been death spasms, though.
I'll scout the area, make sure that--
PFFFT
Steven, DOWN!
BLAM

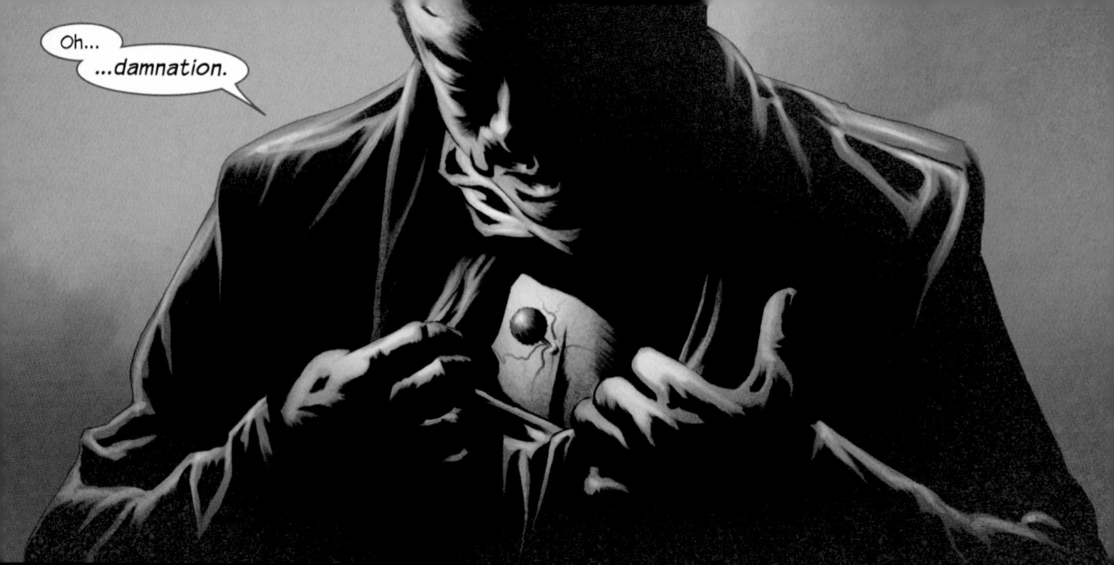
Oh...
...damnation.

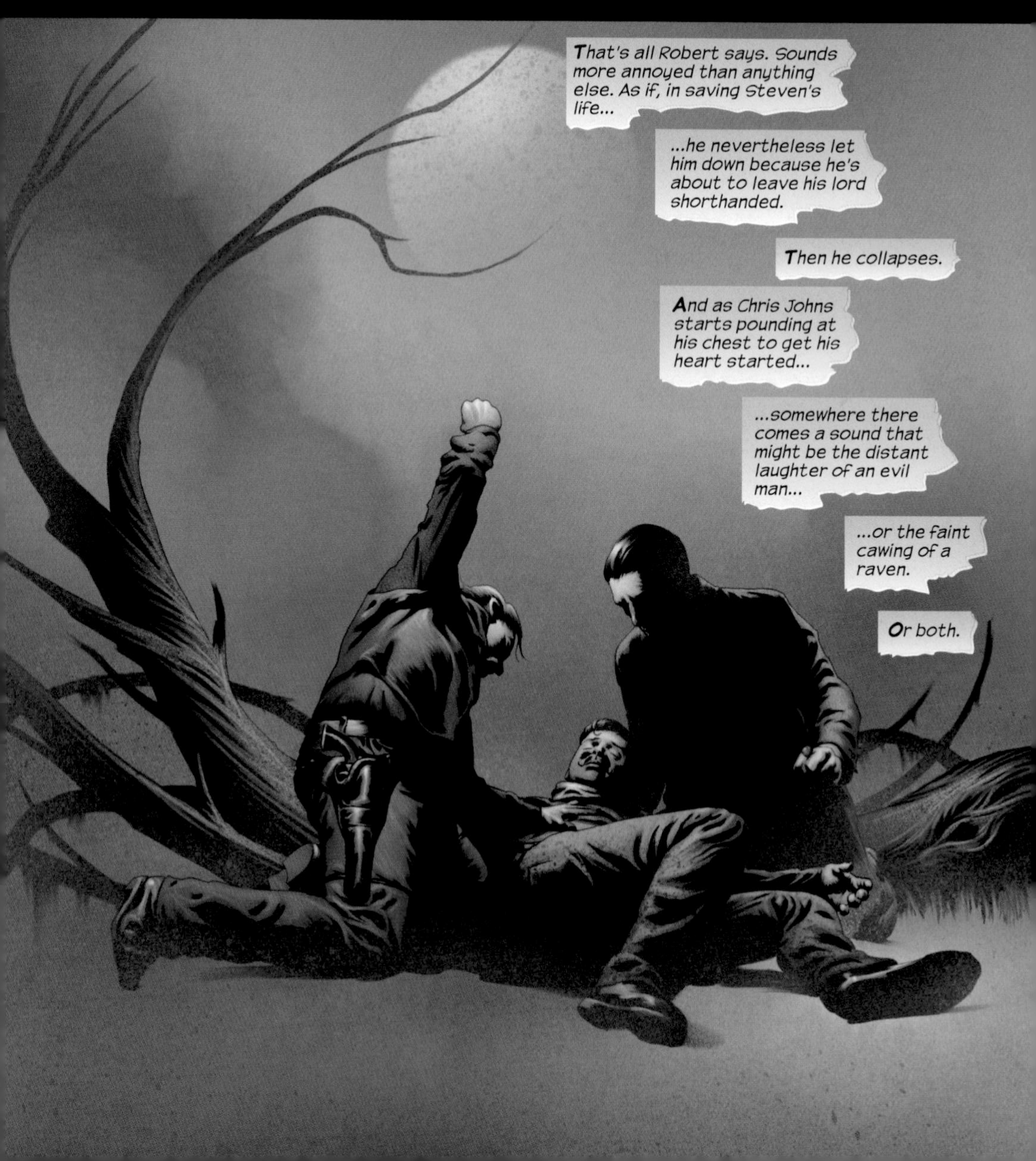
That's all Robert says. Sounds more annoyed than anything else. As if, in saving Steven's life...
...he nevertheless let him down because he's about to leave his lord shorthanded.
Then he collapses.
And as Chris Johns starts pounding at his chest to get his heart started...
...somewhere there comes a sound that might be the distant laughter of an evil man...
...or the faint cawing of a raven.
Or both.

STEPHEN KING

THE DARK TOWER

FALL OF GILEAD

CHAPTER THREE

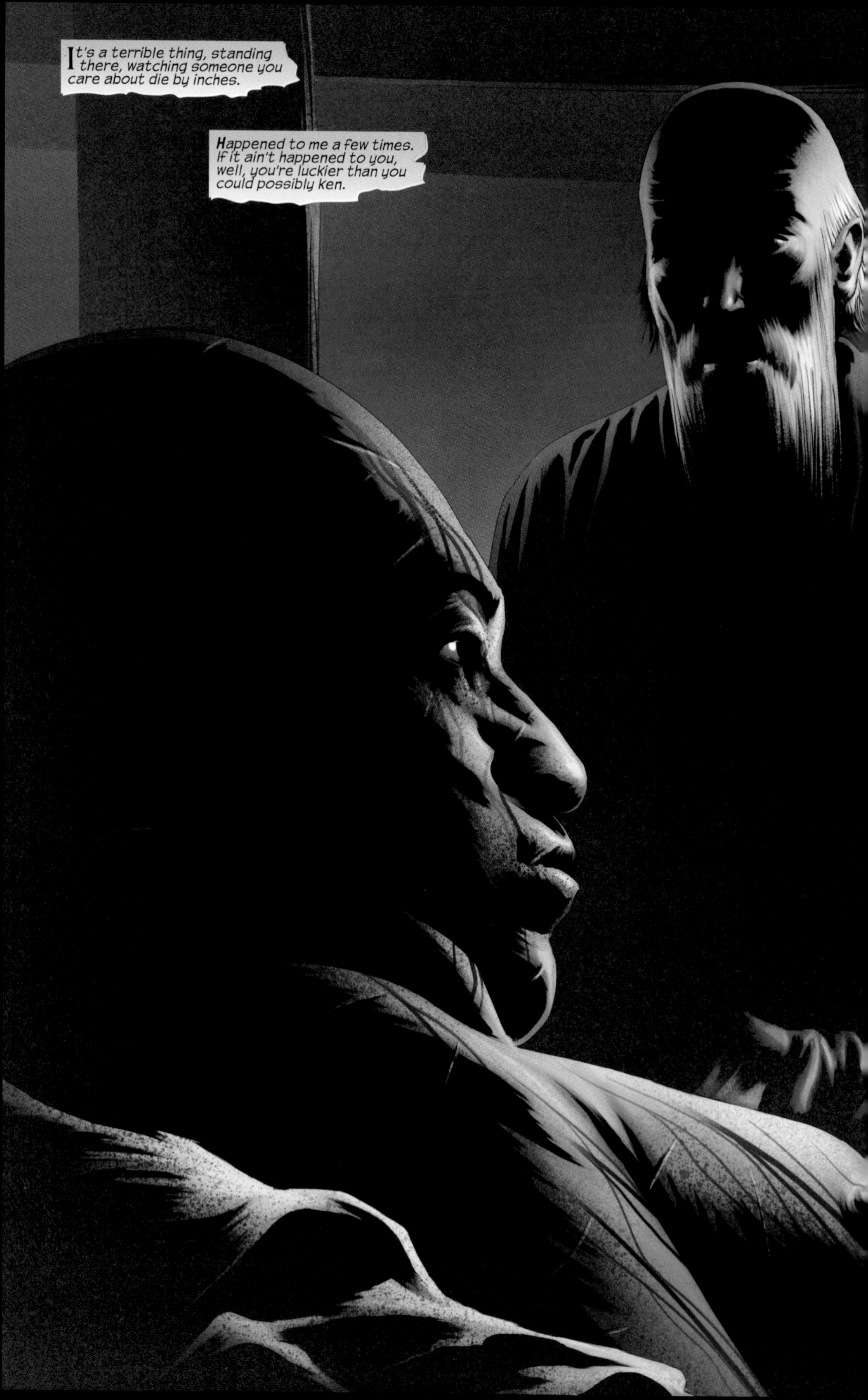
It's a terrible thing, standing there, watching someone you care about die by inches.
Happened to me a few times. If it ain't happened to you, well, you're luckier than you could possibly ken.

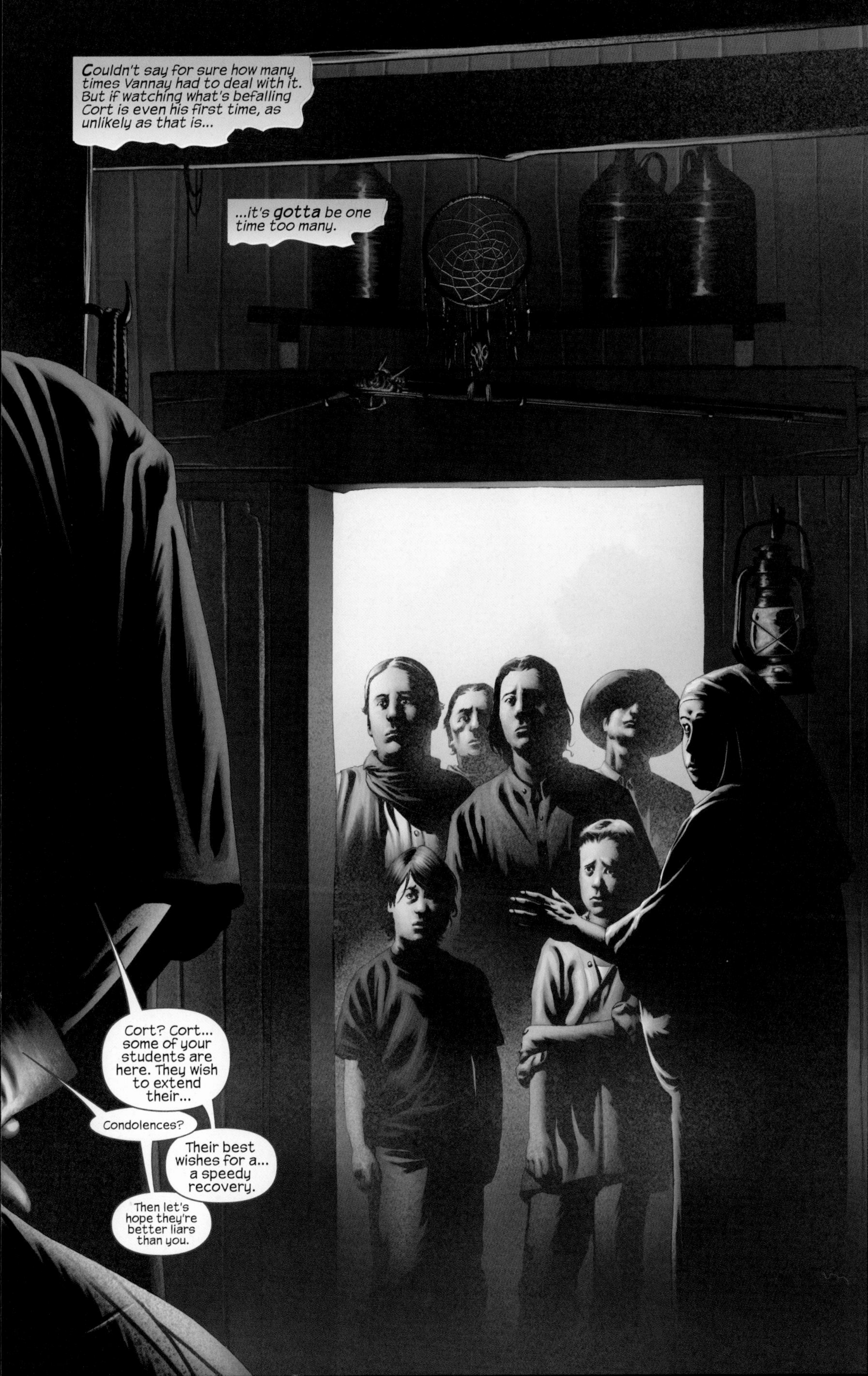
Couldn't say for sure how many times Vannay had to deal with it. But if watching what's befalling Cort is even his first time, as unlikely as that is...
...it's gotta be one time too many.
Cort? Cort... some of your students are here. They wish to extend their...
Condolences?
Their best wishes for a... a speedy recovery.
Then let's hope they're better liars than you.

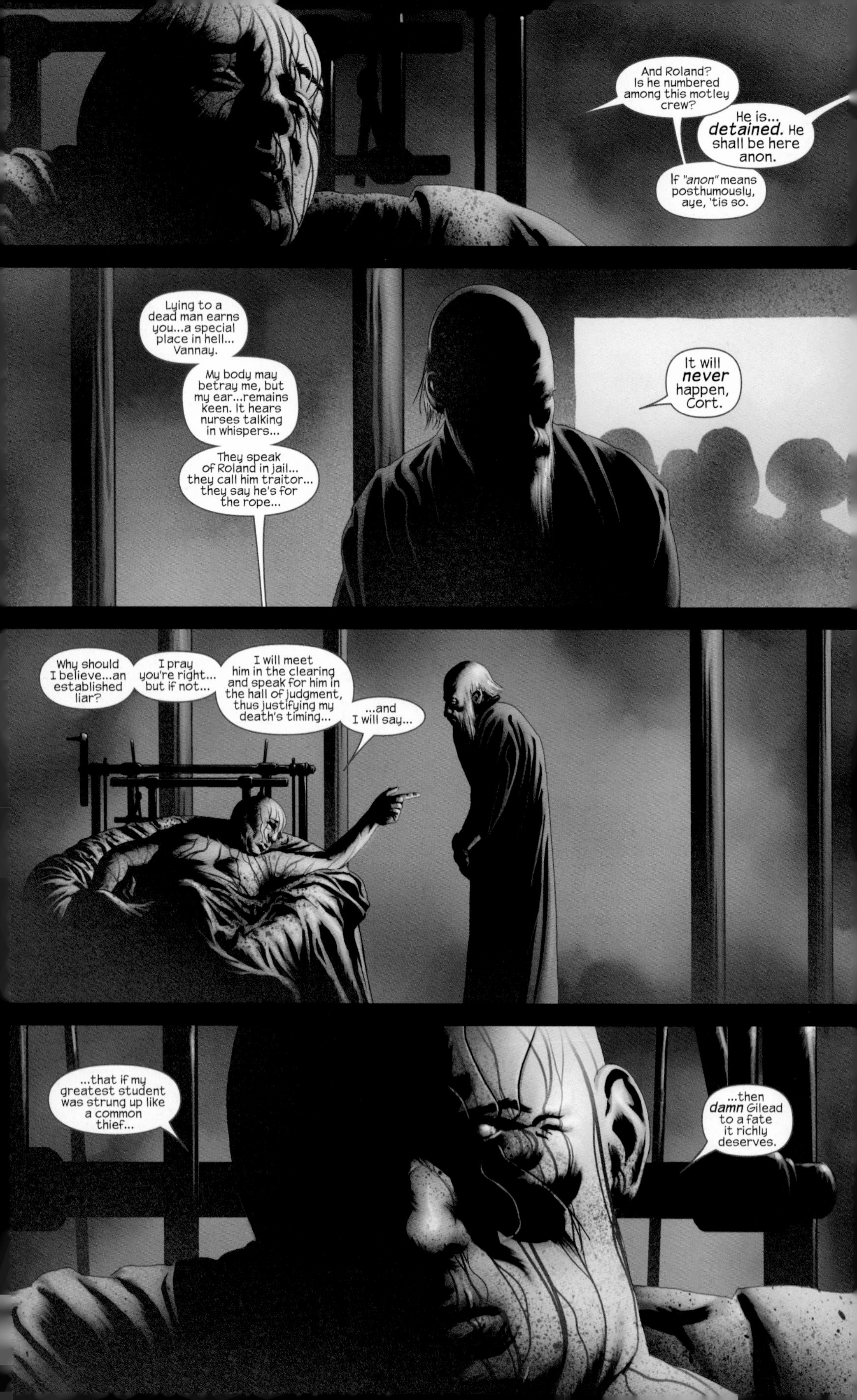
And Roland? Is he numbered among this motley crew?
He is... *detained.* He shall be here anon.
If *"anon"* means posthumously, aye, 'tis so.
Lying to a dead man earns you...a special place in hell... Vannay.
My body may betray me, but my ear...remains keen. It hears nurses talking in whispers...
They speak of Roland in jail... they call him traitor... they say he's for the rope...
It will *never* happen, Cort.
Why should I believe...an established liar?
I pray you're right... but if not...
I will meet him in the clearing and speak for him in the hall of judgment, thus justifying my death's timing...
...and I will say...
...that if my greatest student was strung up like a common thief...
...then *damn* Gilead to a fate it richly deserves.

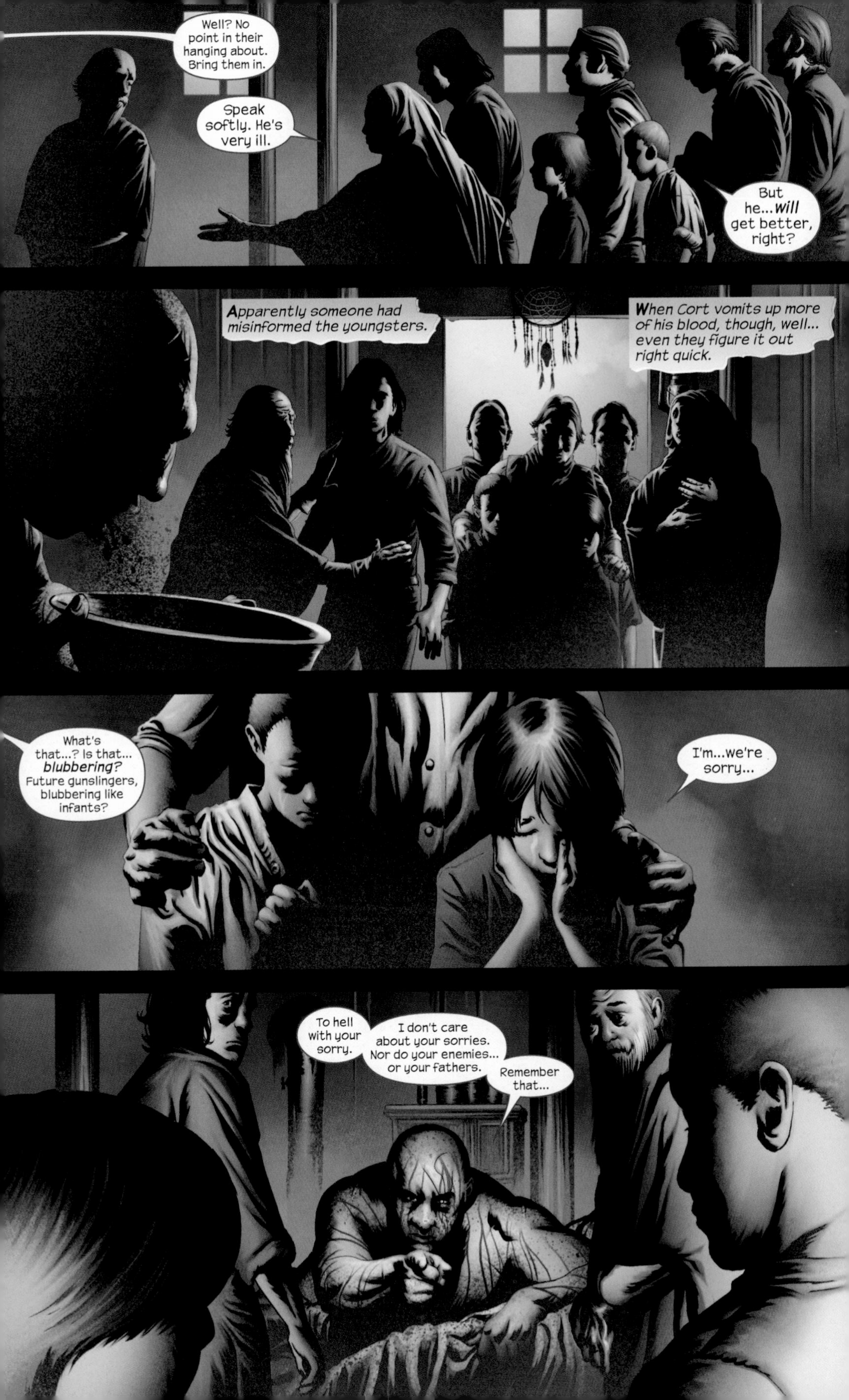
Well? No point in their hanging about. Bring them in.
Speak softly. He's very ill.
But he...*will* get better, right?
Apparently someone had misinformed the youngsters.
When Cort vomits up more of his blood, though, well... even they figure it out right quick.
What's that...? Is that... *blubbering?* Future gunslingers, blubbering like infants?
I'm...we're sorry...
To hell with your sorry.
I don't care about your sorries. Nor do your enemies... or your fathers.
Remember that...

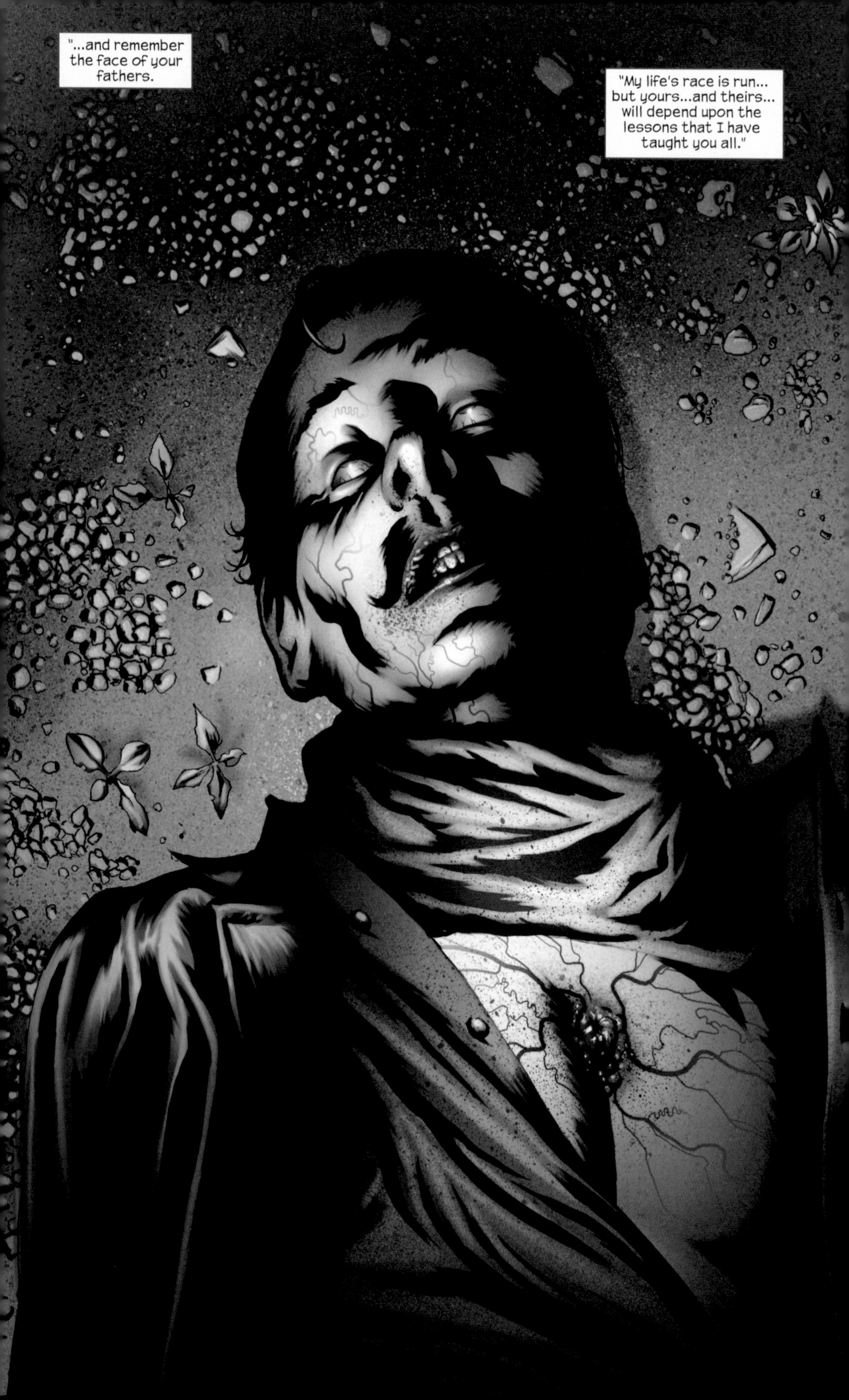
"...and remember the face of your fathers.
"My life's race is run... but yours...and theirs... will depend upon the lessons that I have taught you all."

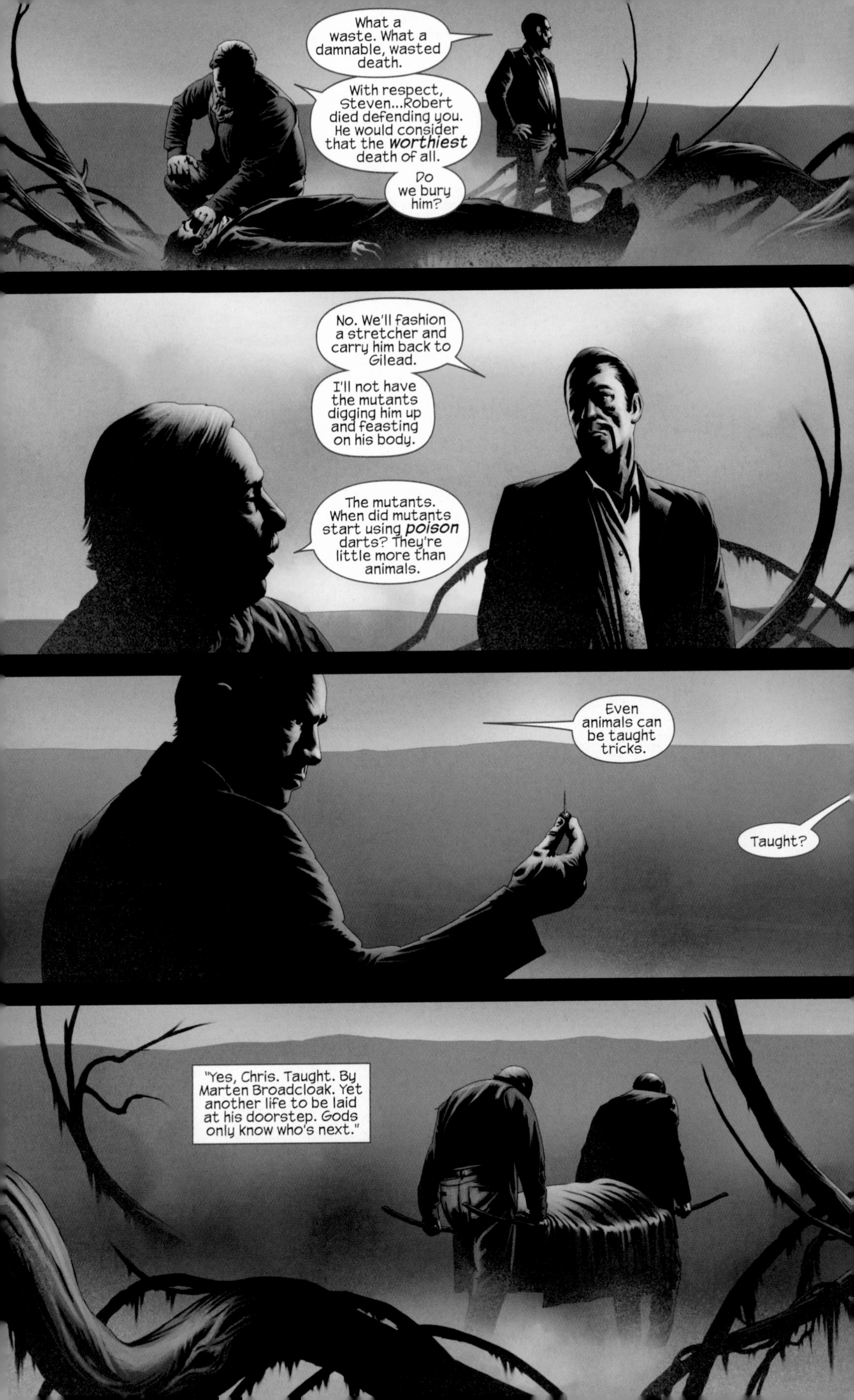
What a waste. What a damnable, wasted death.
With respect, Steven...Robert died defending you. He would consider that the *worthiest* death of all.
Do we bury him?
No. We'll fashion a stretcher and carry him back to Gilead.
I'll not have the mutants digging him up and feasting on his body.
The mutants. When did mutants start using *poison* darts? They're little more than animals.
Even animals can be taught tricks.
Taught?
"Yes, Chris. Taught. By Marten Broadcloak. Yet another life to be laid at his doorstep. Gods only know who's next."

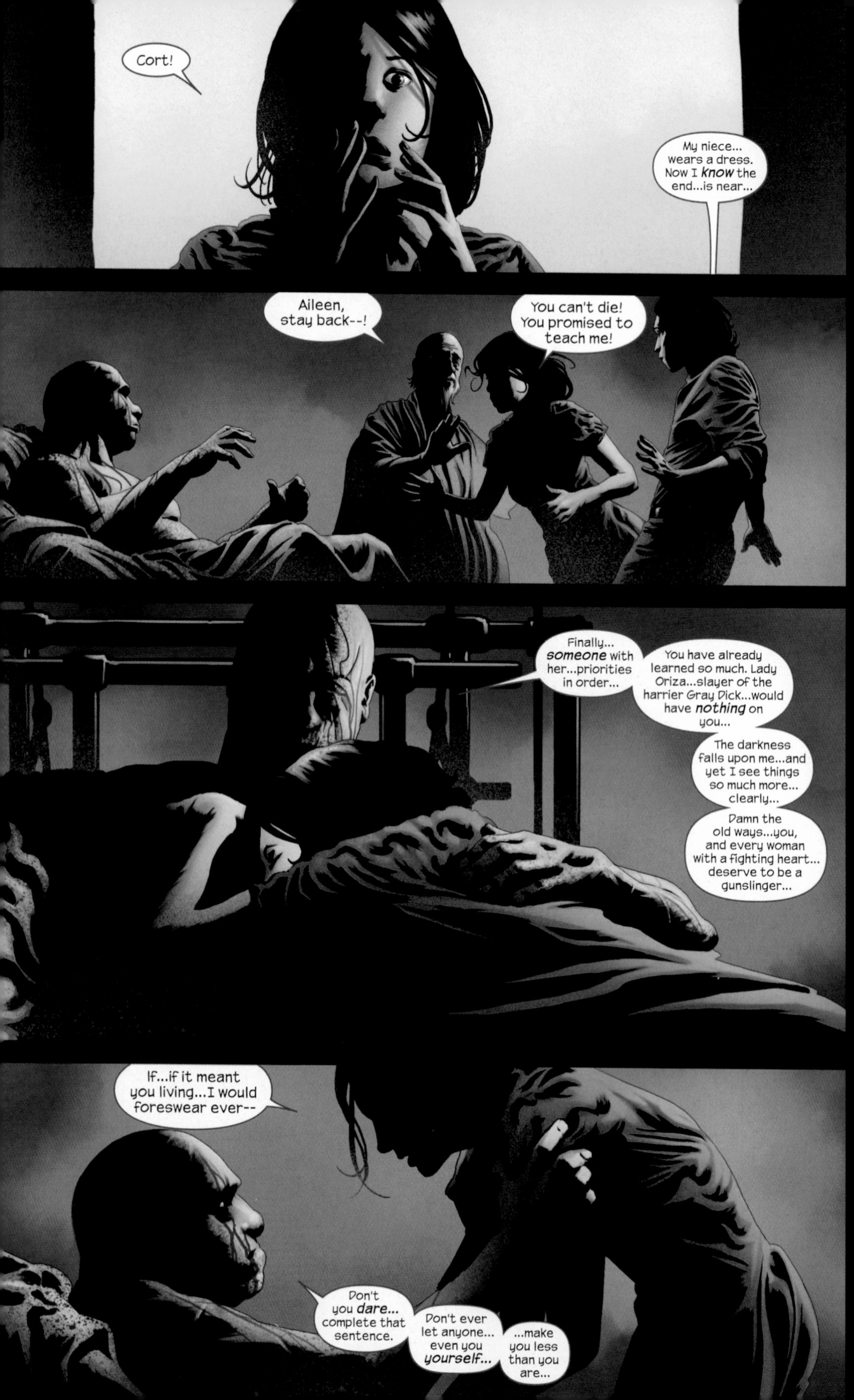
Cort!
My niece... wears a dress. Now I *know* the end...is near...
Aileen, stay back--!
You can't die! You promised to teach me!
Finally... *someone* with her...priorities in order...
You have already learned so much. Lady Oriza...slayer of the harrier Gray Dick...would have *nothing* on you...
The darkness falls upon me...and yet I see things so much more... clearly...
Damn the old ways...you, and every woman with a fighting heart... deserve to be a gunslinger...
If...if it meant you living...I would foreswear ever--
Don't you *dare...* complete that sentence.
Don't ever let anyone... even you *yourself...*
...make you less than you are...

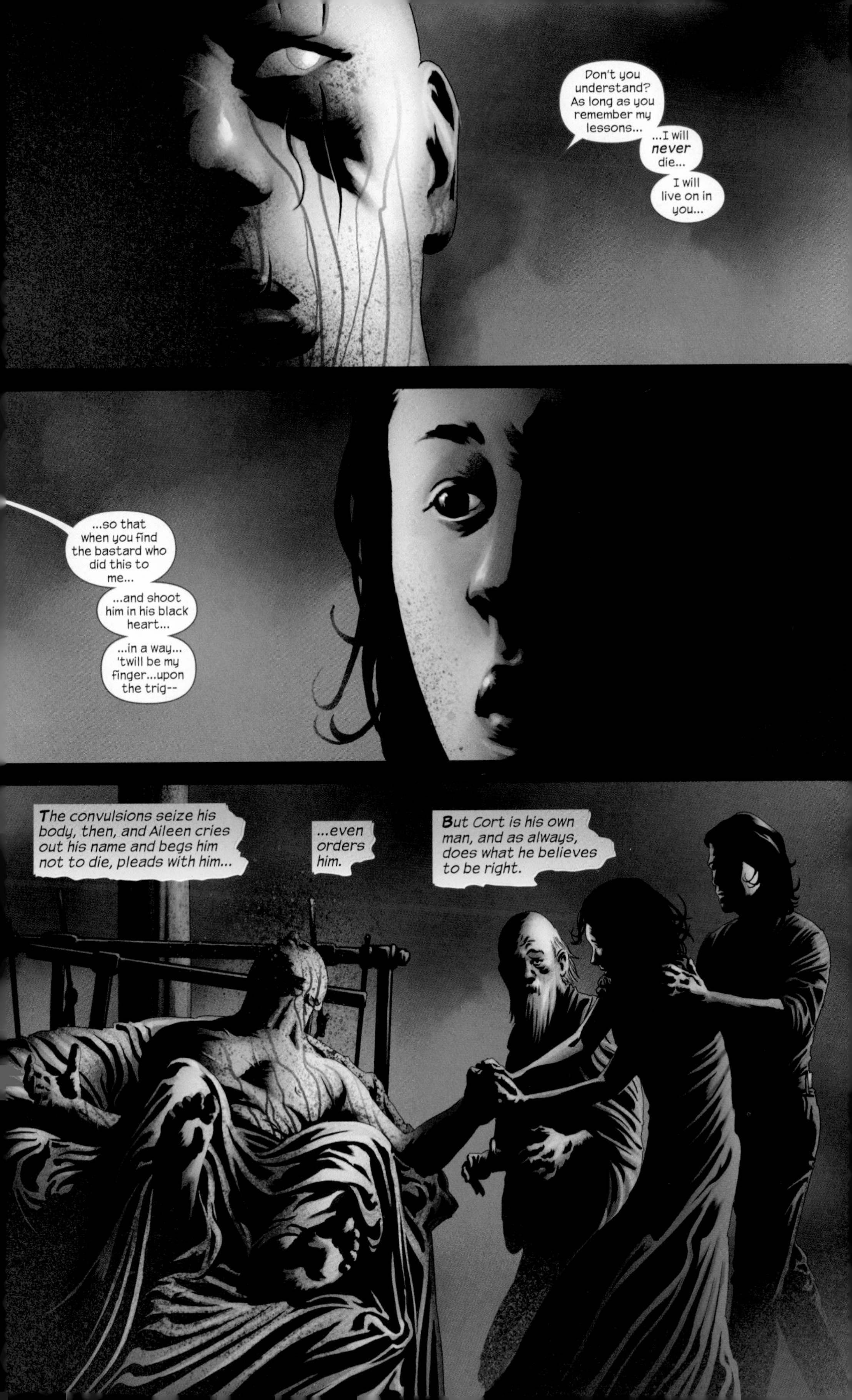
Don't you understand? As long as you remember my lessons...
...I will *never* die...
I will live on in you...
...so that when you find the bastard who did this to me...
...and shoot him in his black heart...
...in a way... 'twill be my finger...upon the trig--
The convulsions seize his body, then, and Aileen cries out his name and begs him not to die, pleads with him...
...even orders him.
But Cort is his own man, and as always, does what he believes to be right.

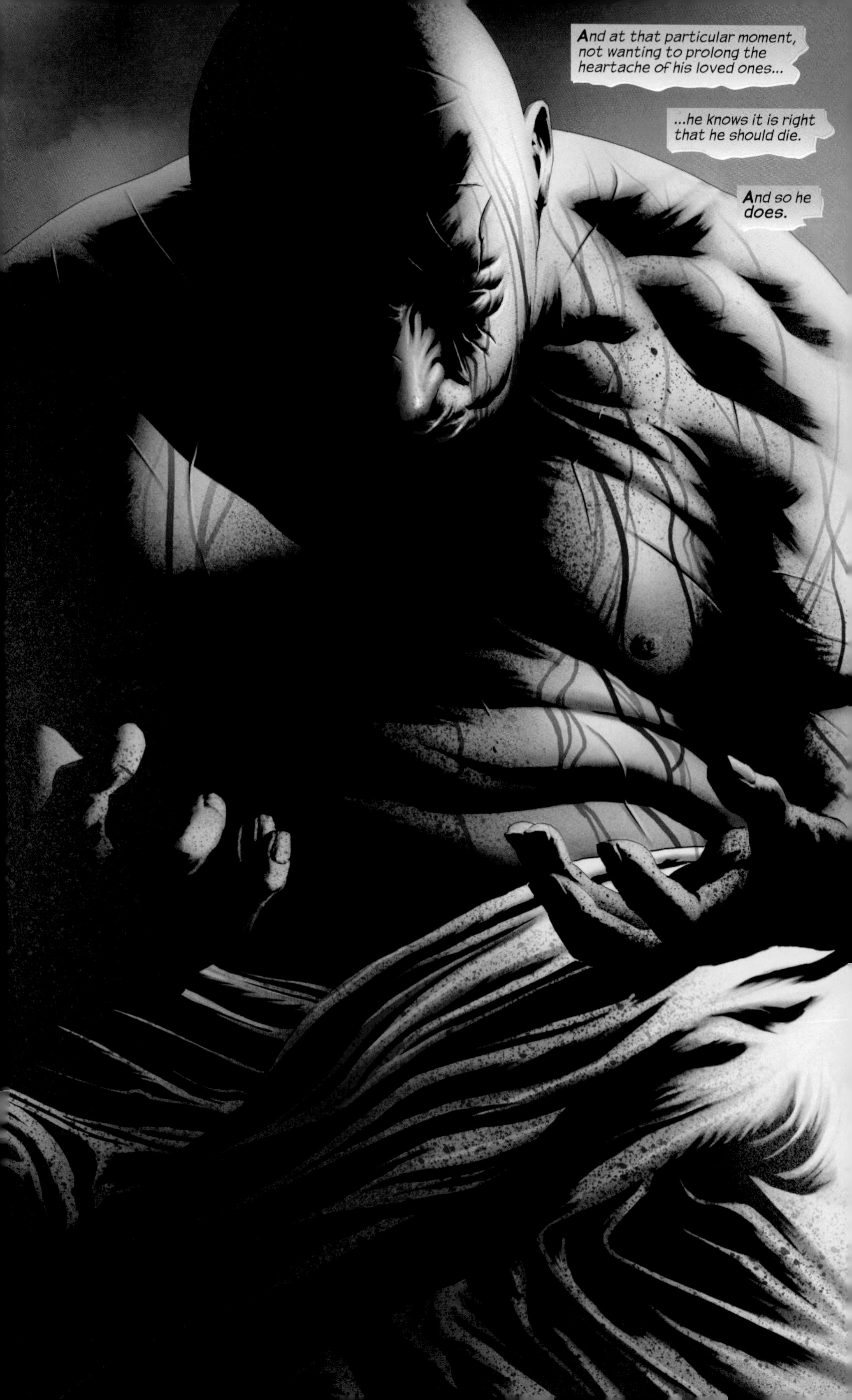
And at that particular moment, not wanting to prolong the heartache of his loved ones...
...he knows it is right that he should die.
And so he does.

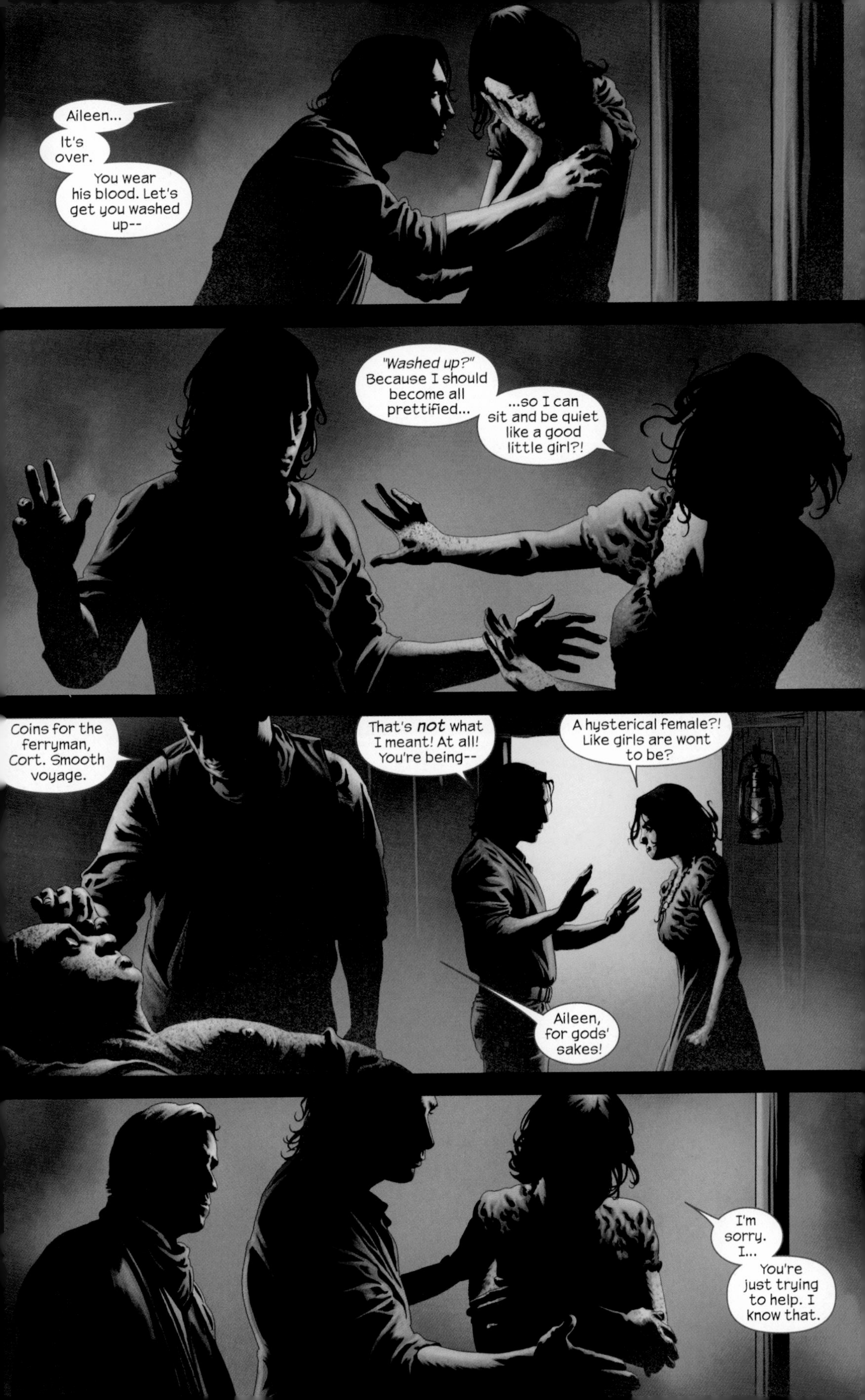
Aileen...
It's over.
You wear his blood. Let's get you washed up--
"Washed up?" Because I should become all prettified...
...so I can sit and be quiet like a good little girl?!
Coins for the ferryman, Cort. Smooth voyage.
That's not what I meant! At all! You're being--
A hysterical female?! Like girls are wont to be?
Aileen, for gods' sakes!
I'm sorry. I...
You're just trying to help. I know that.

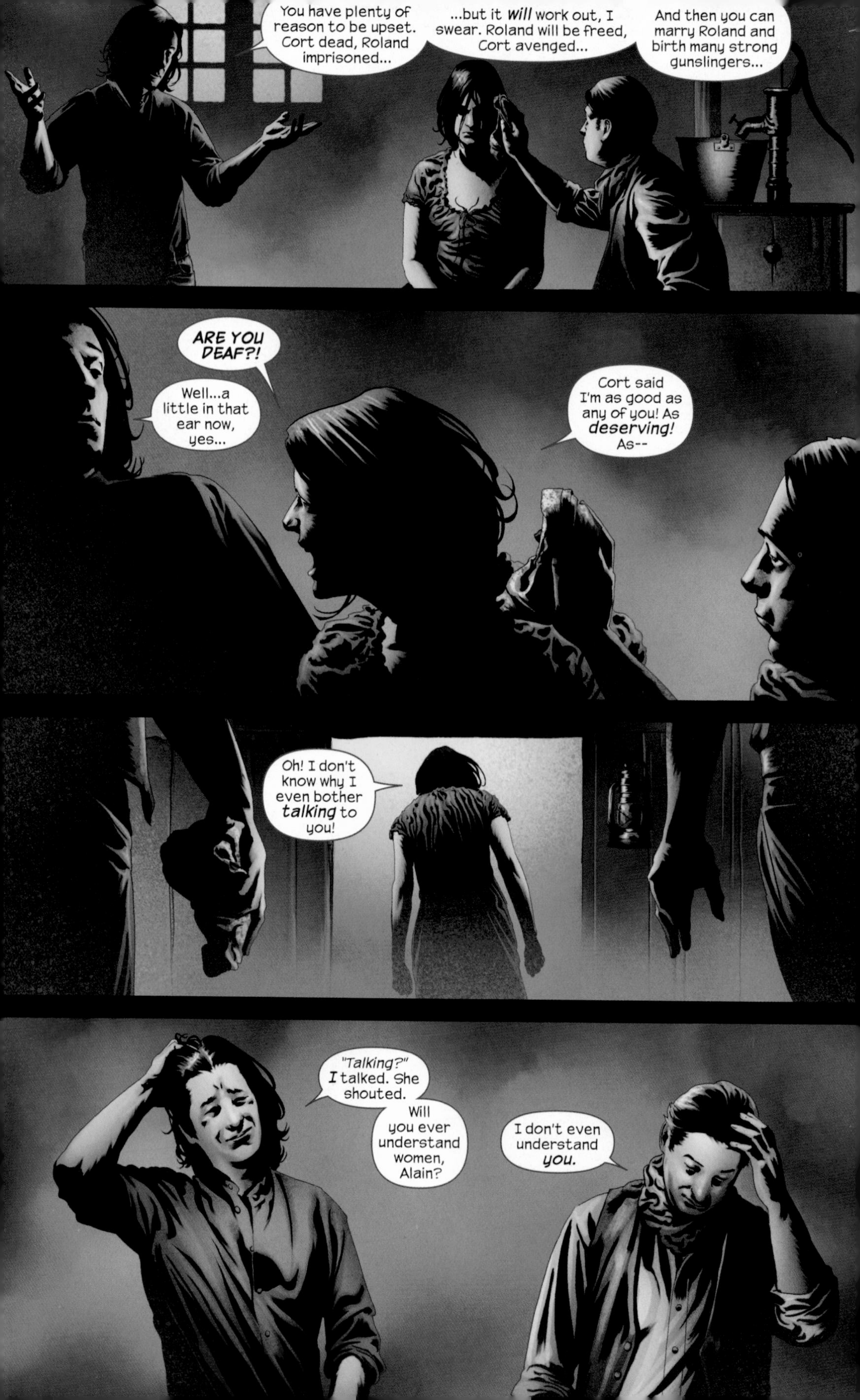

You have plenty of reason to be upset. Cort dead, Roland imprisoned...
...but it *will* work out, I swear. Roland will be freed, Cort avenged...
And then you can marry Roland and birth many strong gunslingers...
ARE YOU DEAF?!
Well...a little in that ear now, yes...
Cort said I'm as good as any of you! As *deserving!* As--
Oh! I don't know why I even bother *talking* to you!
"Talking?" *I* talked. She shouted.
Will you ever understand women, Alain?
I don't even understand *you.*

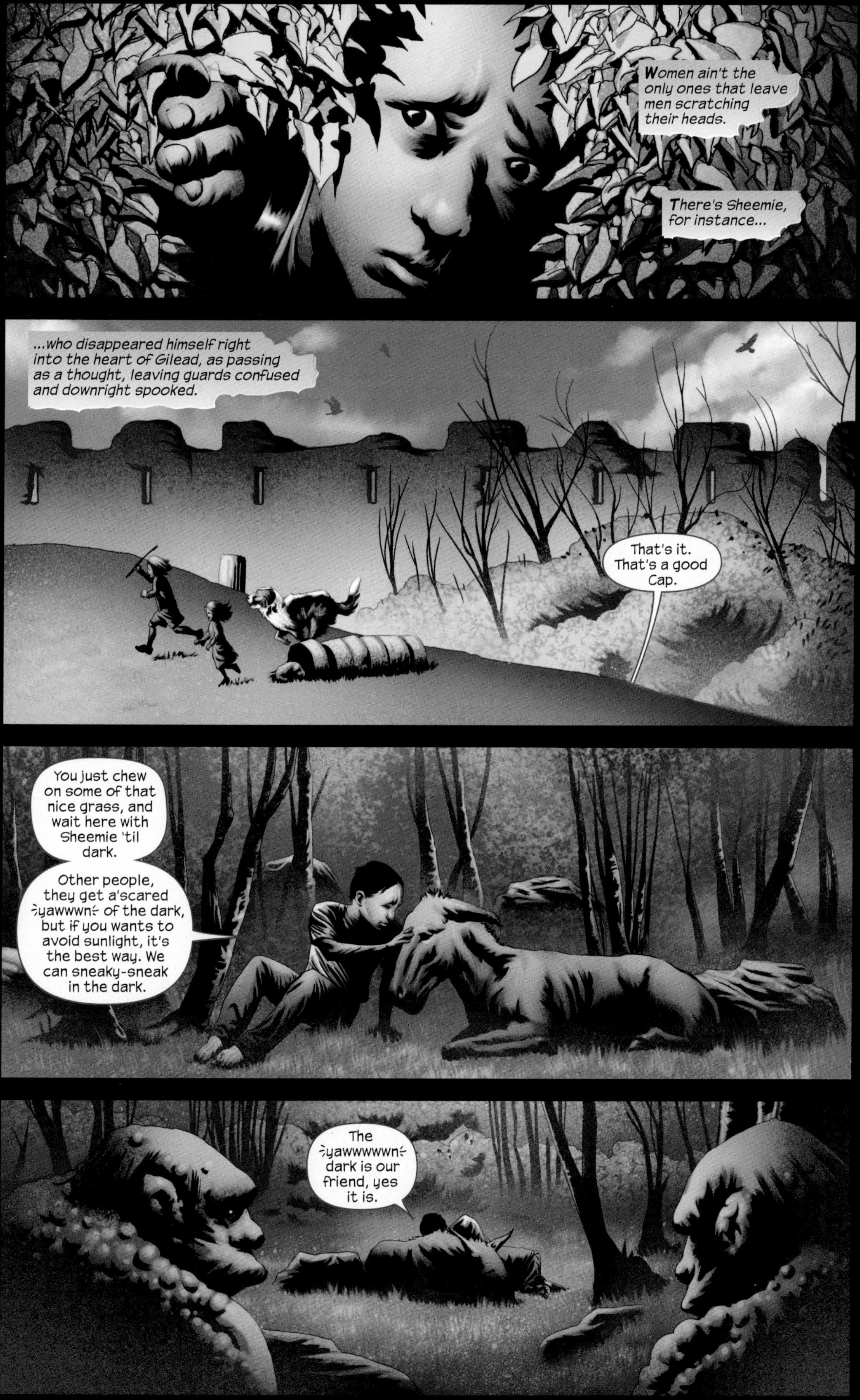
Women ain't the only ones that leave men scratching their heads.
There's Sheemie, for instance...
...who disappeared himself right into the heart of Gilead, as passing as a thought, leaving guards confused and downright spooked.
That's it. That's a good Cap.
You just chew on some of that nice grass, and wait here with Sheemie 'til dark.
Other people, they get a'scared ~yawwwn~ of the dark, but if you wants to avoid sunlight, it's the best way. We can sneaky-sneak in the dark.
The ~yawwwwwn~ dark is our friend, yes it is.

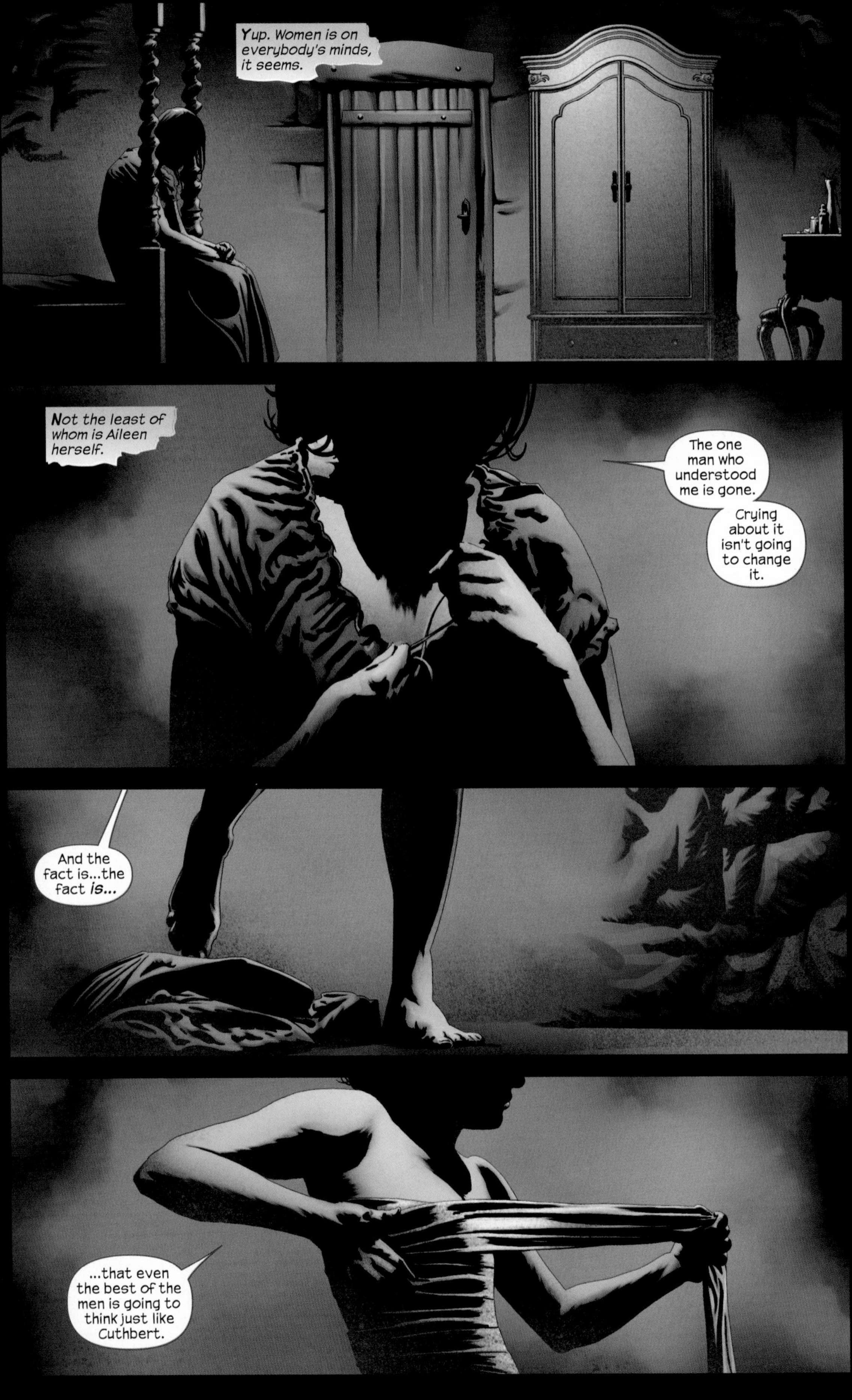
Yup. Women is on everybody's minds, it seems.
Not the least of whom is Aileen herself.
The one man who understood me is gone.
Crying about it isn't going to change it.
And the fact is...the fact is...
...that even the best of the men is going to think just like Cuthbert.

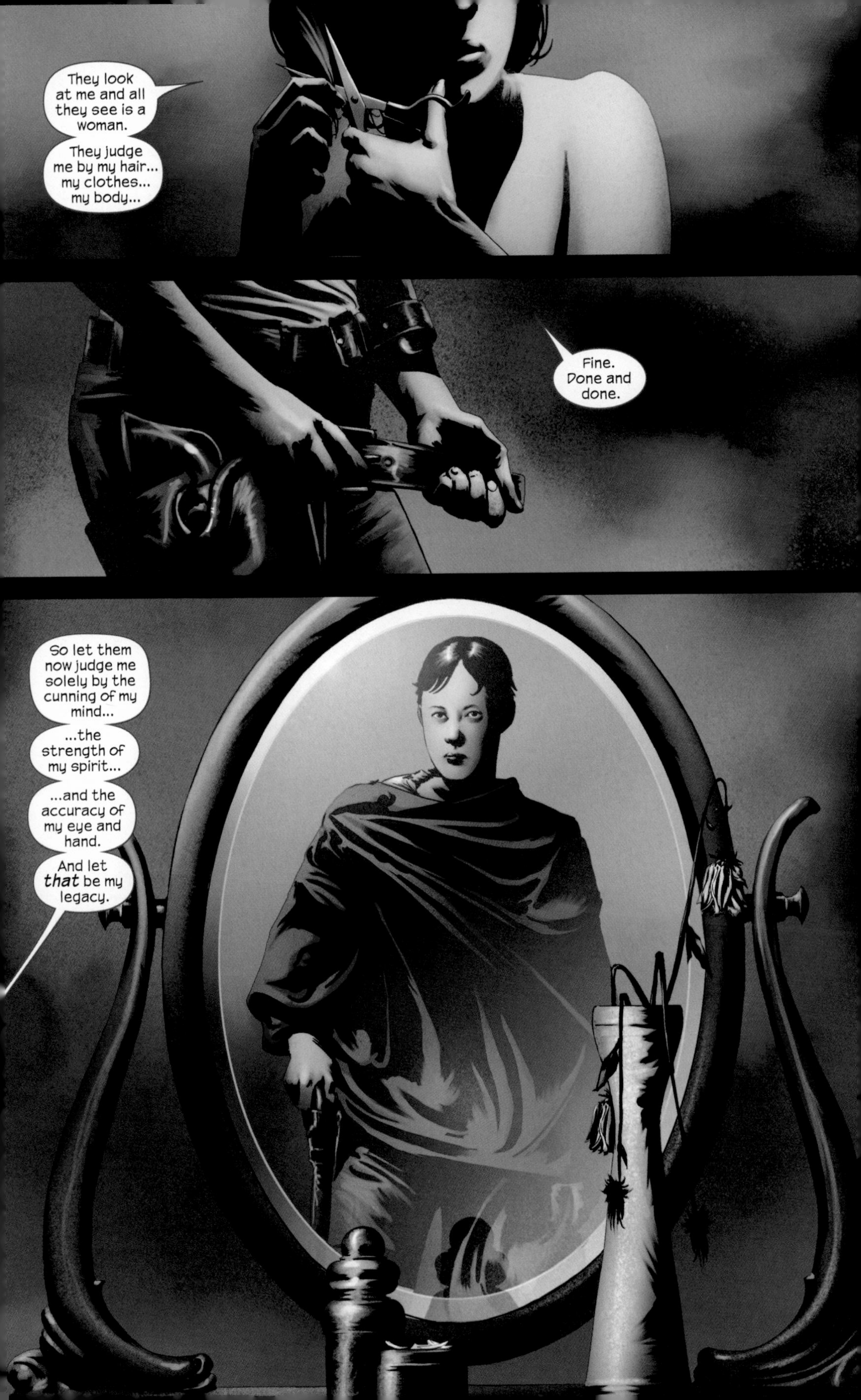

They look at me and all they see is a woman.
They judge me by my hair... my clothes... my body...
Fine. Done and done.
So let them now judge me solely by the cunning of my mind...
...the strength of my spirit...
...and the accuracy of my eye and hand.
And let *that* be my legacy.

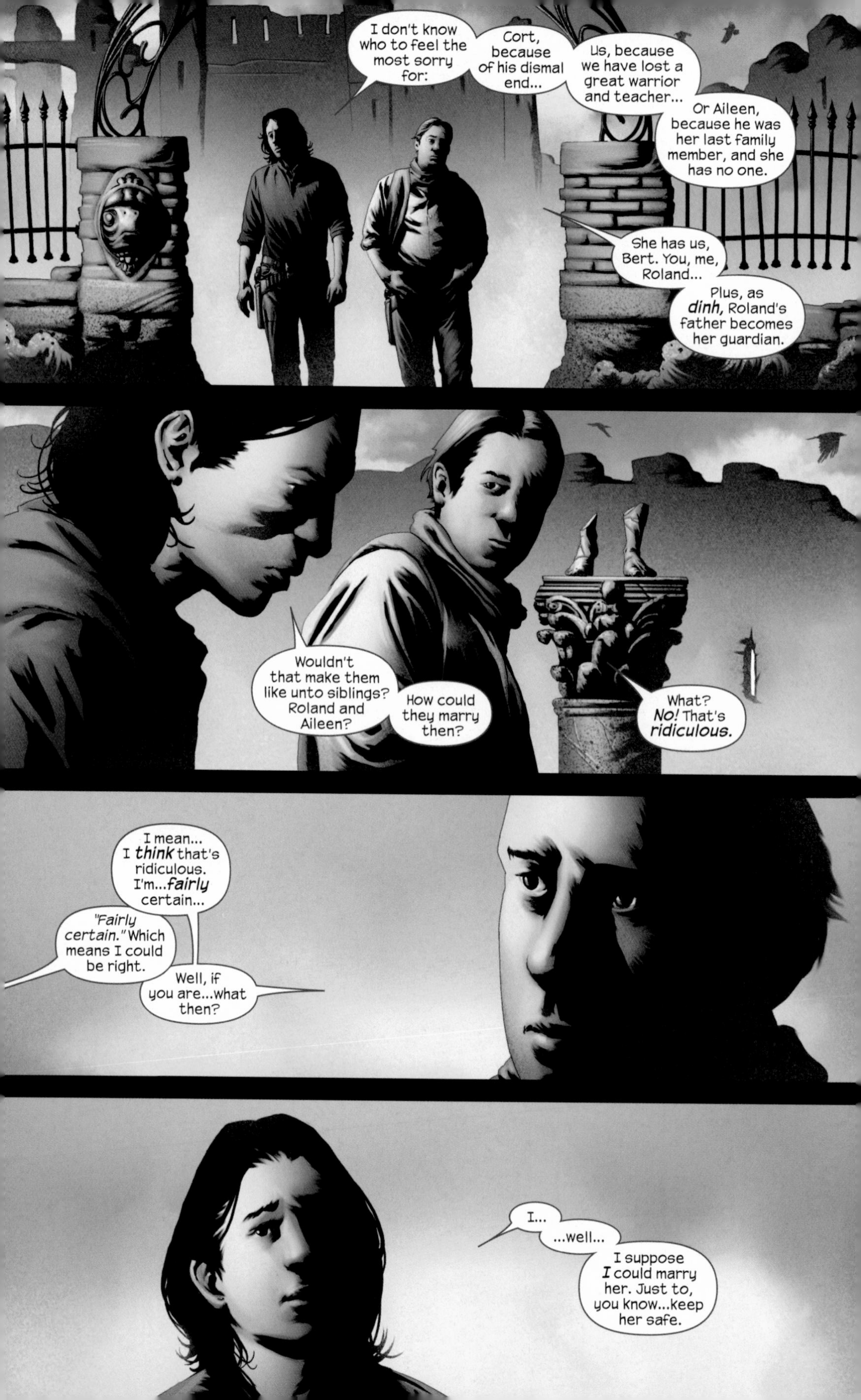
I don't know who to feel the most sorry for:
Cort, because of his dismal end...
Us, because we have lost a great warrior and teacher...
Or Aileen, because he was her last family member, and she has no one.
She has us, Bert. You, me, Roland...
Plus, as *dinh,* Roland's father becomes her guardian.
Wouldn't that make them like unto siblings? Roland and Aileen?
How could they marry then?
What? *No!* That's *ridiculous.*
I mean... I *think* that's ridiculous. I'm...*fairly* certain...
"Fairly certain." Which means I could be right.
Well, if you are...what then?
I...
...well...
I suppose *I* could marry her. Just to, you know...keep her safe.

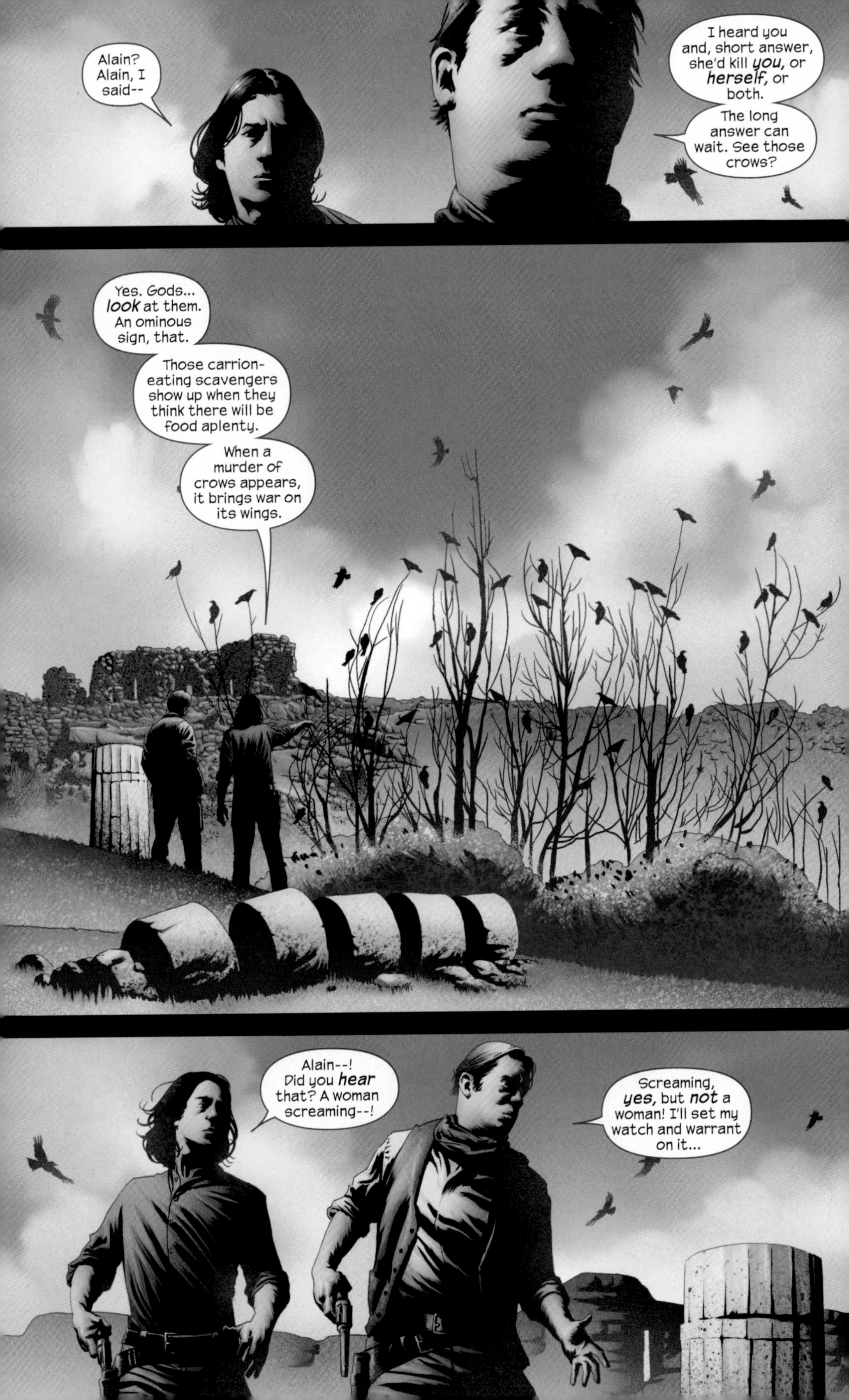
Alain? Alain, I said--
I heard you and, short answer, she'd kill *you,* or *herself,* or both.
The long answer can wait. See those crows?
Yes. Gods... *look* at them. An ominous sign, that.
Those carrion-eating scavengers show up when they think there will be food aplenty.
When a murder of crows appears, it brings war on its wings.
Alain--! Did you *hear* that? A woman screaming--!
Screaming, *yes,* but *not* a woman! I'll set my watch and warrant on it...

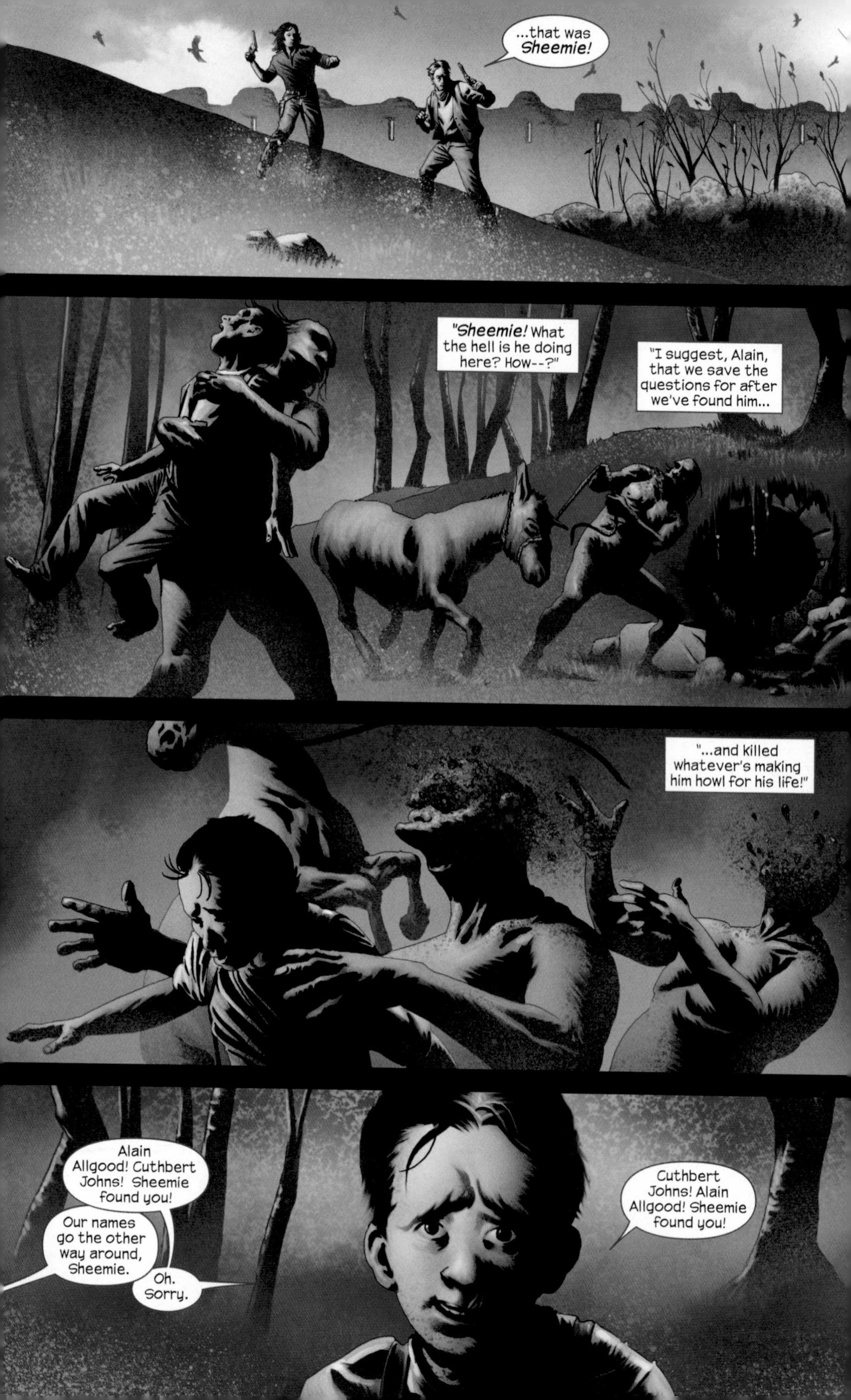
...that was *Sheemie!*
"*Sheemie!* What the hell is he doing here? How--?"
"I suggest, Alain, that we save the questions for after we've found him...
"...and killed whatever's making him howl for his life!"
Alain Allgood! Cuthbert Johns! Sheemie found you!
Our names go the other way around, Sheemie.
Oh. Sorry.
Cuthbert Johns! Alain Allgood! Sheemie found you!

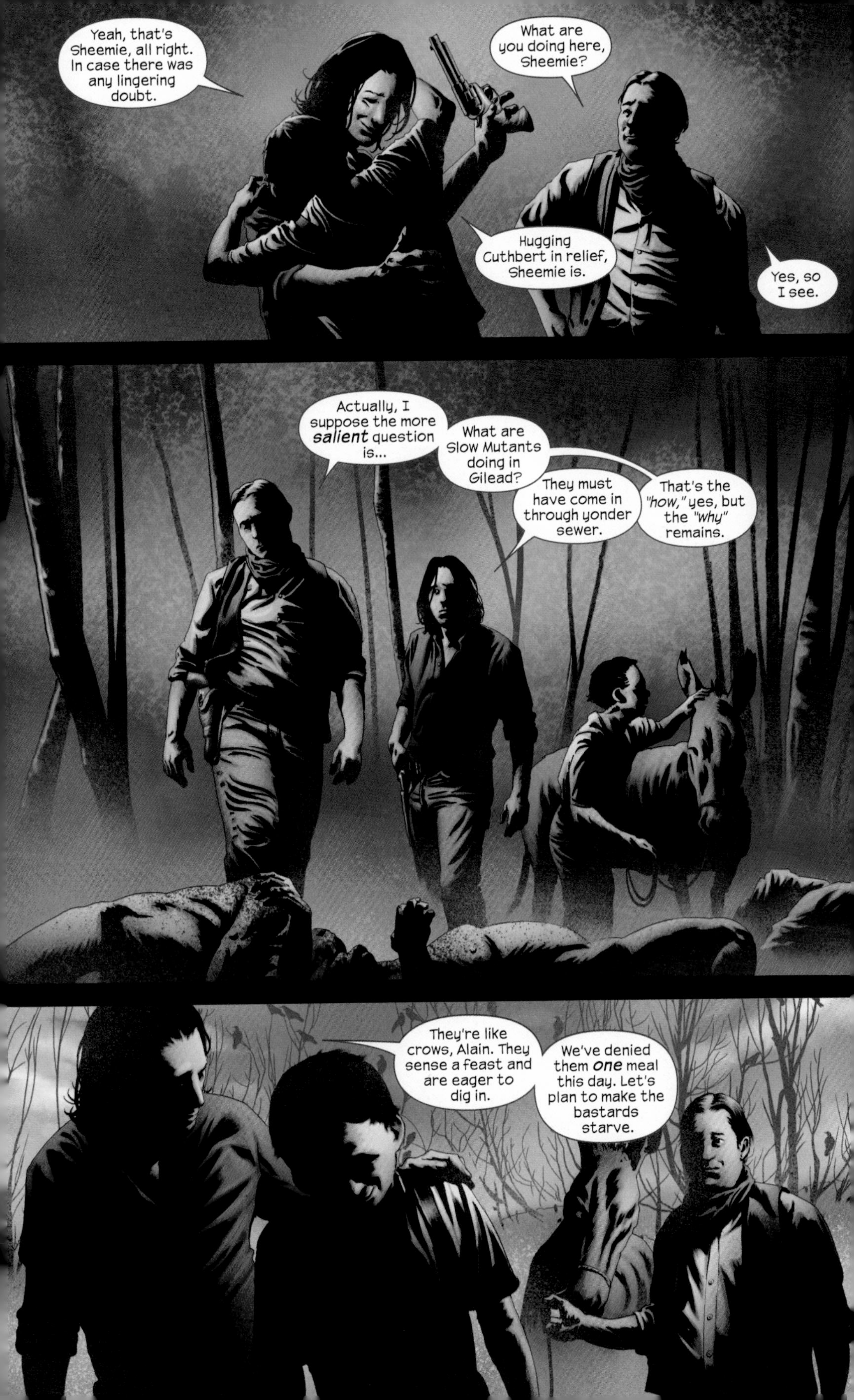
Yeah, that's Sheemie, all right. In case there was any lingering doubt.
What are you doing here, Sheemie?
Hugging Cuthbert in relief, Sheemie is.
Yes, so I see.
Actually, I suppose the more *salient* question is...
What are Slow Mutants doing in Gilead?
They must have come in through yonder sewer.
That's the *"how,"* yes, but the *"why"* remains.
They're like crows, Alain. They sense a feast and are eager to dig in.
We've denied them ***one*** meal this day. Let's plan to make the bastards starve.

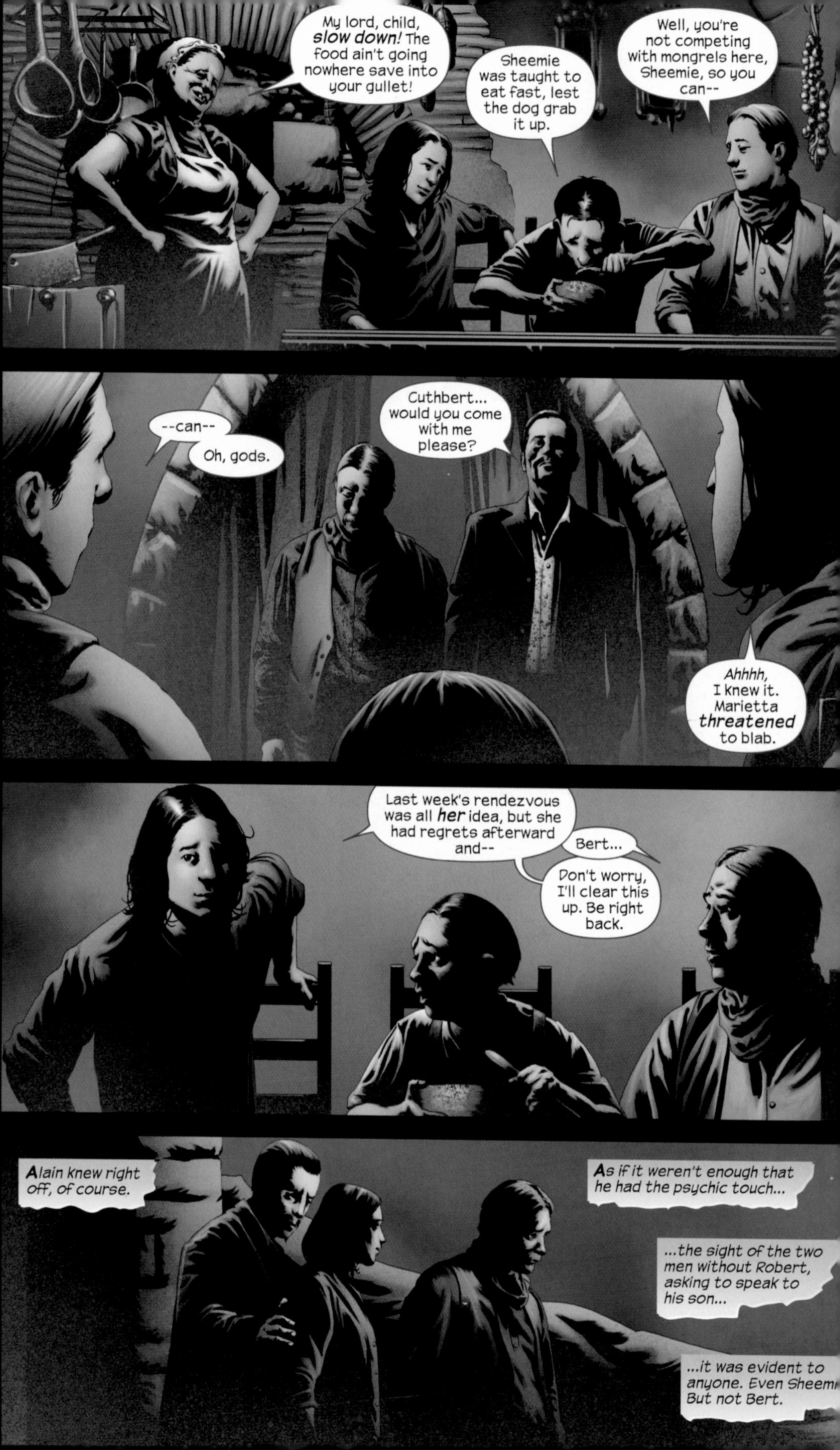
My lord, child, slow down! The food ain't going nowhere save into your gullet!
Sheemie was taught to eat fast, lest the dog grab it up.
Well, you're not competing with mongrels here, Sheemie, so you can--
--can--
Oh, gods.
Cuthbert... would you come with me please?
Ahhhh, I knew it. Marietta threatened to blab.
Last week's rendezvous was all her idea, but she had regrets afterward and--
Bert...
Don't worry, I'll clear this up. Be right back.
Alain knew right off, of course.
As if it weren't enough that he had the psychic touch...
...the sight of the two men without Robert, asking to speak to his son...
...it was evident to anyone. Even Sheemi
But not Bert.

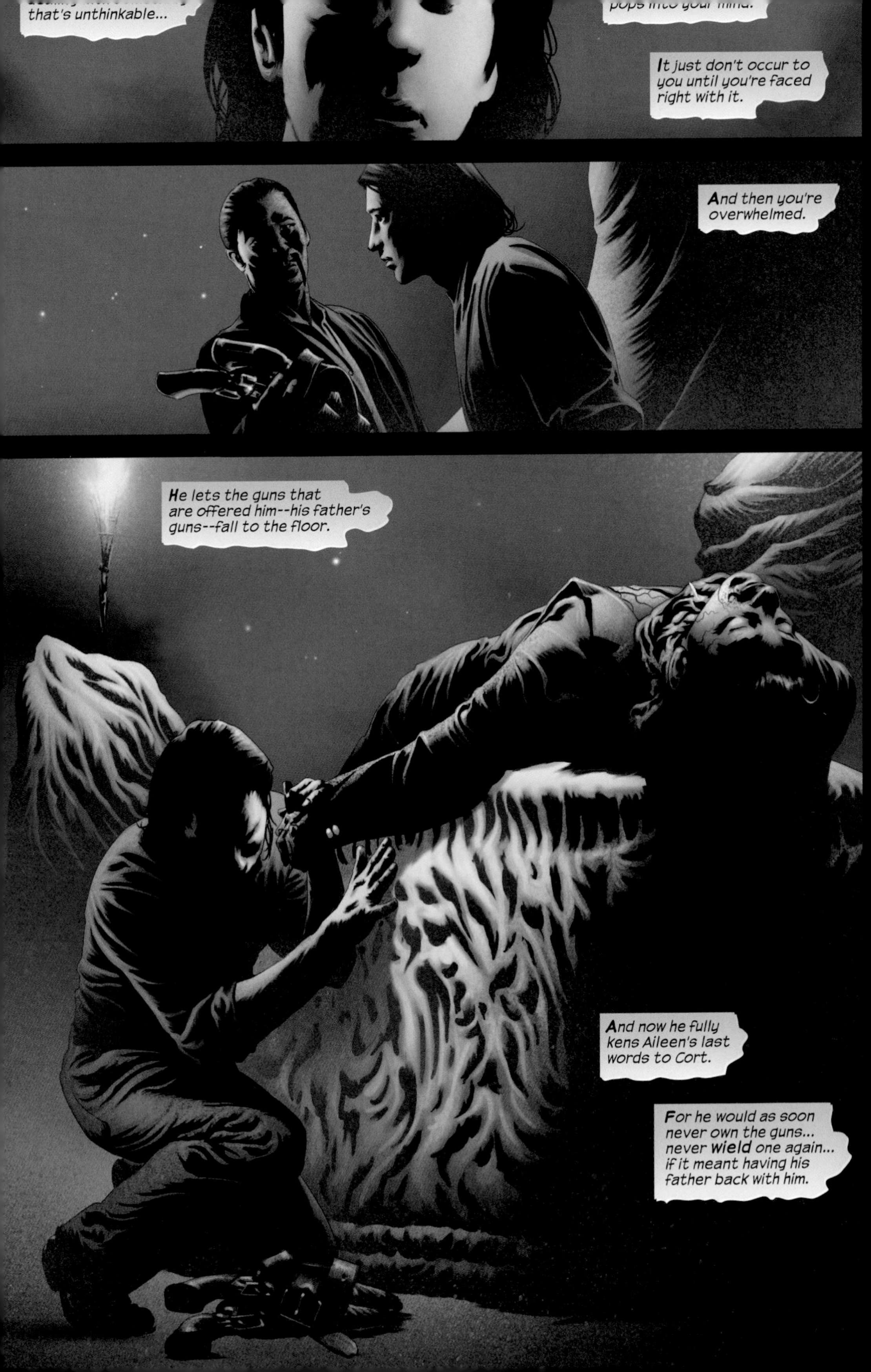

that's unthinkable...
It just don't occur to you until you're faced right with it.
And then you're overwhelmed.
He lets the guns that are offered him--his father's guns--fall to the floor.
And now he fully kens Aileen's last words to Cort.
For he would as soon never own the guns... never wield one again... if it meant having his father back with him.

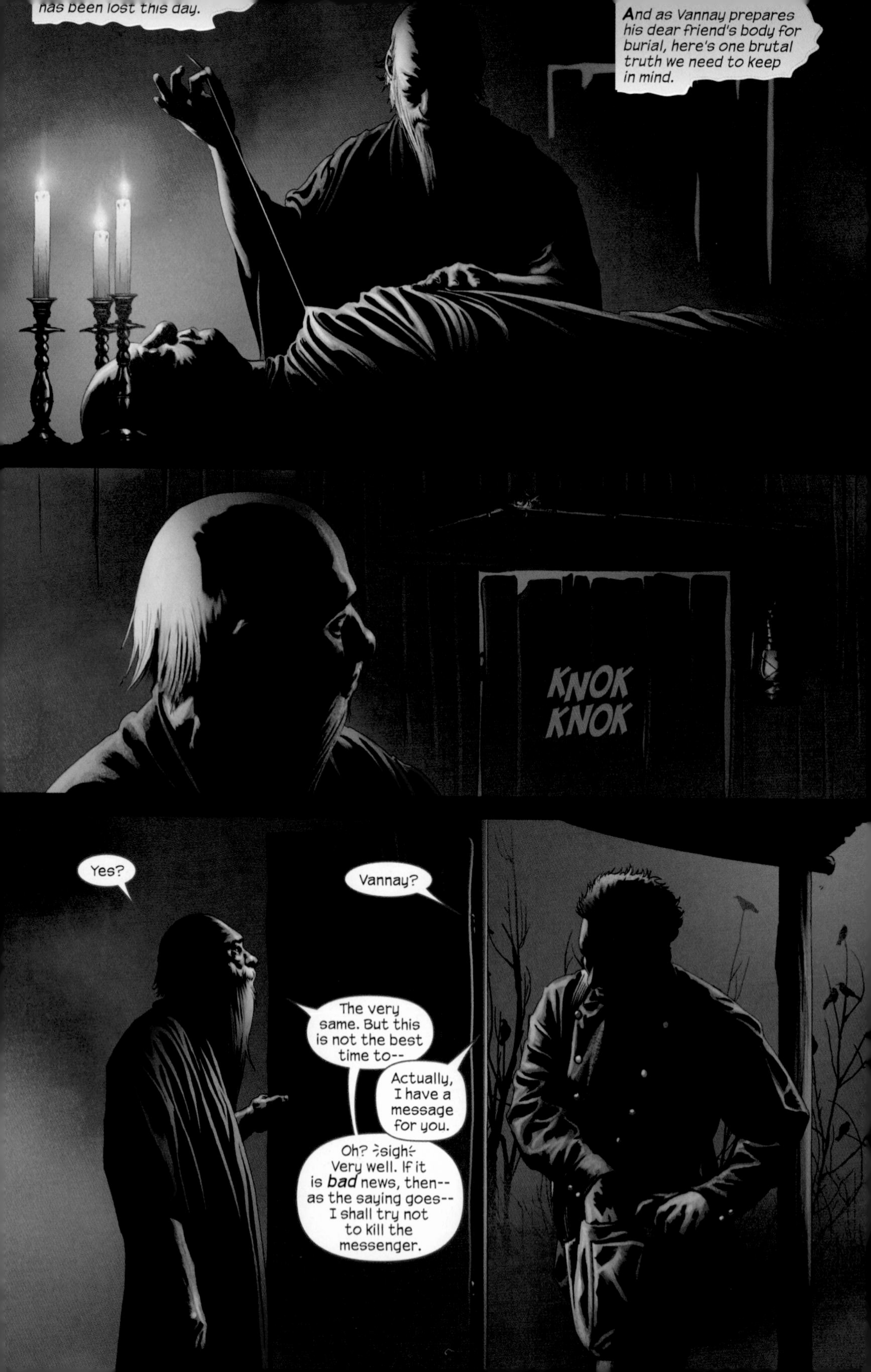
has been lost this day.
And as Vannay prepares his dear friend's body for burial, here's one brutal truth we need to keep in mind.
KNOK KNOK
Yes?
Vannay?
The very same. But this is not the best time to--
Actually, I have a message for you.
Oh? -sigh- Very well. If it is bad news, then--as the saying goes--I shall try not to kill the messenger.

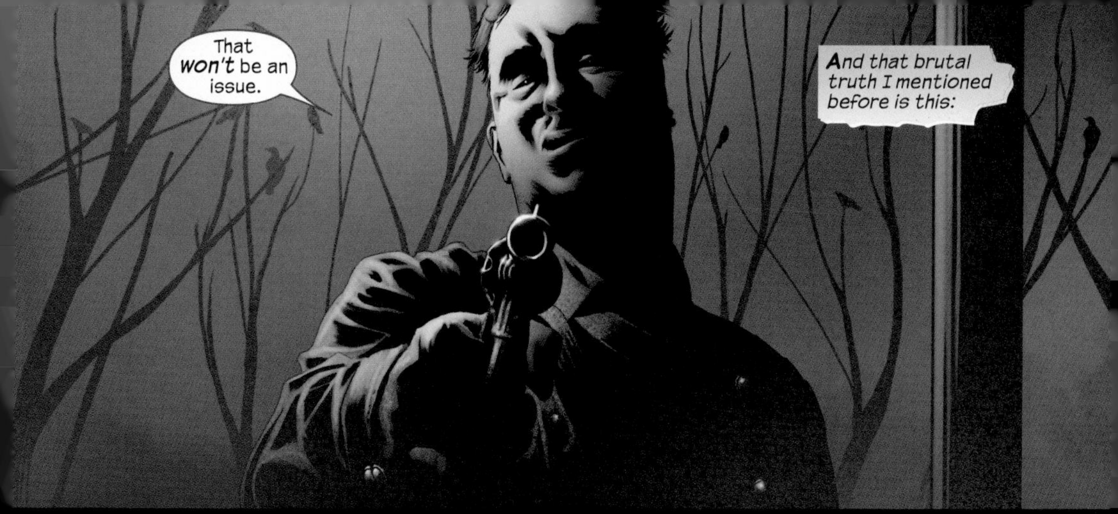
That *won't* be an issue.
And that brutal truth I mentioned before is this:

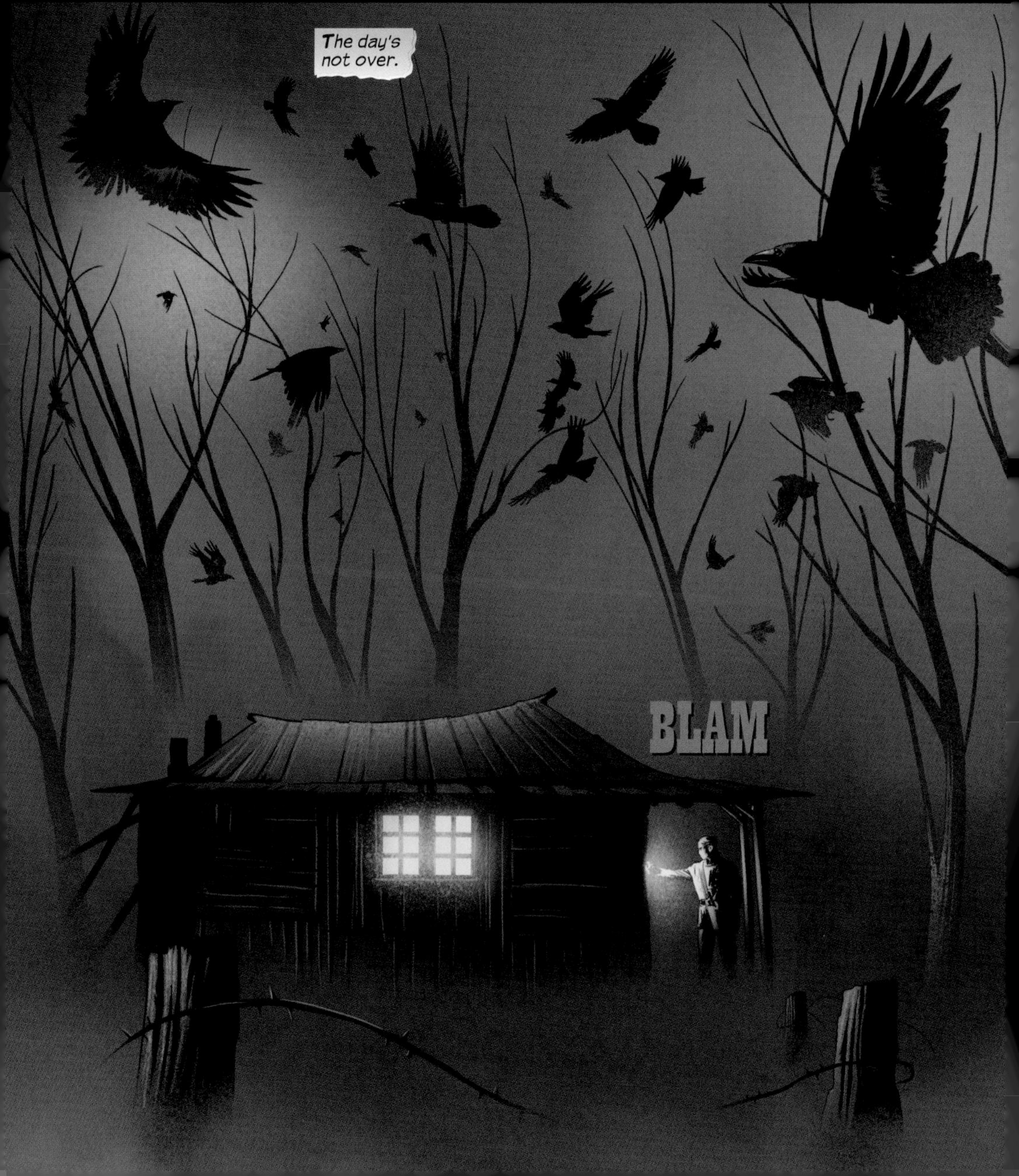
The day's not over.
BLAM

STEPHEN KING

THE DARK TOWER

FALL OF GILEAD

CHAPTER FOUR

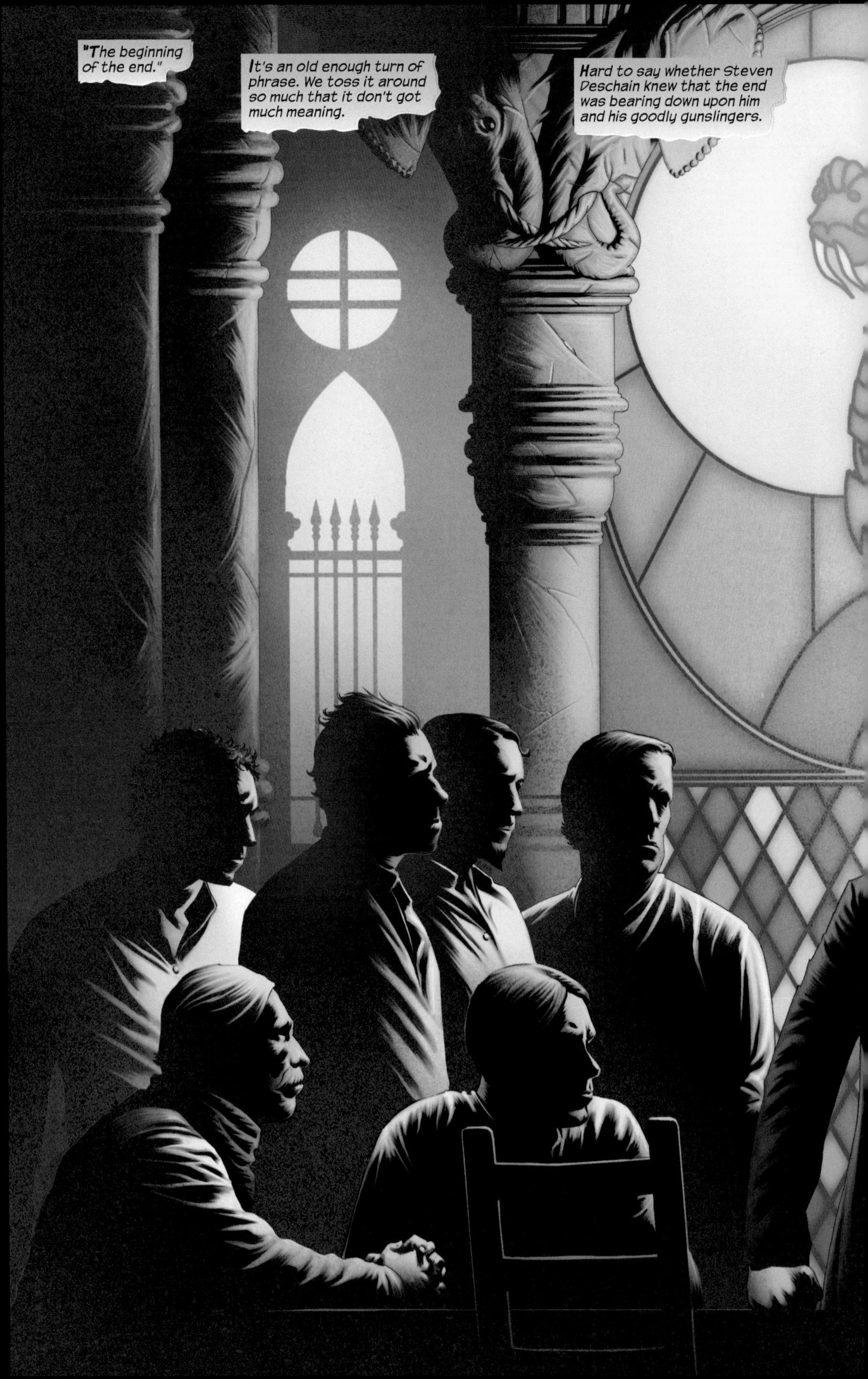
"The beginning of the end."
It's an old enough turn of phrase. We toss it around so much that it don't got much meaning.
Hard to say whether Steven Deschain knew that the end was bearing down upon him and his goodly gunslingers.

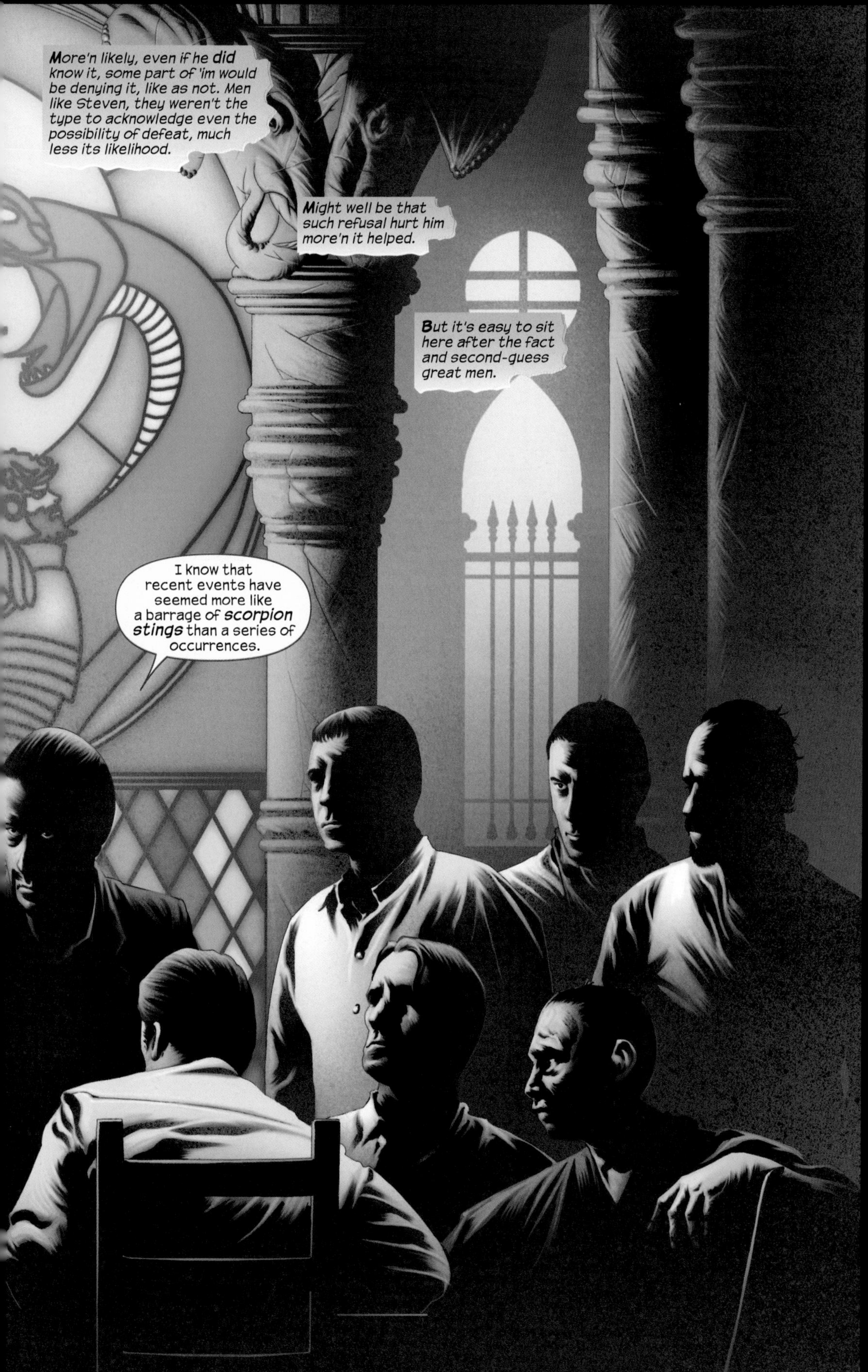
More'n likely, even if he did know it, some part of 'im would be denying it, like as not. Men like Steven, they weren't the type to acknowledge even the possibility of defeat, much less its likelihood.
Might well be that such refusal hurt him more'n it helped.
But it's easy to sit here after the fact and second-guess great men.
I know that recent events have seemed more like a barrage of scorpion stings than a series of occurrences.

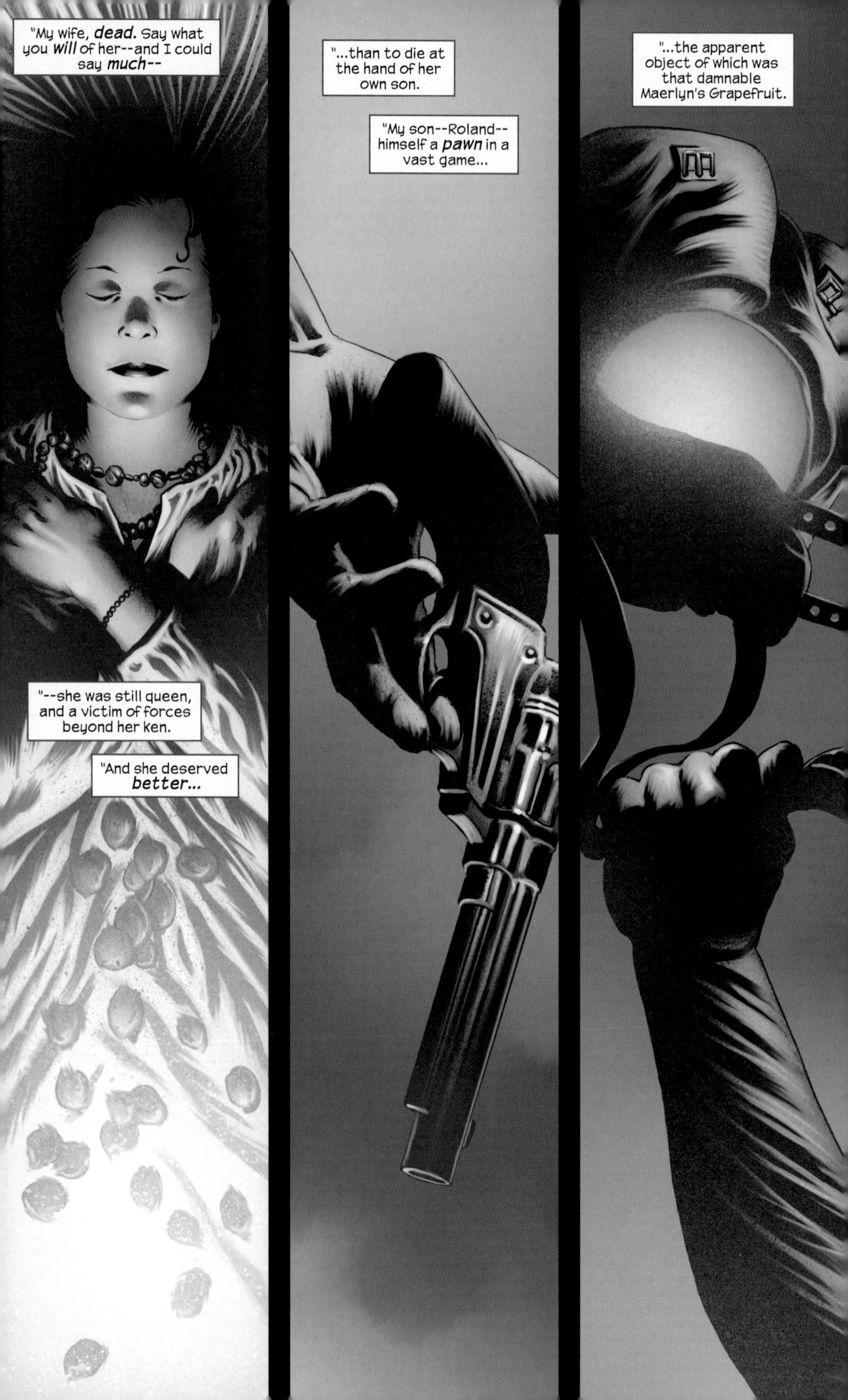
"My wife, dead. Say what you will of her--and I could say much--
"--she was still queen, and a victim of forces beyond her ken.
"And she deserved better...
"...than to die at the hand of her own son.
"My son--Roland--himself a pawn in a vast game...
"...the apparent object of which was that damnable Maerlyn's Grapefruit.

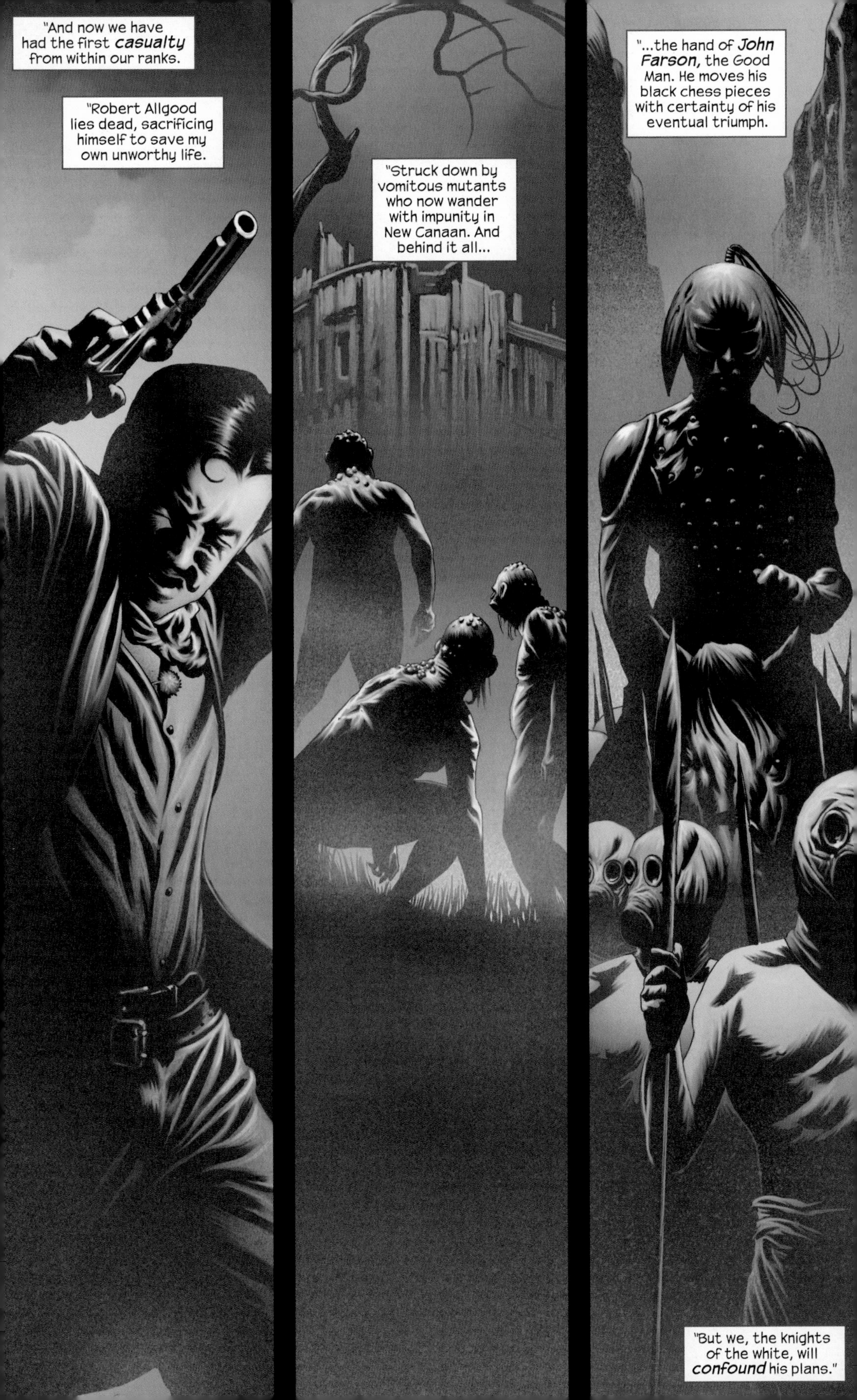
"And now we have had the first *casualty* from within our ranks.
"Robert Allgood lies dead, sacrificing himself to save my own unworthy life.
"Struck down by vomitous mutants who now wander with impunity in New Canaan. And behind it all...
"...the hand of *John Farson,* the Good Man. He moves his black chess pieces with certainty of his eventual triumph.
"But we, the knights of the white, will *confound* his plans."

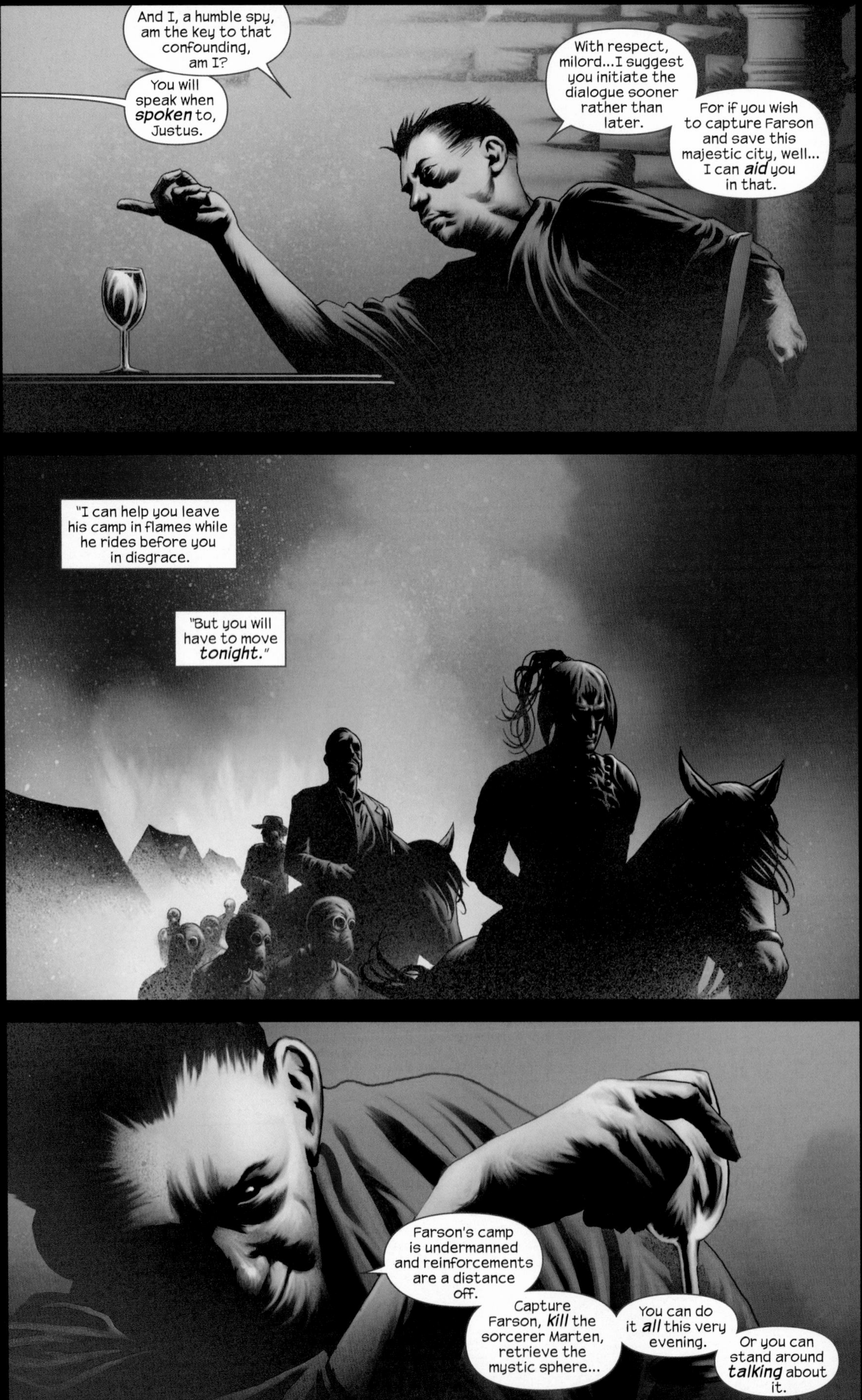

And I, a humble spy, am the key to that confounding, am I?
You will speak when *spoken* to, Justus.
With respect, milord...I suggest you initiate the dialogue sooner rather than later.
For if you wish to capture Farson and save this majestic city, well... I can *aid* you in that.
"I can help you leave his camp in flames while he rides before you in disgrace.
"But you will have to move *tonight.*"
Farson's camp is undermanned and reinforcements are a distance off.
Capture Farson, *kill* the sorcerer Marten, retrieve the mystic sphere...
You can do it *all* this very evening.
Or you can stand around *talking* about it.

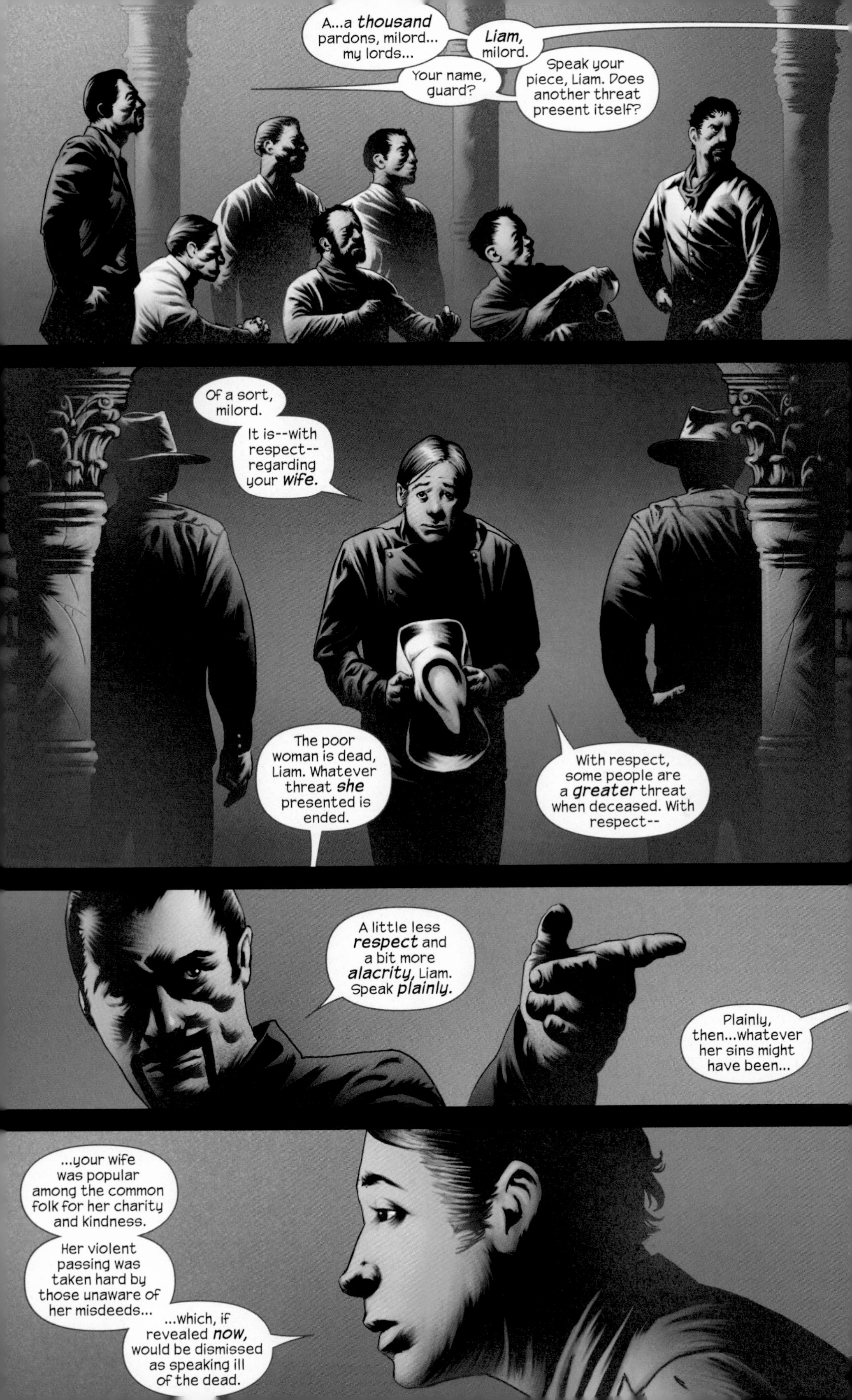
A...a *thousand* pardons, milord... my lords...
Your name, guard?
Liam, milord.
Speak your piece, Liam. Does another threat present itself?
Of a sort, milord.
It is--with respect--regarding your *wife.*
The poor woman is dead, Liam. Whatever threat *she* presented is ended.
With respect, some people are a *greater* threat when deceased. With respect--
A little less *respect* and a bit more *alacrity,* Liam. Speak *plainly.*
Plainly, then...whatever her sins might have been...
...your wife was popular among the common folk for her charity and kindness.
Her violent passing was taken hard by those unaware of her misdeeds...
...which, if revealed *now,* would be dismissed as speaking ill of the dead.

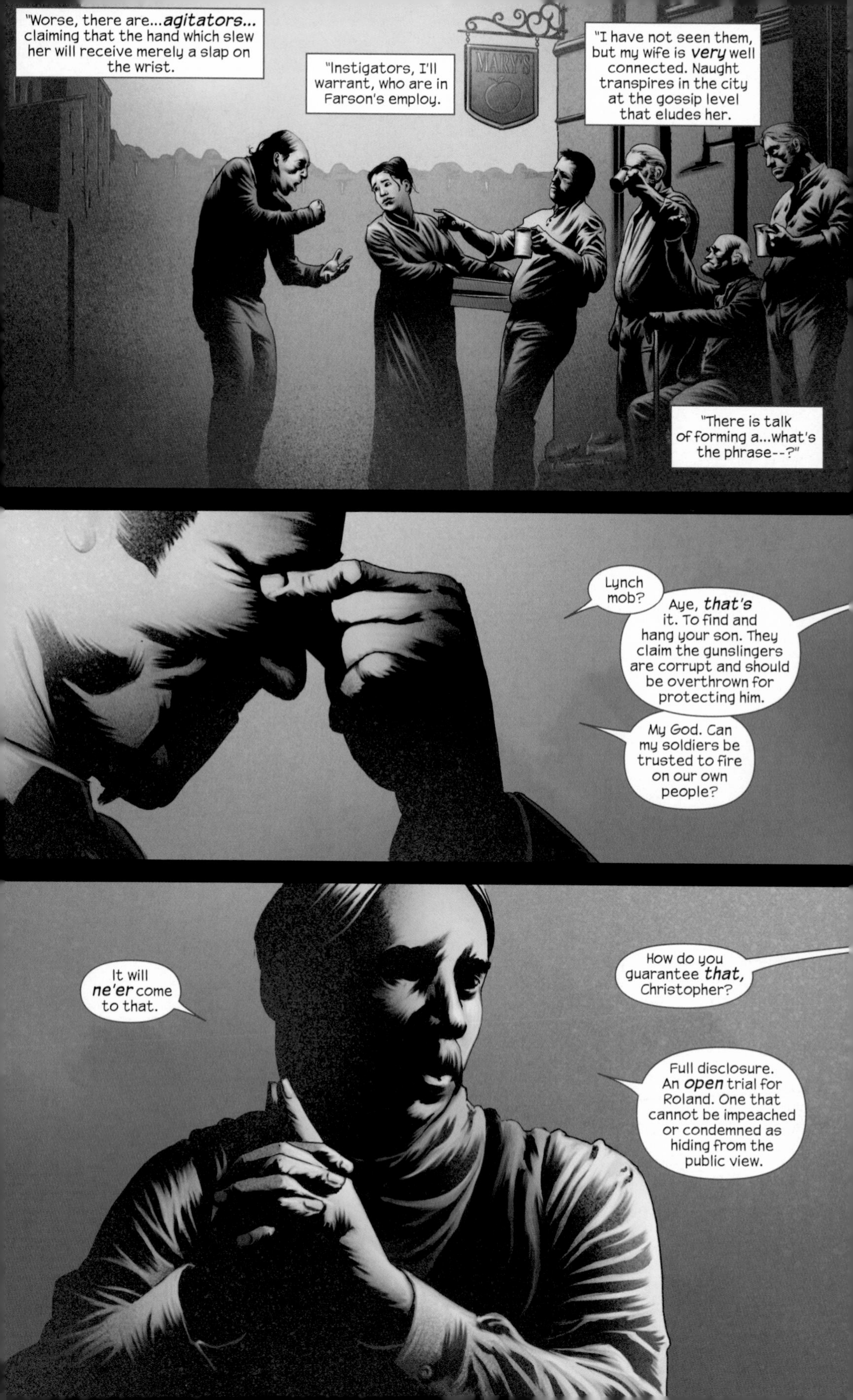
"Worse, there are...*agitators...* claiming that the hand which slew her will receive merely a slap on the wrist.
"Instigators, I'll warrant, who are in Farson's employ.
MARY'S
"I have not seen them, but my wife is *very* well connected. Naught transpires in the city at the gossip level that eludes her.
"There is talk of forming a...what's the phrase--?"
Lynch mob?
Aye, *that's* it. To find and hang your son. They claim the gunslingers are corrupt and should be overthrown for protecting him.
My God. Can my soldiers be trusted to fire on our own people?
It will *ne'er* come to that.
How do you guarantee *that,* Christopher?
Full disclosure. An *open* trial for Roland. One that cannot be impeached or condemned as hiding from the public view.

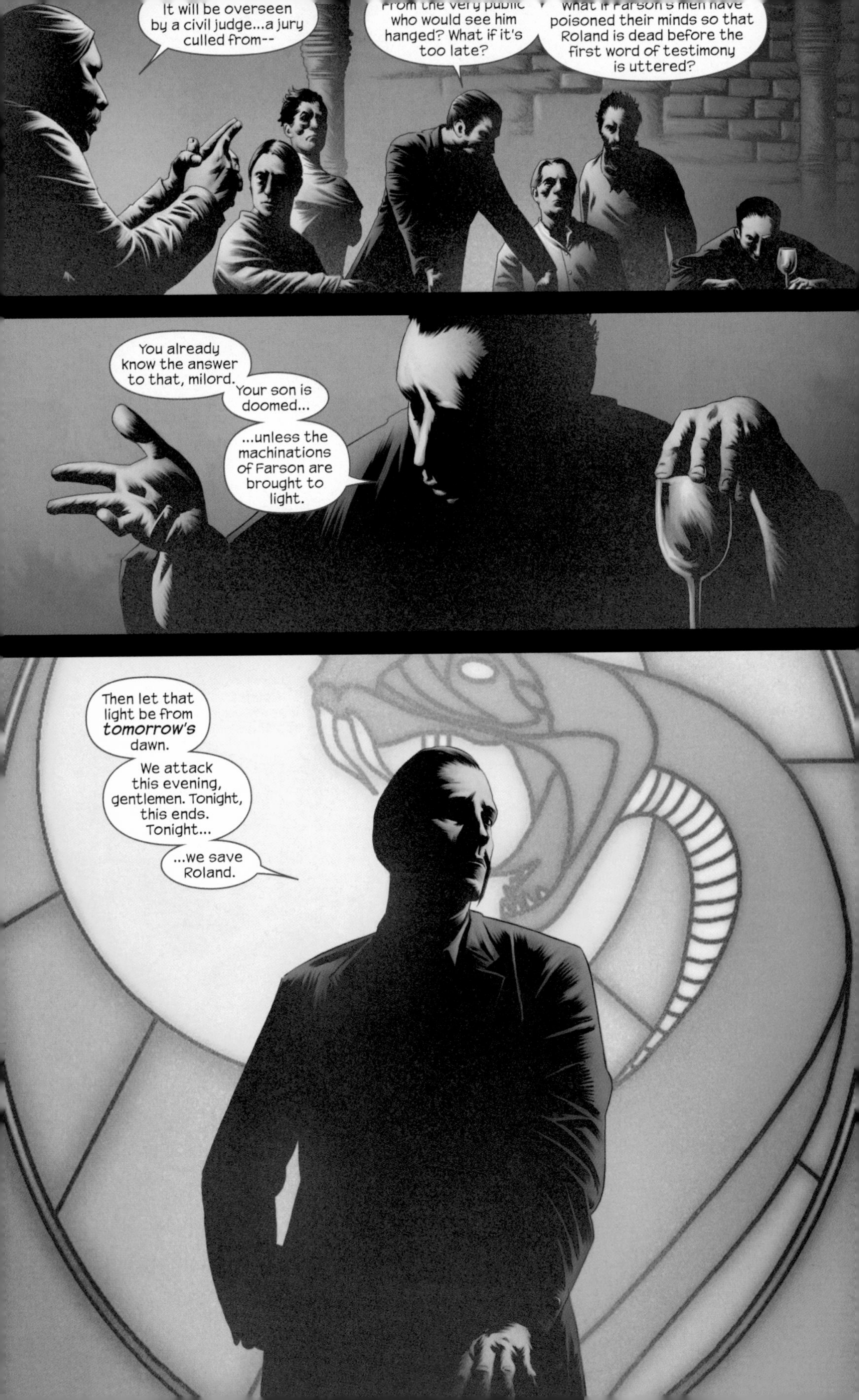
It will be overseen by a civil judge...a jury culled from--
From the very public who would see him hanged? What if it's too late?
What if Farson's men have poisoned their minds so that Roland is dead before the first word of testimony is uttered?
You already know the answer to that, milord.
Your son is doomed...
...unless the machinations of Farson are brought to light.
Then let that light be from *tomorrow's* dawn.
We attack this evening, gentlemen. Tonight, this ends. Tonight...
...we save Roland.

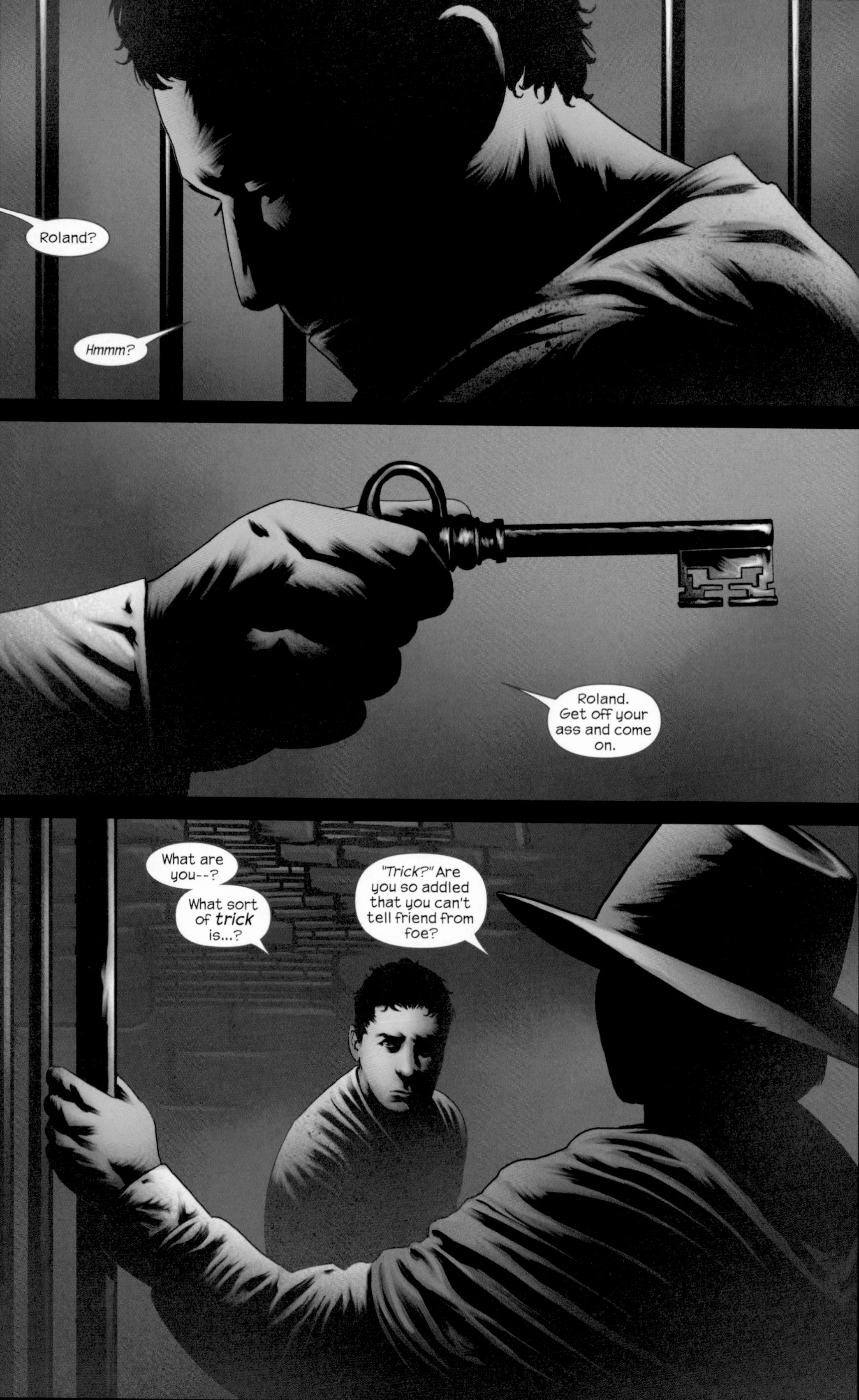
Roland?
Hmmm?
Roland. Get off your ass and come on.
What are you--?
What sort of *trick* is...?
"*Trick?*" Are you so addled that you can't tell friend from foe?

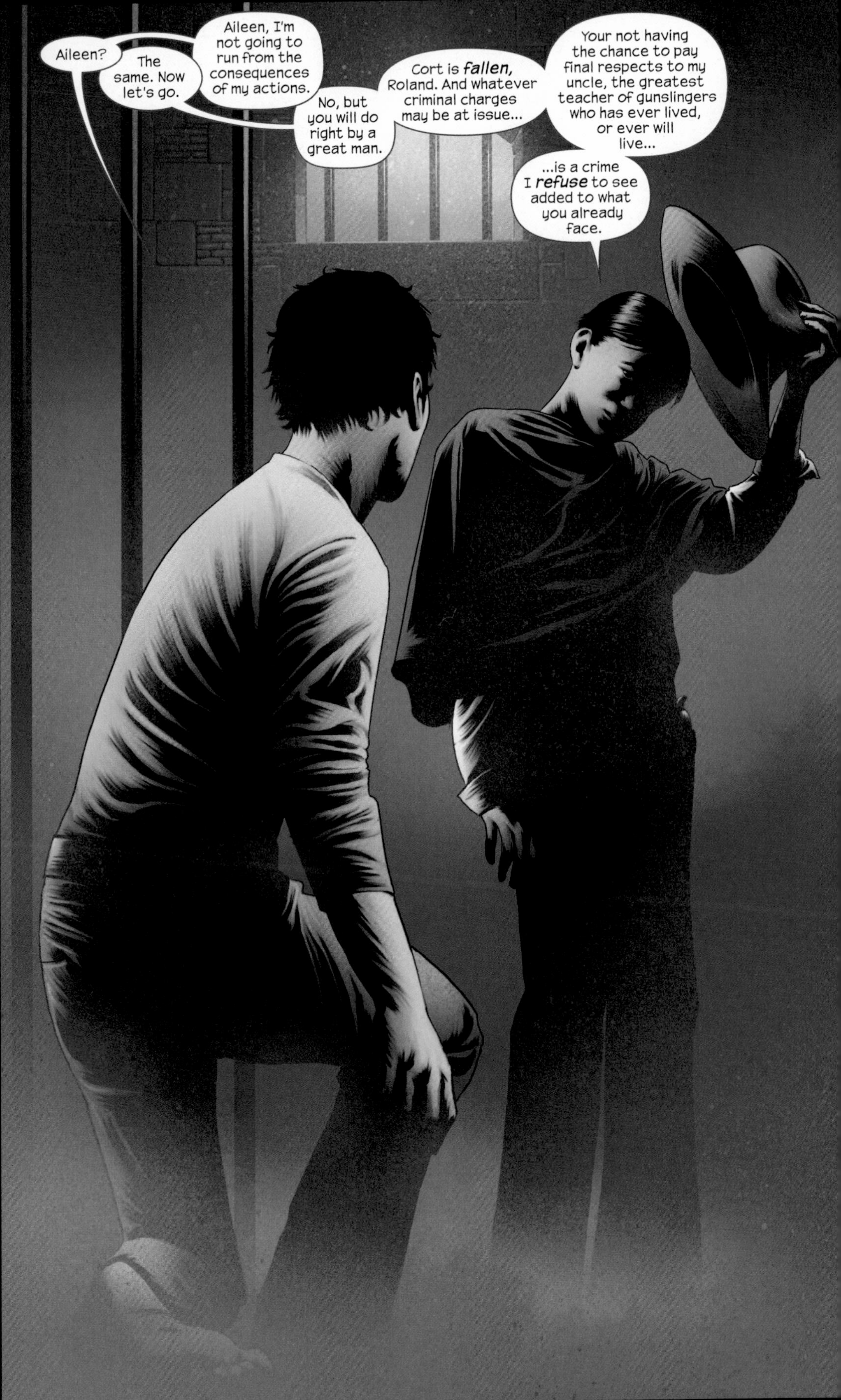
Aileen?
The same. Now let's go.
Aileen, I'm not going to run from the consequences of my actions.
No, but you will do right by a great man.
Cort is *fallen,* Roland. And whatever criminal charges may be at issue...
Your not having the chance to pay final respects to my uncle, the greatest teacher of gunslingers who has ever lived, or ever will live...
...is a crime I *refuse* to see added to what you already face.

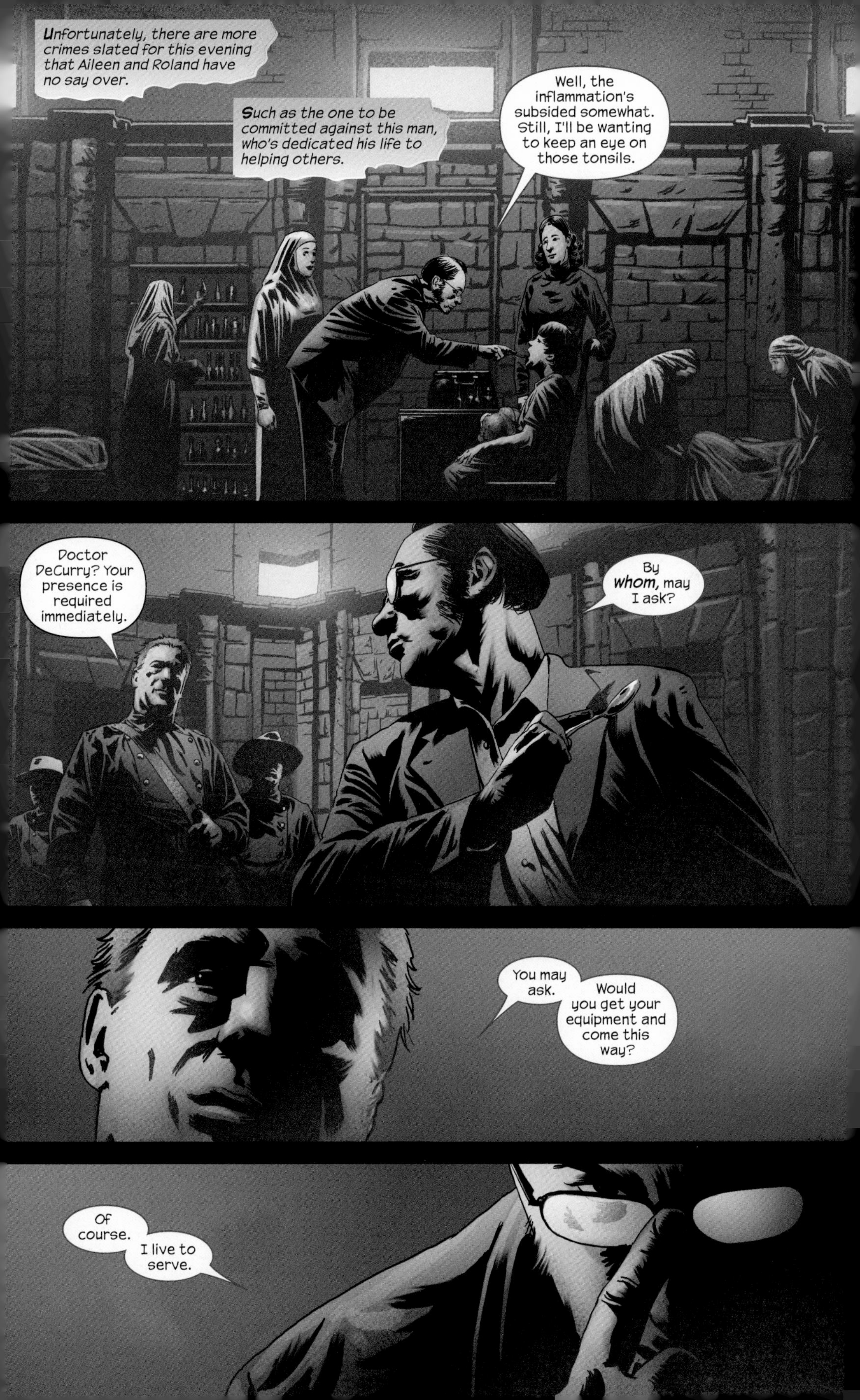
Unfortunately, there are more crimes slated for this evening that Aileen and Roland have no say over.
Such as the one to be committed against this man, who's dedicated his life to helping others.
Well, the inflammation's subsided somewhat. Still, I'll be wanting to keep an eye on those tonsils.
Doctor DeCurry? Your presence is required immediately.
By whom, may I ask?
You may ask.
Would you get your equipment and come this way?
Of course.
I live to serve.

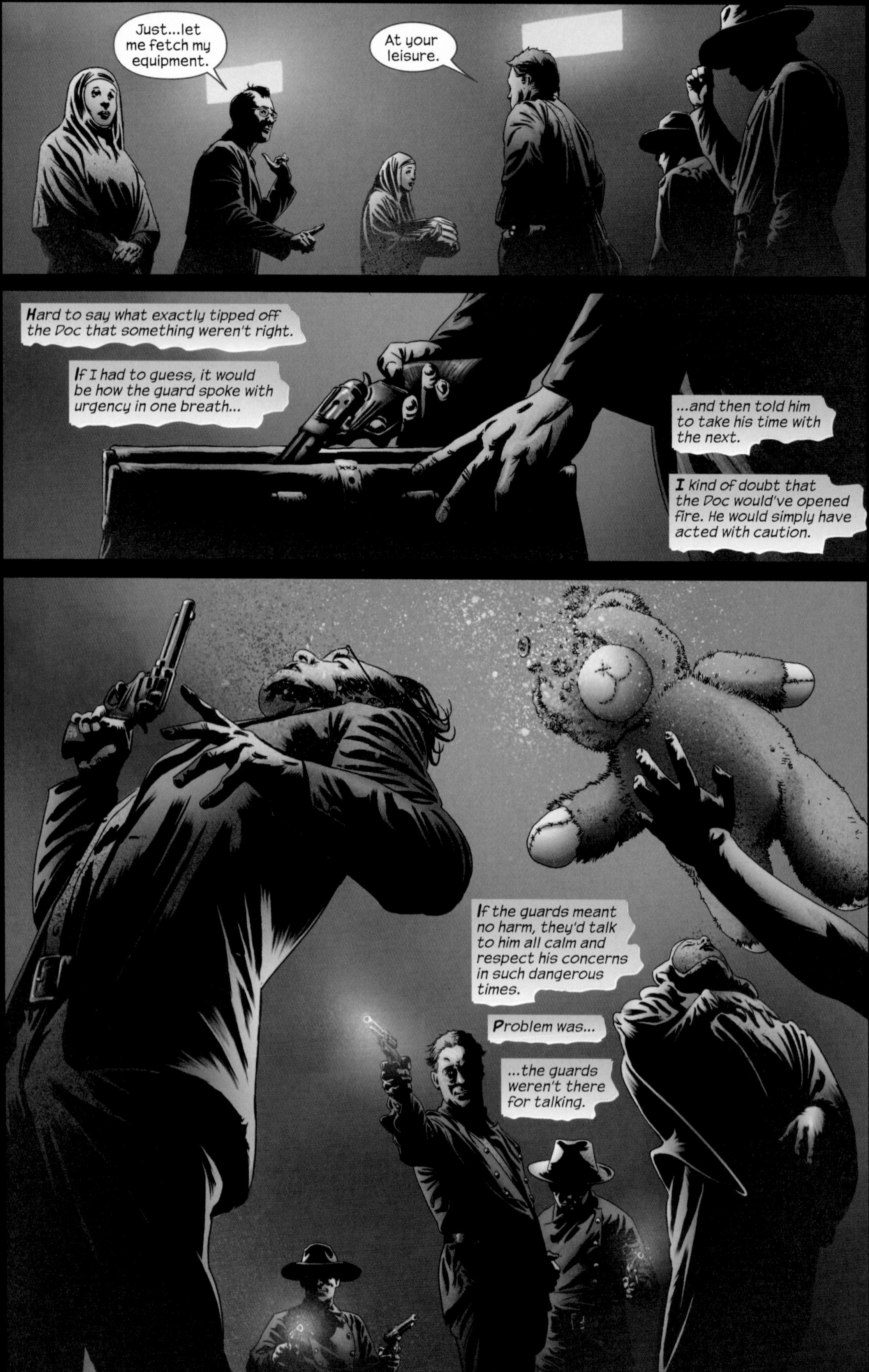
Just...let me fetch my equipment.
At your leisure.
Hard to say what exactly tipped off the Doc that something weren't right.
If I had to guess, it would be how the guard spoke with urgency in one breath...
...and then told him to take his time with the next.
I kind of doubt that the Doc would've opened fire. He would simply have acted with caution.
If the guards meant no harm, they'd talk to him all calm and respect his concerns in such dangerous times.
Problem was...
...the guards weren't there for talking.

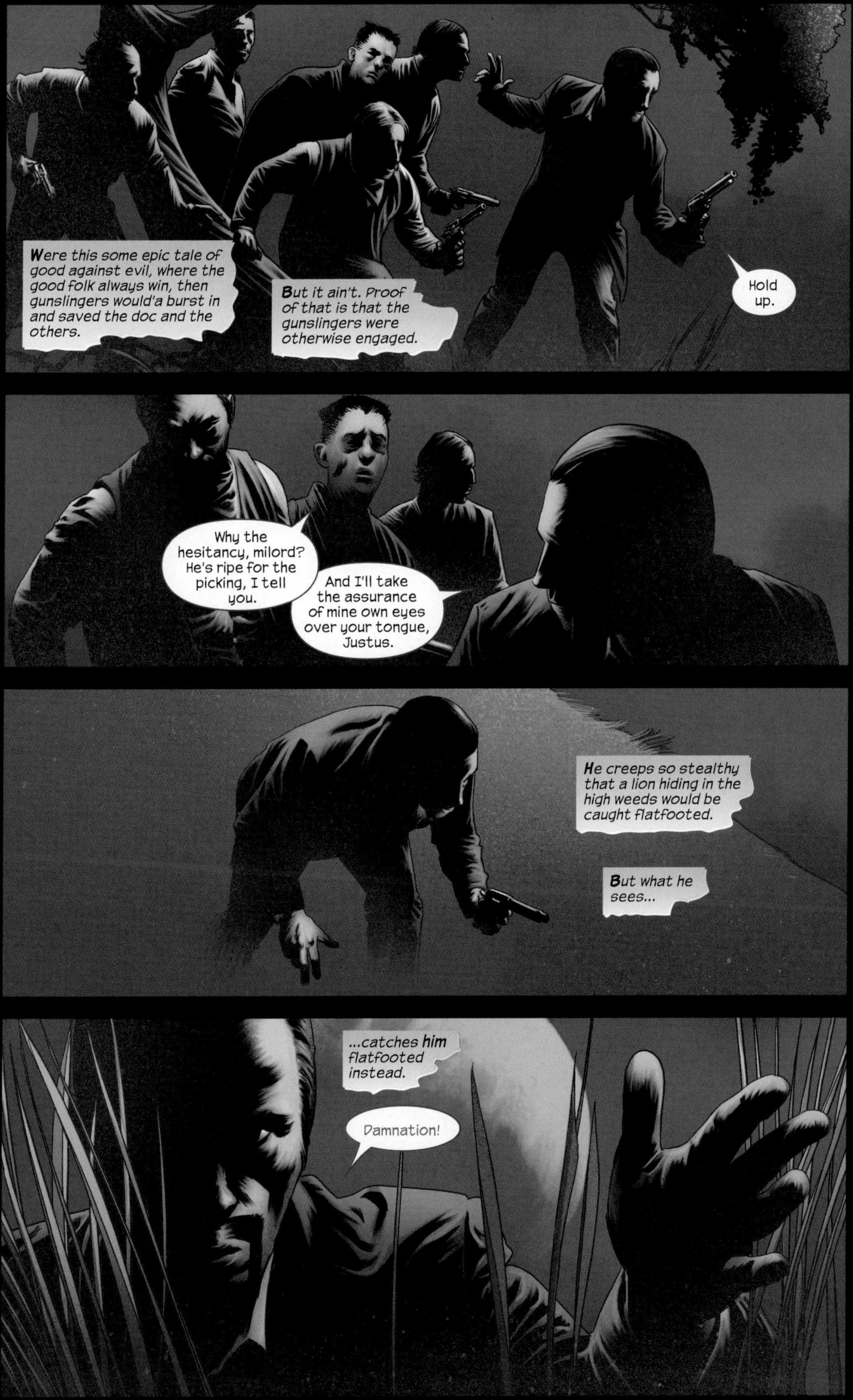
Were this some epic tale of good against evil, where the good folk always win, then gunslingers would'a burst in and saved the doc and the others.
But it ain't. Proof of that is that the gunslingers were otherwise engaged.
Hold up.
Why the hesitancy, milord? He's ripe for the picking, I tell you.
And I'll take the assurance of mine own eyes over your tongue, Justus.
He creeps so stealthy that a lion hiding in the high weeds would be caught flatfooted.
But what he sees...
...catches him flatfooted instead.
Damnation!

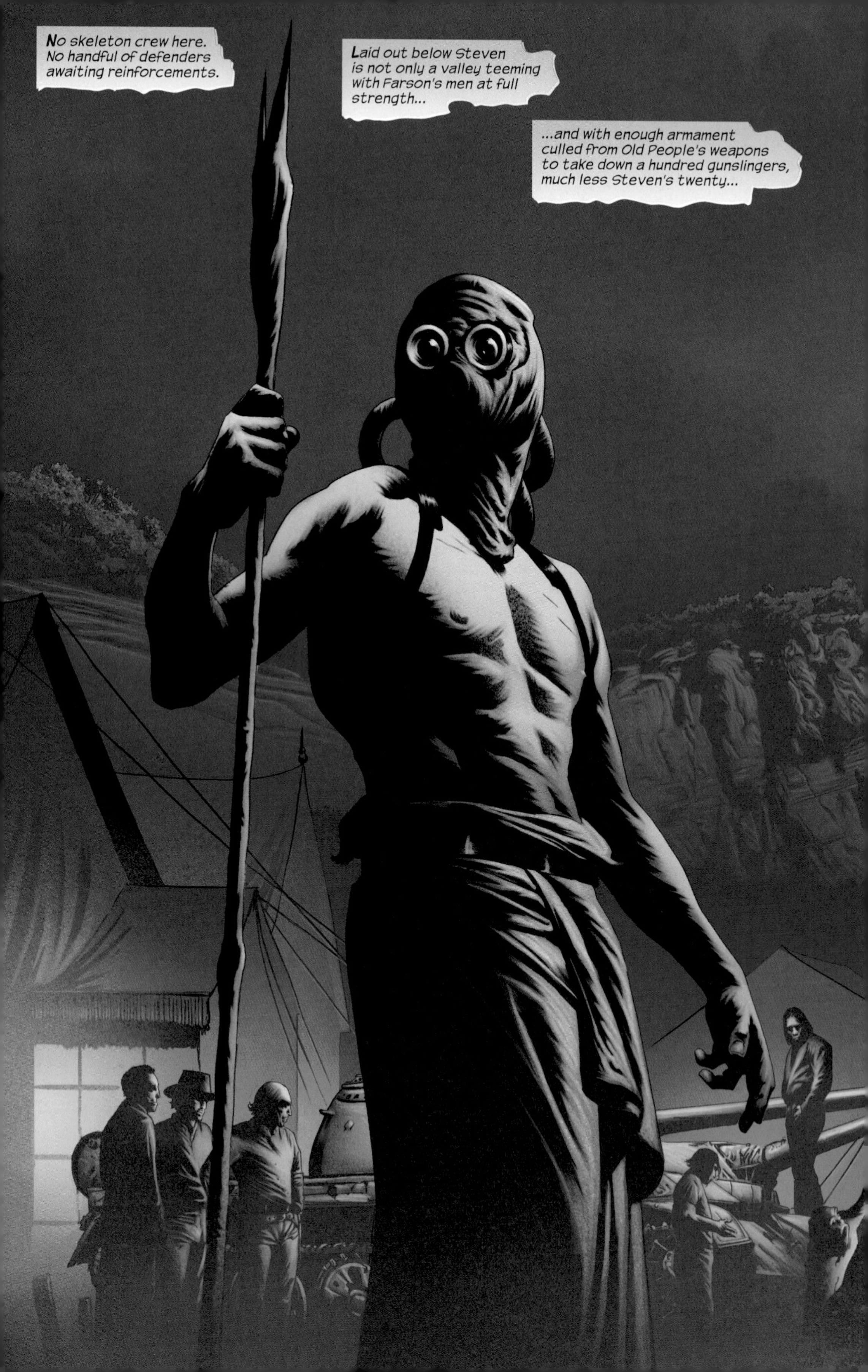
No skeleton crew here. No handful of defenders awaiting reinforcements.
Laid out below Steven is not only a valley teeming with Farson's men at full strength...
...and with enough armament culled from Old People's weapons to take down a hundred gunslingers, much less Steven's twenty...

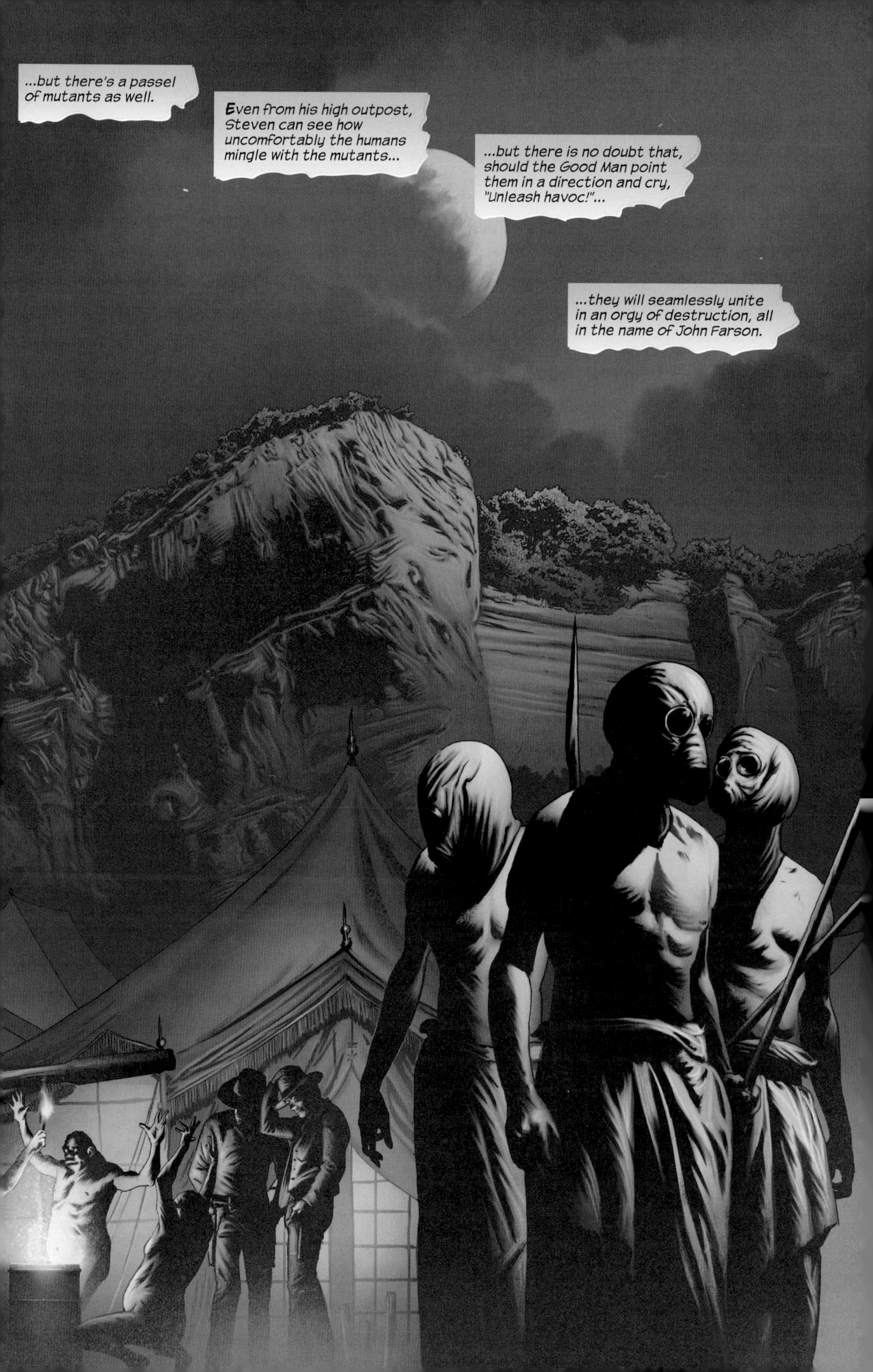
...but there's a passel of mutants as well.
Even from his high outpost, Steven can see how uncomfortably the humans mingle with the mutants...
...but there is no doubt that, should the Good Man point them in a direction and cry, "Unleash havoc!"...
...they will seamlessly unite in an orgy of destruction, all in the name of John Farson.

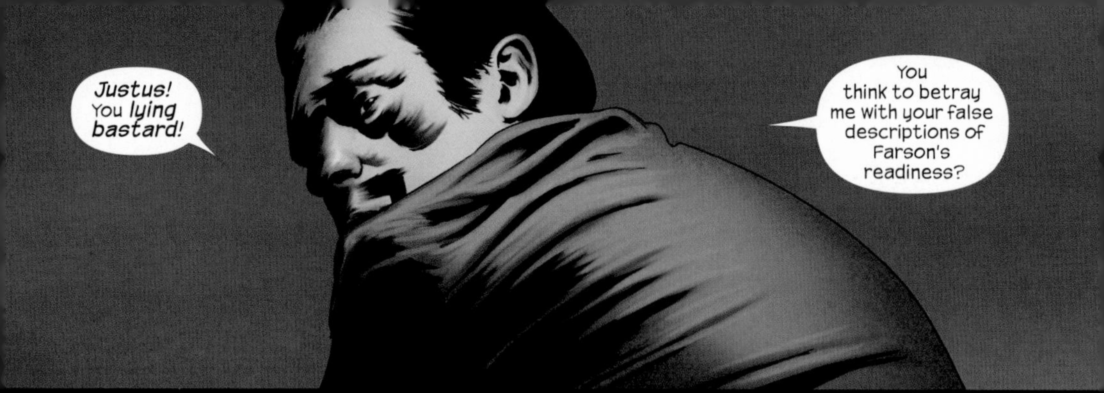
Justus! You *lying* bastard!
You think to betray me with your false descriptions of Farson's readiness?

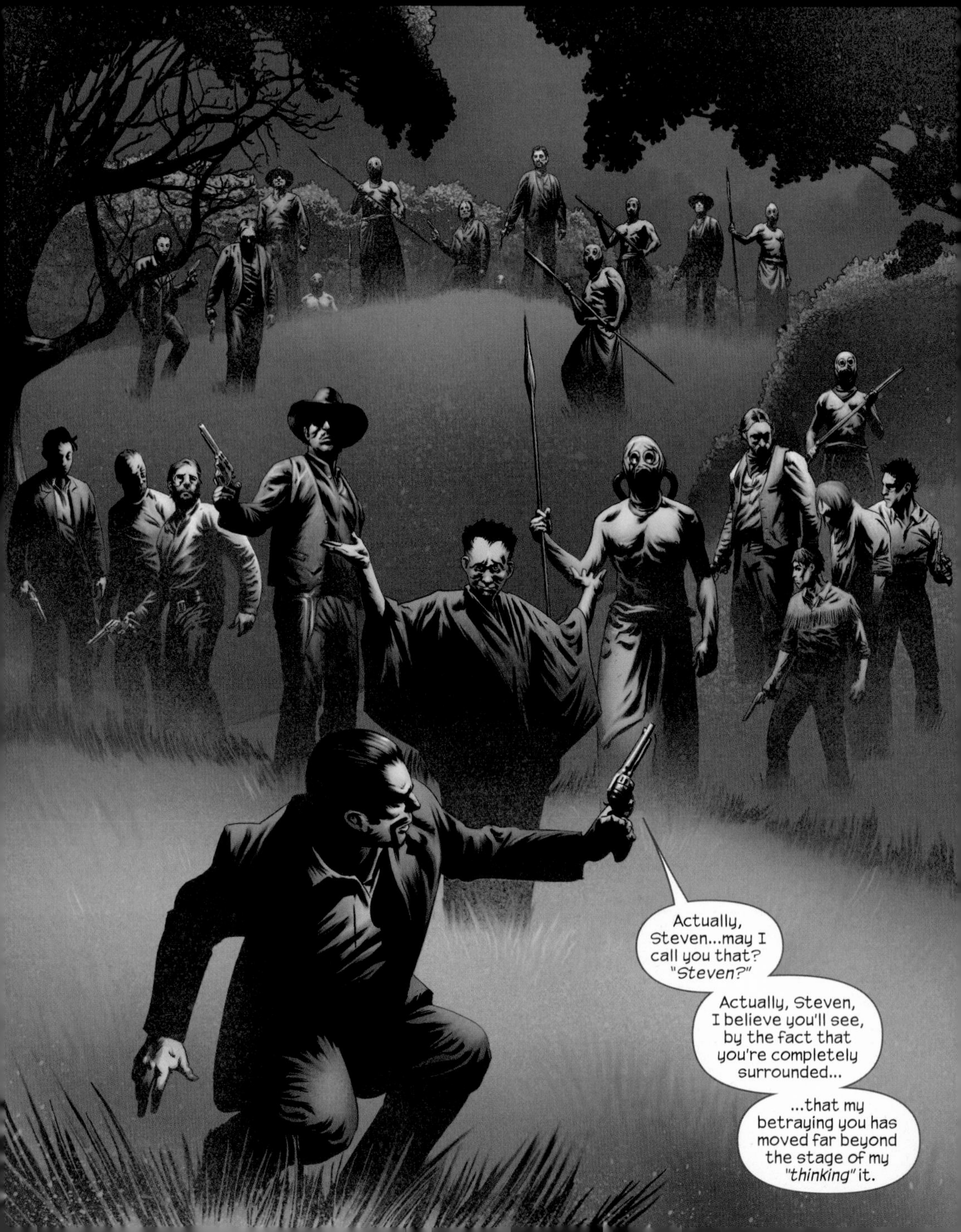
Actually, Steven...may I call you that? *"Steven?"*
Actually, Steven, I believe you'll see, by the fact that you're completely surrounded...
...that my betraying you has moved far beyond the stage of my *"thinking"* it.

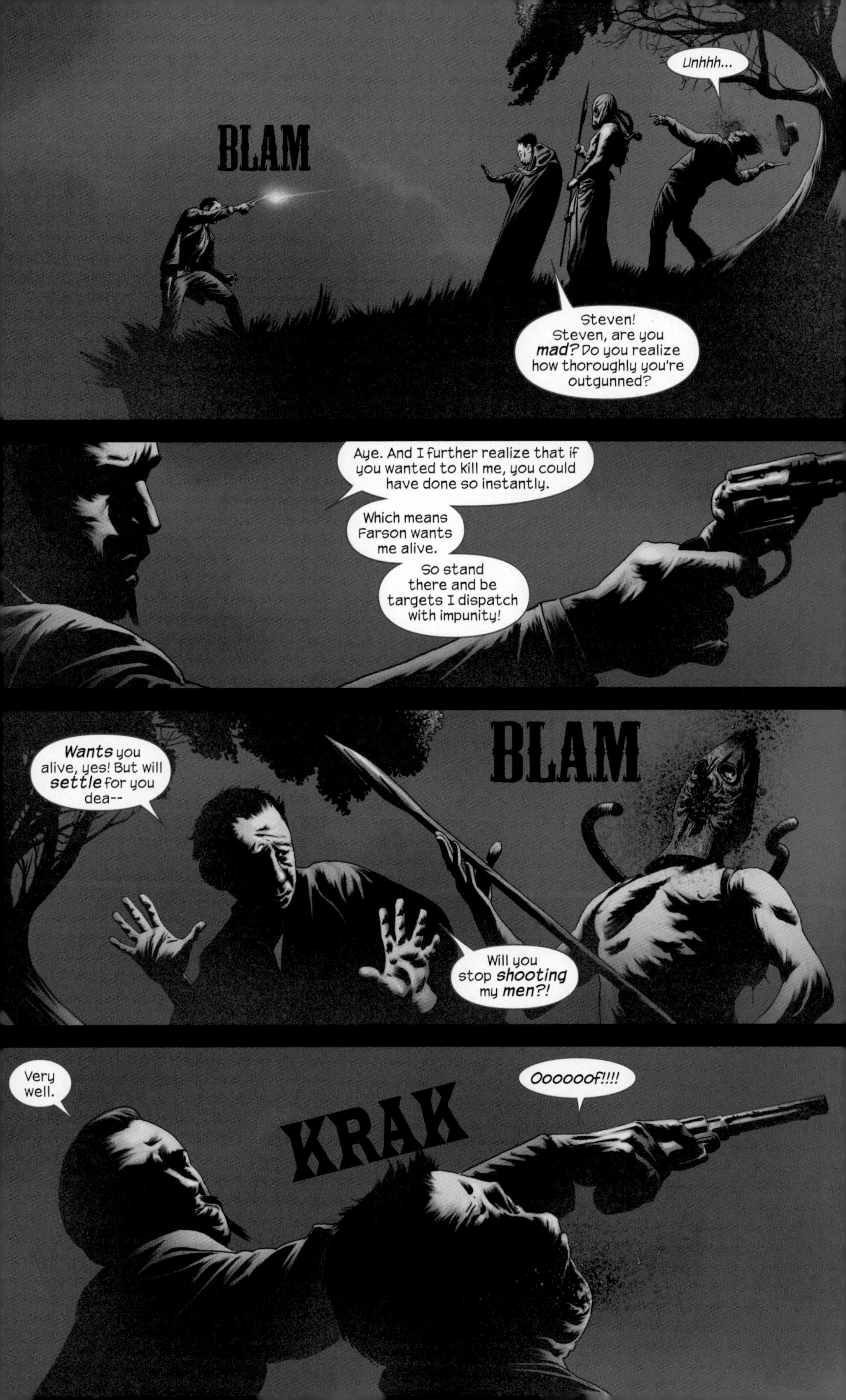
BLAM
Unhhh...
Steven! Steven, are you *mad?* Do you realize how thoroughly you're outgunned?
Aye. And I further realize that if you wanted to kill me, you could have done so instantly.
Which means Farson wants me alive.
So stand there and be targets I dispatch with impunity!
Wants you alive, yes! But will *settle* for you dea--
BLAM
Will you stop *shooting* my *men?!*
Very well.
KRAK
Ooooooof!!!!

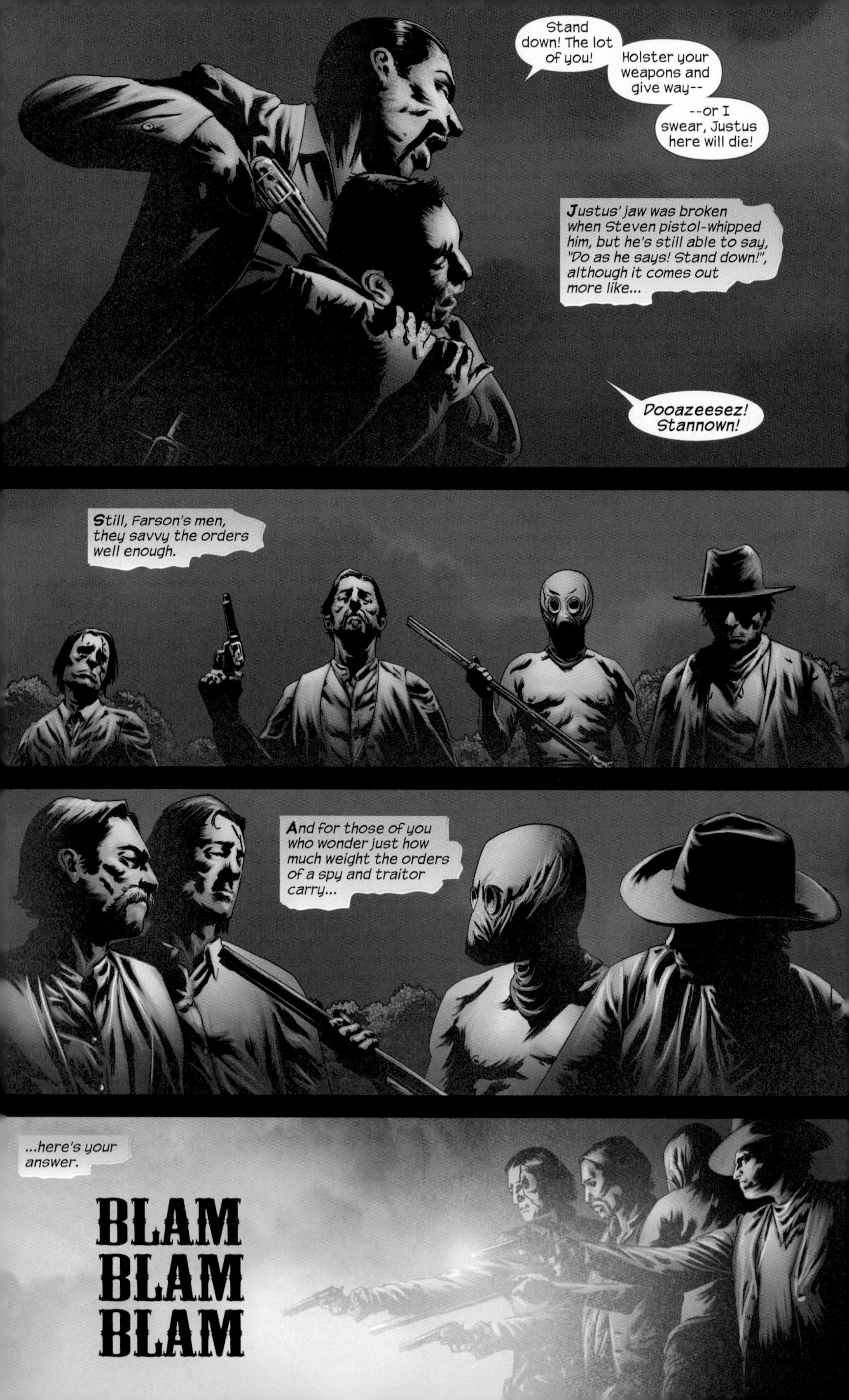

Stand down! The lot of you!
Holster your weapons and give way--
--or I swear, Justus here will die!
Justus' jaw was broken when Steven pistol-whipped him, but he's still able to say, "Do as he says! Stand down!", although it comes out more like...
Dooazeesez! Stannown!
Still, Farson's men, they savvy the orders well enough.
And for those of you who wonder just how much weight the orders of a spy and traitor carry...
...here's your answer.
BLAM
BLAM
BLAM

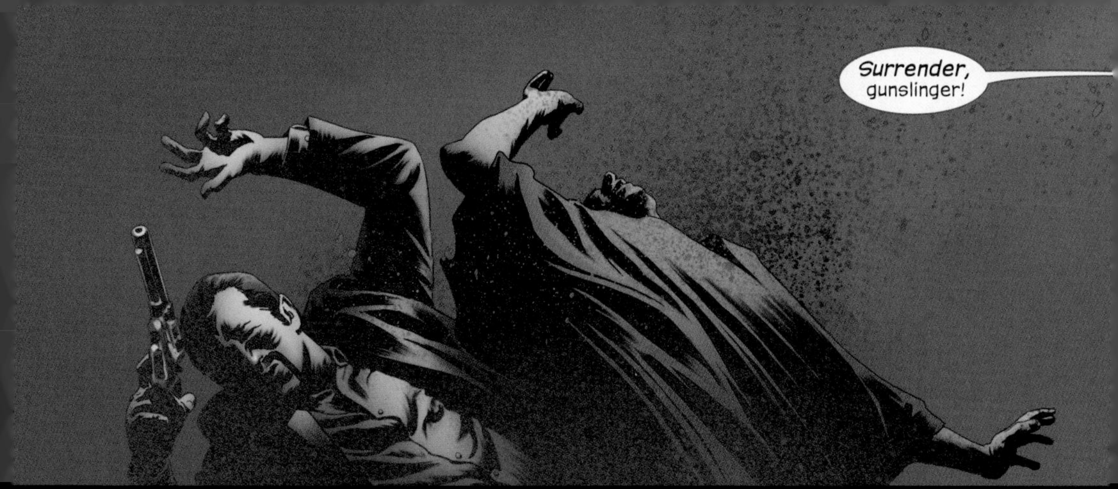
Surrender, gunslinger!

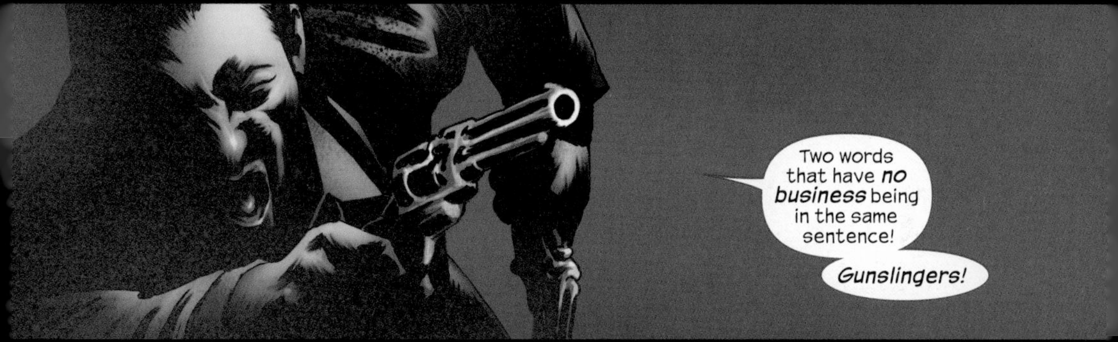
Two words that have no business being in the same sentence!
Gunslingers!

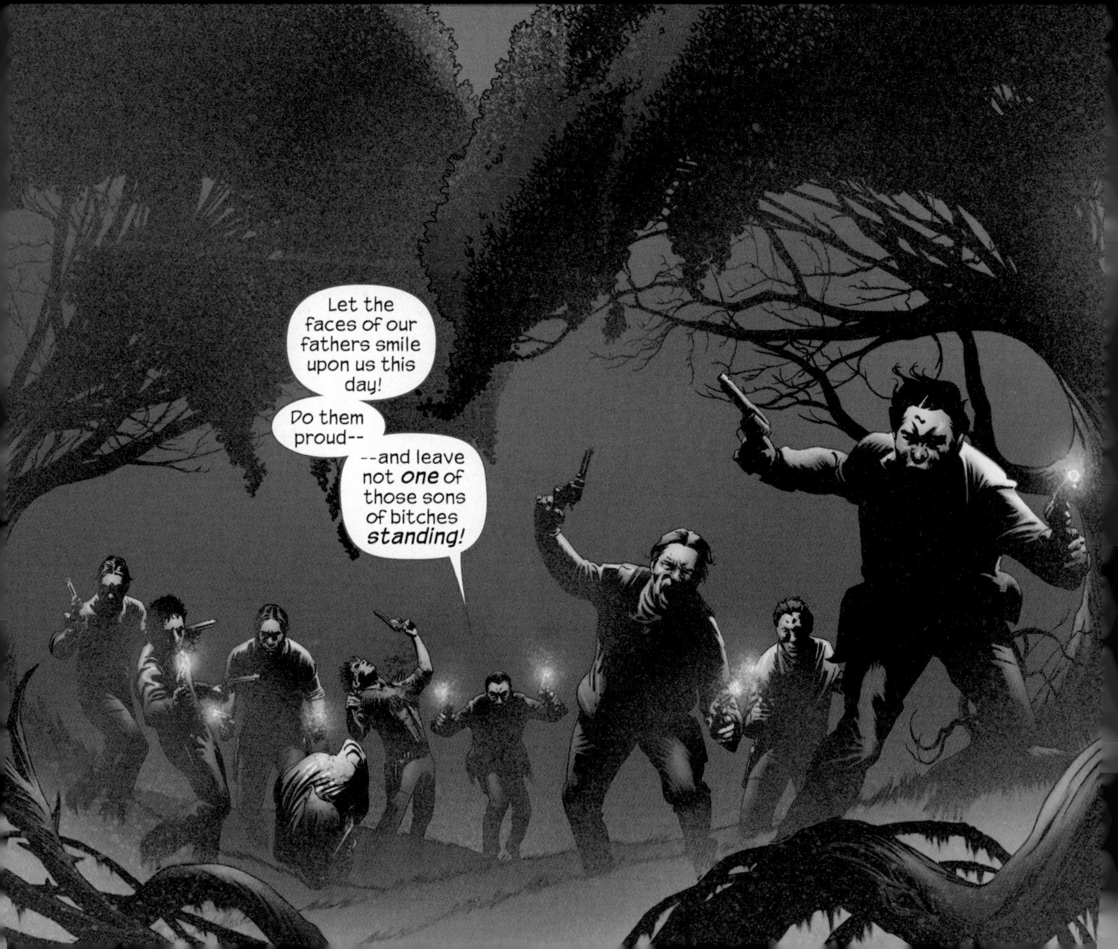
Let the faces of our fathers smile upon us this day!
Do them proud--
--and leave not one of those sons of bitches standing!

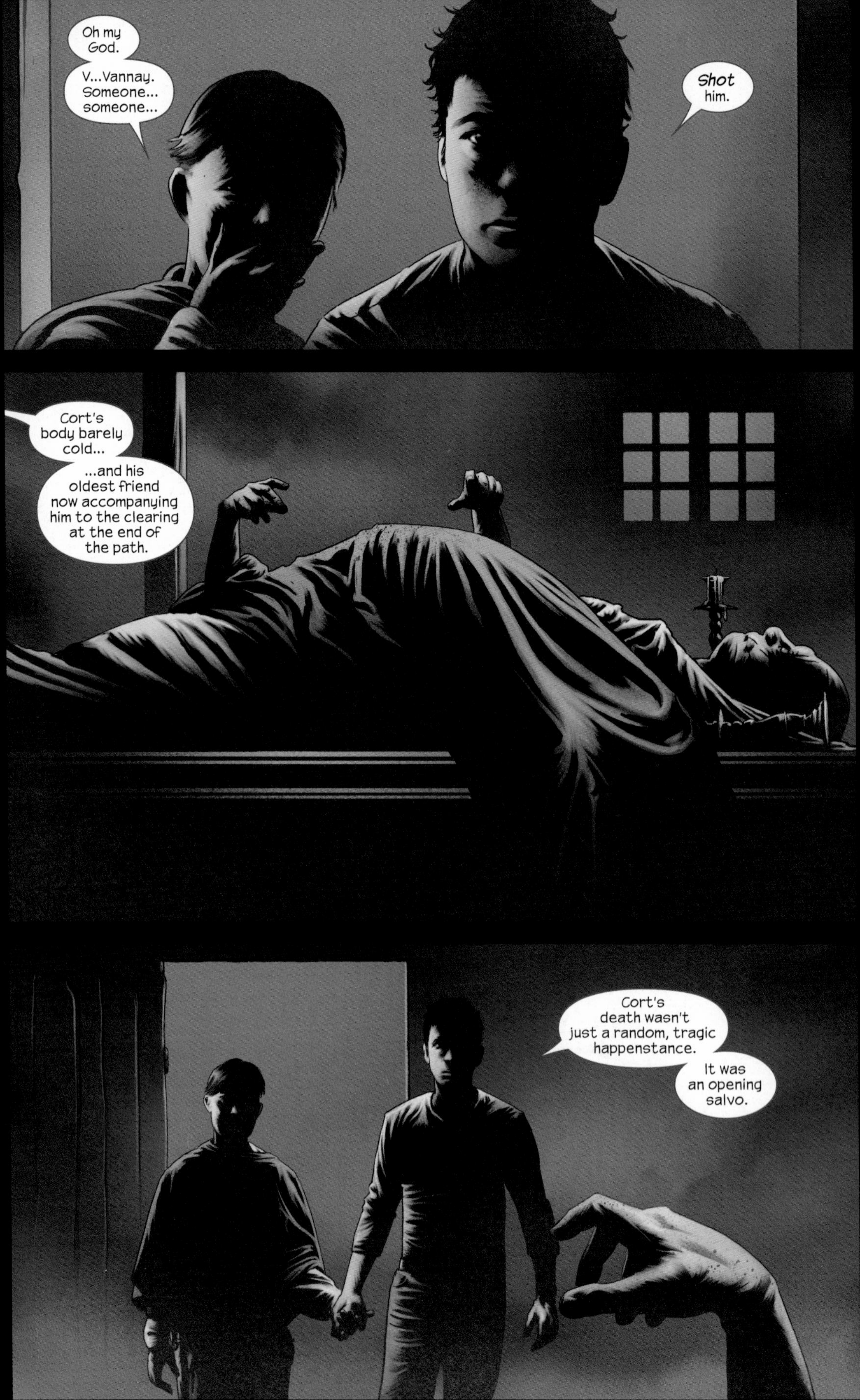
Oh my God.
V...Vannay. Someone... someone...
Shot him.
Cort's body barely cold...
...and his oldest friend now accompanying him to the clearing at the end of the path.
Cort's death wasn't just a random, tragic happenstance.
It was an opening salvo.

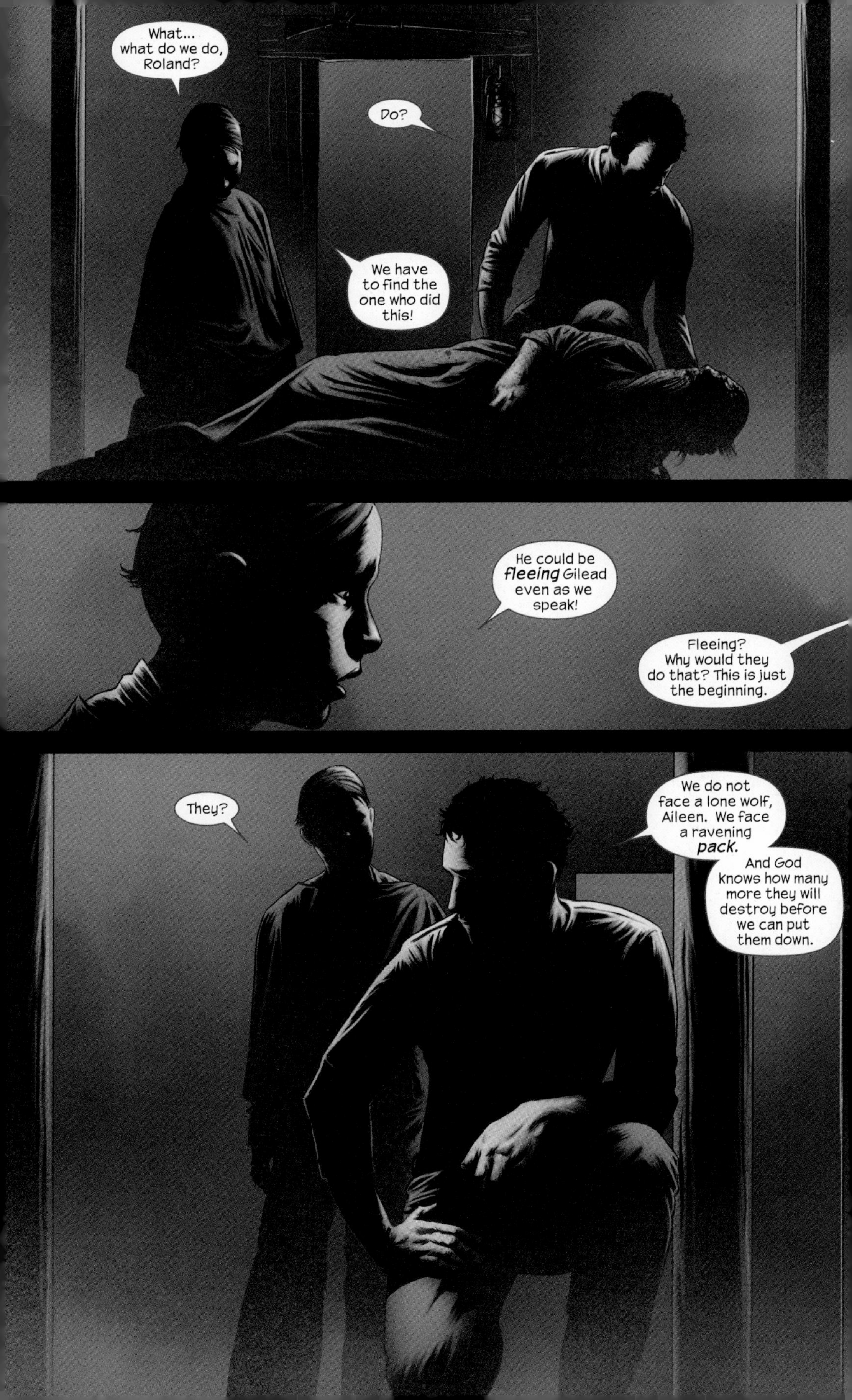
What... what do we do, Roland?
Do?
We have to find the one who did this!
He could be *fleeing* Gilead even as we speak!
Fleeing? Why would they do that? This is just the beginning.
They?
We do not face a lone wolf, Aileen. We face a ravening *pack.*
And God knows how many more they will destroy before we can put them down.

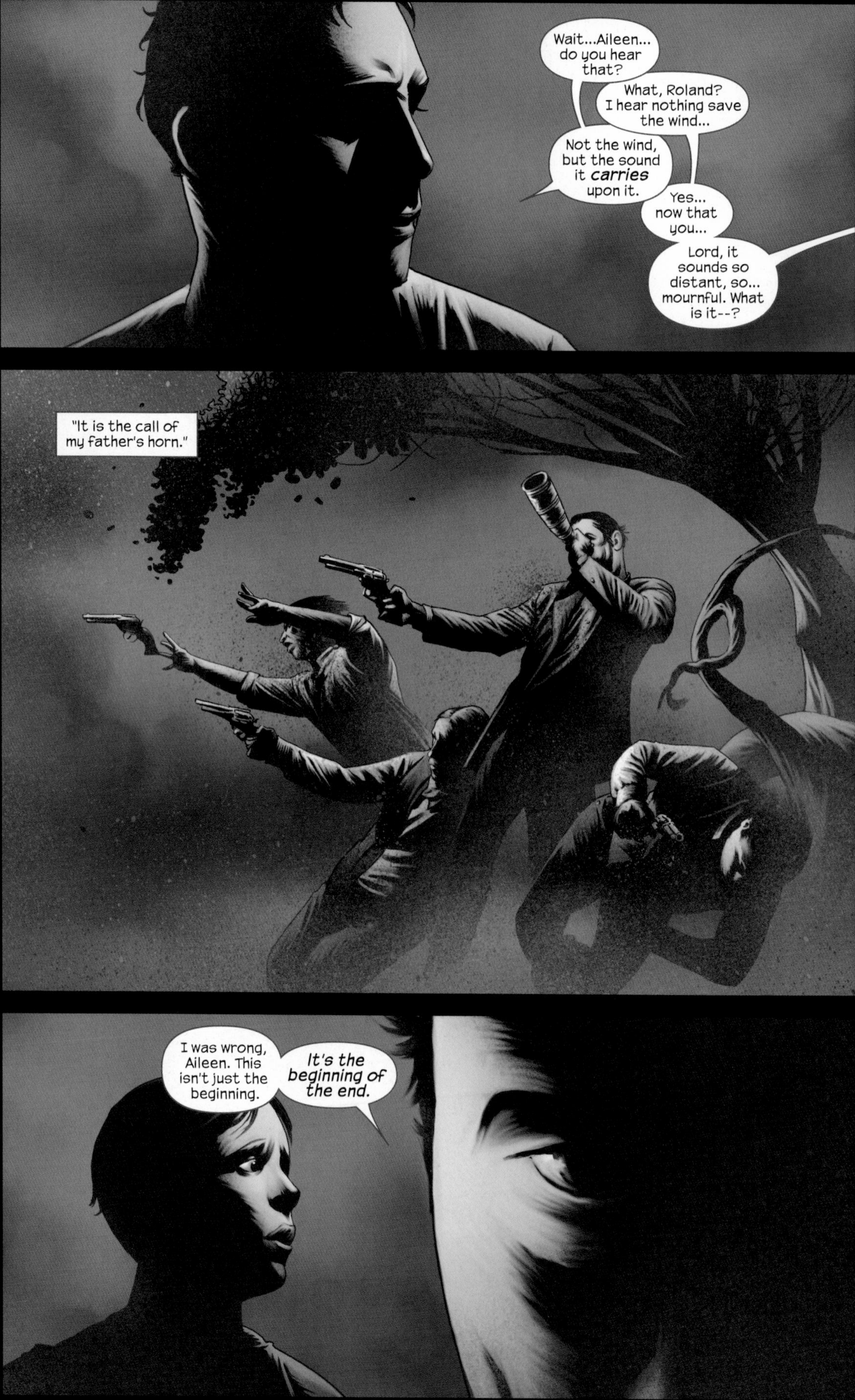
Wait...Aileen... do you hear that?
What, Roland? I hear nothing save the wind...
Not the wind, but the sound it carries upon it.
Yes... now that you...
Lord, it sounds so distant, so... mournful. What is it--?
"It is the call of my father's horn."
I was wrong, Aileen. This isn't just the beginning.
It's the beginning of the end.

STEPHEN KING

THE DARK TOWER

FALL OF GILEAD

CHAPTER FIVE

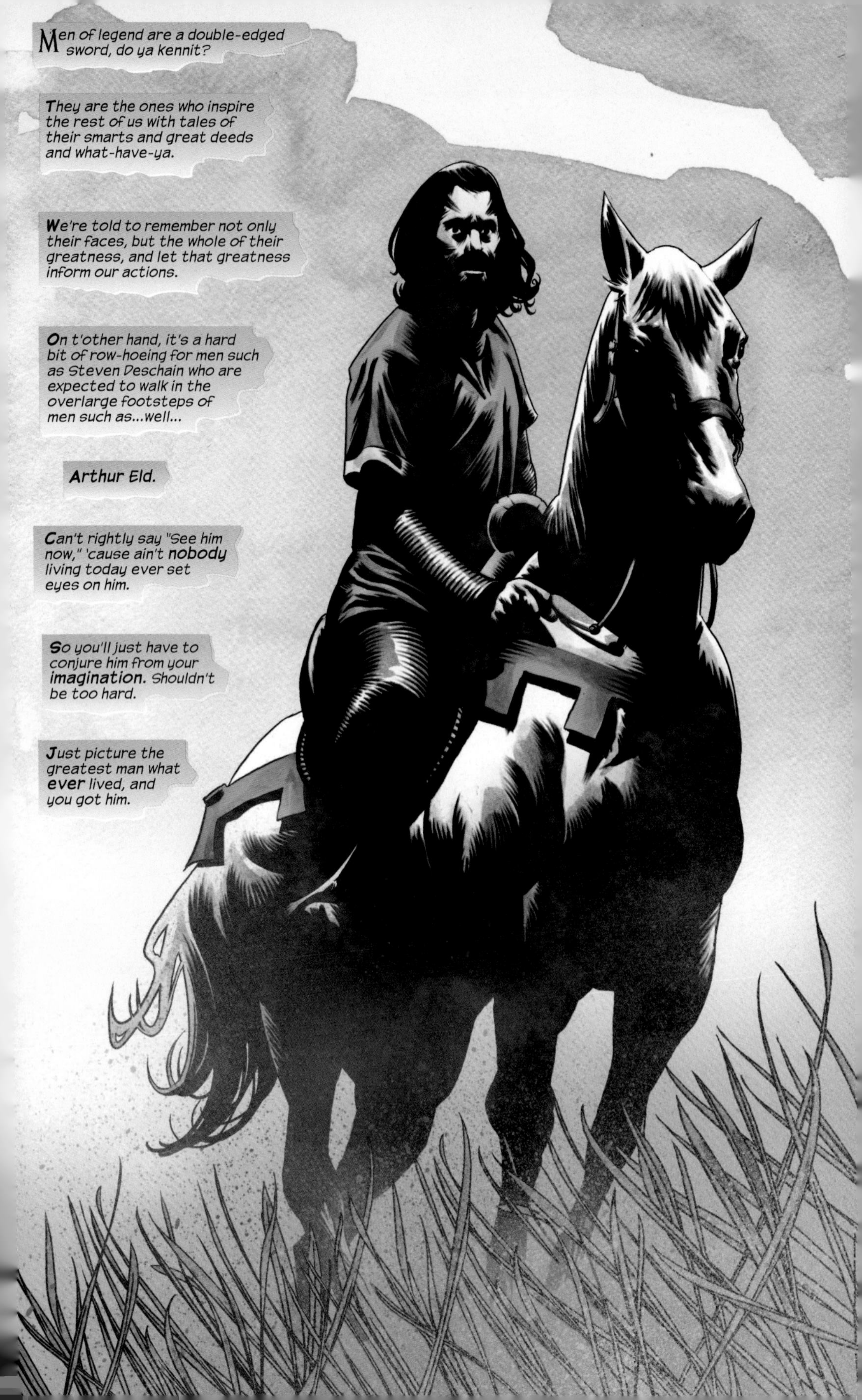

Men of legend are a double-edged sword, do ya kennit?
They are the ones who inspire the rest of us with tales of their smarts and great deeds and what-have-ya.
We're told to remember not only their faces, but the whole of their greatness, and let that greatness inform our actions.
On t'other hand, it's a hard bit of row-hoeing for men such as Steven Deschain who are expected to walk in the overlarge footsteps of men such as...well...
Arthur Eld.
Can't rightly say "See him now," 'cause ain't nobody living today ever set eyes on him.
So you'll just have to conjure him from your imagination. Shouldn't be too hard.
Just picture the greatest man what ever lived, and you got him.

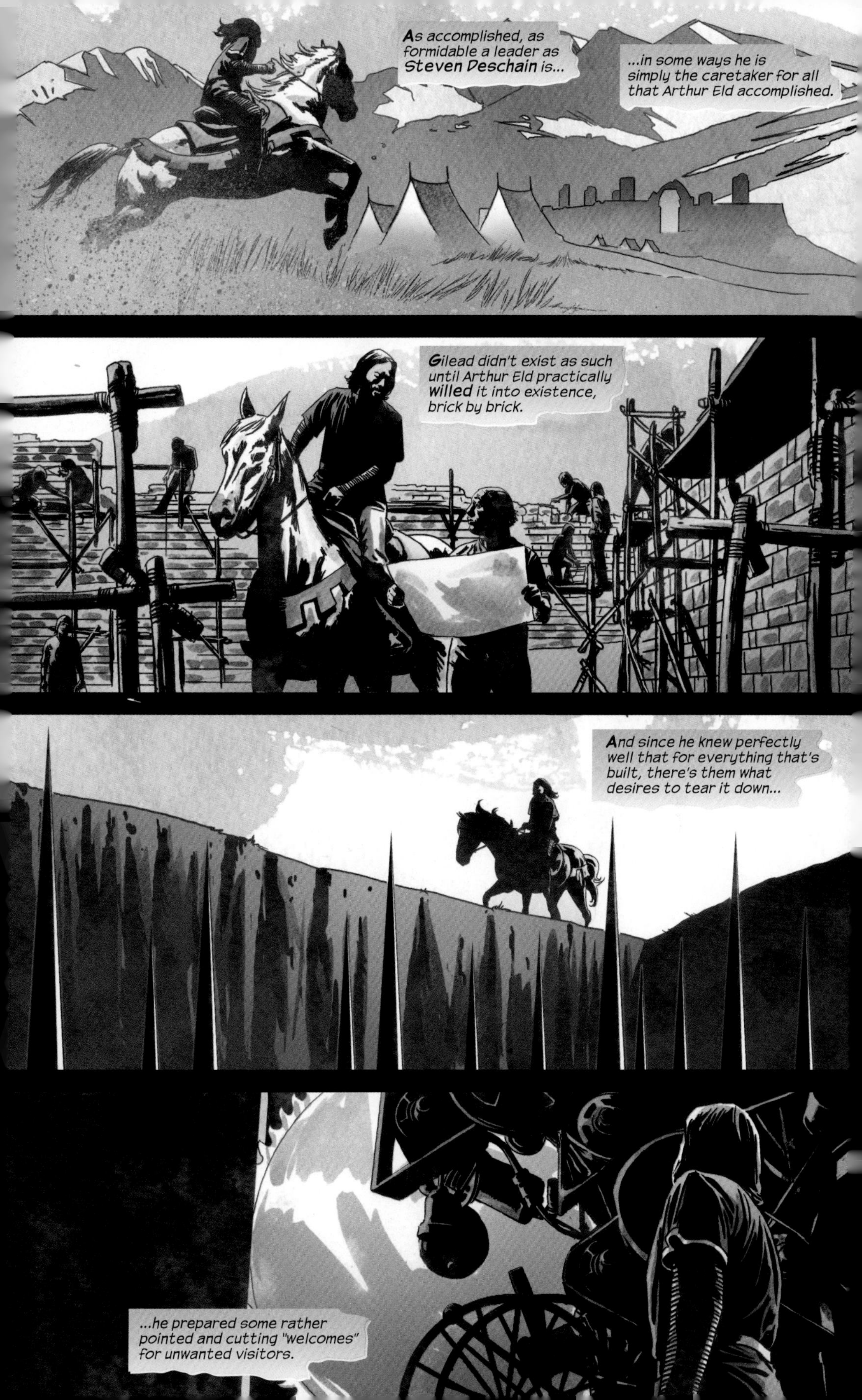
As accomplished, as formidable a leader as Steven Deschain is...
...in some ways he is simply the caretaker for all that Arthur Eld accomplished.
Gilead didn't exist as such until Arthur Eld practically willed it into existence, brick by brick.
And since he knew perfectly well that for everything that's built, there's them what desires to tear it down...
...he prepared some rather pointed and cutting "welcomes" for unwanted visitors.

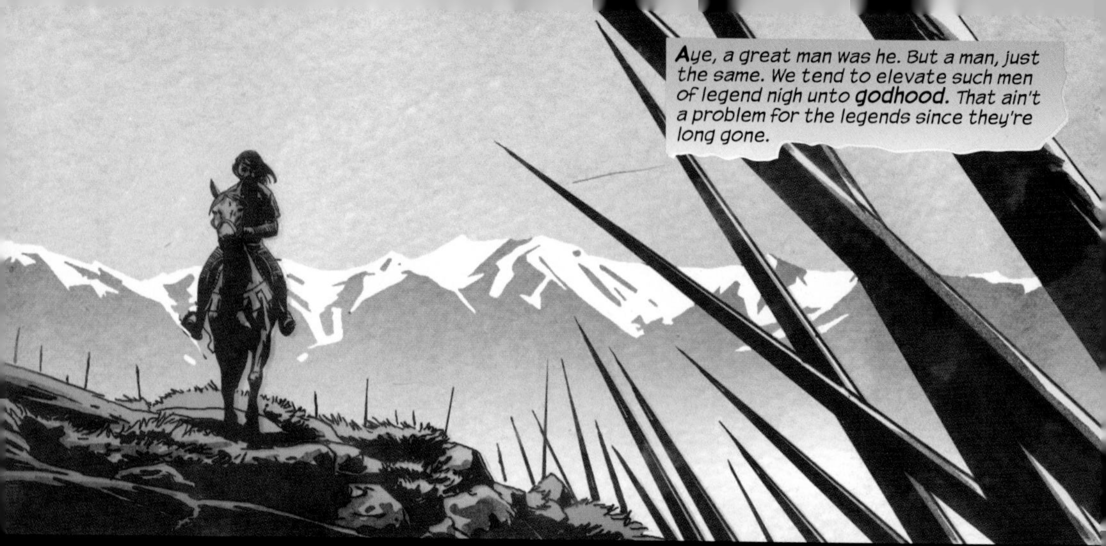
Aye, a great man was he. But a man, just the same. We tend to elevate such men of legend nigh unto godhood. That ain't a problem for the legends since they're long gone.

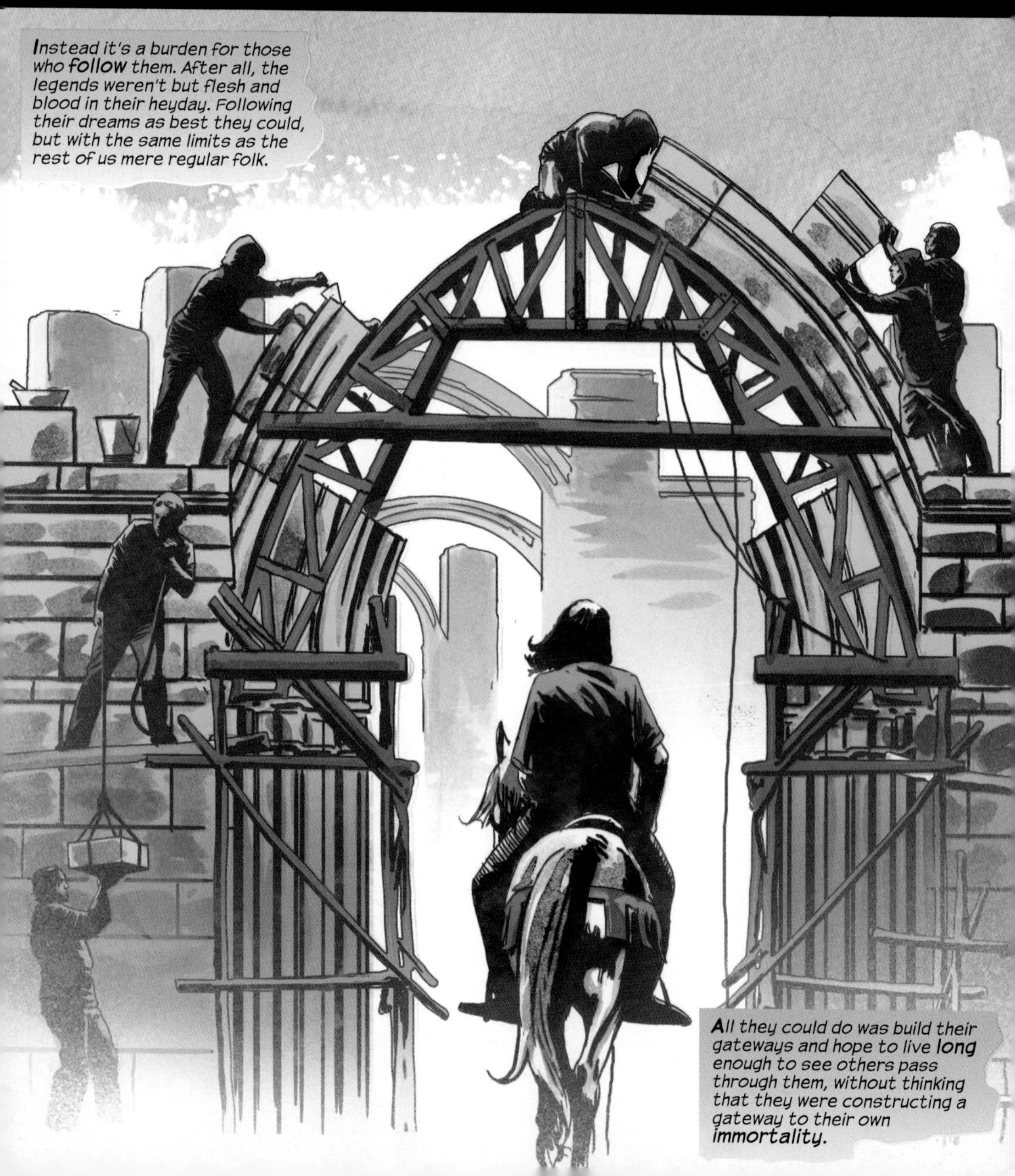
Instead it's a burden for those who follow them. After all, the legends weren't but flesh and blood in their heyday. Following their dreams as best they could, but with the same limits as the rest of us mere regular folk.
All they could do was build their gateways and hope to live long enough to see others pass through them, without thinking that they were constructing a gateway to their own immortality.

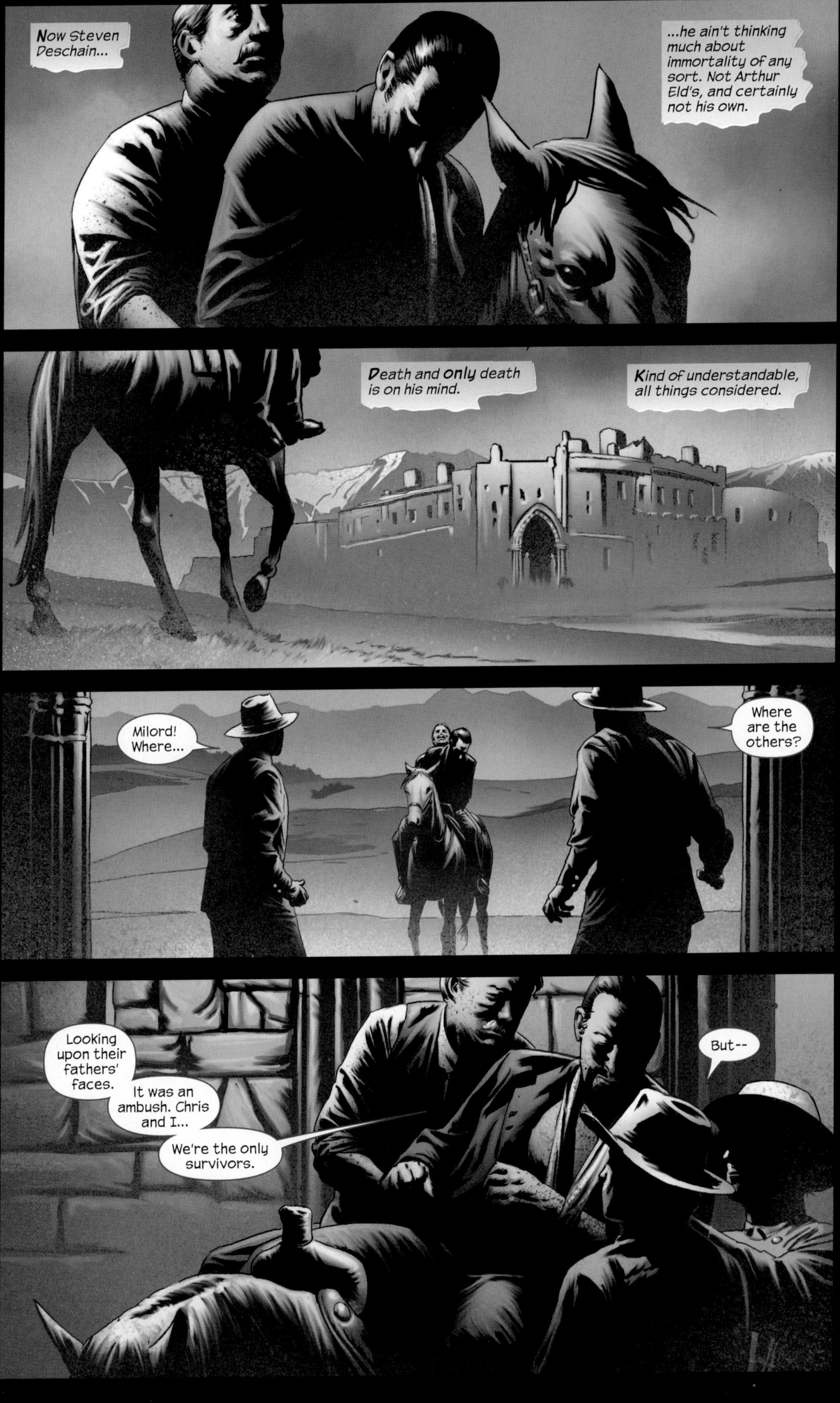
Now Steven Deschain...
...he ain't thinking much about immortality of any sort. Not Arthur Eld's, and certainly not his own.
Death and only death is on his mind.
Kind of understandable, all things considered.
Milord! Where...
Where are the others?
Looking upon their fathers' faces.
It was an ambush. Chris and I...
We're the only survivors.
But--

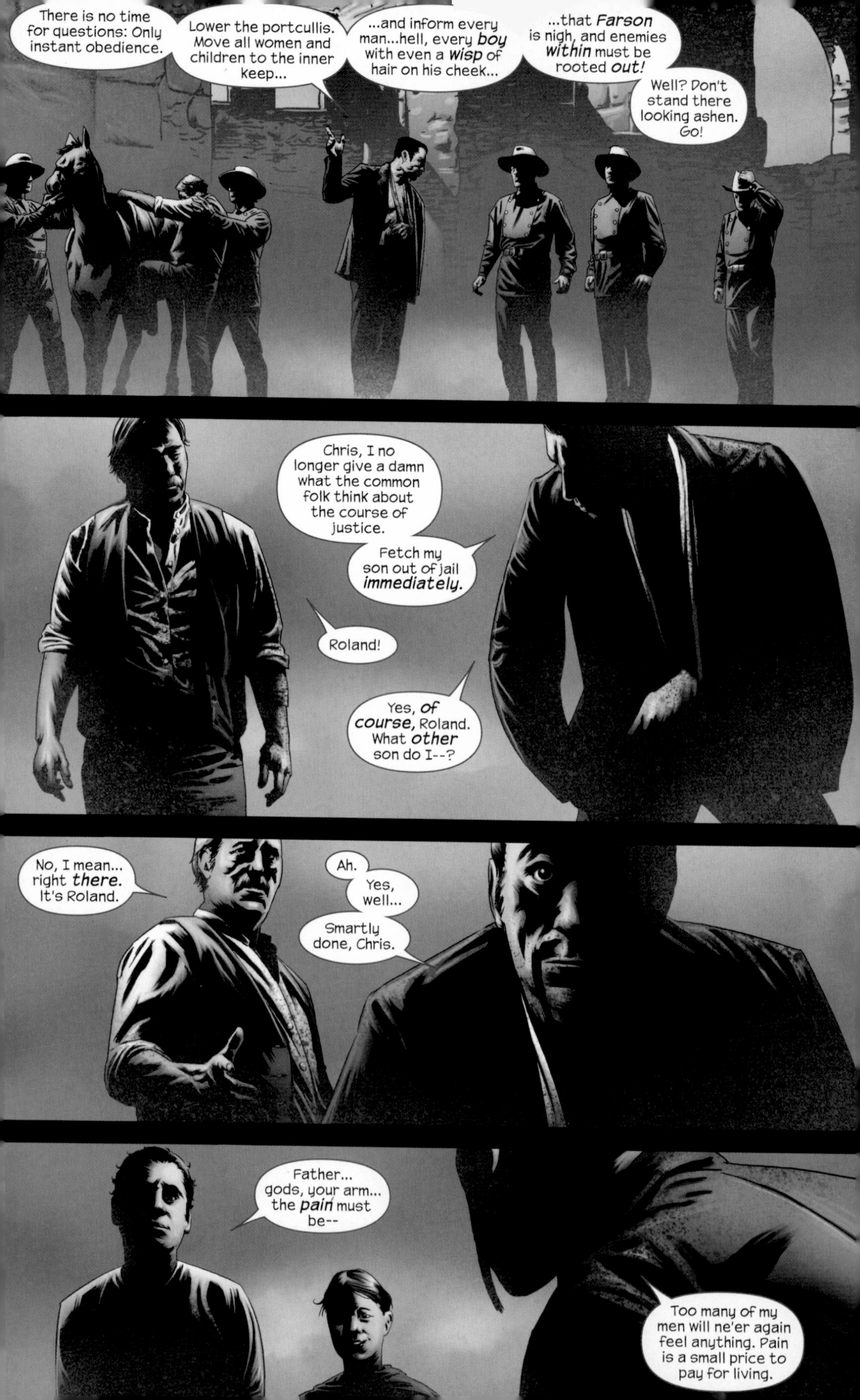
There is no time for questions: Only instant obedience.
Lower the portcullis. Move all women and children to the inner keep...
...and inform every man...hell, every boy with even a wisp of hair on his cheek...
...that Farson is nigh, and enemies within must be rooted out!
Well? Don't stand there looking ashen. Go!
Chris, I no longer give a damn what the common folk think about the course of justice.
Fetch my son out of jail immediately.
Roland!
Yes, of course, Roland. What other son do I--?
No, I mean... right there. It's Roland.
Ah.
Yes, well...
Smartly done, Chris.
Father... gods, your arm... the pain must be--
Too many of my men will ne'er again feel anything. Pain is a small price to pay for living.

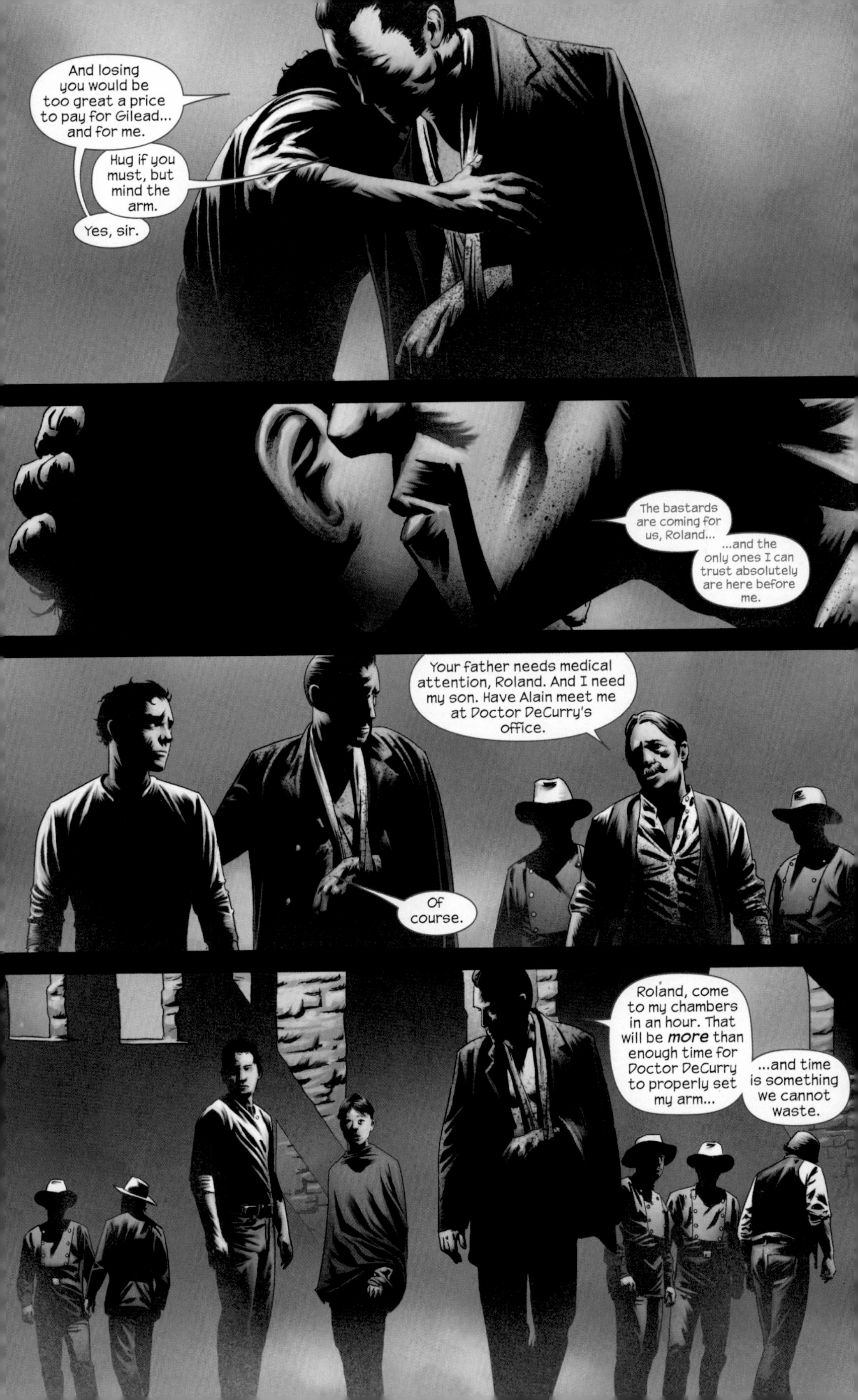
And losing you would be too great a price to pay for Gilead... and for me.
Hug if you must, but mind the arm.
Yes, sir.
The bastards are coming for us, Roland...
...and the only ones I can trust absolutely are here before me.
Your father needs medical attention, Roland. And I need my son. Have Alain meet me at Doctor DeCurry's office.
Of course.
Roland, come to my chambers in an hour. That will be *more* than enough time for Doctor DeCurry to properly set my arm...
...and time is something we cannot waste.

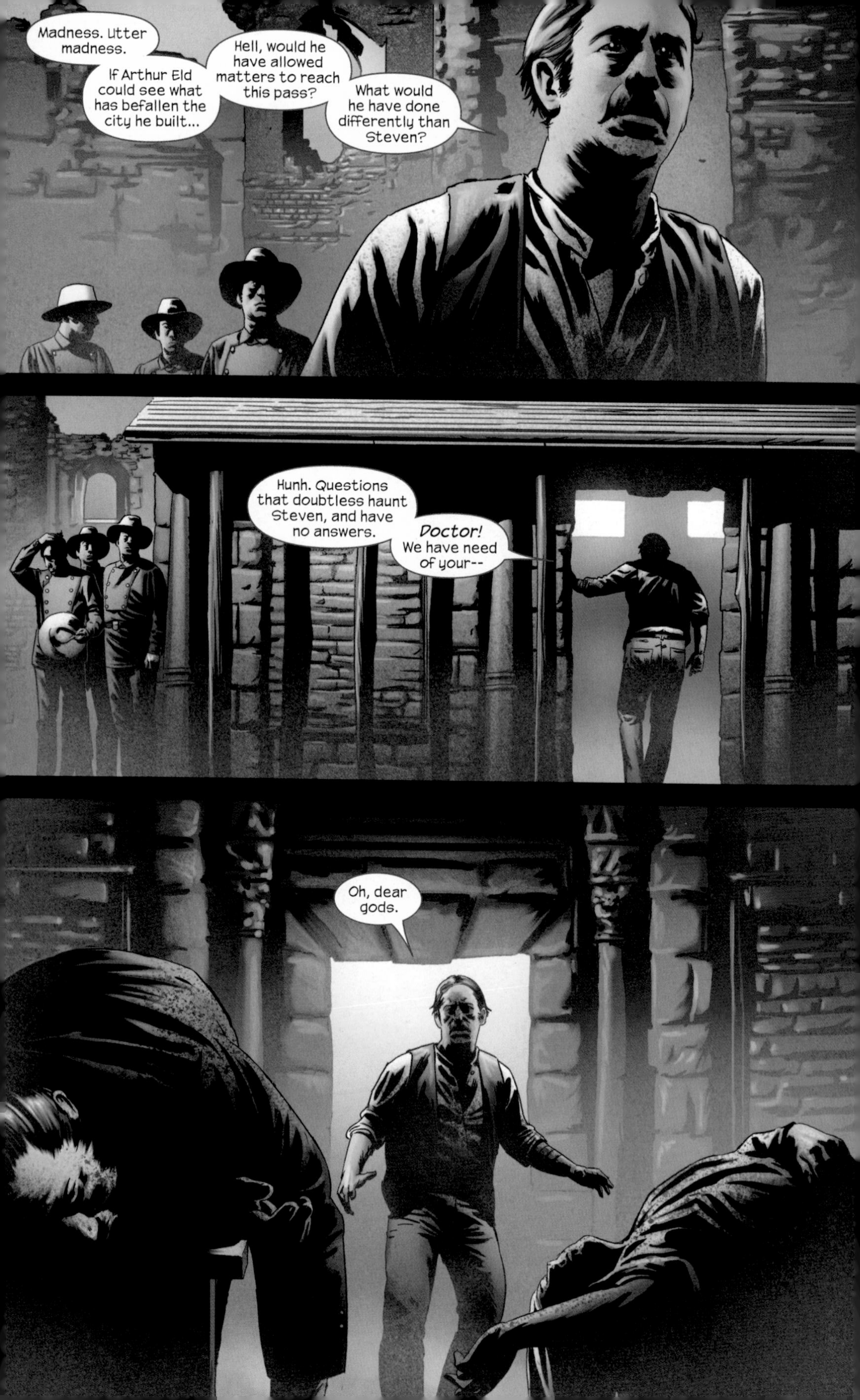

Madness. Utter madness.
If Arthur Eld could see what has befallen the city he built...
Hell, would he have allowed matters to reach this pass?
What would he have done differently than Steven?
Hunh. Questions that doubtless haunt Steven, and have no answers.
Doctor! We have need of your--
Oh, dear gods.

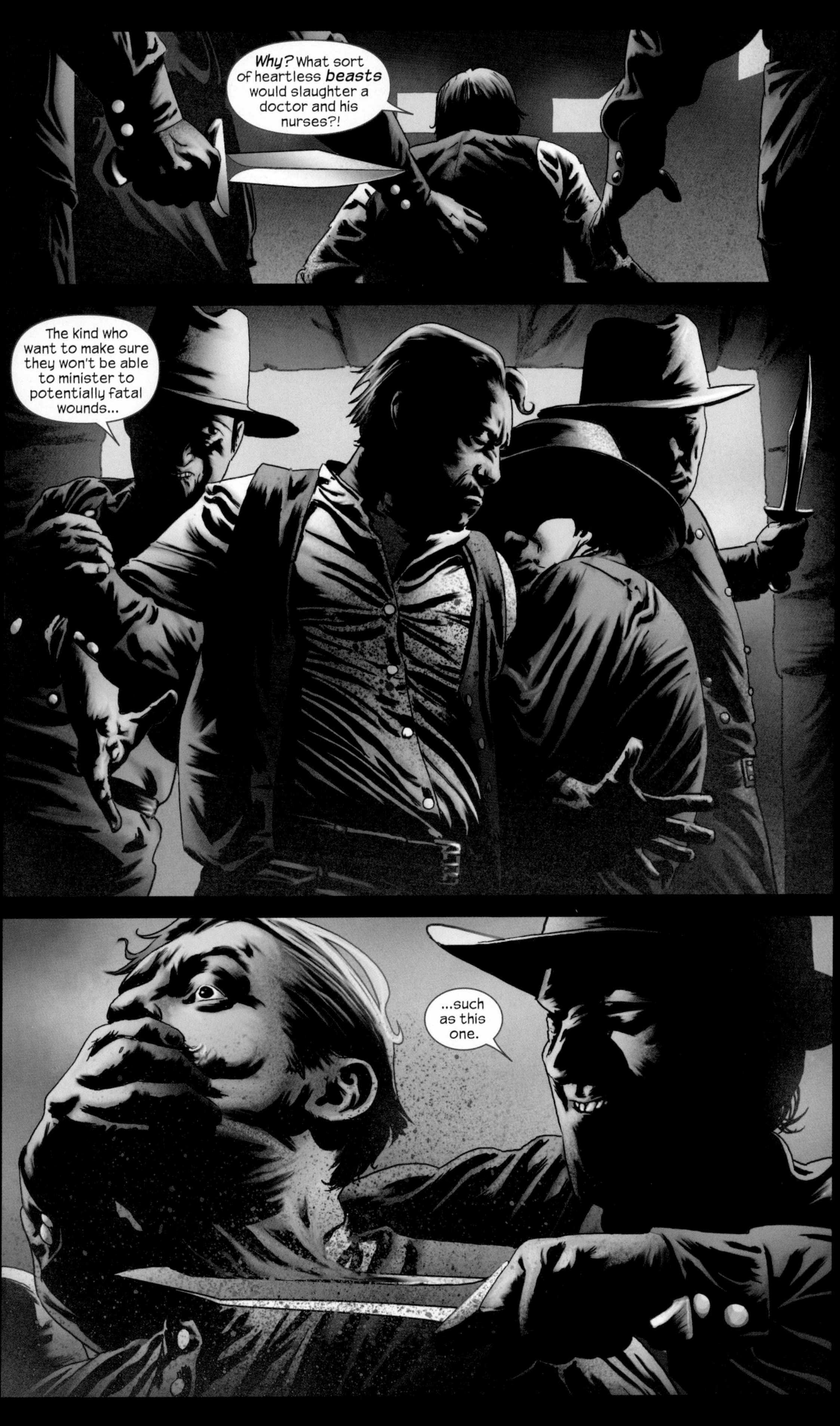
Why? What sort of heartless ***beasts*** would slaughter a doctor and his nurses?!
The kind who want to make sure they won't be able to minister to potentially fatal wounds...
...such as this one.

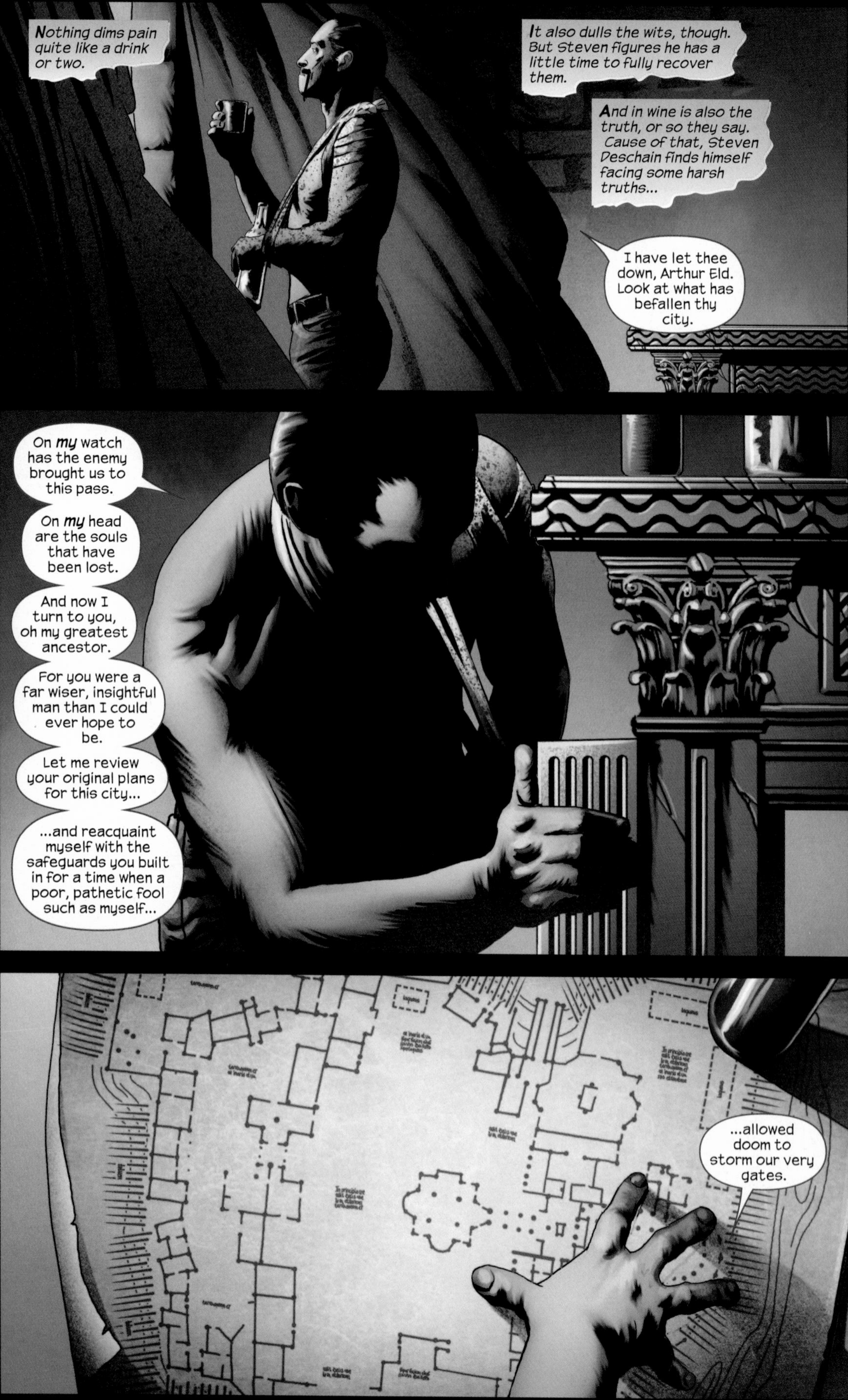
Nothing dims pain quite like a drink or two.
It also dulls the wits, though. But Steven figures he has a little time to fully recover them.
And in wine is also the truth, or so they say. 'Cause of that, Steven Deschain finds himself facing some harsh truths...
I have let thee down, Arthur Eld. Look at what has befallen thy city.
On my watch has the enemy brought us to this pass.
On my head are the souls that have been lost.
And now I turn to you, oh my greatest ancestor.
For you were a far wiser, insightful man than I could ever hope to be.
Let me review your original plans for this city...
...and reacquaint myself with the safeguards you built in for a time when a poor, pathetic fool such as myself...
...allowed doom to storm our very gates.

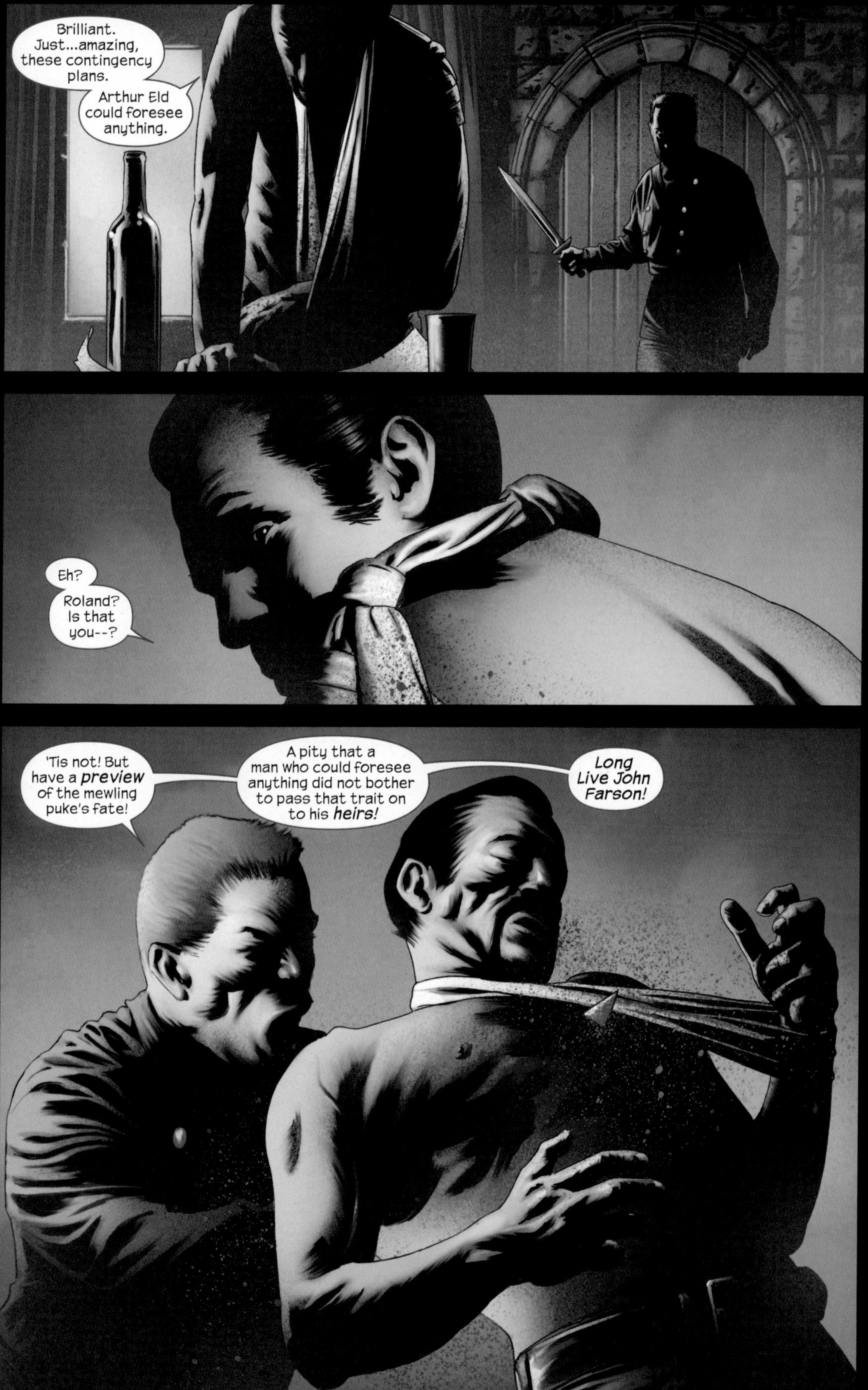
Brilliant. Just...amazing, these contingency plans.
Arthur Eld could foresee anything.
Eh?
Roland? Is that you--?
'Tis not! But have a *preview* of the mewling puke's fate!
A pity that a man who could foresee anything did not bother to pass that trait on to his *heirs!*
Long Live John Farson!

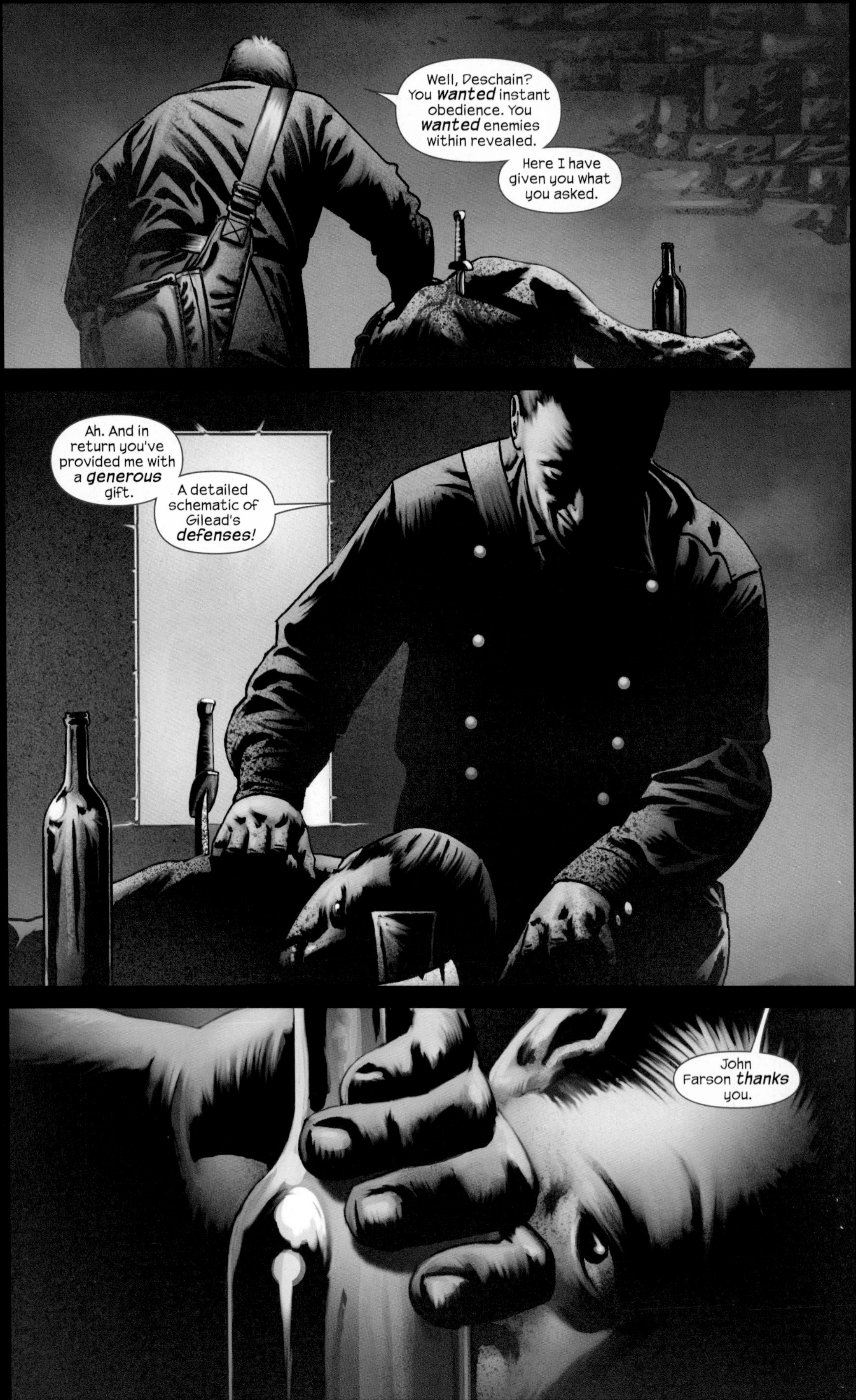
Well, Deschain? You wanted instant obedience. You wanted enemies within revealed.
Here I have given you what you asked.
Ah. And in return you've provided me with a generous gift.
A detailed schematic of Gilead's defenses!
John Farson thanks you.

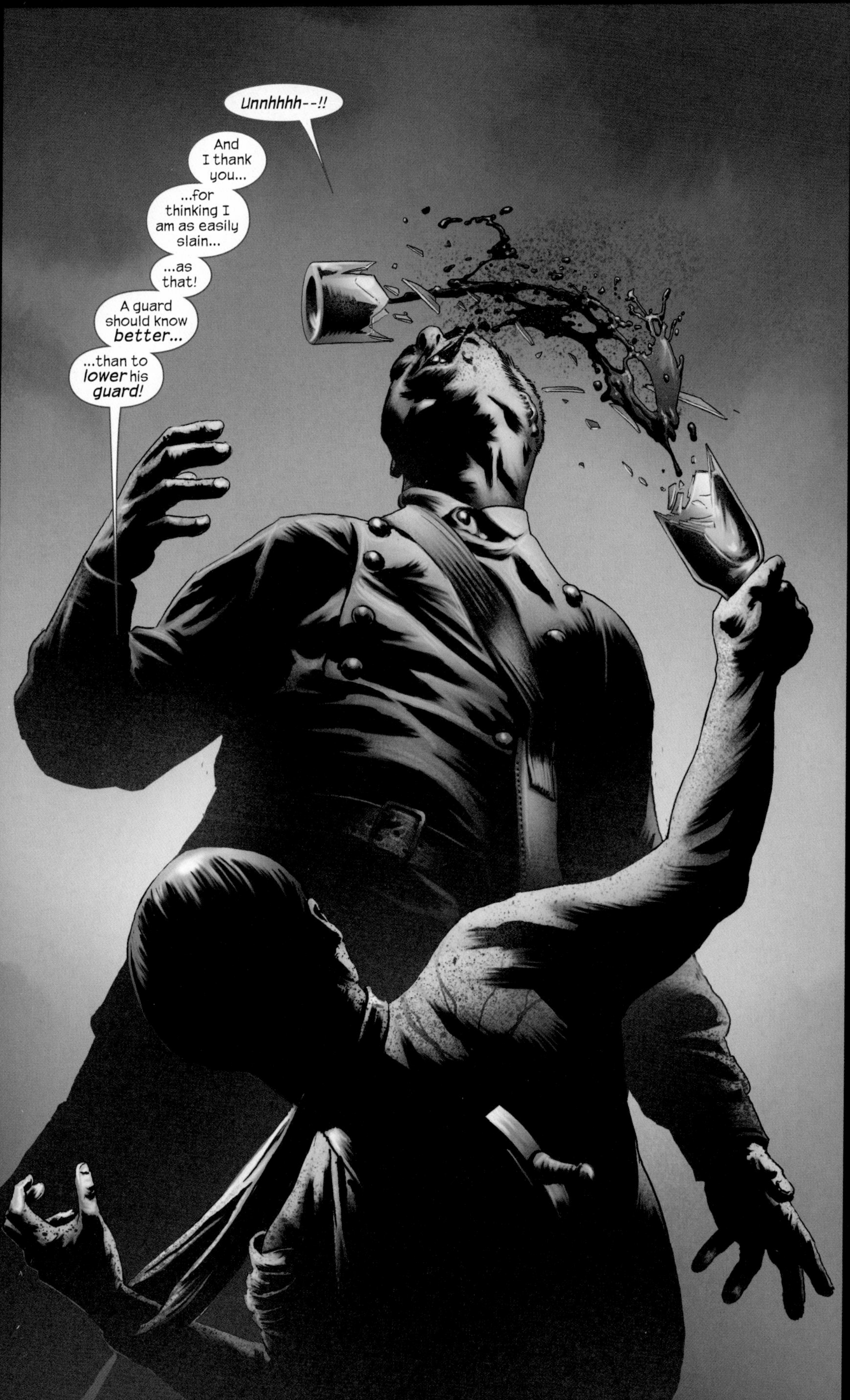
Unnhhhh--!!
And I thank you...
...for thinking I am as easily slain...
...as that!
A guard should know *better...*
...than to *lower* his *guard!*

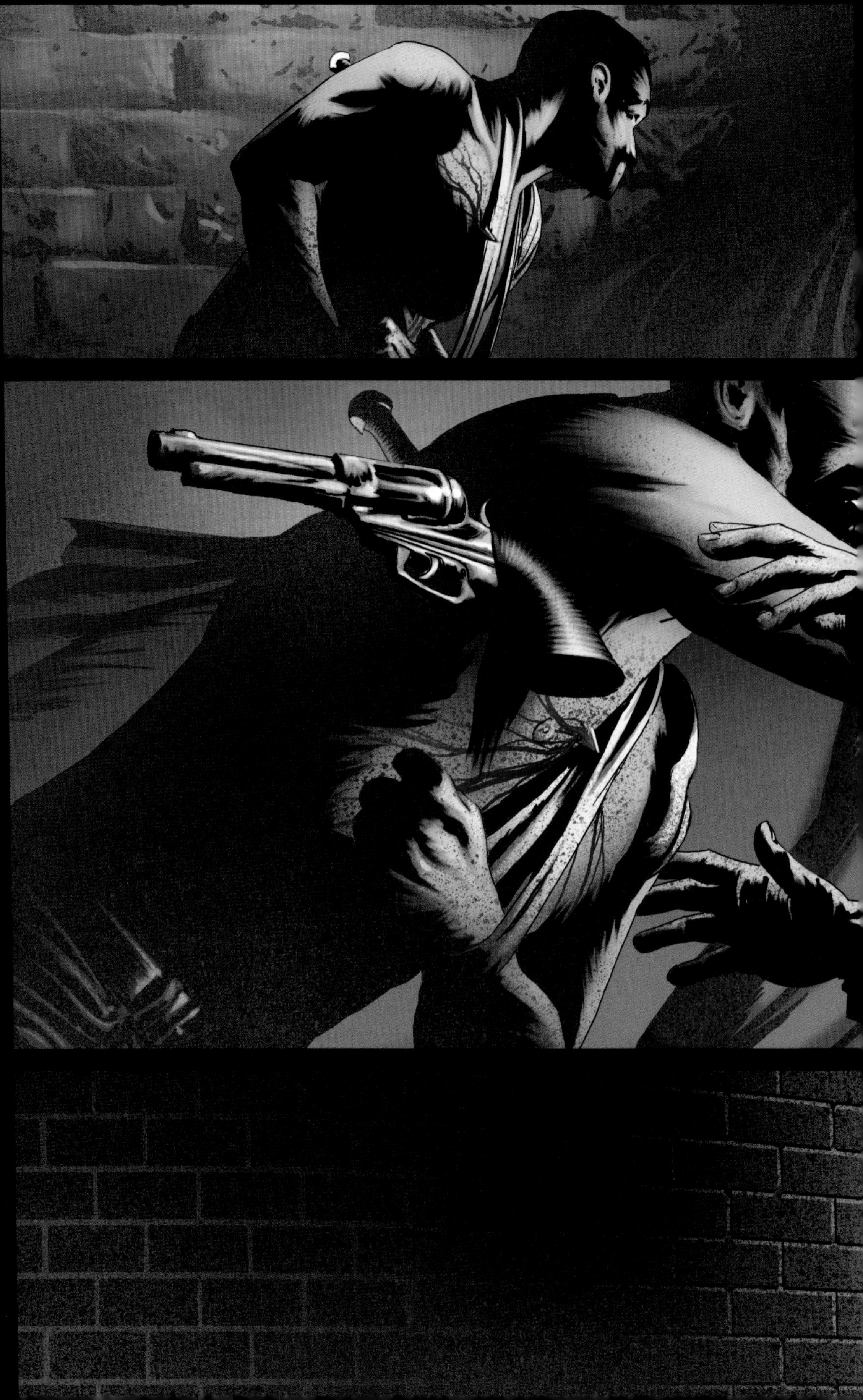

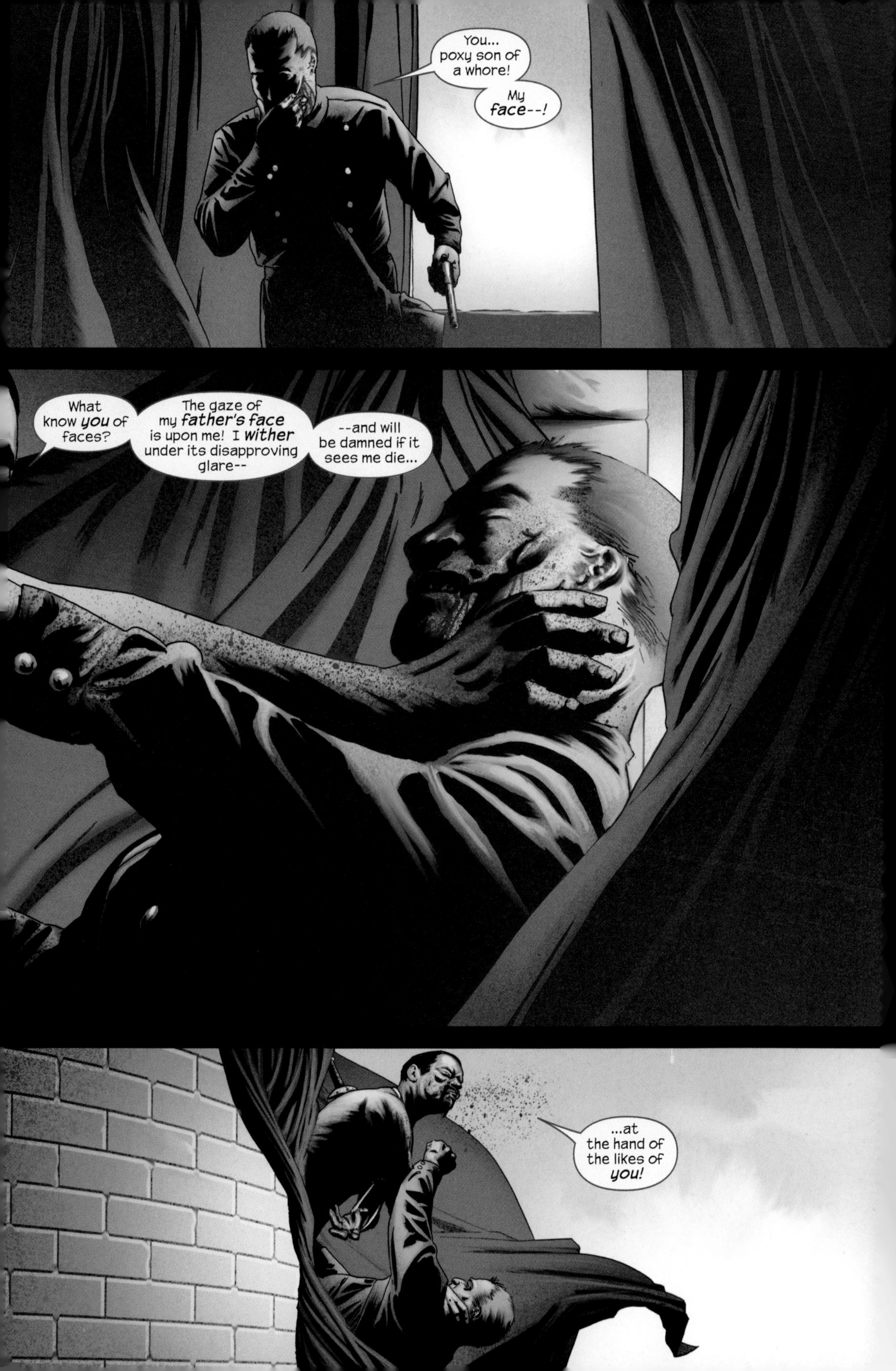

You... poxy son of a whore!
My face--!
What know you of faces?
The gaze of my father's face is upon me! I wither under its disapproving glare--
--and will be damned if it sees me die...
...at the hand of the likes of you!

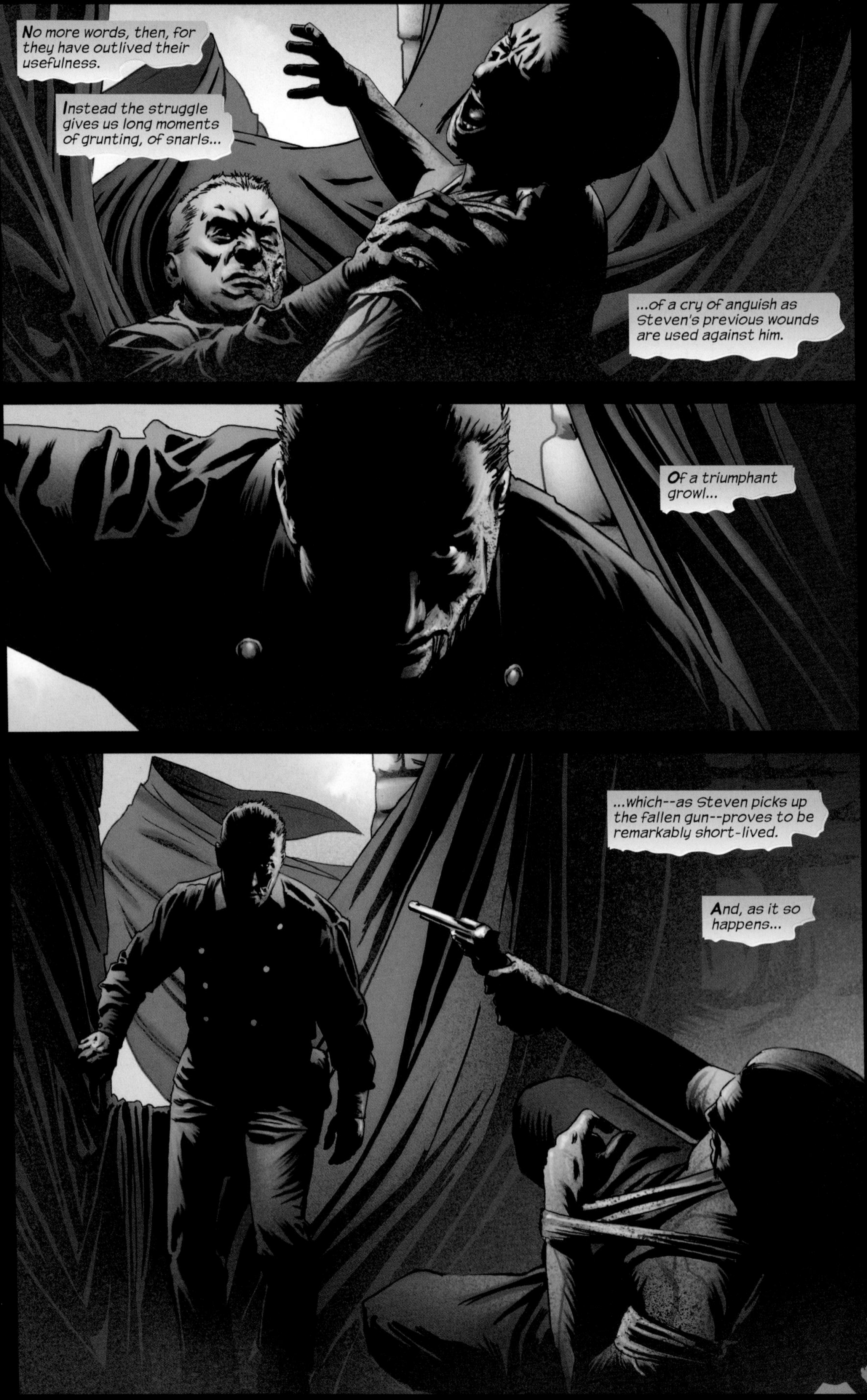
No more words, then, for they have outlived their usefulness.
Instead the struggle gives us long moments of grunting, of snarls...
...of a cry of anguish as Steven's previous wounds are used against him.
Of a triumphant growl...
...which--as Steven picks up the fallen gun--proves to be remarkably short-lived.
And, as it so happens...

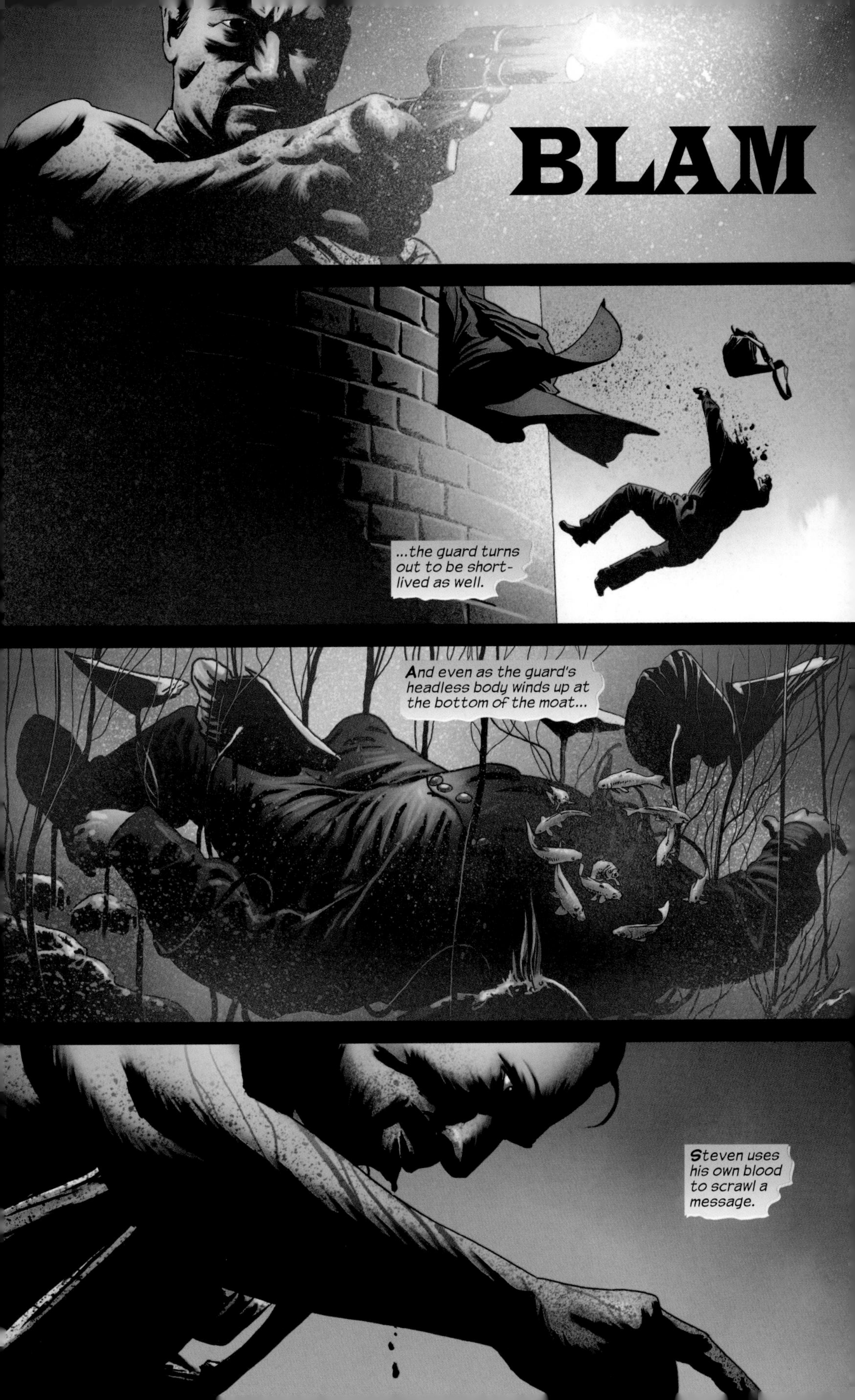
BLAM
...the guard turns out to be short-lived as well.
And even as the guard's headless body winds up at the bottom of the moat...
Steven uses his own blood to scrawl a message.

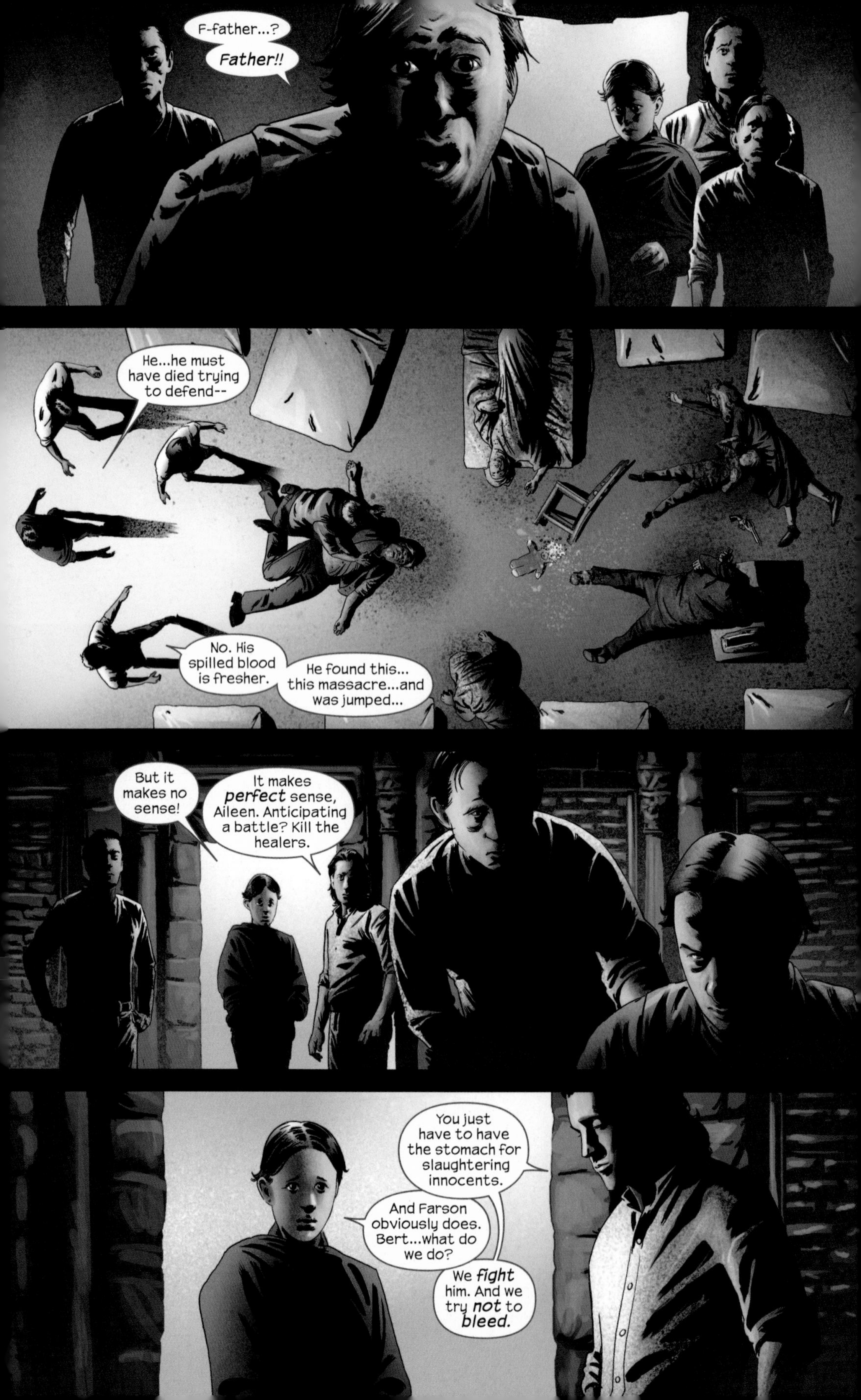
F-father...?
Father!!
He...he must have died trying to defend--
No. His spilled blood is fresher.
He found this... this massacre...and was jumped...
But it makes no sense!
It makes *perfect* sense, Aileen. Anticipating a battle? Kill the healers.
You just have to have the stomach for slaughtering innocents.
And Farson obviously does. Bert...what do we do?
We *fight* him. And we try *not* to *bleed*.

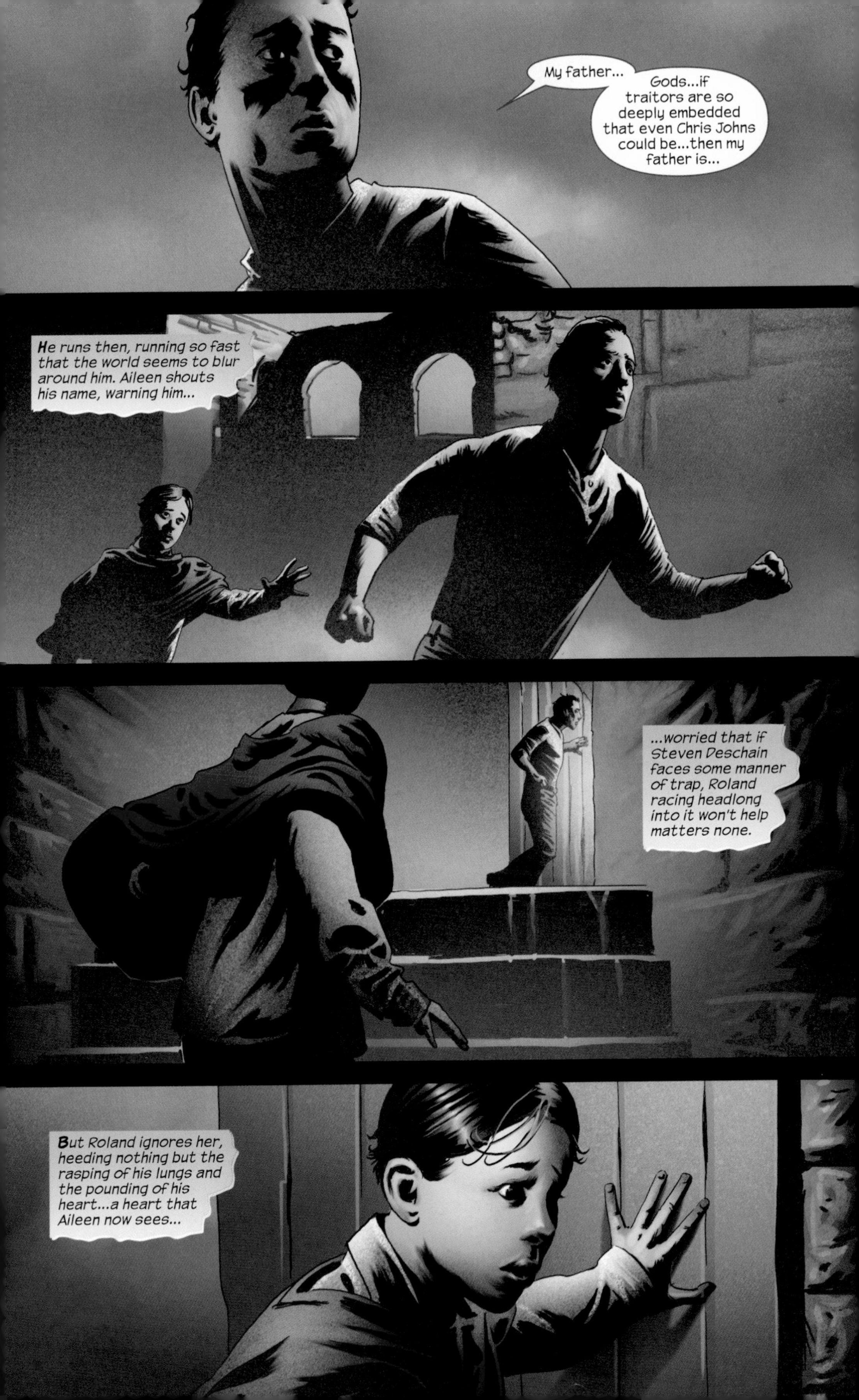
My father...
Gods...if traitors are so deeply embedded that even Chris Johns could be...then my father is...
He runs then, running so fast that the world seems to blur around him. Aileen shouts his name, warning him...
...worried that if Steven Deschain faces some manner of trap, Roland racing headlong into it won't help matters none.
But Roland ignores her, heeding nothing but the rasping of his lungs and the pounding of his heart...a heart that Aileen now sees...

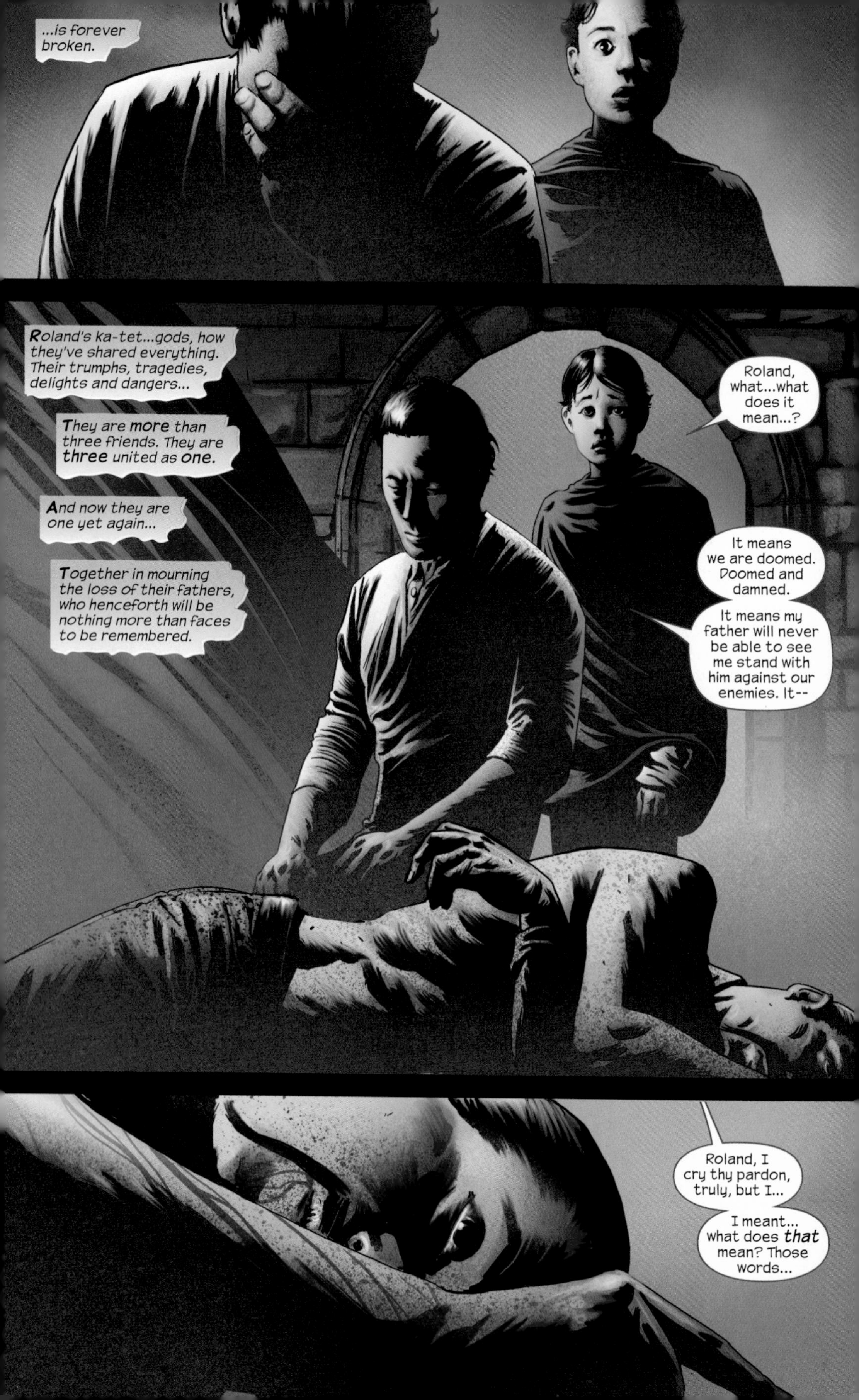
...is forever broken.
Roland's ka-tet...gods, how they've shared everything. Their trumphs, tragedies, delights and dangers...
They are more than three friends. They are three united as one.
And now they are one yet again...
Together in mourning the loss of their fathers, who henceforth will be nothing more than faces to be remembered.
Roland, what...what does it mean...?
It means we are doomed. Doomed and damned.
It means my father will never be able to see me stand with him against our enemies. It--
Roland, I cry thy pardon, truly, but I...
I meant... what does that mean? Those words...

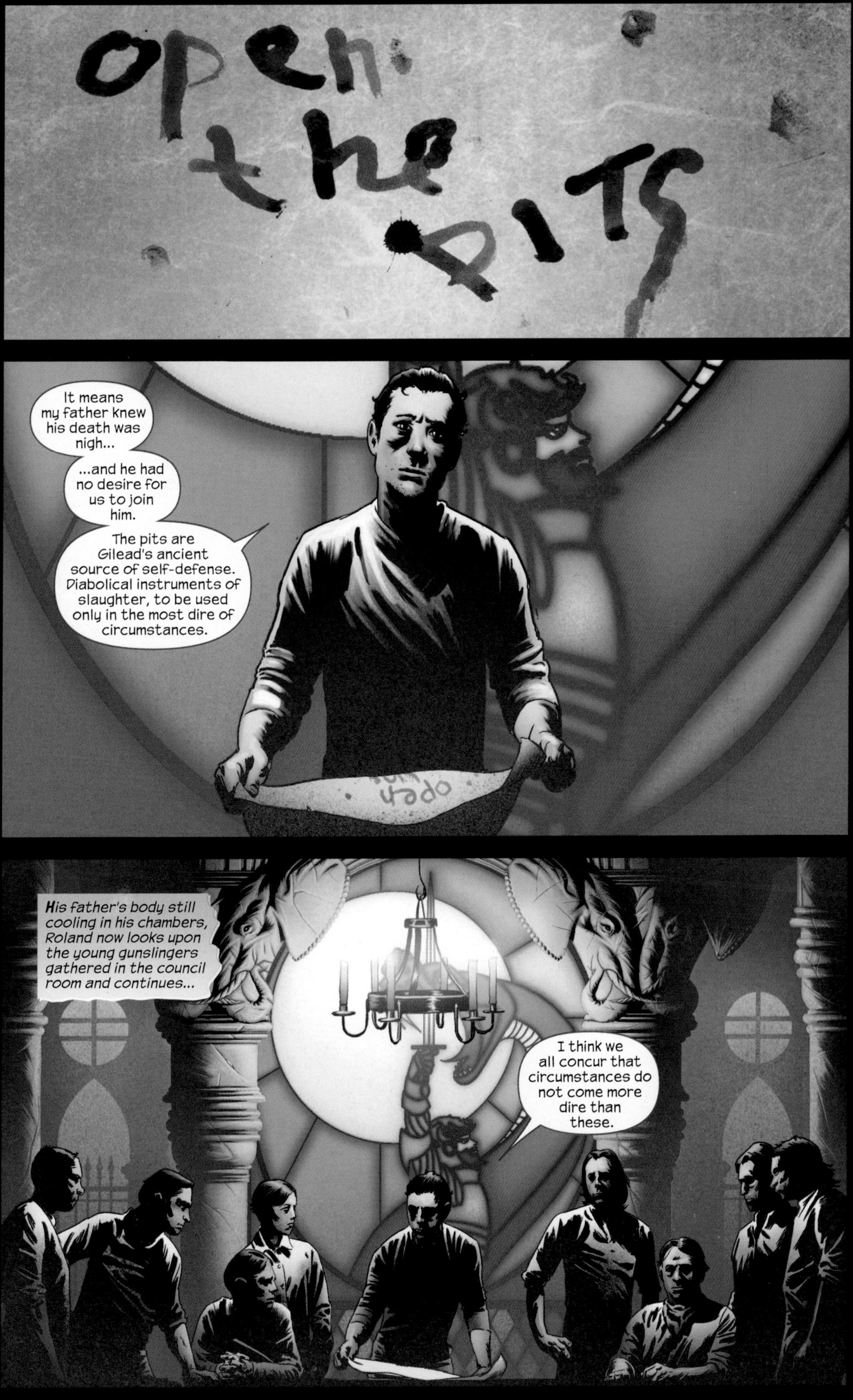
open the pits
It means my father knew his death was nigh...
...and he had no desire for us to join him.
The pits are Gilead's ancient source of self-defense. Diabolical instruments of slaughter, to be used only in the most dire of circumstances.
open
His father's body still cooling in his chambers, Roland now looks upon the young gunslingers gathered in the council room and continues...
I think we all concur that circumstances do not come more dire than these.

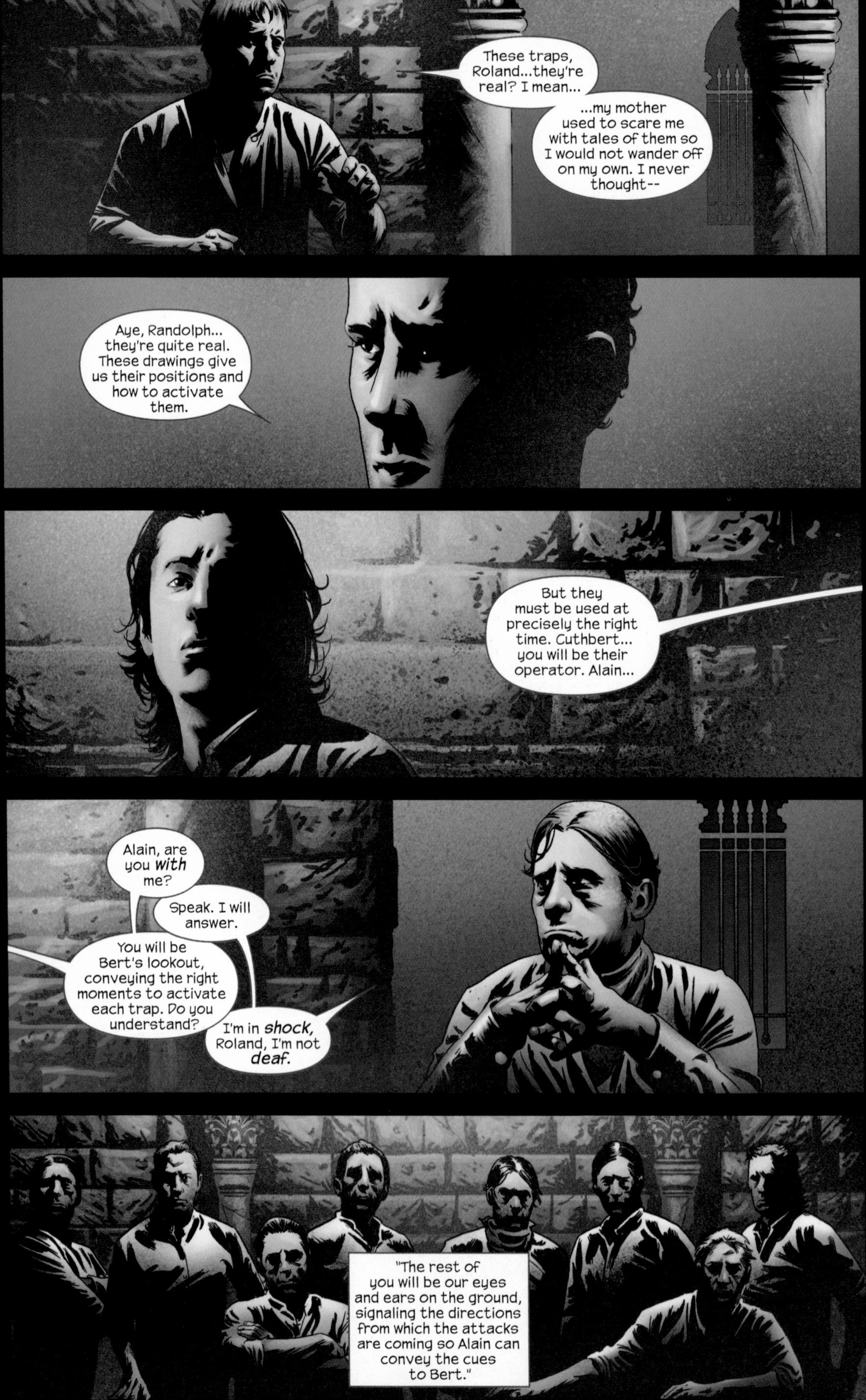
These traps, Roland...they're real? I mean...
...my mother used to scare me with tales of them so I would not wander off on my own. I never thought--
Aye, Randolph... they're quite real. These drawings give us their positions and how to activate them.
But they must be used at precisely the right time. Cuthbert... you will be their operator. Alain...
Alain, are you *with* me?
Speak. I will answer.
You will be Bert's lookout, conveying the right moments to activate each trap. Do you understand?
I'm in *shock,* Roland, I'm not *deaf.*
"The rest of you will be our eyes and ears on the ground, signaling the directions from which the attacks are coming so Alain can convey the cues to Bert."

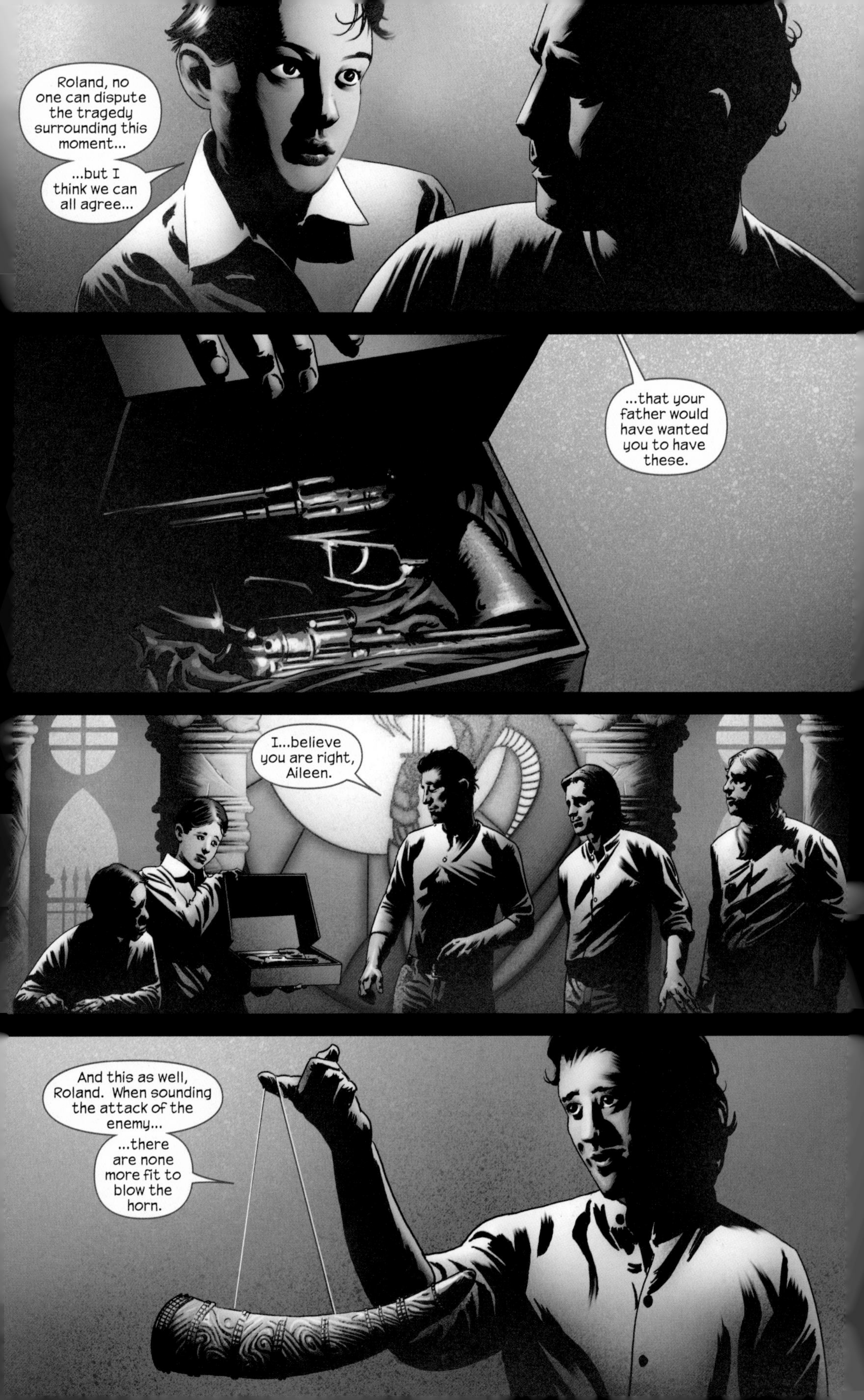
Roland, no one can dispute the tragedy surrounding this moment...
...but I think we can all agree...
...that your father would have wanted you to have these.
I...believe you are right, Aileen.
And this as well, Roland. When sounding the attack of the enemy...
...there are none more fit to blow the horn.

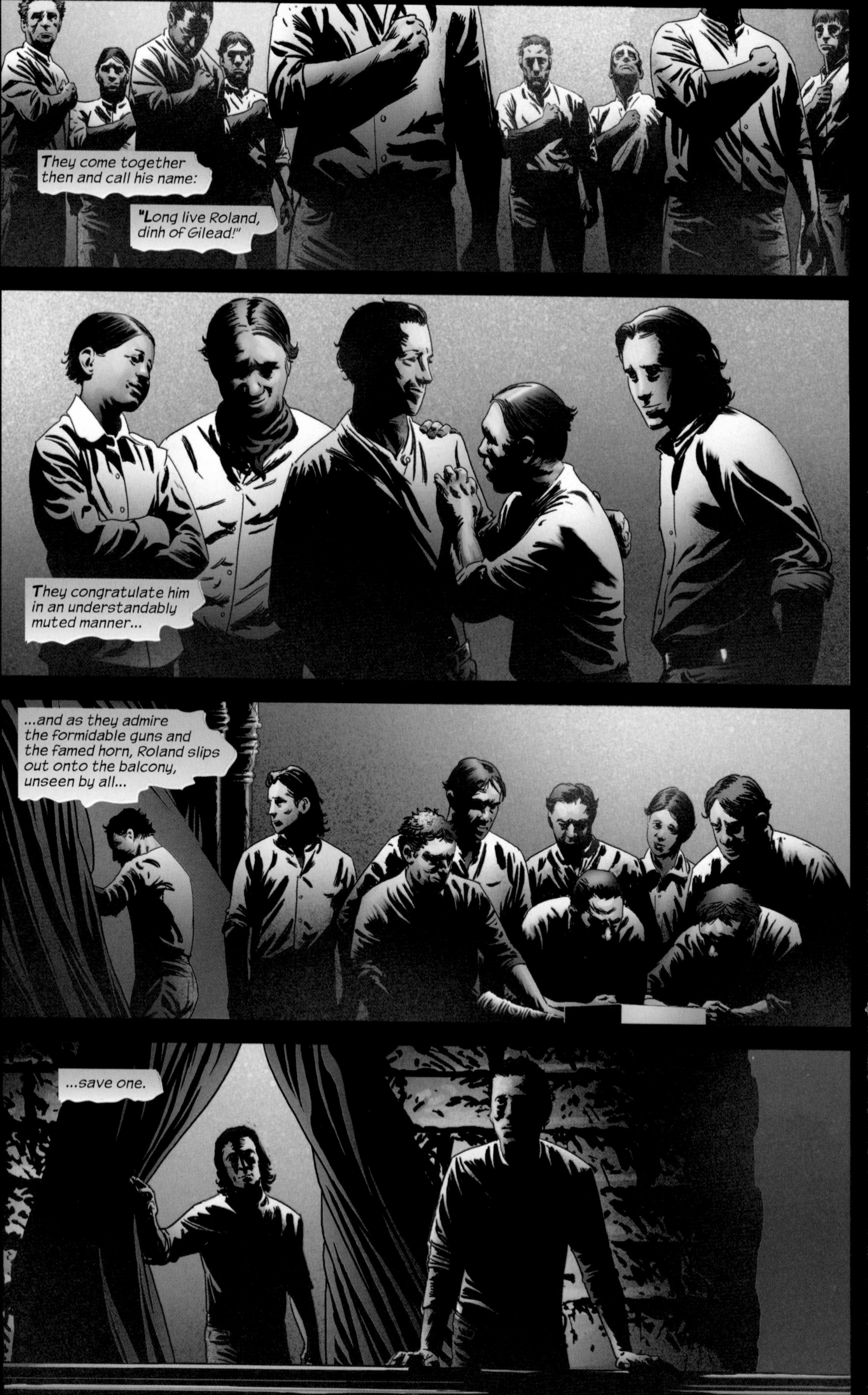
They come together then and call his name:
"Long live Roland, dinh of Gilead!"
They congratulate him in an understandably muted manner...
...and as they admire the formidable guns and the famed horn, Roland slips out onto the balcony, unseen by all...
...save one.

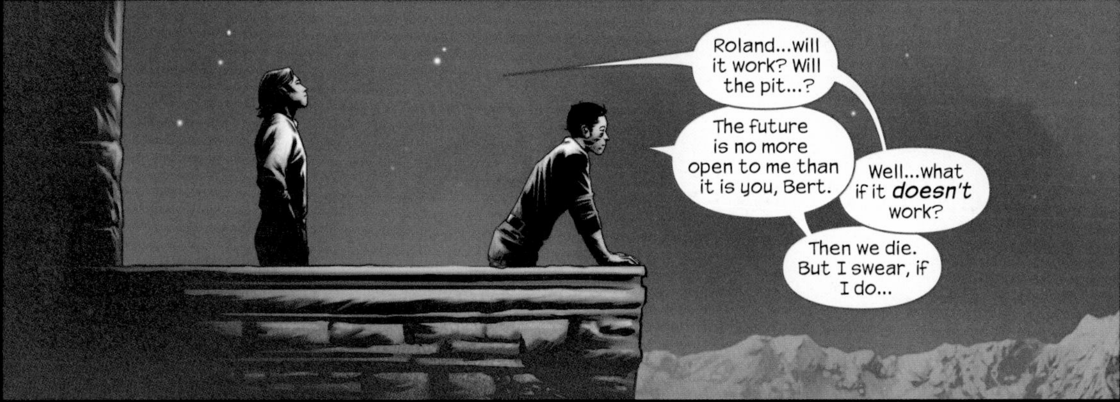
Roland...will it work? Will the pit...?
The future is no more open to me than it is you, Bert.
Well...what if it *doesn't* work?
Then we die. But I swear, if I do...

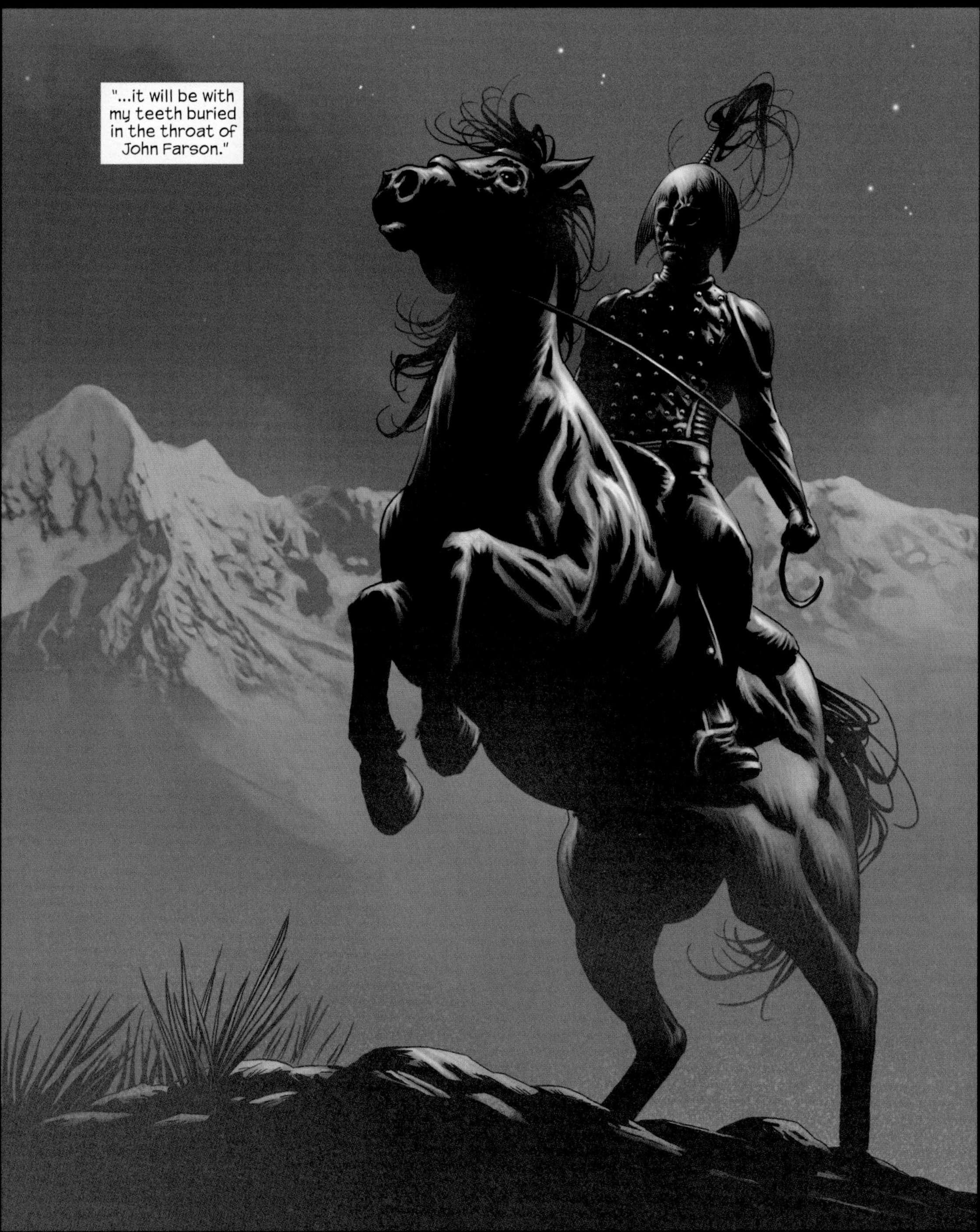
"...it will be with my teeth buried in the throat of John Farson."

STEPHEN KING

THE DARK TOWER

FALL OF GILEAD

CHAPTER SIX

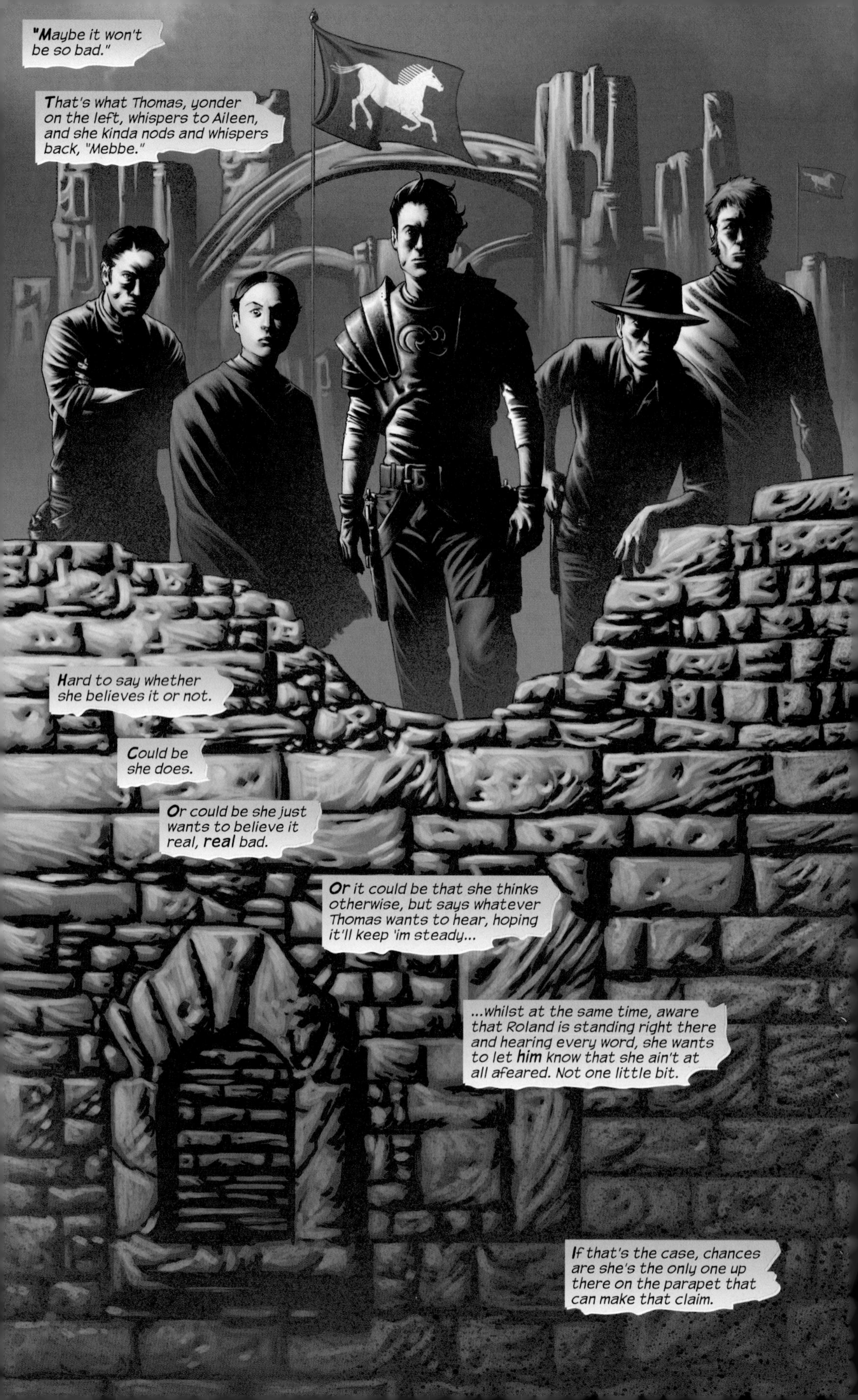
"Maybe it won't be so bad."
That's what Thomas, yonder on the left, whispers to Aileen, and she kinda nods and whispers back, "Mebbe."
Hard to say whether she believes it or not.
Could be she does.
Or could be she just wants to believe it real, real bad.
Or it could be that she thinks otherwise, but says whatever Thomas wants to hear, hoping it'll keep 'im steady...
...whilst at the same time, aware that Roland is standing right there and hearing every word, she wants to let him know that she ain't at all afeared. Not one little bit.
If that's the case, chances are she's the only one up there on the parapet that can make that claim.

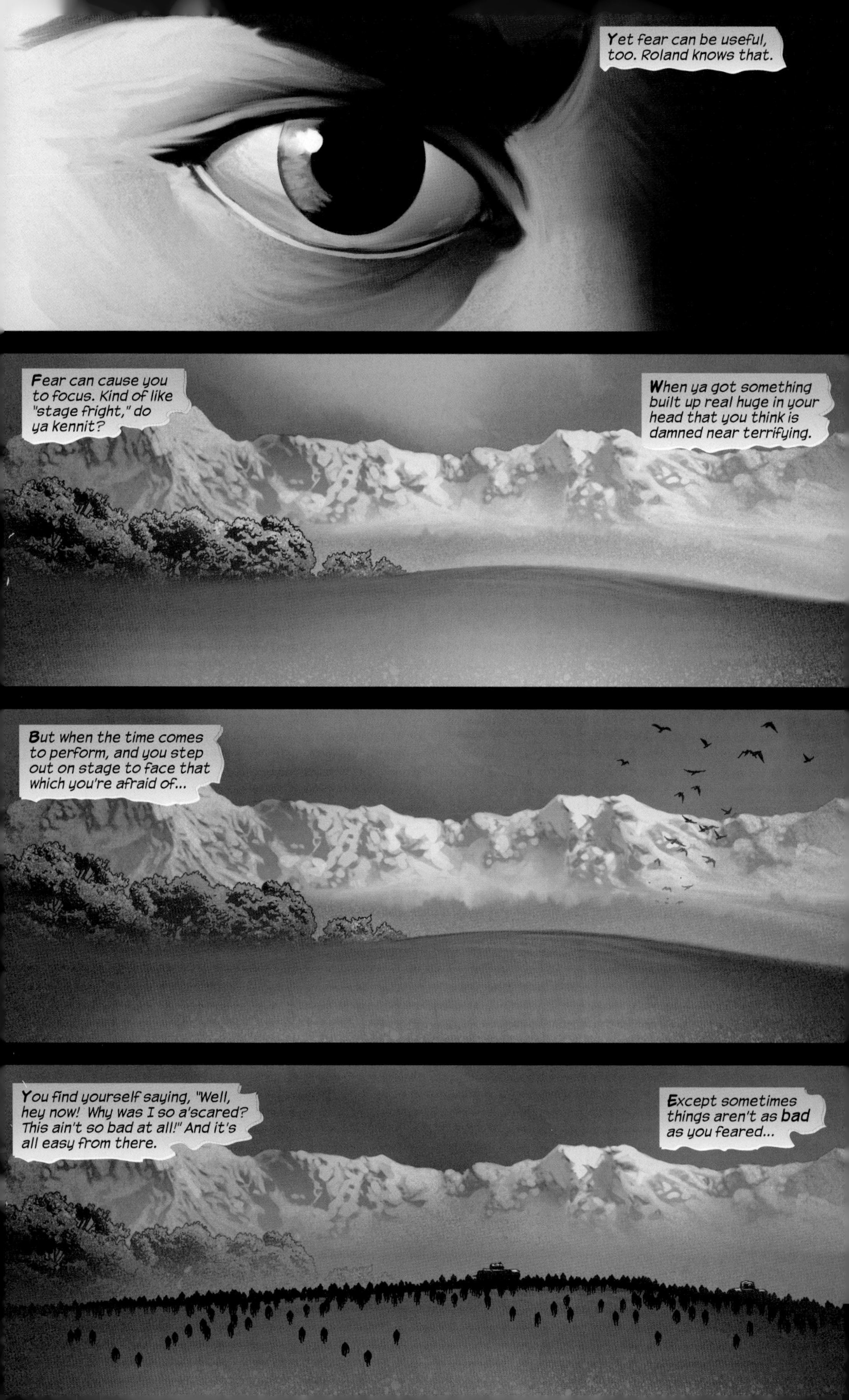

Yet fear can be useful, too. Roland knows that.
Fear can cause you to focus. Kind of like "stage fright," do ya kennit?
When ya got something built up real huge in your head that you think is damned near terrifying.
But when the time comes to perform, and you step out on stage to face that which you're afraid of...
You find yourself saying, "Well, hey now! Why was I so a'scared? This ain't so bad at all!" And it's all easy from there.
Except sometimes things aren't as bad as you feared...

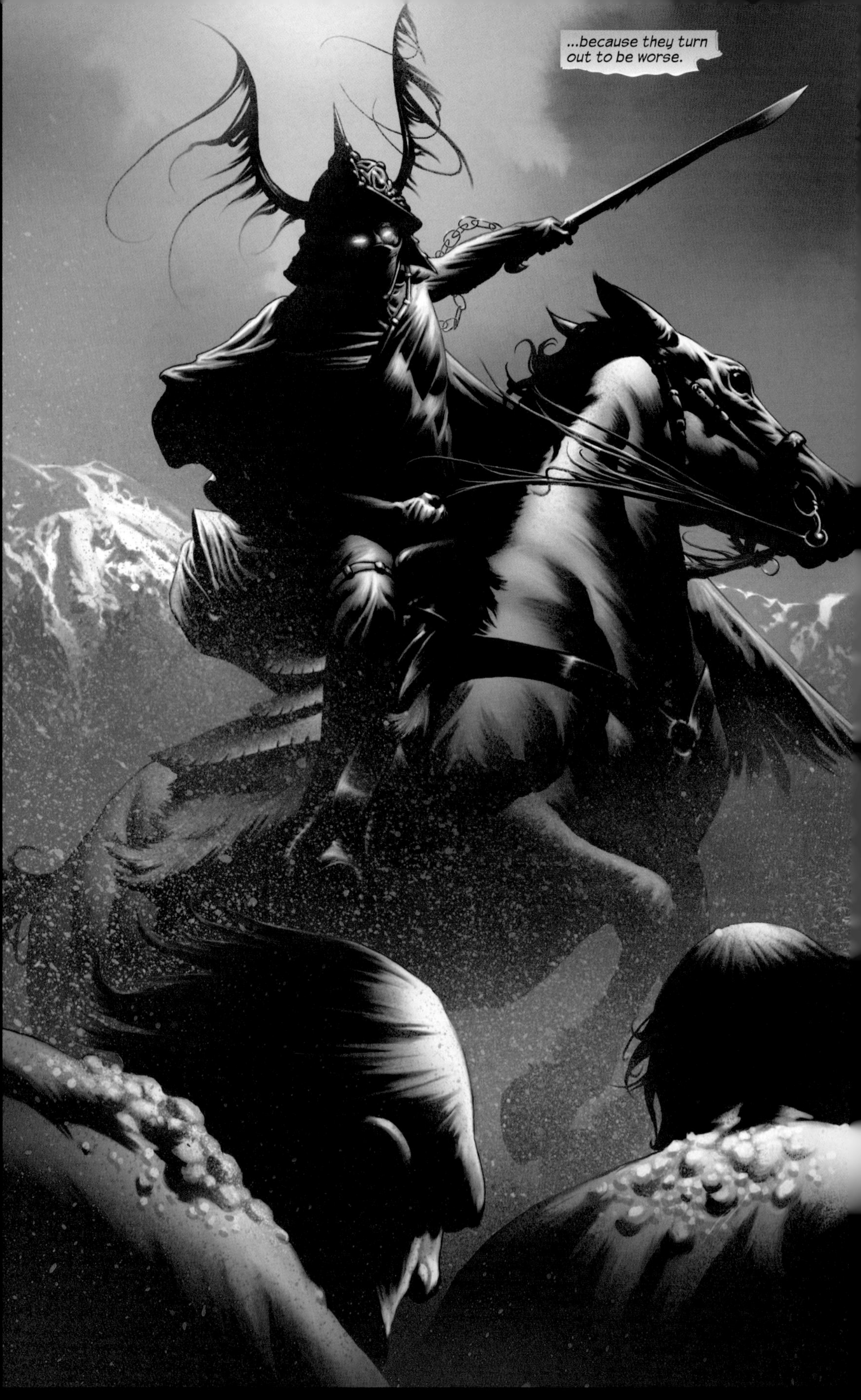
...because they turn out to be worse.

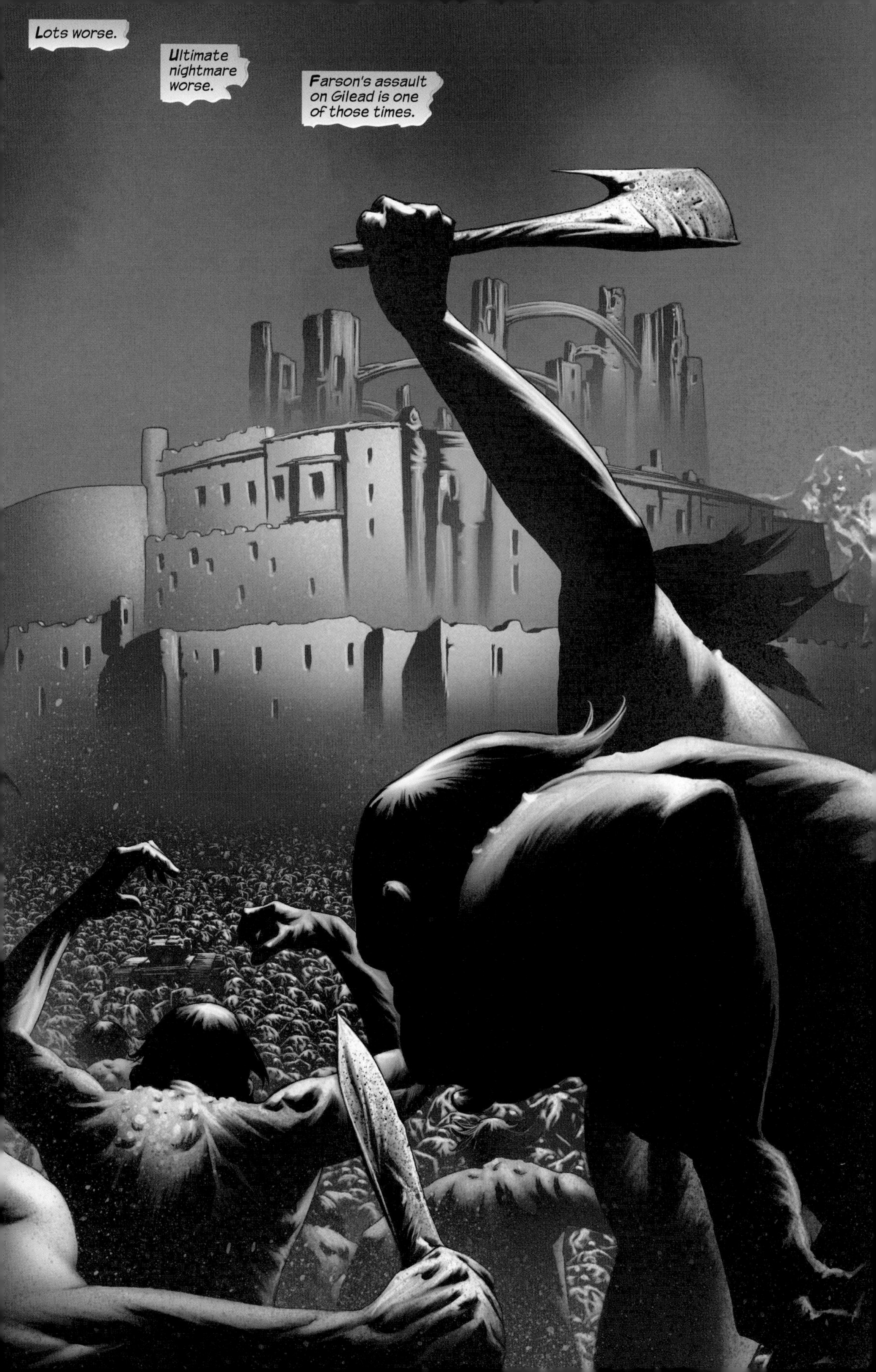
Lots worse.
Ultimate nightmare worse.
Farson's assault on Gilead is one of those times.

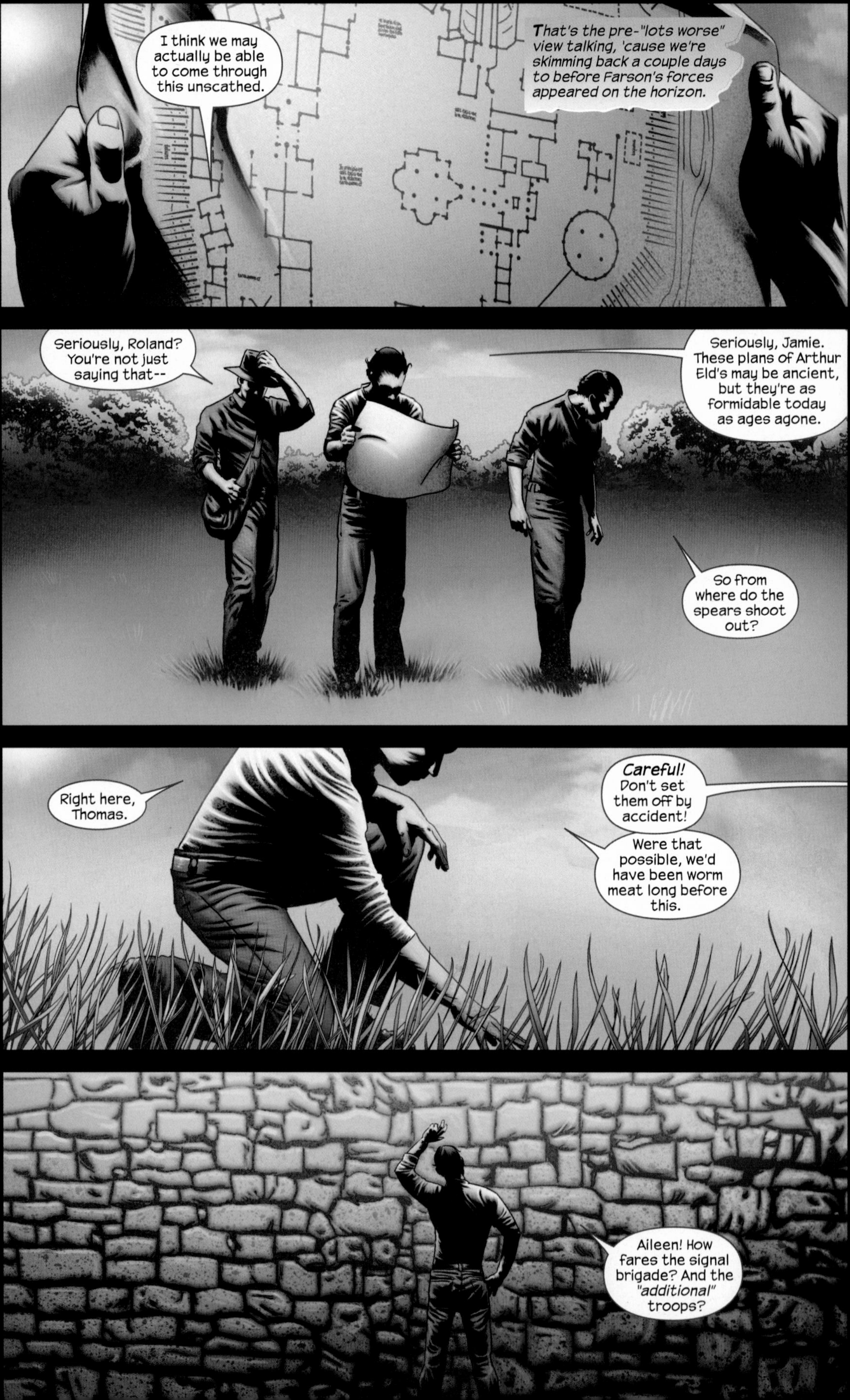
I think we may actually be able to come through this unscathed.
That's the pre-"lots worse" view talking, 'cause we're skimming back a couple days to before Farson's forces appeared on the horizon.
Seriously, Roland? You're not just saying that--
Seriously, Jamie. These plans of Arthur Eld's may be ancient, but they're as formidable today as ages agone.
So from where do the spears shoot out?
Right here, Thomas.
Careful! Don't set them off by accident!
Were that possible, we'd have been worm meat long before this.
Aileen! How fares the signal brigade? And the "additional" troops?

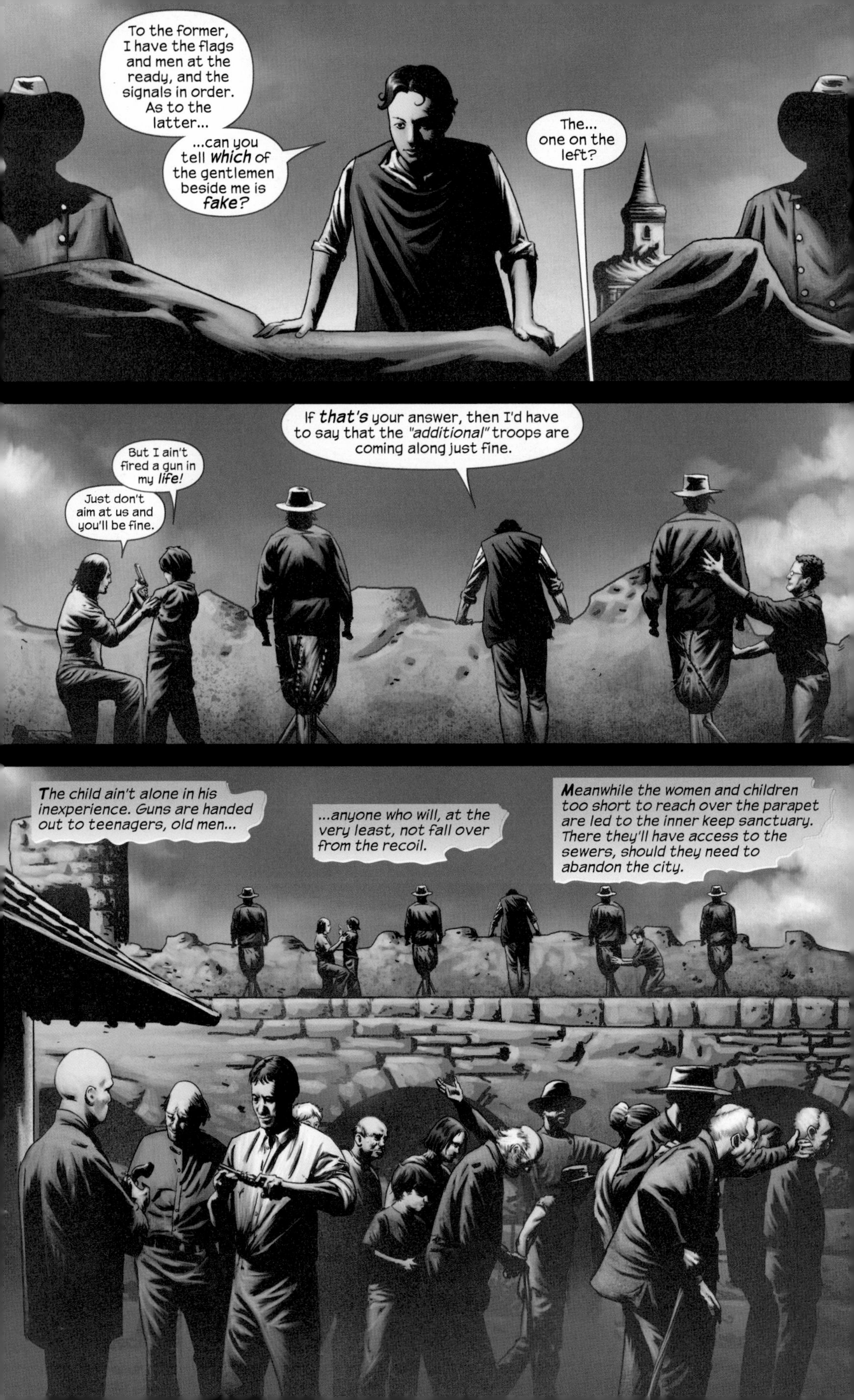
To the former, I have the flags and men at the ready, and the signals in order. As to the latter...
...can you tell *which* of the gentlemen beside me is *fake?*
The... one on the left?
If *that's* your answer, then I'd have to say that the *"additional"* troops are coming along just fine.
But I ain't fired a gun in my *life!*
Just don't aim at us and you'll be fine.
The child ain't alone in his inexperience. Guns are handed out to teenagers, old men...
...anyone who will, at the very least, not fall over from the recoil.
Meanwhile the women and children too short to reach over the parapet are led to the inner keep sanctuary. There they'll have access to the sewers, should they need to abandon the city.

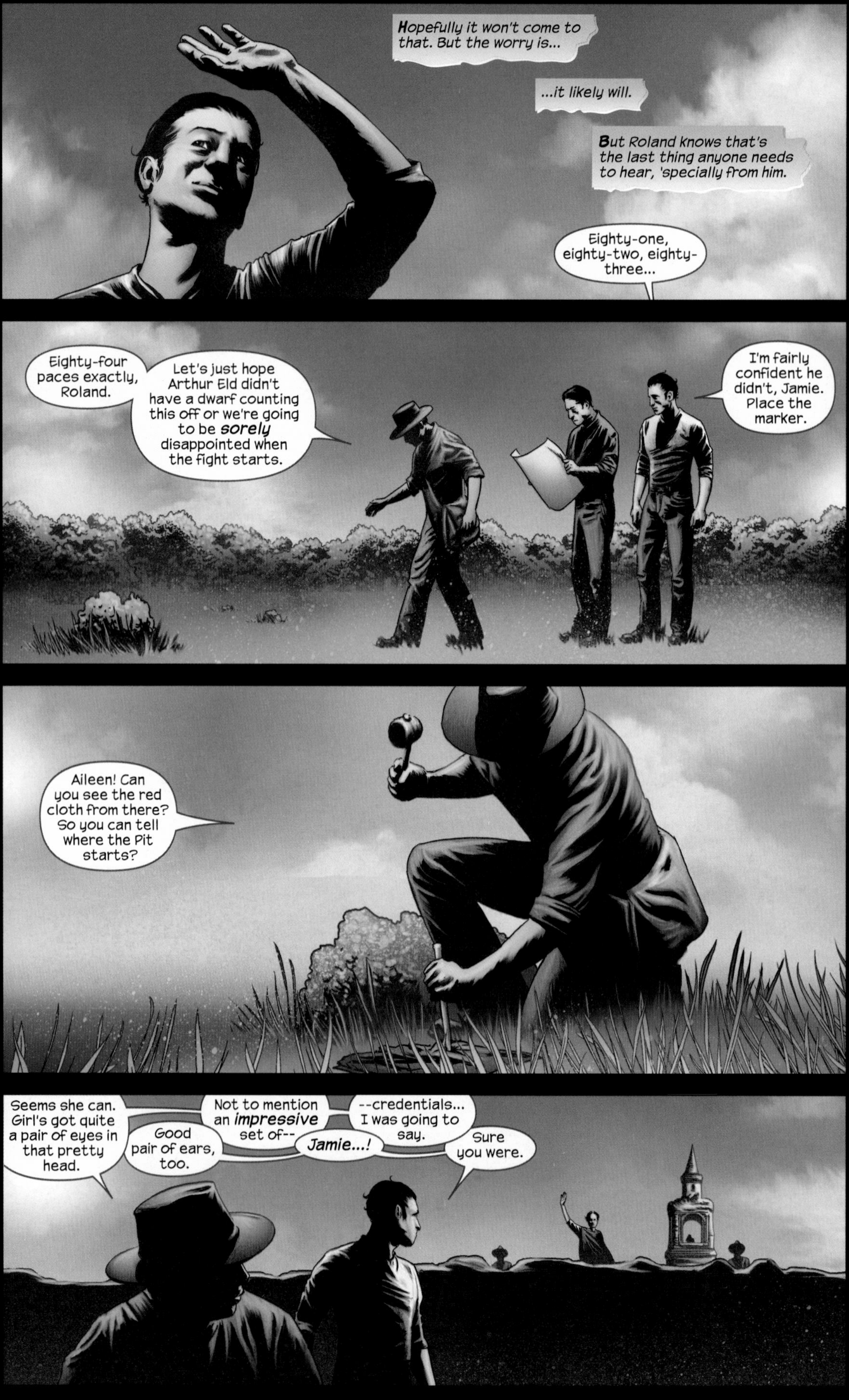
Hopefully it won't come to that. But the worry is...
...it likely will.
But Roland knows that's the last thing anyone needs to hear, 'specially from him.
Eighty-one, eighty-two, eighty-three...
Eighty-four paces exactly, Roland.
Let's just hope Arthur Eld didn't have a dwarf counting this off or we're going to be sorely disappointed when the fight starts.
I'm fairly confident he didn't, Jamie. Place the marker.
Aileen! Can you see the red cloth from there? So you can tell where the Pit starts?
Seems she can. Girl's got quite a pair of eyes in that pretty head.
Good pair of ears, too.
Not to mention an impressive set of--
Jamie...!
--credentials... I was going to say.
Sure you were.

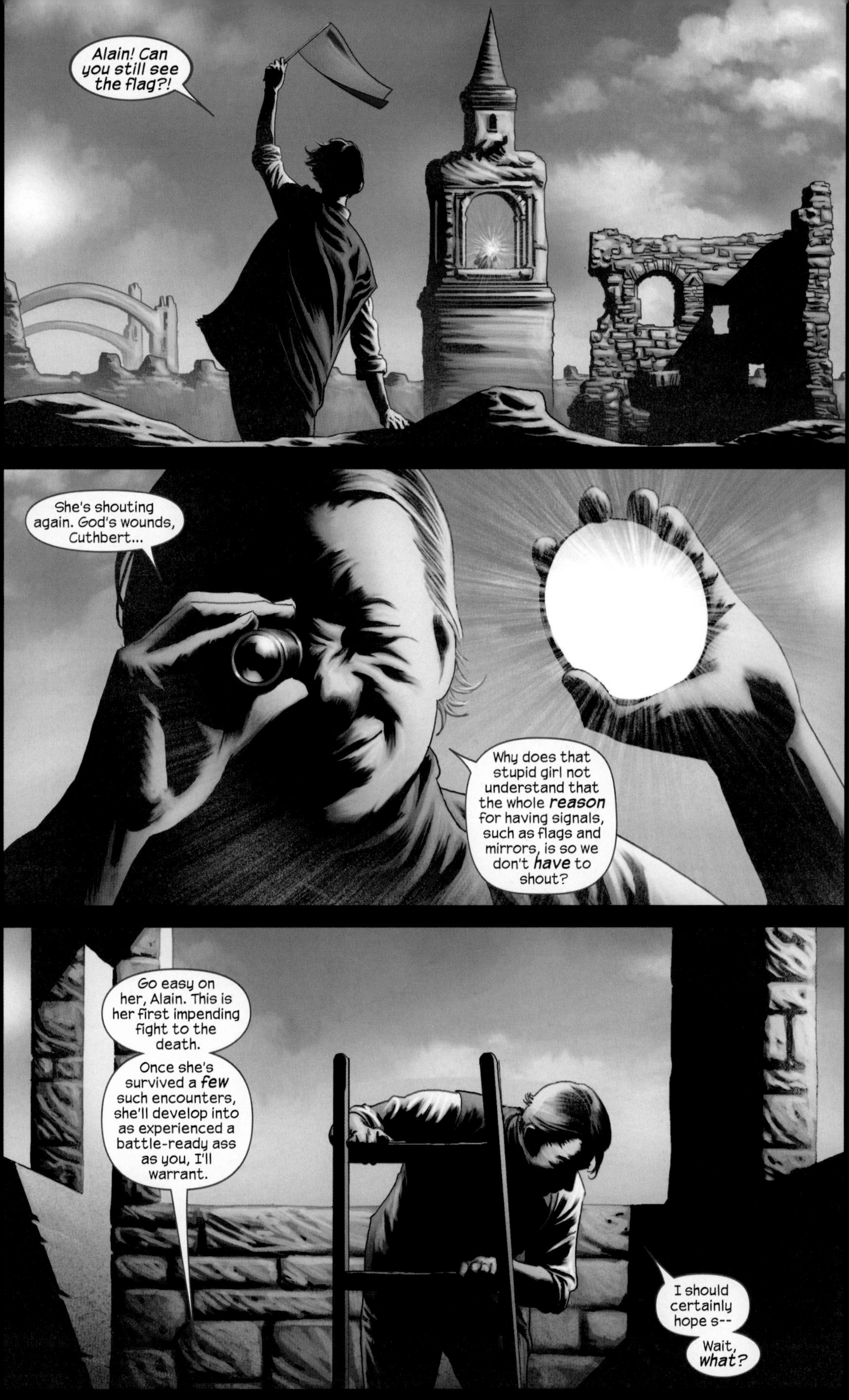
Alain! Can you still see the flag?!
She's shouting again. God's wounds, Cuthbert...
Why does that stupid girl not understand that the whole *reason* for having signals, such as flags and mirrors, is so we don't *have* to shout?
Go easy on her, Alain. This is her first impending fight to the death.
Once she's survived a *few* such encounters, she'll develop into as experienced a battle-ready ass as you, I'll warrant.
I should certainly hope s--
Wait, *what*?

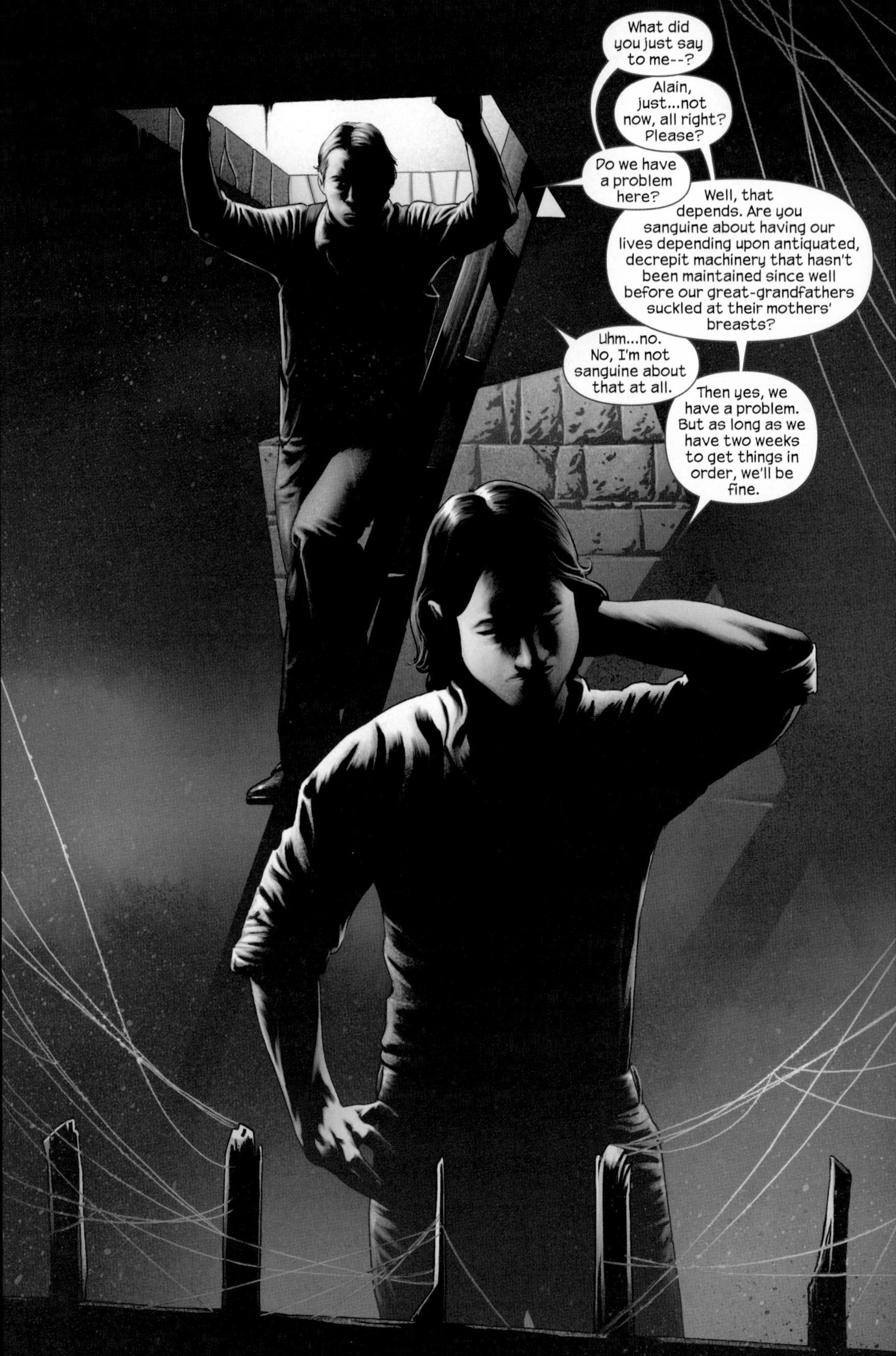
What did you just say to me--?
Alain, just...not now, all right? Please?
Do we have a problem here?
Well, that depends. Are you sanguine about having our lives depending upon antiquated, decrepit machinery that hasn't been maintained since well before our great-grandfathers suckled at their mothers' breasts?
Uhm...no. No, I'm not sanguine about that at all.
Then yes, we have a problem. But as long as we have two weeks to get things in order, we'll be fine.

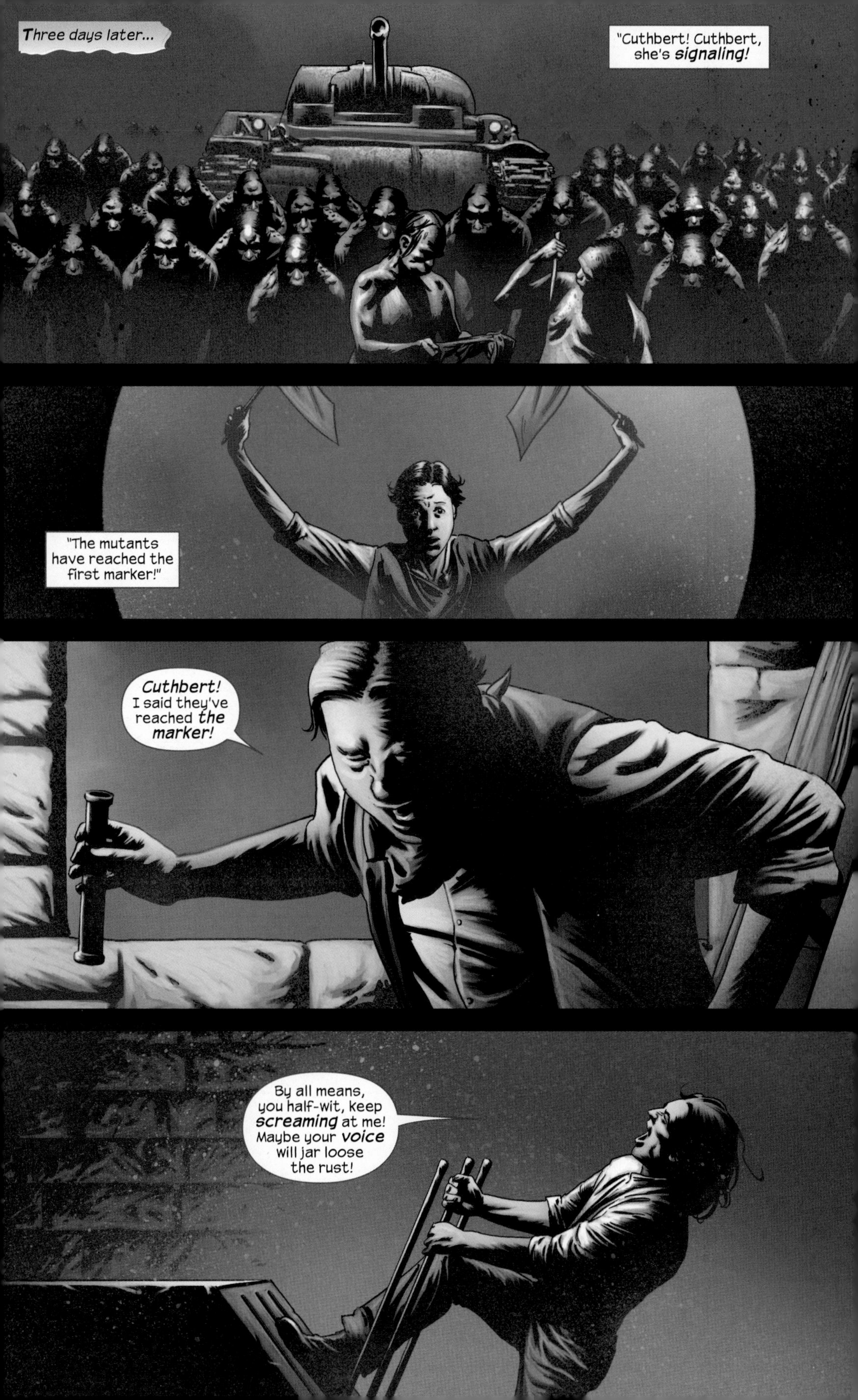
Three days later...
"Cuthbert! Cuthbert, she's signaling!
"The mutants have reached the first marker!"
Cuthbert! I said they've reached the marker!
By all means, you half-wit, keep screaming at me! Maybe your voice will jar loose the rust!

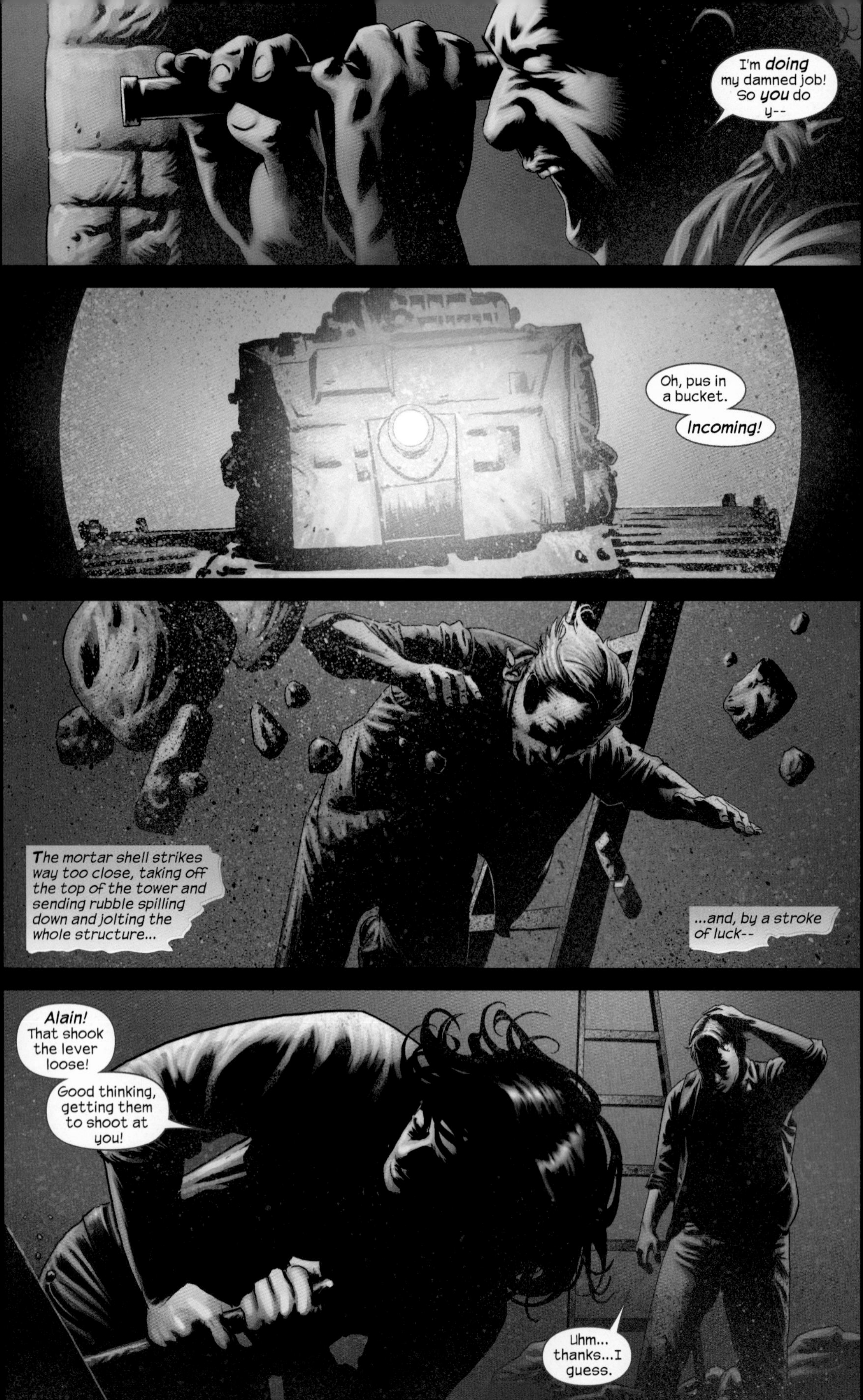
I'm doing my damned job! So you do y--
Oh, pus in a bucket.
Incoming!
The mortar shell strikes way too close, taking off the top of the tower and sending rubble spilling down and jolting the whole structure...
...and, by a stroke of luck--
Alain! That shook the lever loose!
Good thinking, getting them to shoot at you!
Uhm... thanks...I guess.

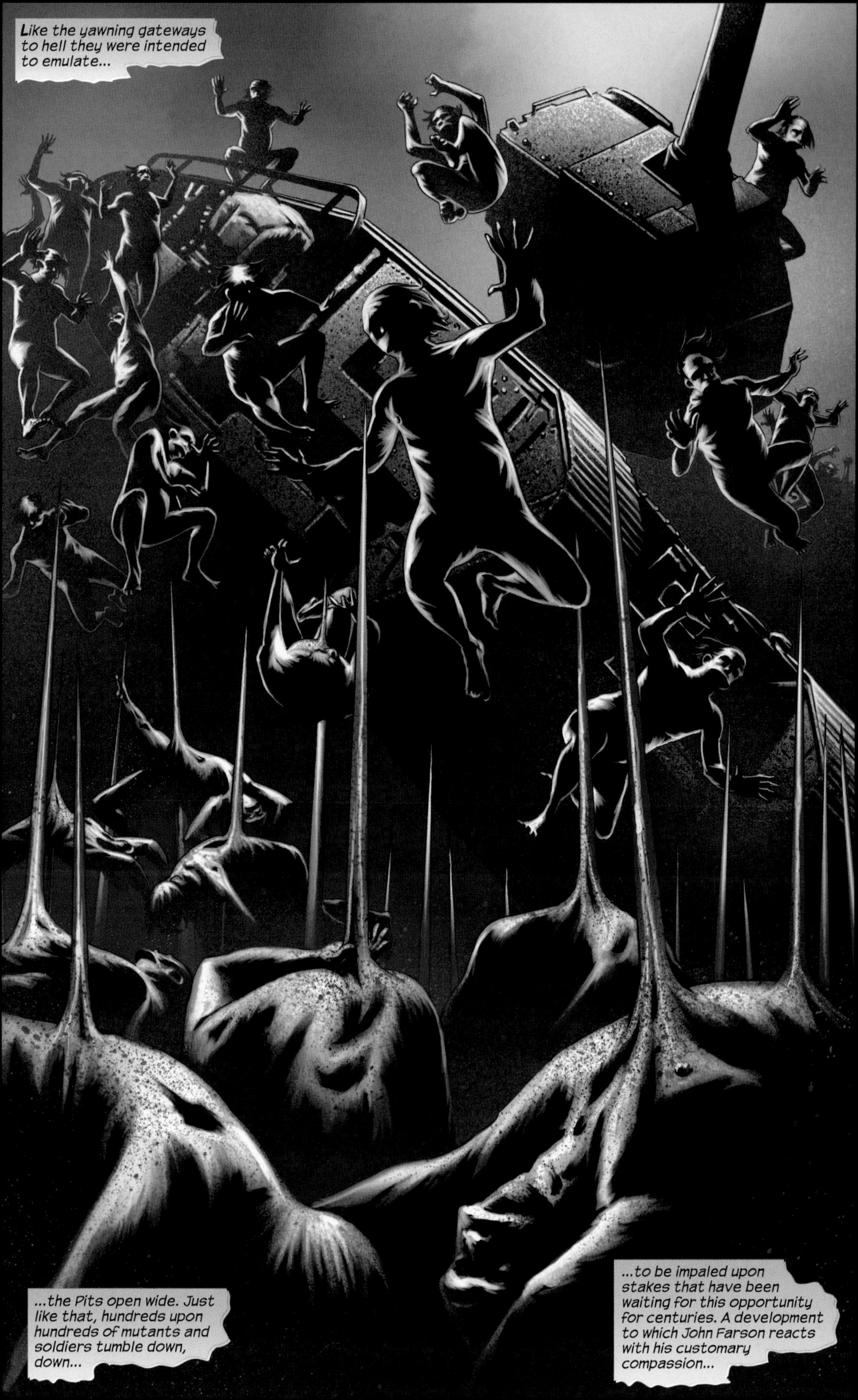
Like the yawning gateways to hell they were intended to emulate...
...the Pits open wide. Just like that, hundreds upon hundreds of mutants and soldiers tumble down, down...
...to be impaled upon stakes that have been waiting for this opportunity for centuries. A development to which John Farson reacts with his customary compassion...

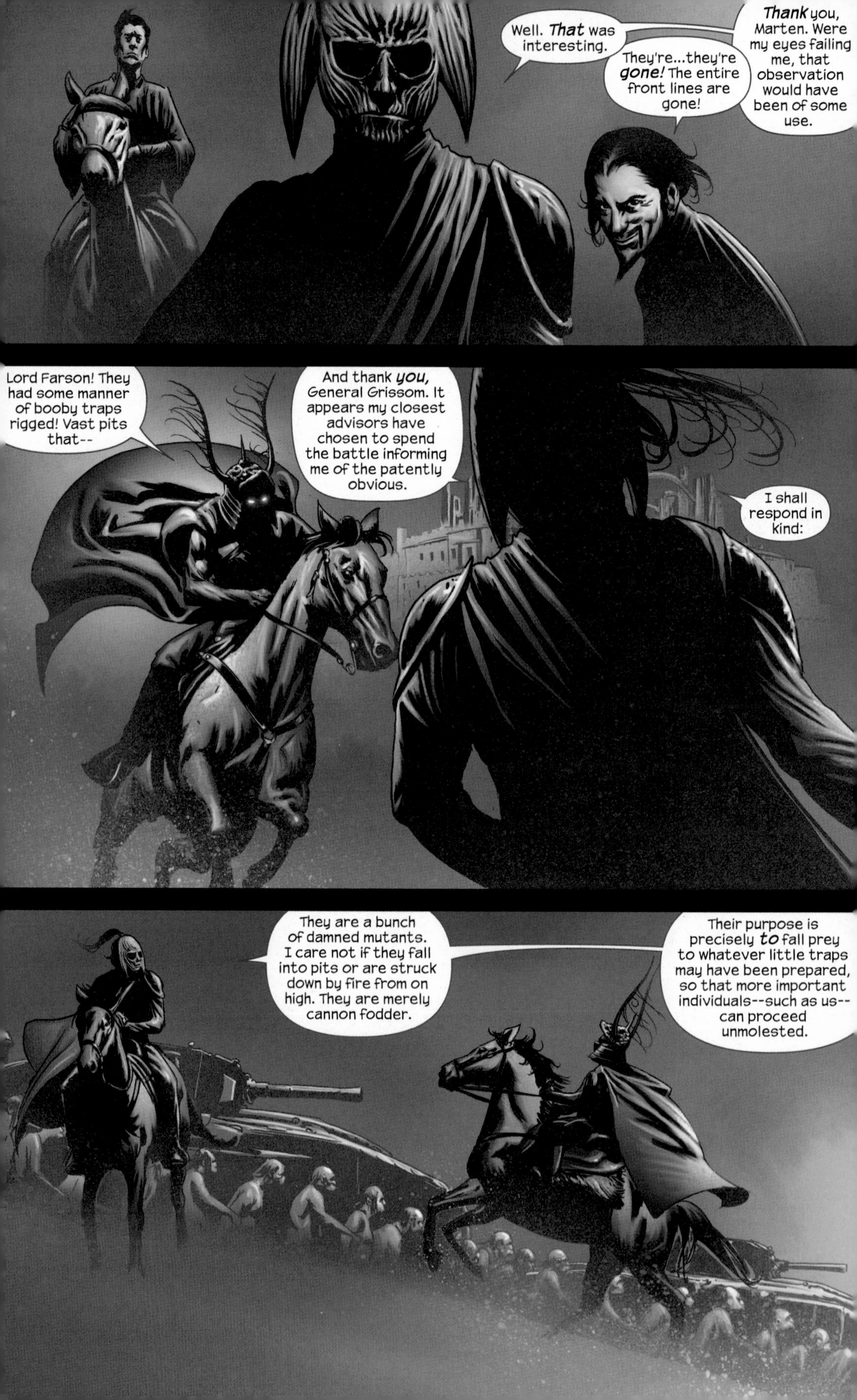
Well. *That* was interesting.
They're...they're *gone!* The entire front lines are gone!
Thank you, Marten. Were my eyes failing me, that observation would have been of some use.
Lord Farson! They had some manner of booby traps rigged! Vast pits that--
And thank *you,* General Grissom. It appears my closest advisors have chosen to spend the battle informing me of the patently obvious.
I shall respond in kind:
They are a bunch of damned mutants. I care not if they fall into pits or are struck down by fire from on high. They are merely cannon fodder.
Their purpose is precisely *to* fall prey to whatever little traps may have been prepared, so that more important individuals--such as us--can proceed unmolested.

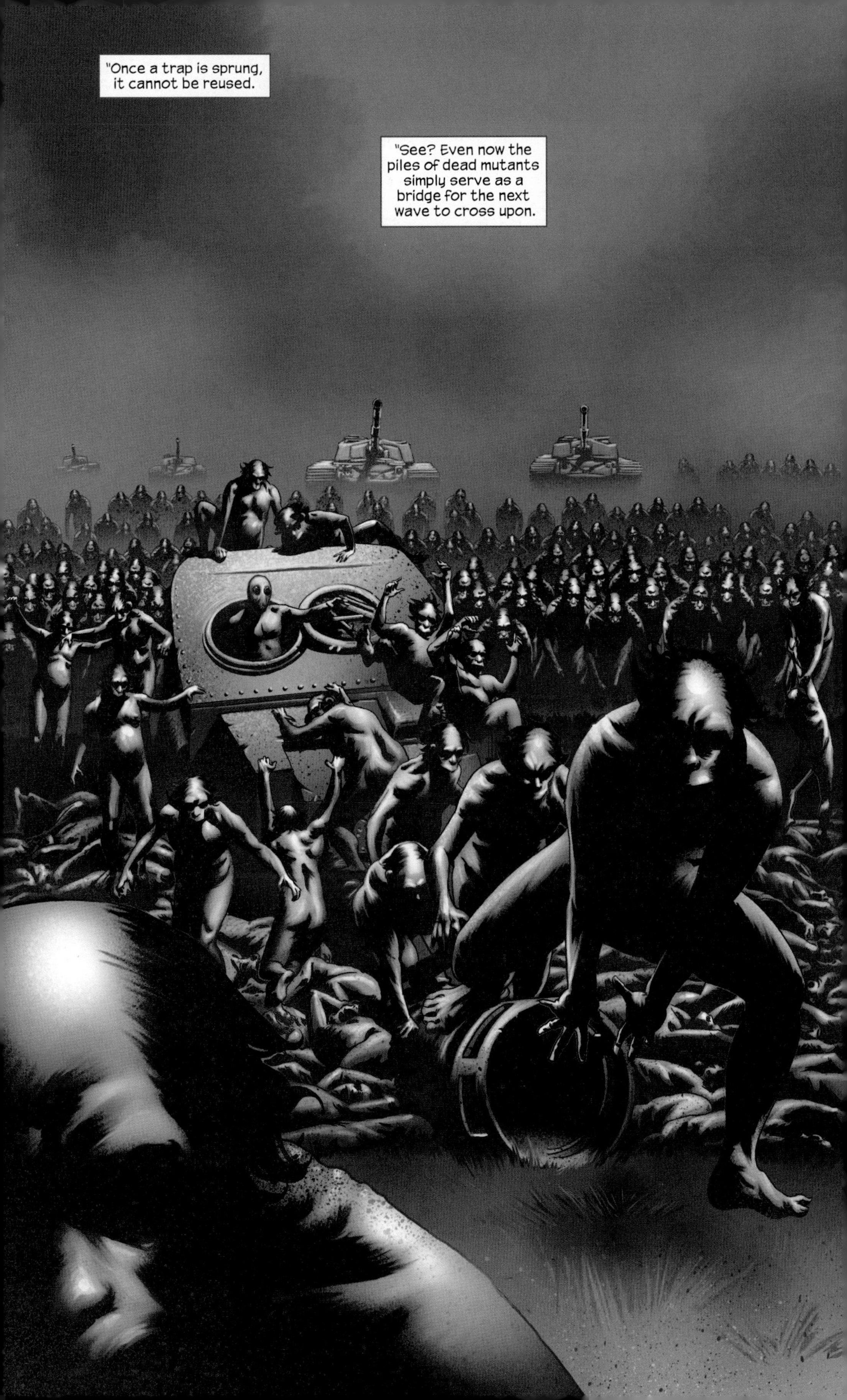

"Once a trap is sprung, it cannot be reused.
"See? Even now the piles of dead mutants simply serve as a bridge for the next wave to cross upon.

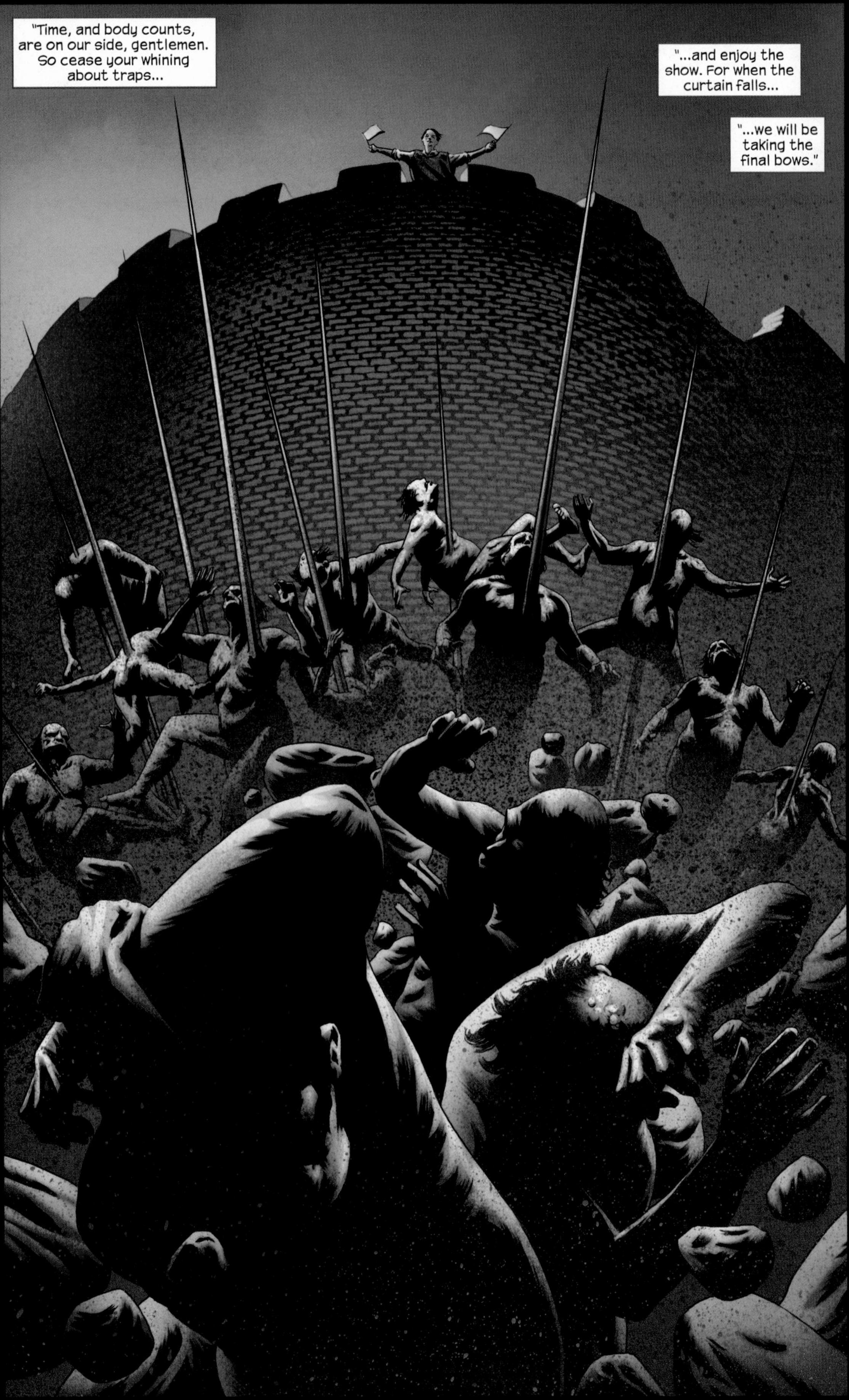
"Time, and body counts, are on our side, gentlemen. So cease your whining about traps...
"...and enjoy the show. For when the curtain falls...
"...we will be taking the final bows."

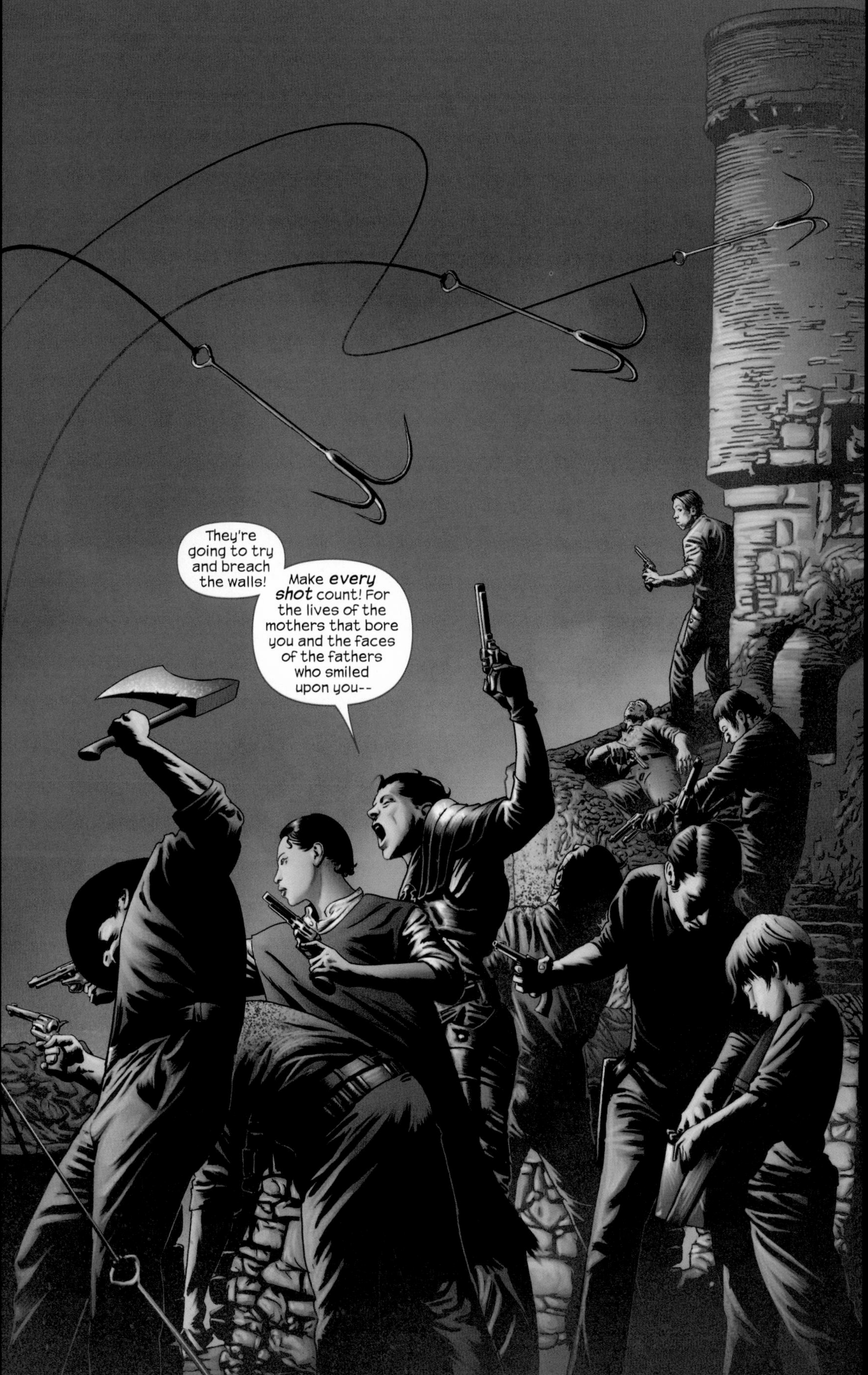
They're going to try and breach the walls!
Make *every shot* count! For the lives of the mothers that bore you and the faces of the fathers who smiled upon you--

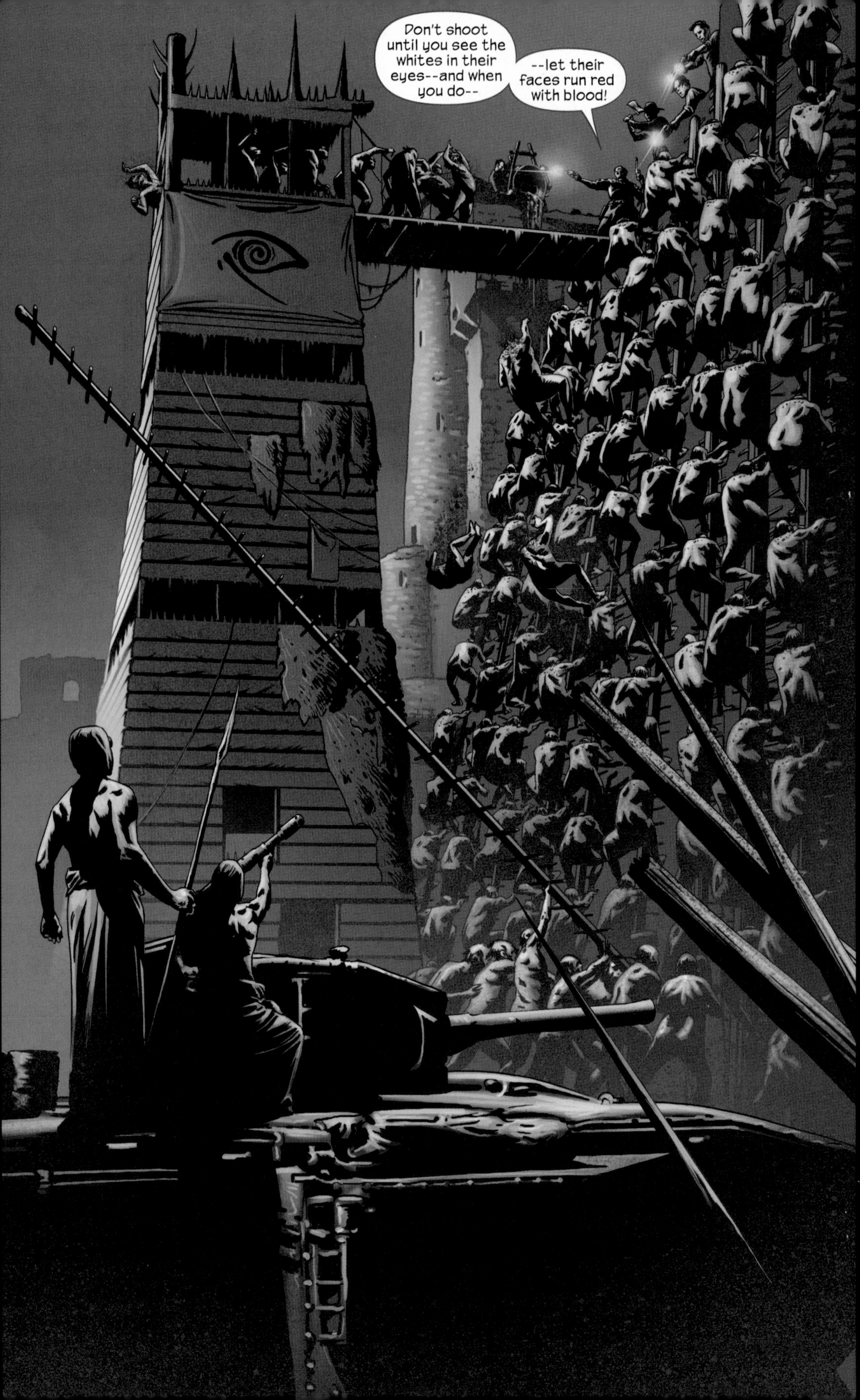
Don't shoot until you see the whites in their eyes--and when you do--
--let their faces run red with blood!

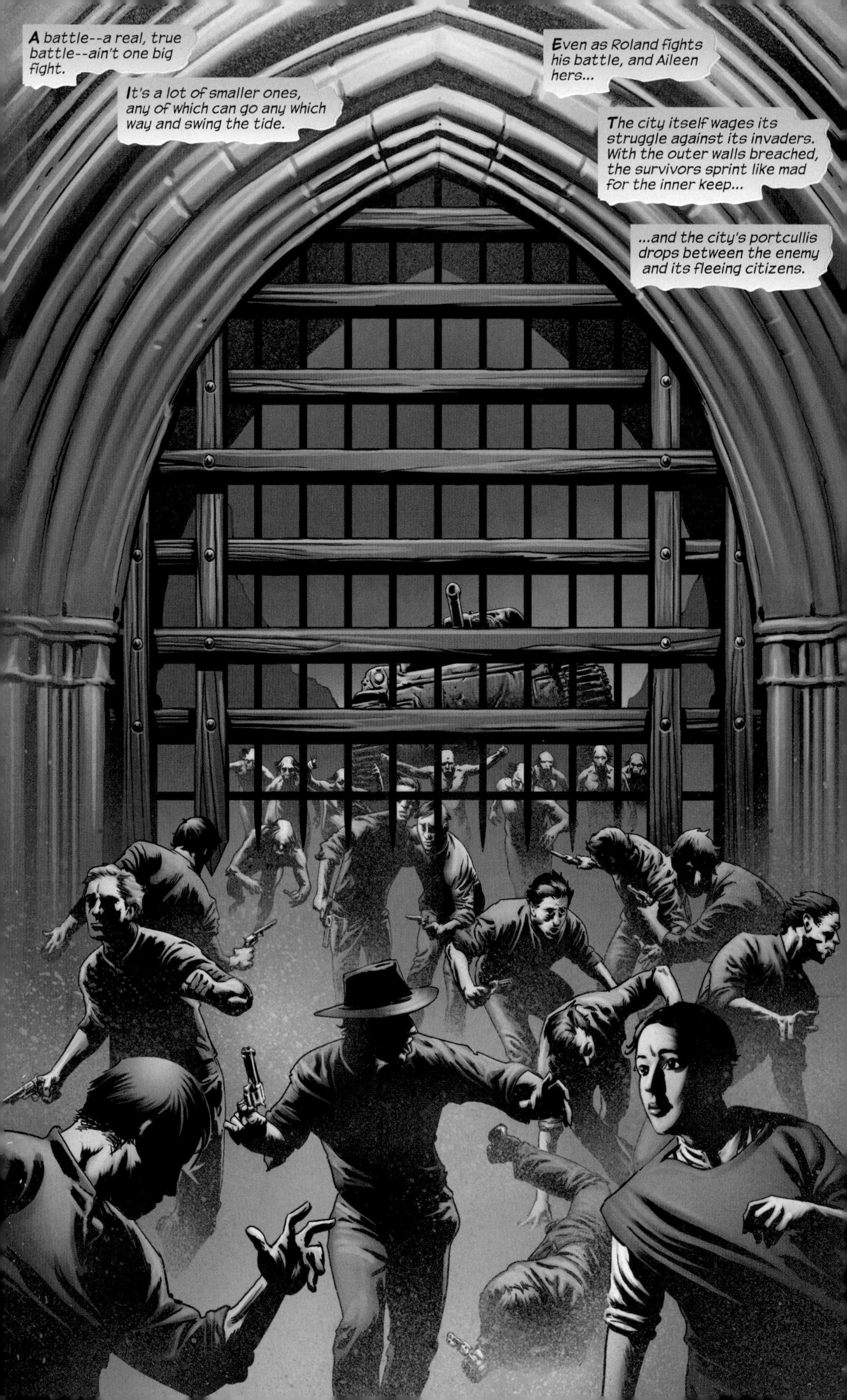
A battle--a real, true battle--ain't one big fight.
It's a lot of smaller ones, any of which can go any which way and swing the tide.
Even as Roland fights his battle, and Aileen hers...
The city itself wages its struggle against its invaders. With the outer walls breached, the survivors sprint like mad for the inner keep...
...and the city's portcullis drops between the enemy and its fleeing citizens.

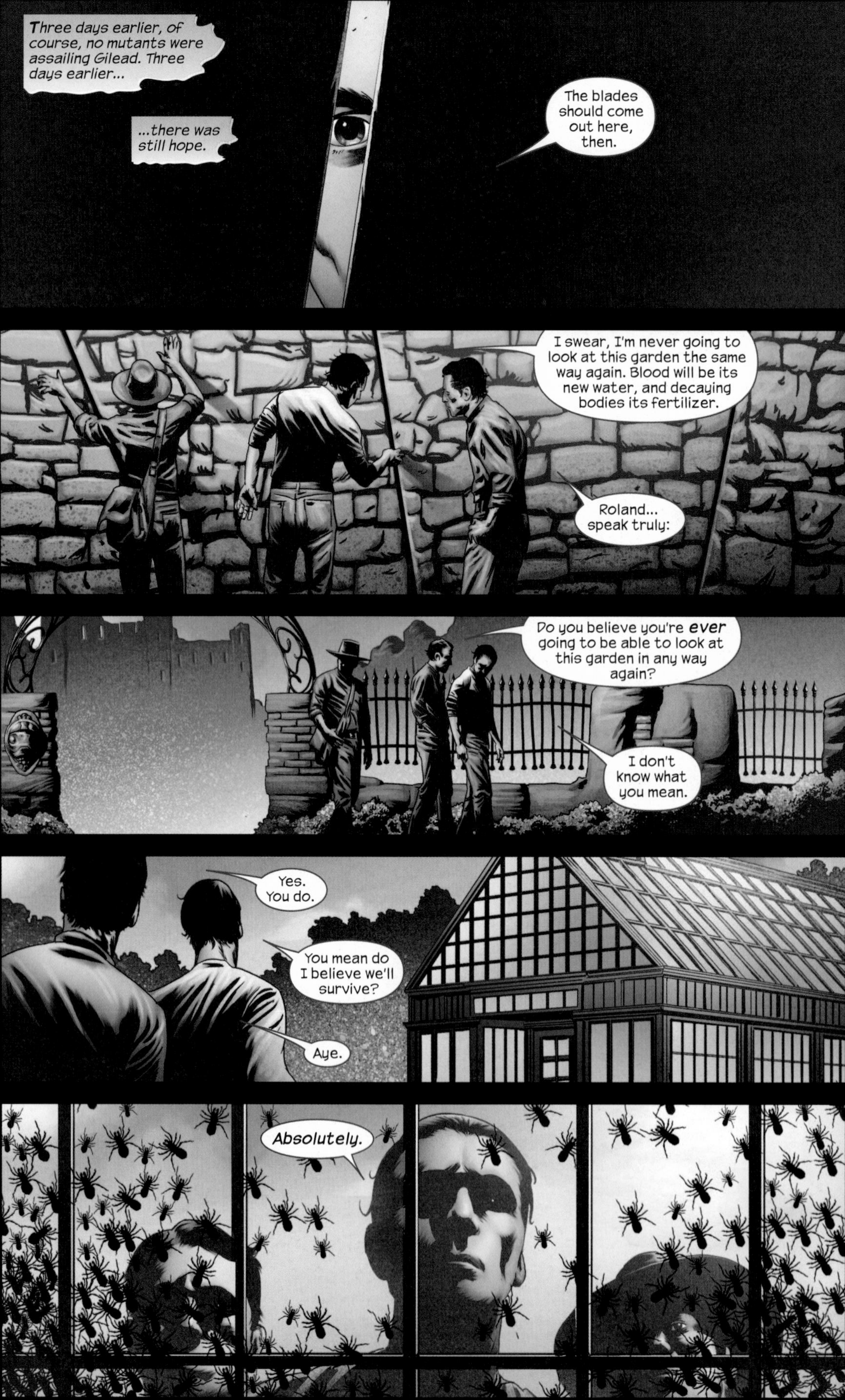
Three days earlier, of course, no mutants were assailing Gilead. Three days earlier...
...there was still hope.
The blades should come out here, then.
I swear, I'm never going to look at this garden the same way again. Blood will be its new water, and decaying bodies its fertilizer.
Roland... speak truly:
Do you believe you're *ever* going to be able to look at this garden in any way again?
I don't know what you mean.
Yes. You do.
You mean do I believe we'll survive?
Aye.
Absolutely.

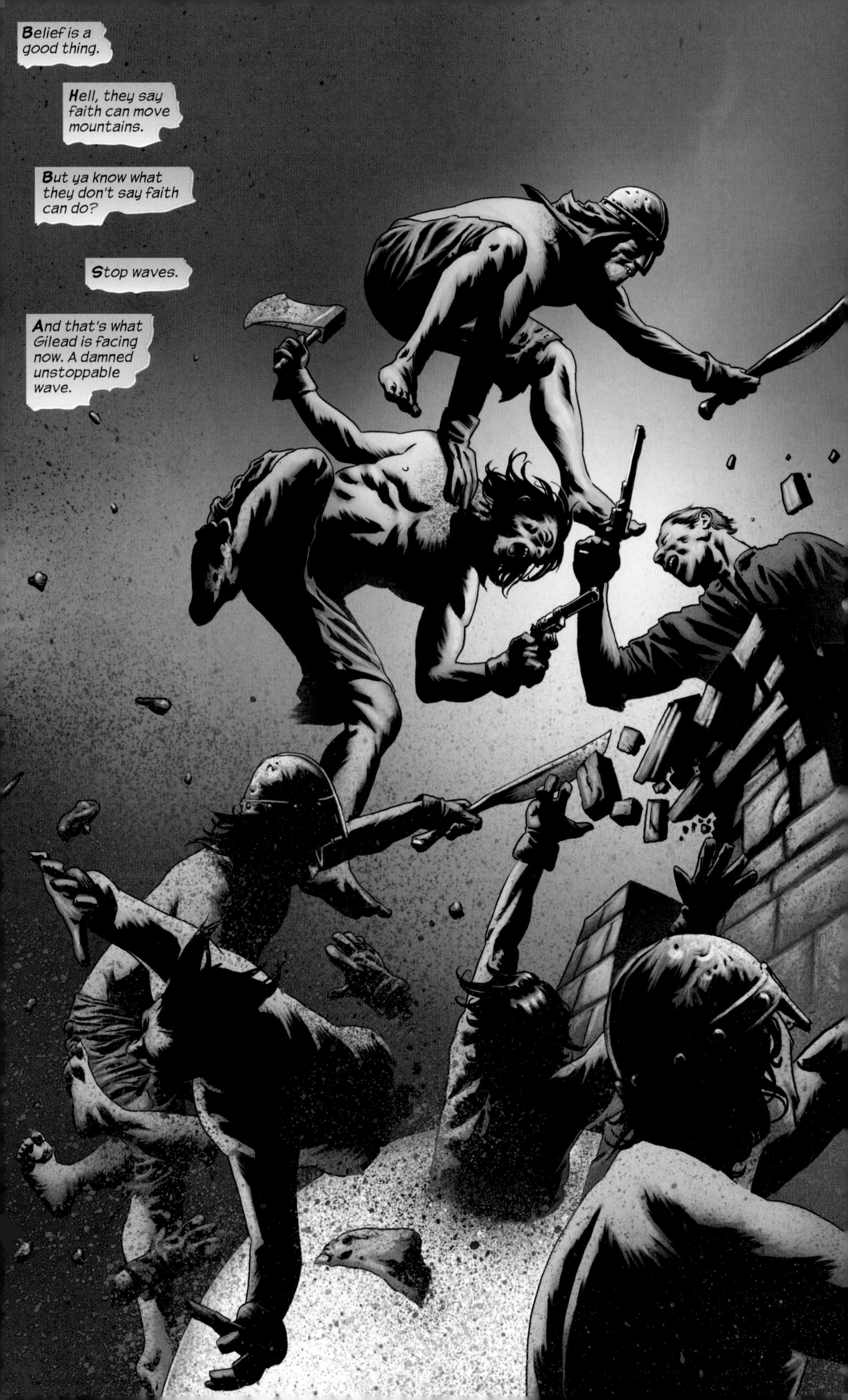
Belief is a good thing.
Hell, they say faith can move mountains.
But ya know what they don't say faith can do?
Stop waves.
And that's what Gilead is facing now. A damned unstoppable wave.

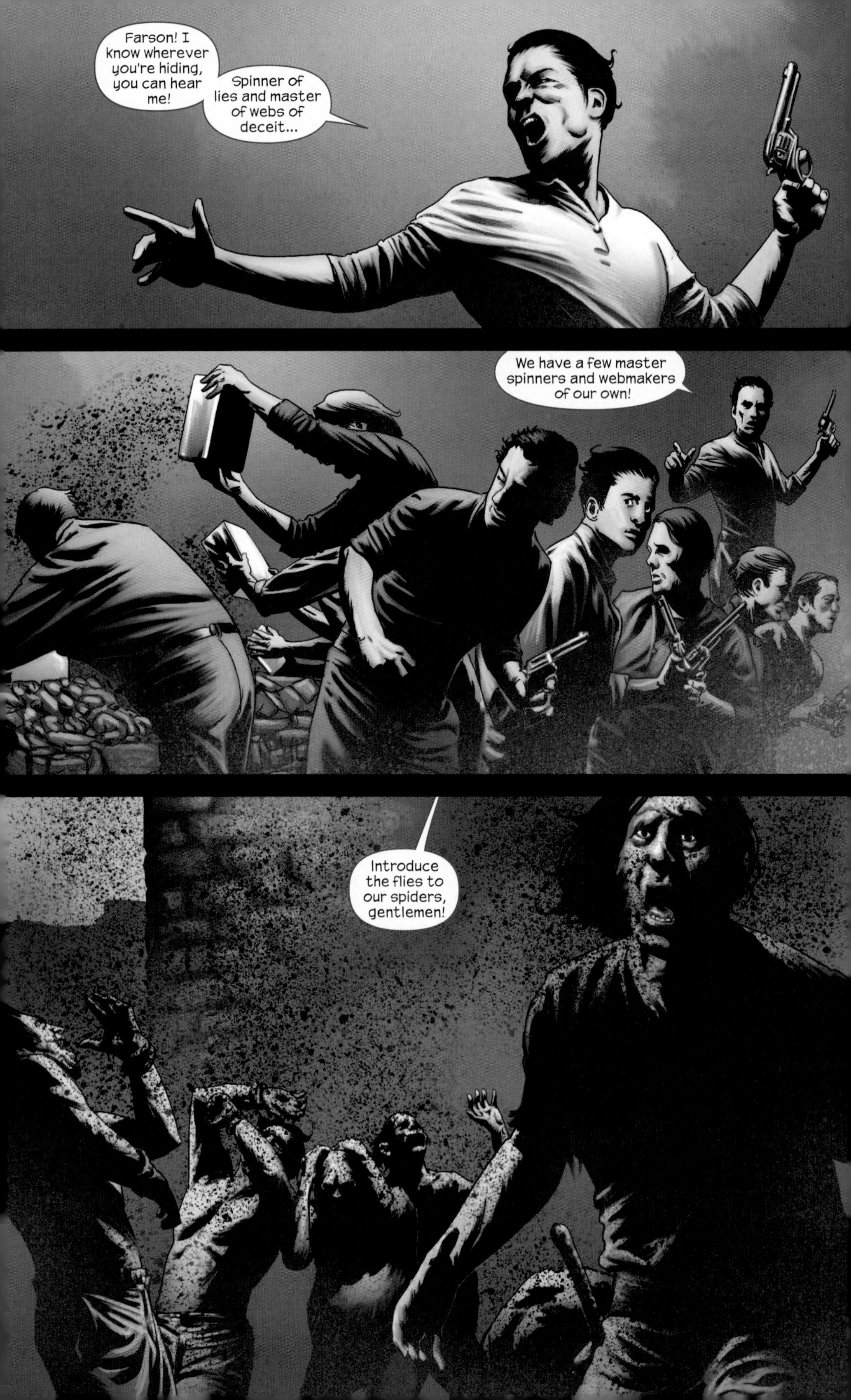

Farson! I know wherever you're hiding, you can hear me!
Spinner of lies and master of webs of deceit...
We have a few master spinners and webmakers of our own!
Introduce the flies to our spiders, gentlemen!

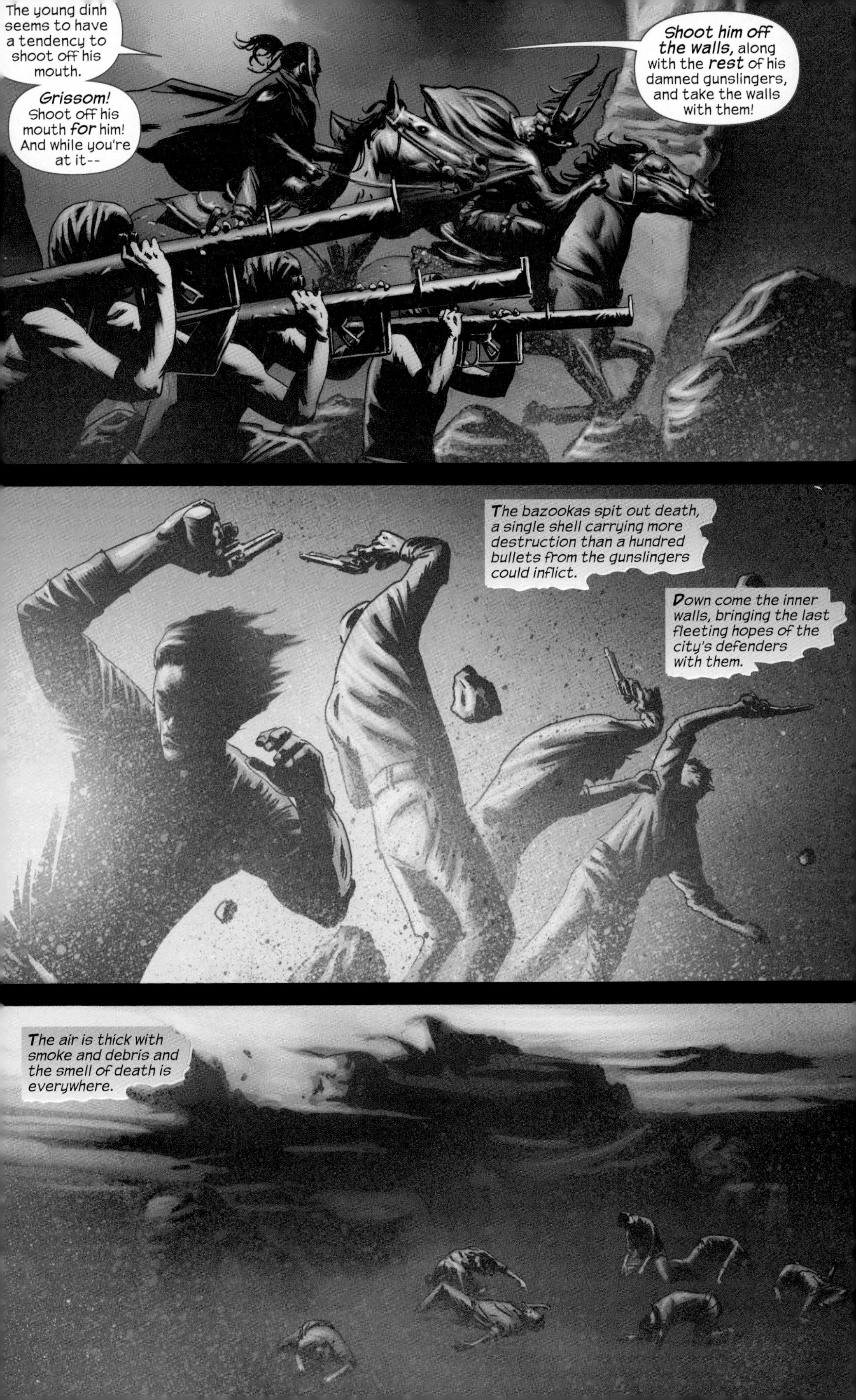

The young dinh seems to have a tendency to shoot off his mouth.
Grissom! Shoot off his mouth for him! And while you're at it--
Shoot him off the walls, along with the rest of his damned gunslingers, and take the walls with them!
The bazookas spit out death, a single shell carrying more destruction than a hundred bullets from the gunslingers could inflict.
Down come the inner walls, bringing the last fleeting hopes of the city's defenders with them.
The air is thick with smoke and debris and the smell of death is everywhere.

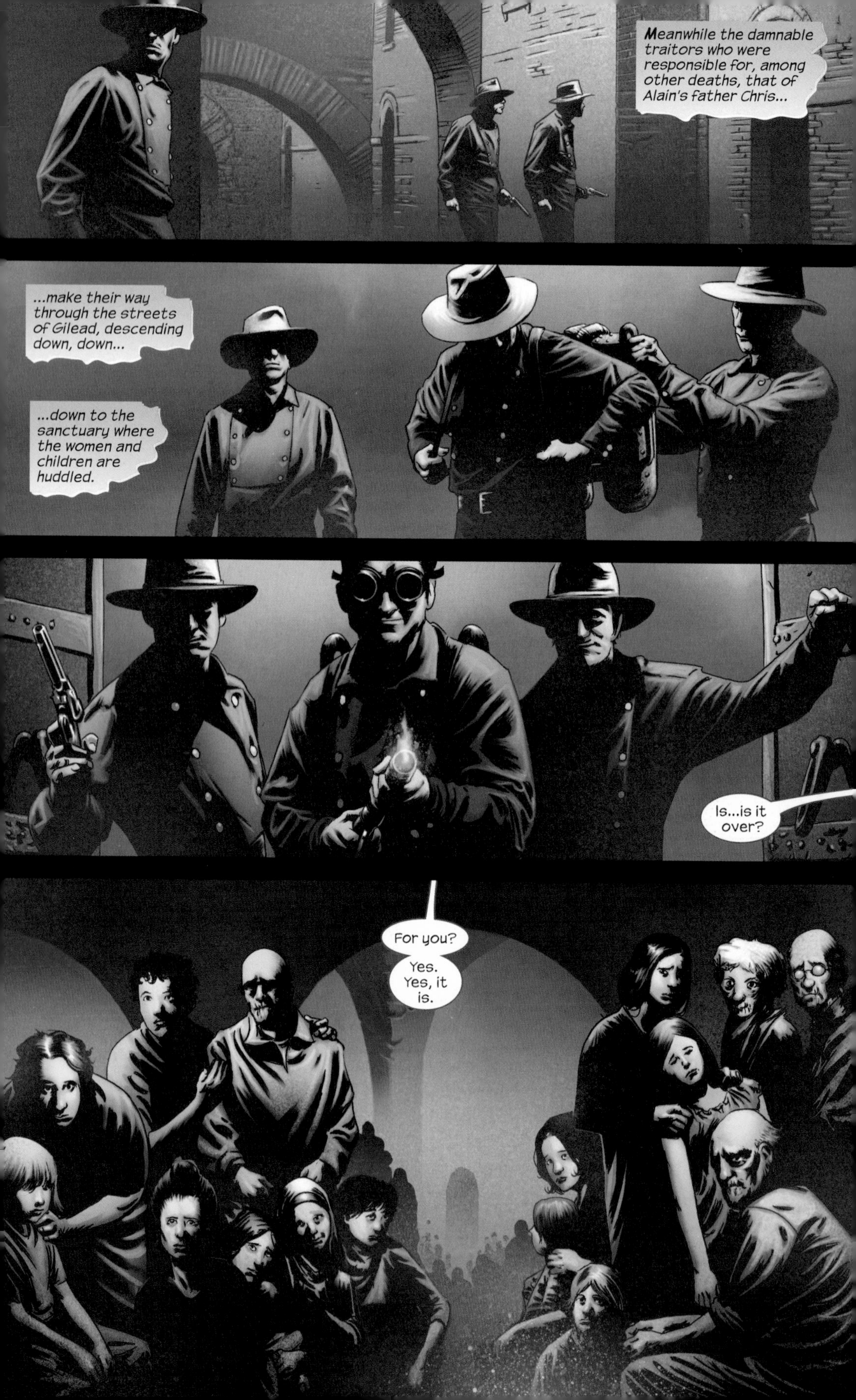
Meanwhile the damnable traitors who were responsible for, among other deaths, that of Alain's father Chris...
...make their way through the streets of Gilead, descending down, down...
...down to the sanctuary where the women and children are huddled.
Is...is it over?
For you?
Yes. Yes, it is.

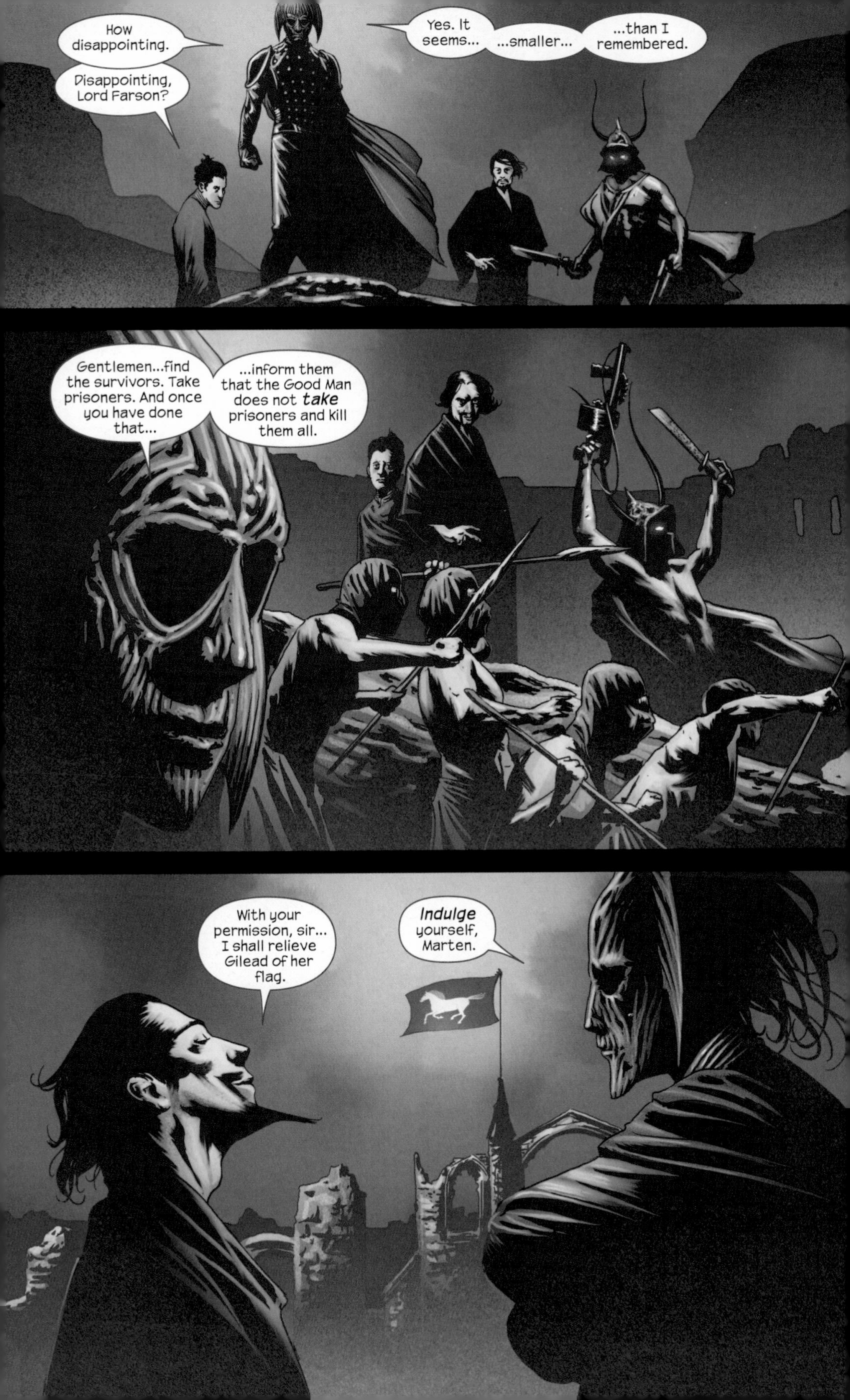
How disappointing.
Disappointing, Lord Farson?
Yes. It seems...
...smaller...
...than I remembered.
Gentlemen...find the survivors. Take prisoners. And once you have done that...
...inform them that the Good Man does not *take* prisoners and kill them all.
With your permission, sir... I shall relieve Gilead of her flag.
Indulge yourself, Marten.

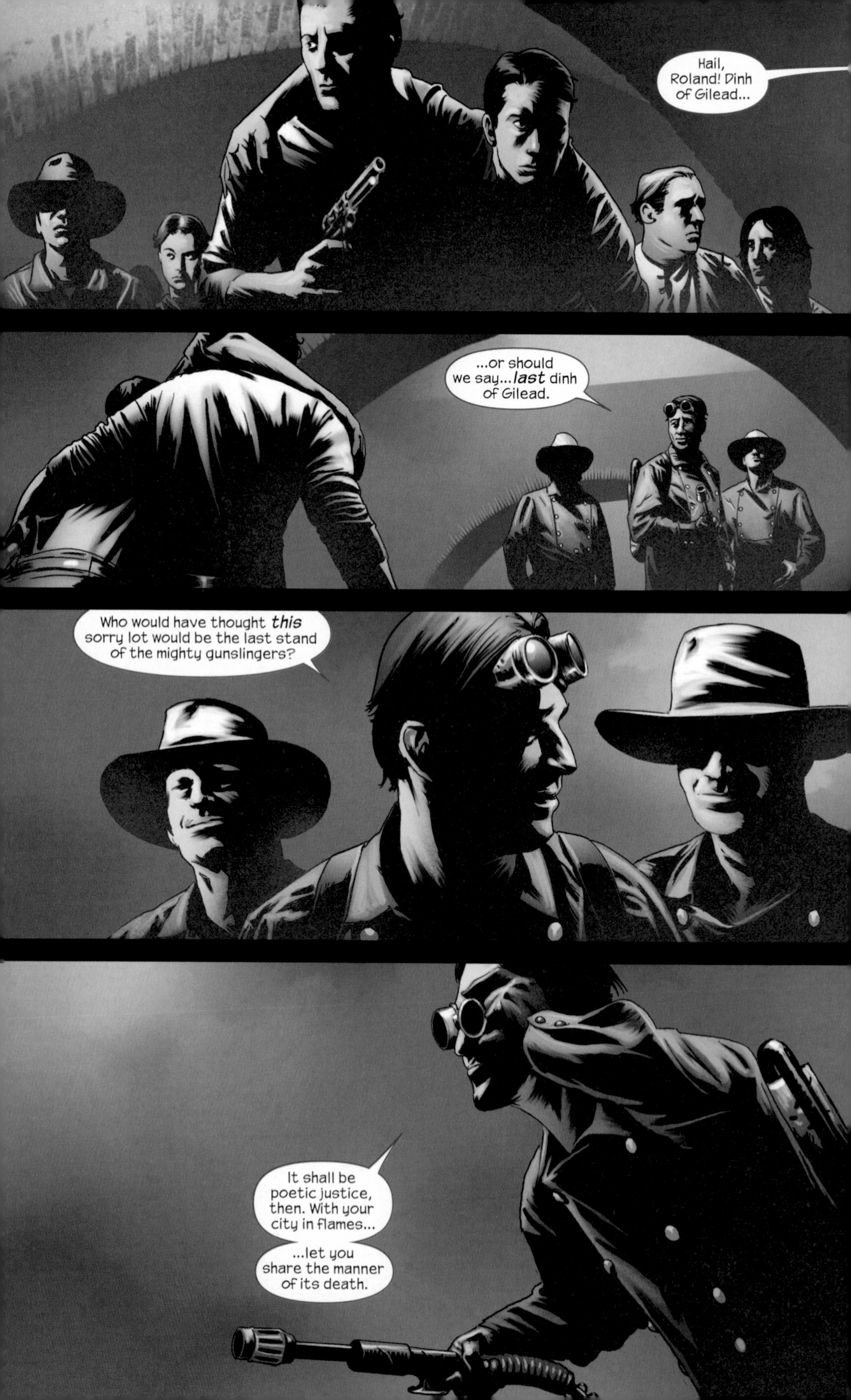
Hail, Roland! Dinh of Gilead...
...or should we say...last dinh of Gilead.
Who would have thought this sorry lot would be the last stand of the mighty gunslingers?
It shall be poetic justice, then. With your city in flames...
...let you share the manner of its death.

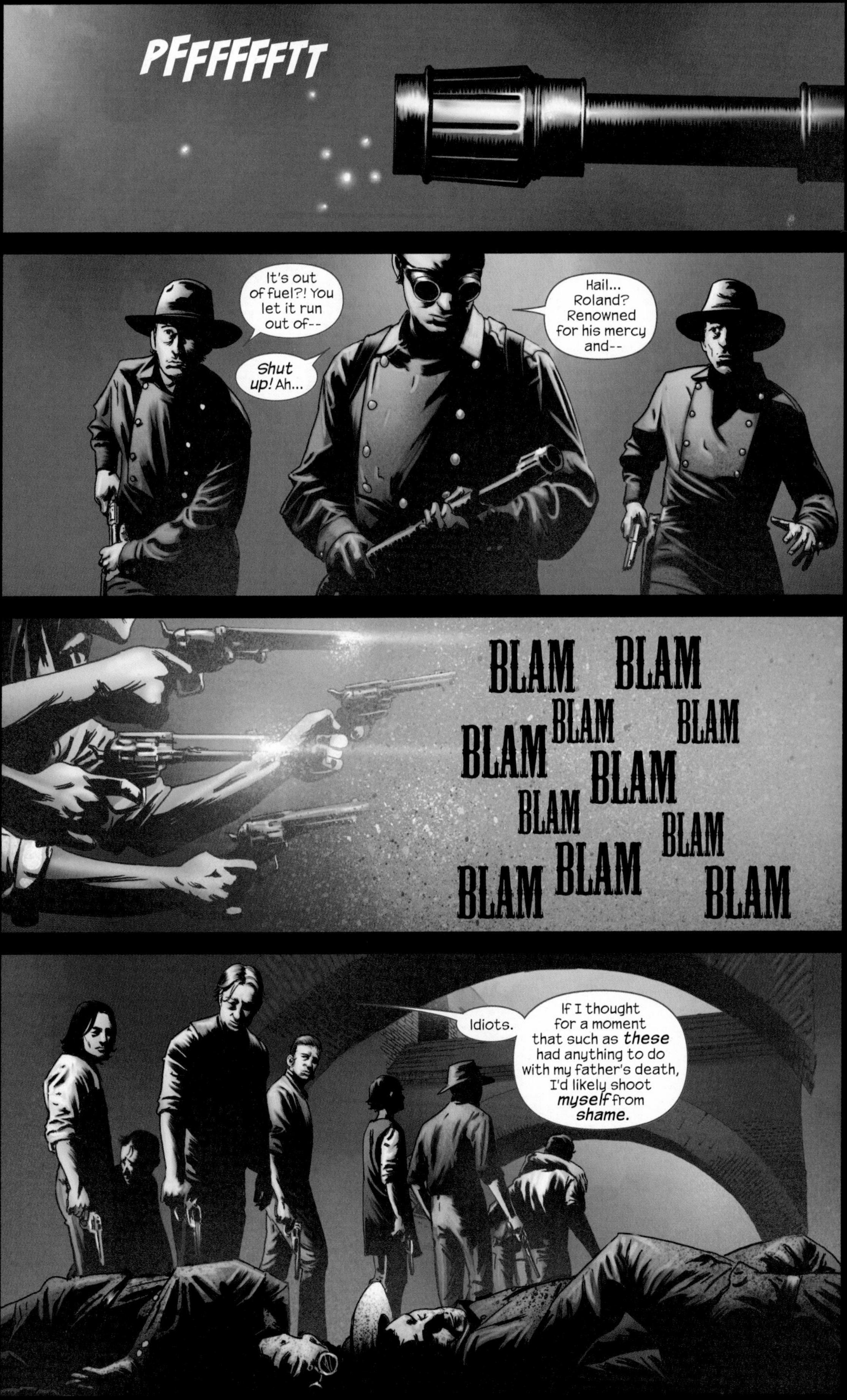
PFFFFFFTT
It's out of fuel!?! You let it run out of--
Shut up! Ah...
Hail... Roland? Renowned for his mercy and--
BLAM BLAM BLAM BLAM BLAM BLAM BLAM BLAM BLAM BLAM BLAM BLAM
Idiots.
If I thought for a moment that such as *these* had anything to do with my father's death, I'd likely shoot *myself* from *shame.*

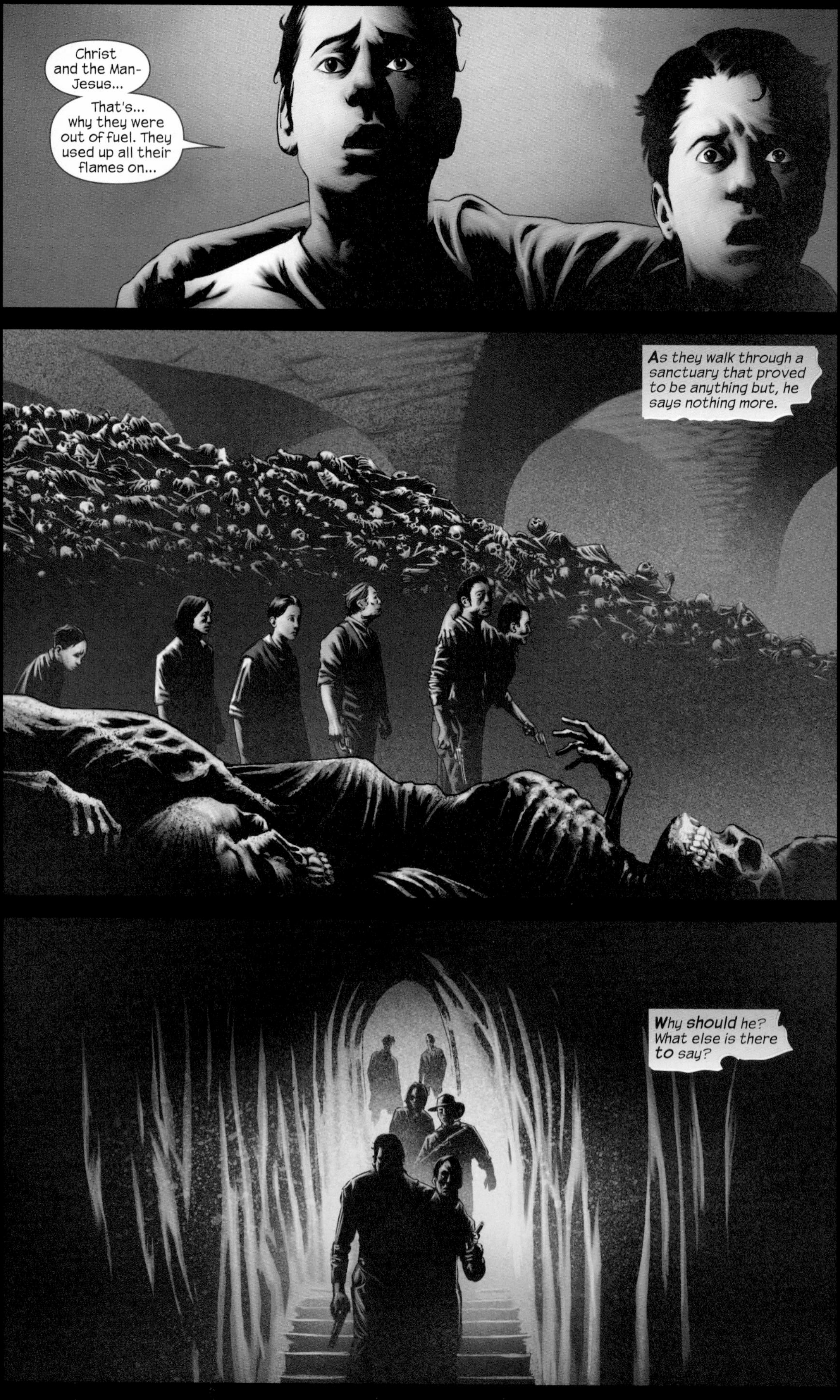
Christ and the Man-Jesus...
That's... why they were out of fuel. They used up all their flames on...
As they walk through a sanctuary that proved to be anything but, he says nothing more.
Why should he? What else is there to say?

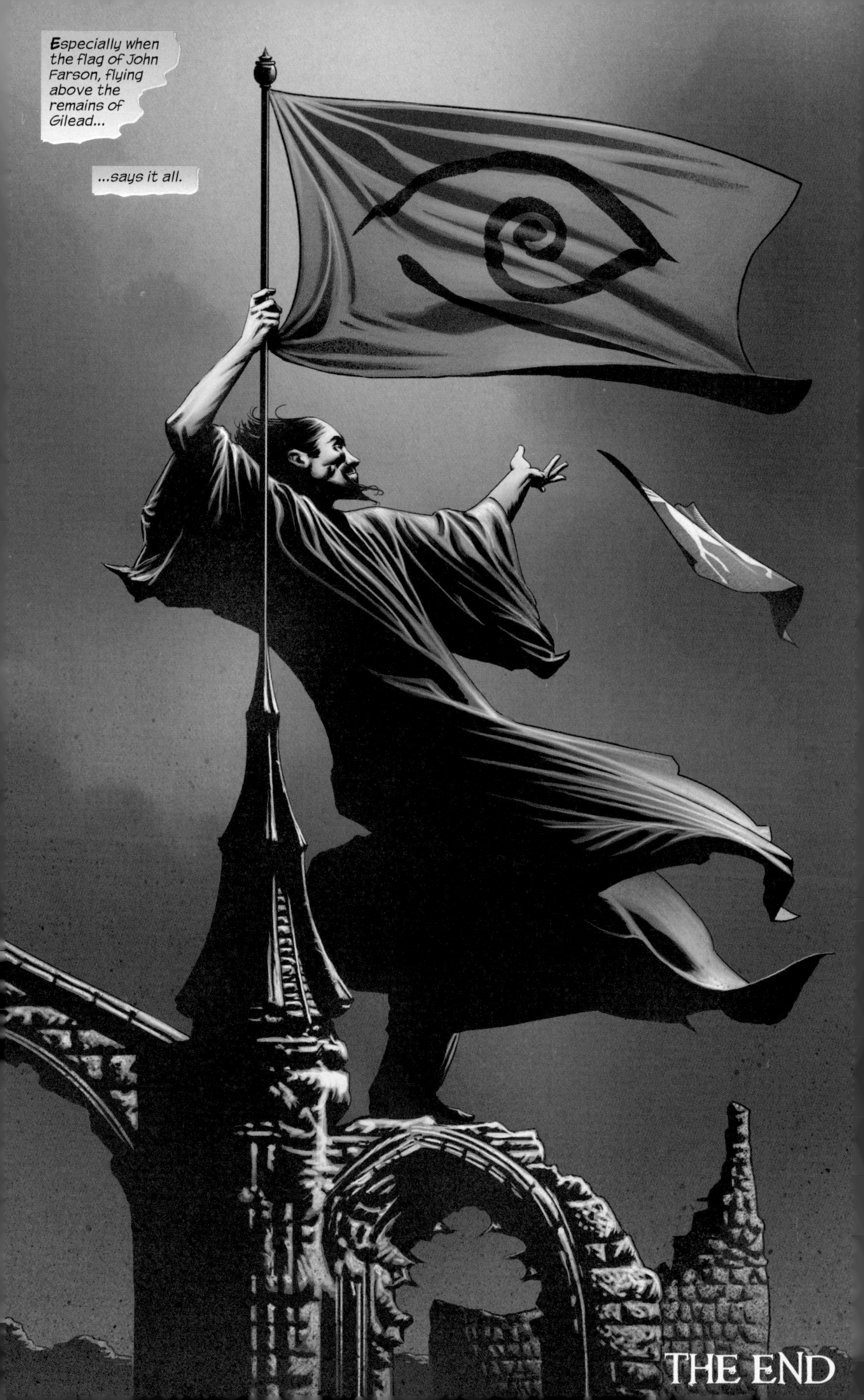
Especially when the flag of John Farson, flying above the remains of Gilead...
...says it all.
THE END

The story continues in...

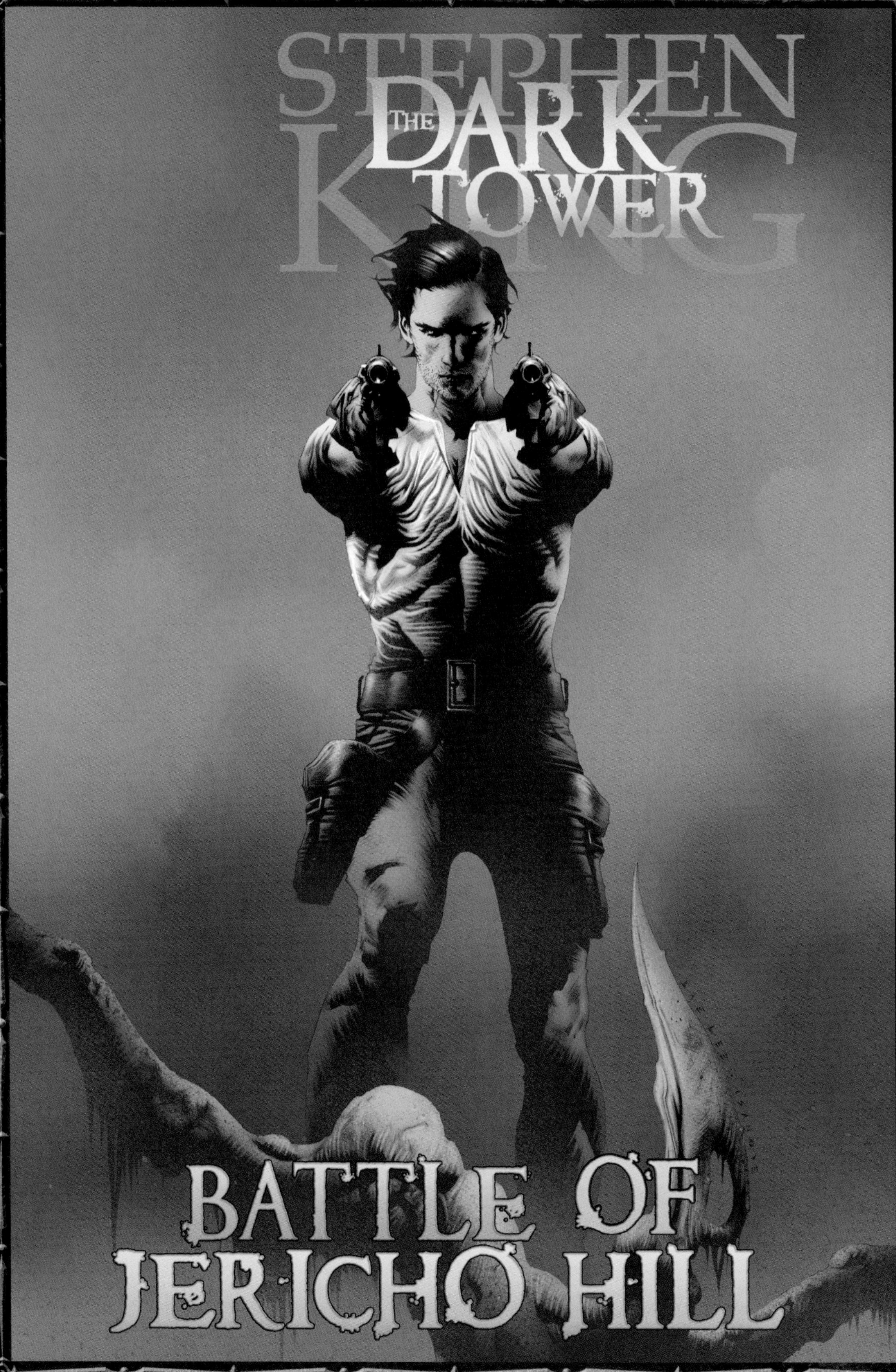
STEPHEN KING
THE DARK TOWER
BATTLE OF JERICHO HILL

THE DARK TOWER READING CHRONOLOGY

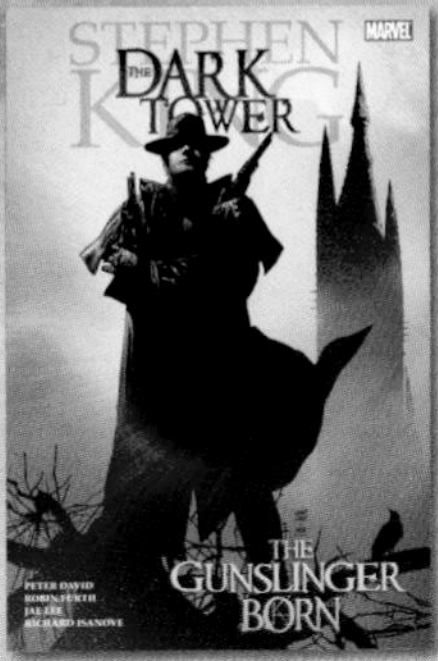
STEPHEN KING
THE DARK TOWER
MARVEL
THE GUNSLINGER BORN

BOOK 1

THE DARK TOWER
THE GUNSLINGER BORN

ISBN: 978-0-7851-2144-2

A man's quest begins with a boy's test.

The world of Roland Deschain — the world of the Dark Tower — has been a thirty-year obsession for Stephen King. And now, King carries his masterwork of fantasy to Marvel, bringing stunning new textures to his epic story!

The Gunslinger Born seamlessly integrates the wonder of Mid-World and the story of its hard-bitten cast of characters into the finest Marvel Comics storytelling tradition.

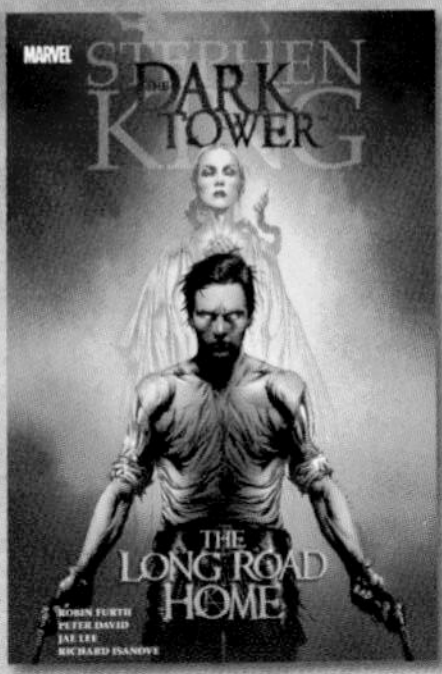
MARVEL
STEPHEN KING
THE DARK TOWER
THE LONG ROAD HOME

BOOK 2

THE DARK TOWER
THE LONG ROAD HOME

ISBN: 978-0-7851-2709-3

The gunslinger is born into a harsh world of mystery and violence.

Susan Delgado is dead. Clay Reynolds and the vestiges of the Big Coffin Hunters are in pursuit. The ka-tet fragments as evil abounds. It will be a long road home.

With Roland seemingly lost inside the haunted world of Maerlyn's Grapefruit, and the dark forces therein tugging at his soul, it will take all the courage of his ka-tet to get him out of Hambry and back home. But as the Dogan stirs, portending an evil of which Roland and his ka-tet have no ken, it may very well be that the gunslinger born walks a long road home to death.

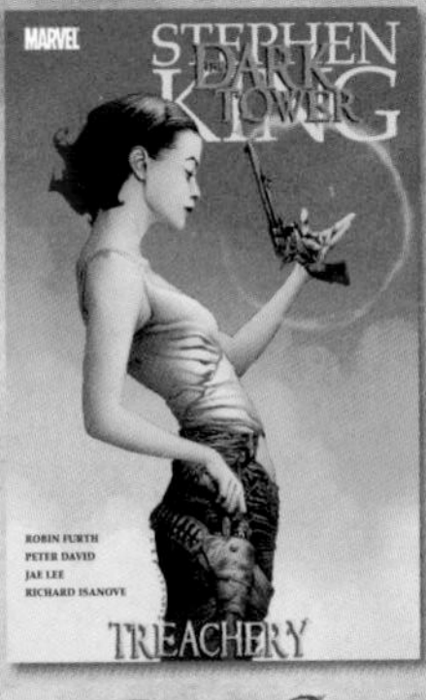
MARVEL
STEPHEN KING
DARK TOWER
TREACHERY

BOOK 3

THE DARK TOWER
TREACHERY

ISBN: 978-0-7851-3574-6

From the creative team that brought Roland's early adventures to life in *Dark Tower: The Gunslinger Born* and *Dark Tower: The Long Road Home* comes the third chapter of this dark saga of friendship, betrayal and a cosmic quest as conceived by master storyteller Stephen King.

The Sorcerer Cover by Richard Isanove

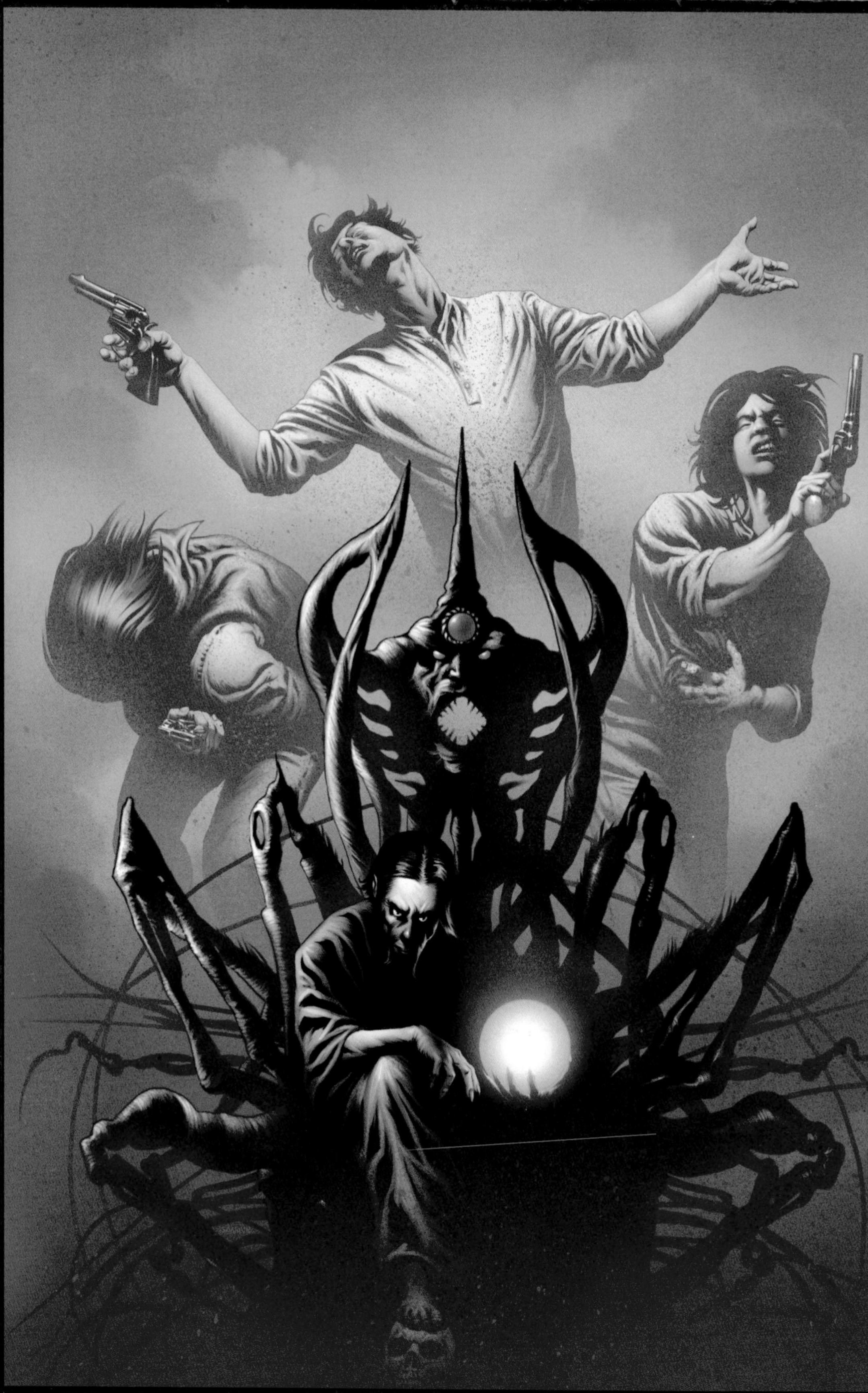

Dark Tower: Fall of Gilead #1 Cover by Jae Lee & Richard Isanove

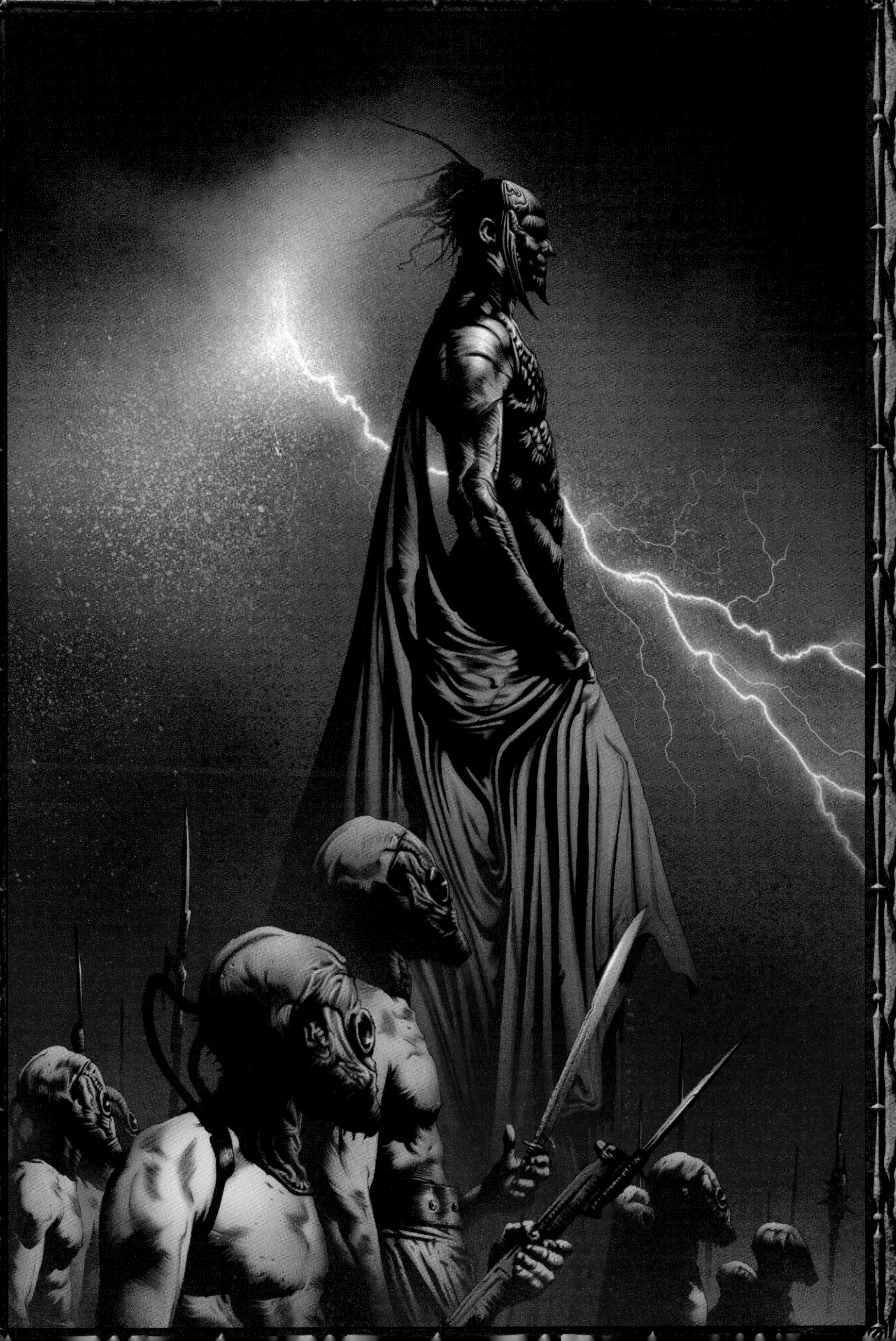

Dark Tower: Fall of Gilead #1 Variant Cover by Adi Granov

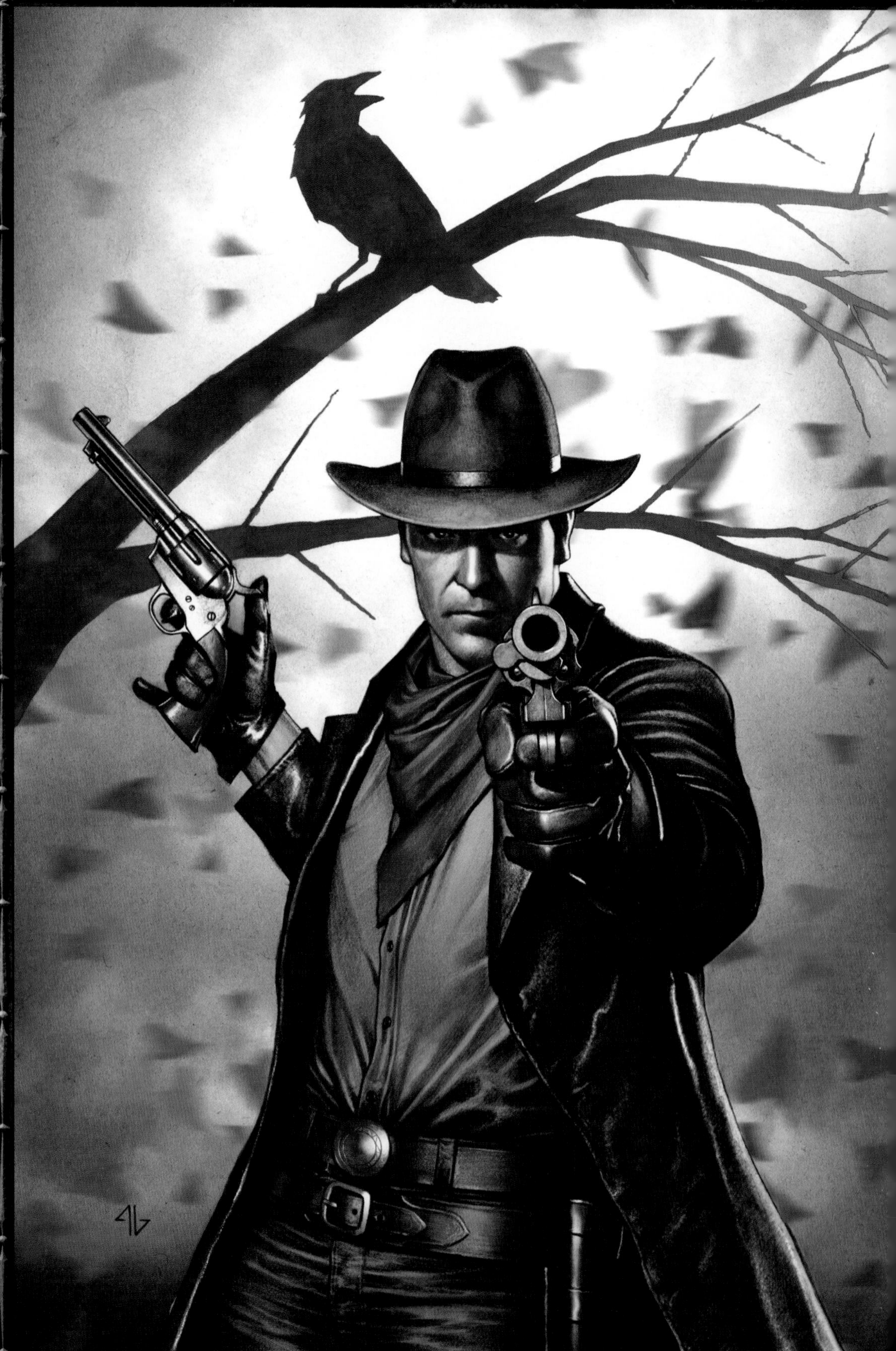

Dark Tower: Fall of Gilead #1 Sketch Variant Cover by Richard Isanove

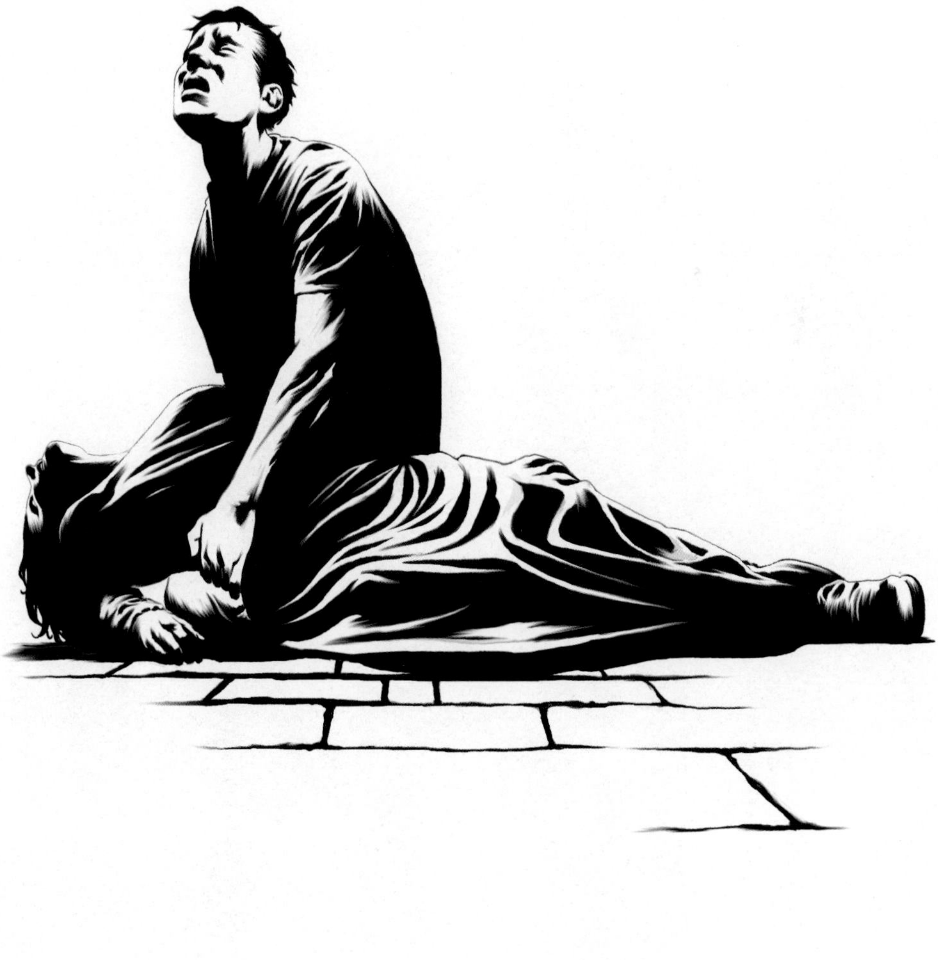

Dark Tower: Fall of Gilead **#2** Cover by Richard Isanove

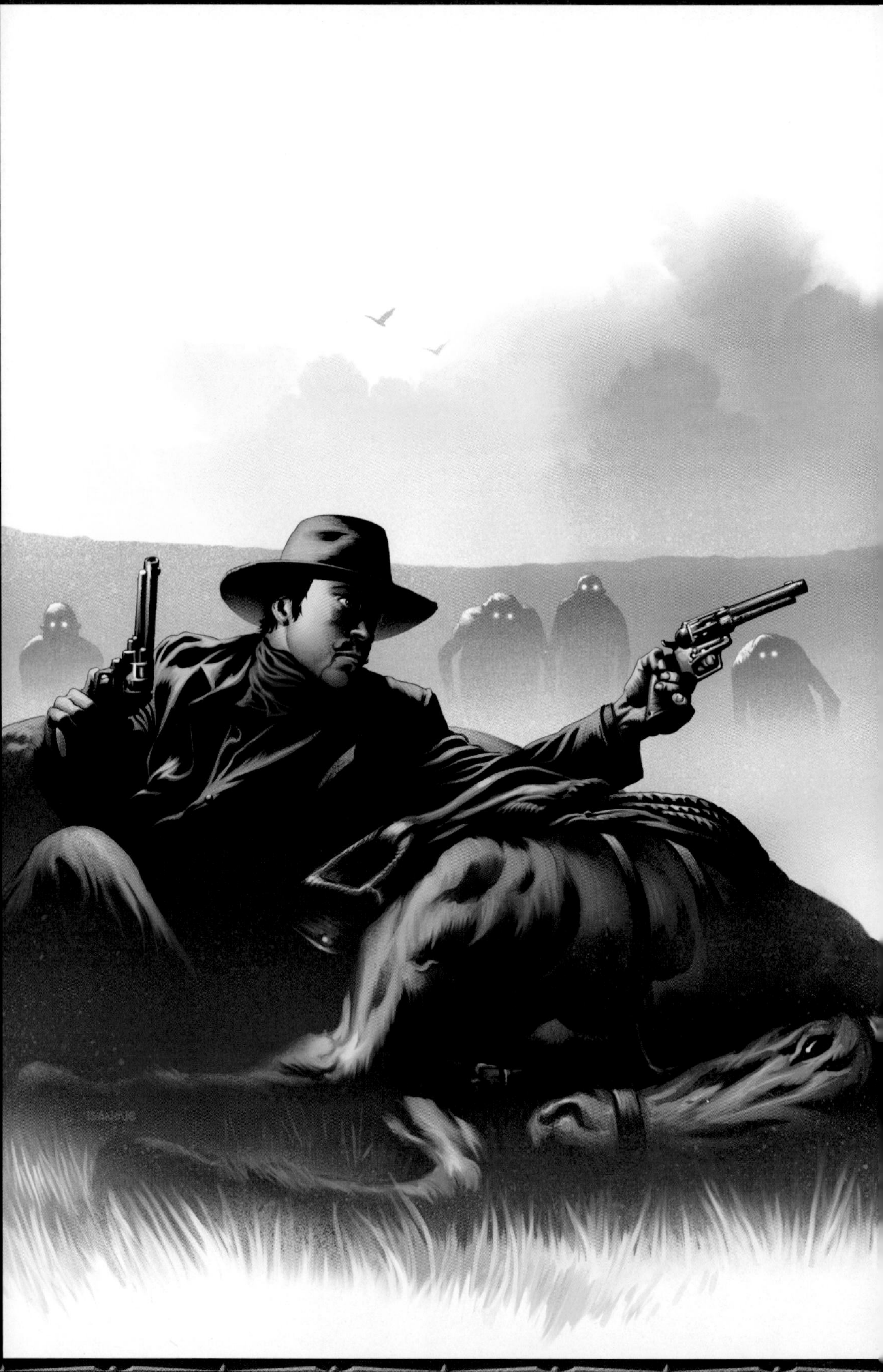
ISANOVE

Dark Tower: Fall of Gilead **#2** Sketch Variant Cover by Richard Isanove

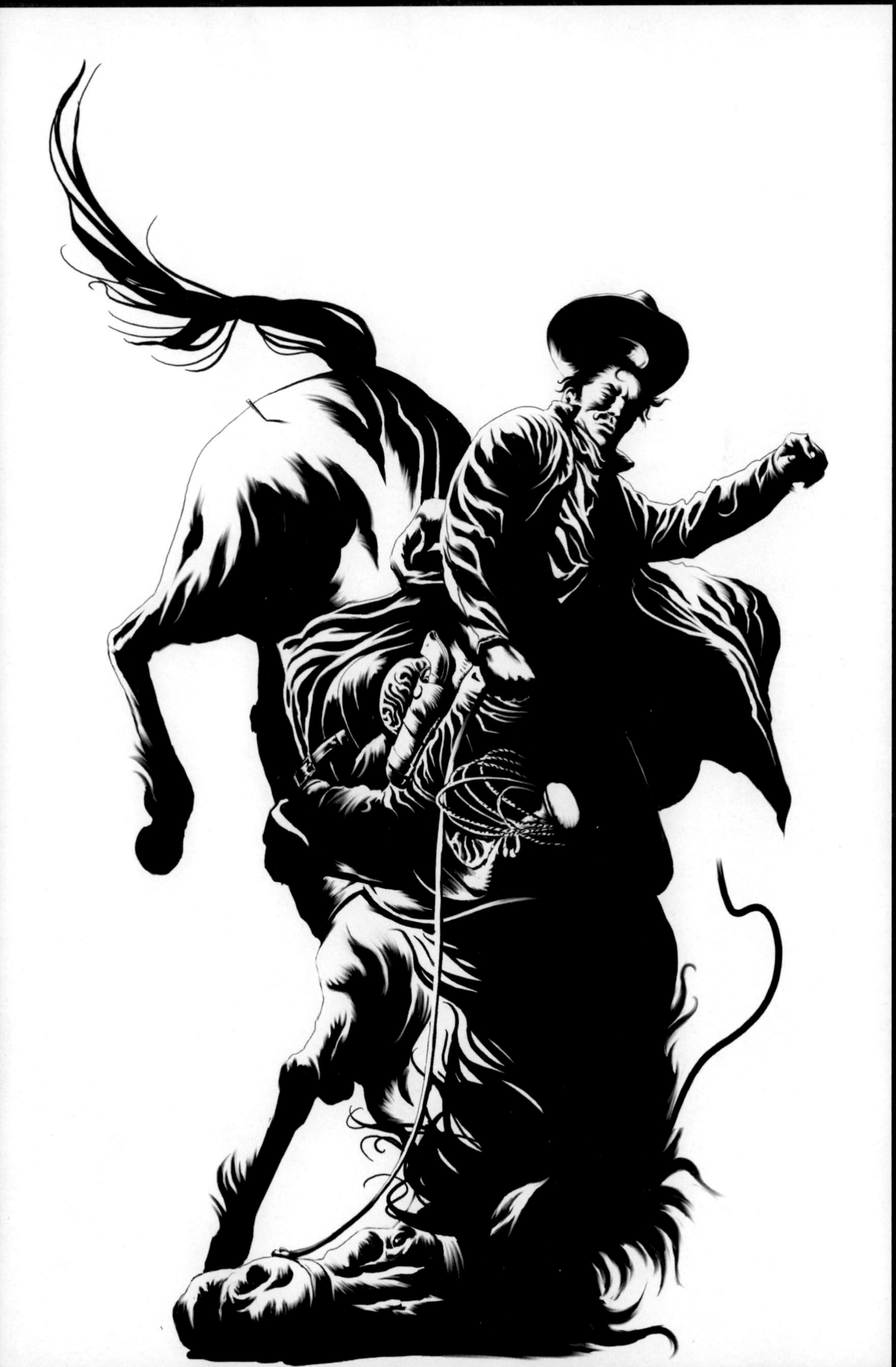

Dark Tower: Fall of Gilead #2 Variant Cover by Tommy Lee Edwards

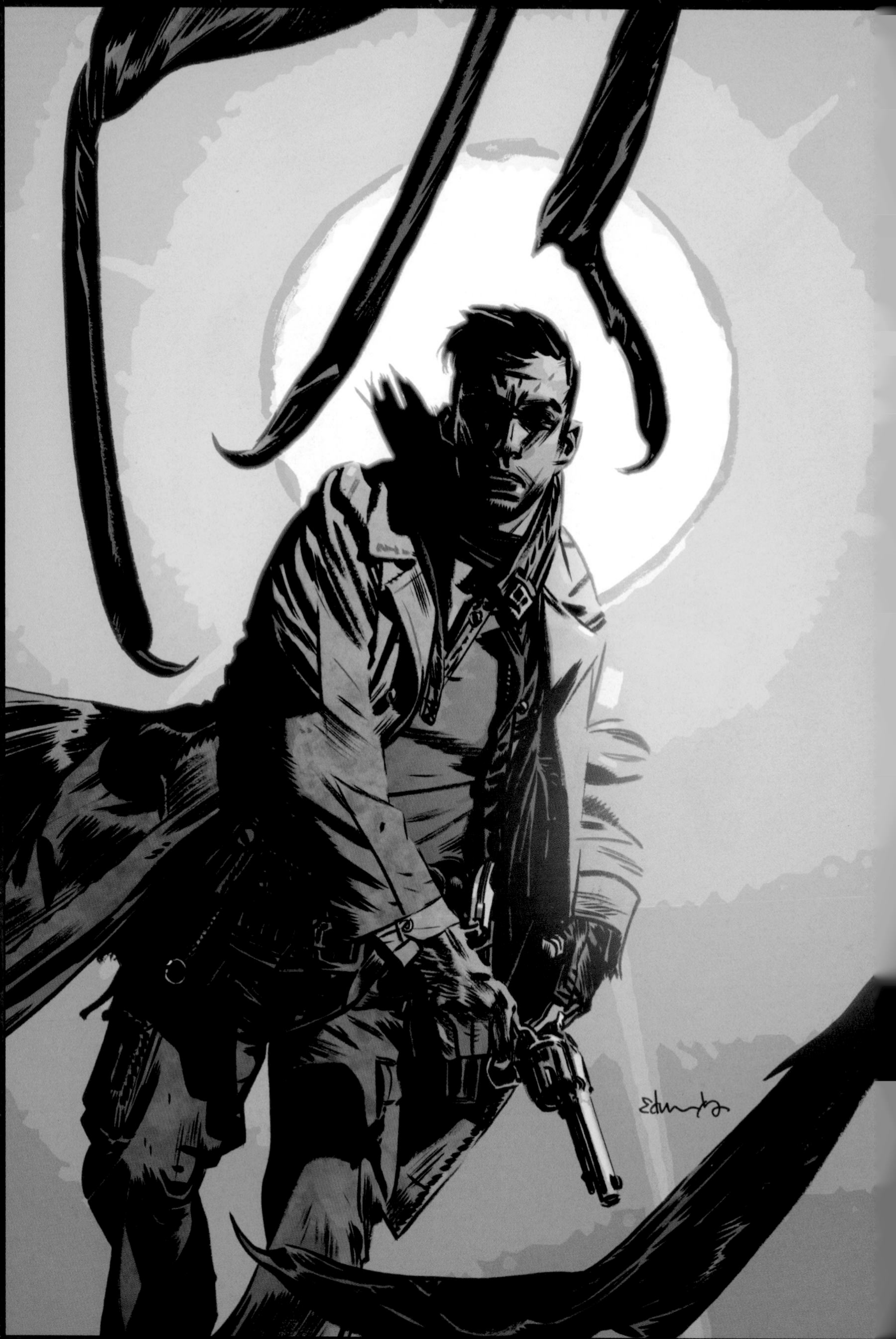

Dark Tower: Fall of Gilead #3 Variant Cover by Mitch Breitweiser

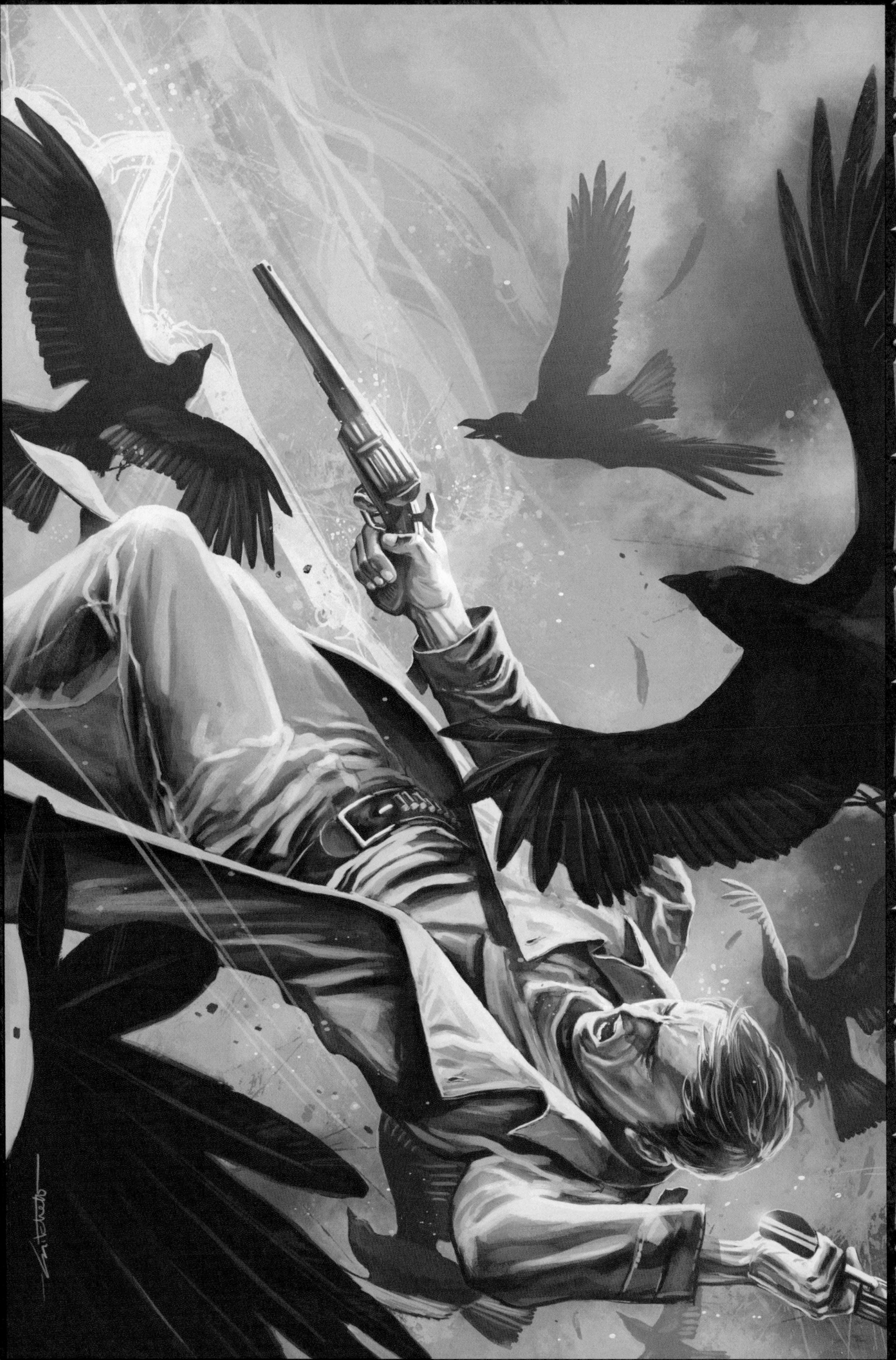

Dark Tower: Fall of Gilead #3 Cover by Richard Isanove

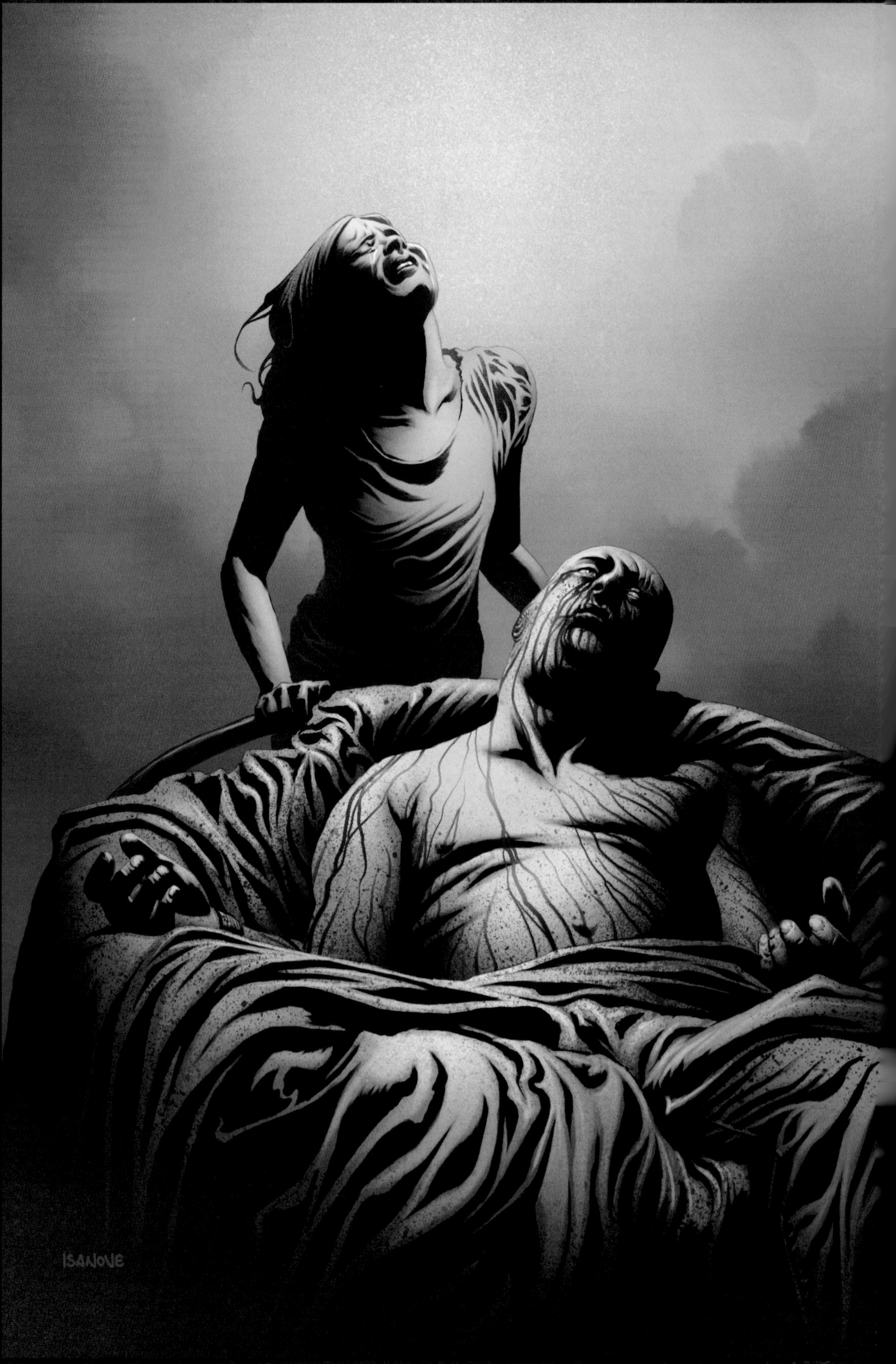
ISANOVE

Dark Tower: Fall of Gilead #3 Sketch Variant Cover by Richard Isanove

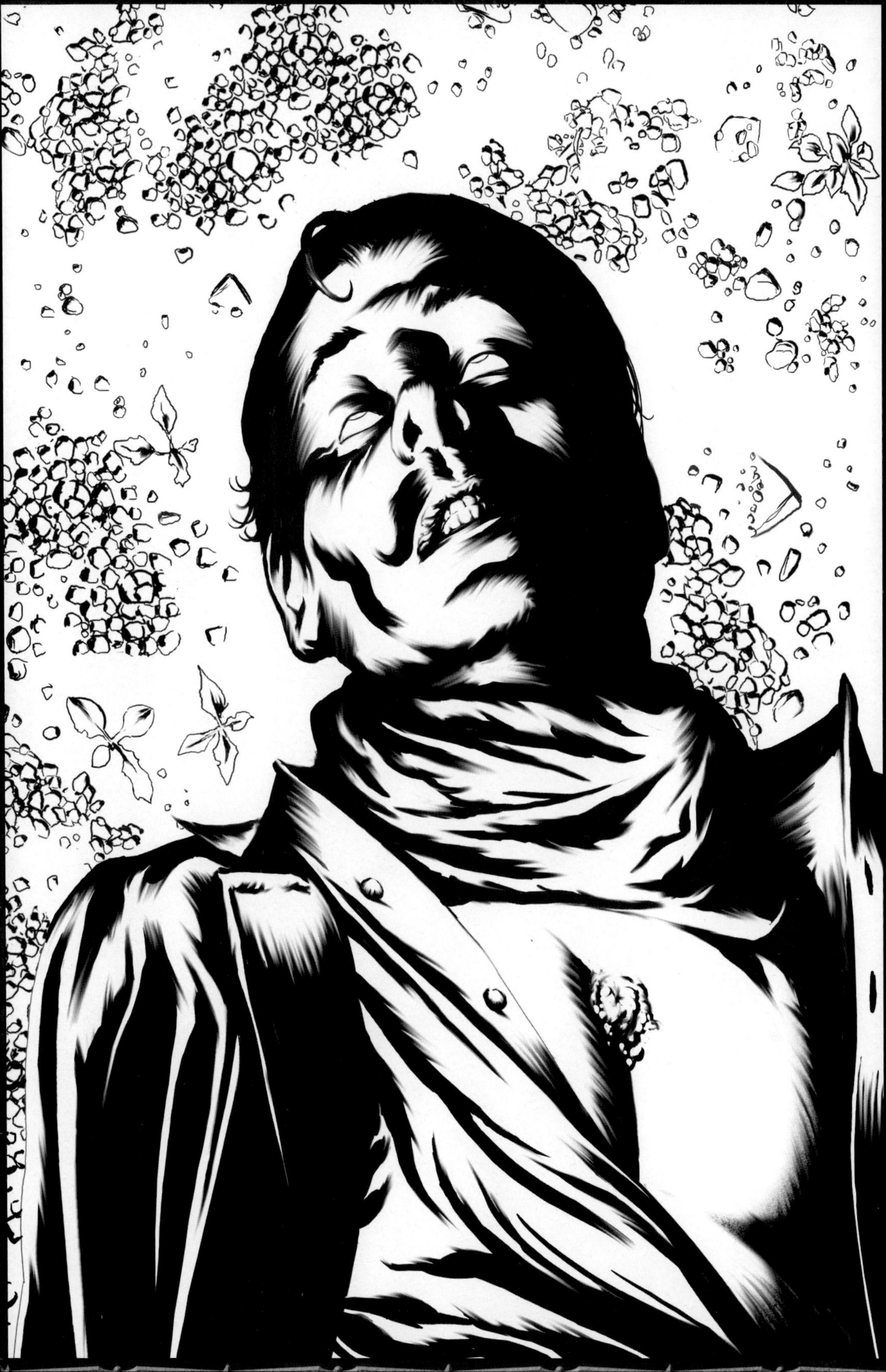

Dark Tower: Fall of Gilead #4 Cover by Richard Isanove

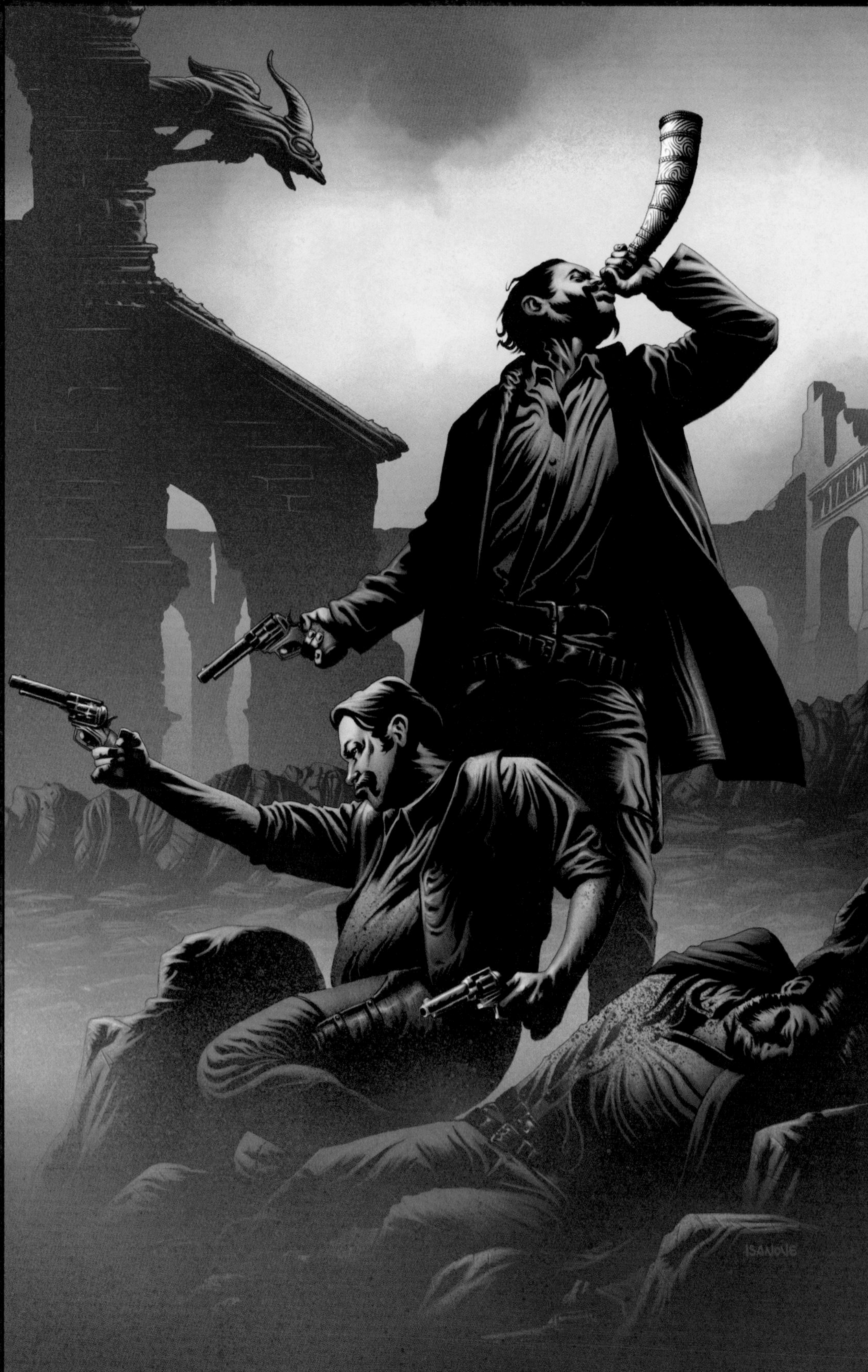
ISANOVE

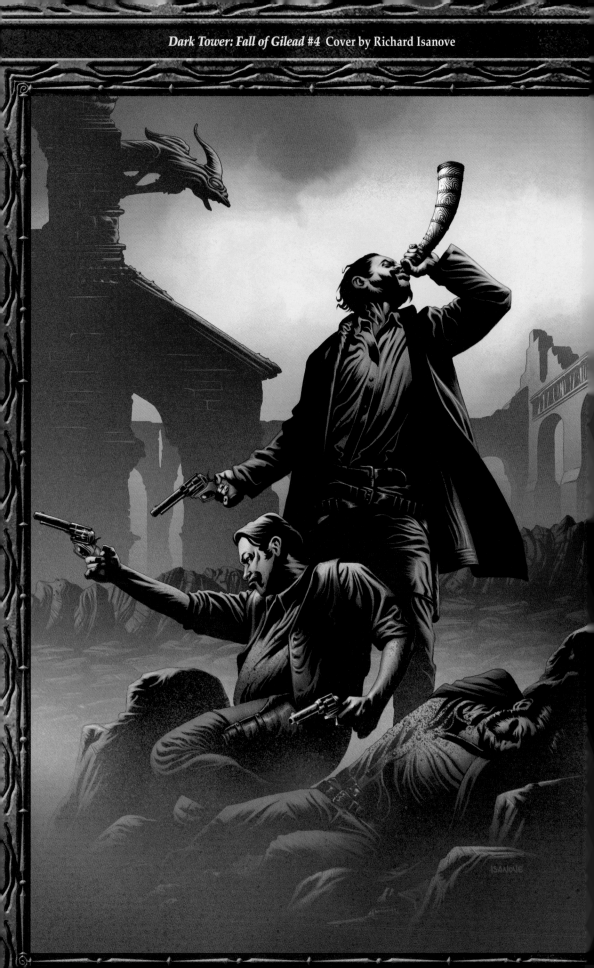

Dark Tower: Fall of Gilead #4 Sketch Variant Cover by Richard Isanove

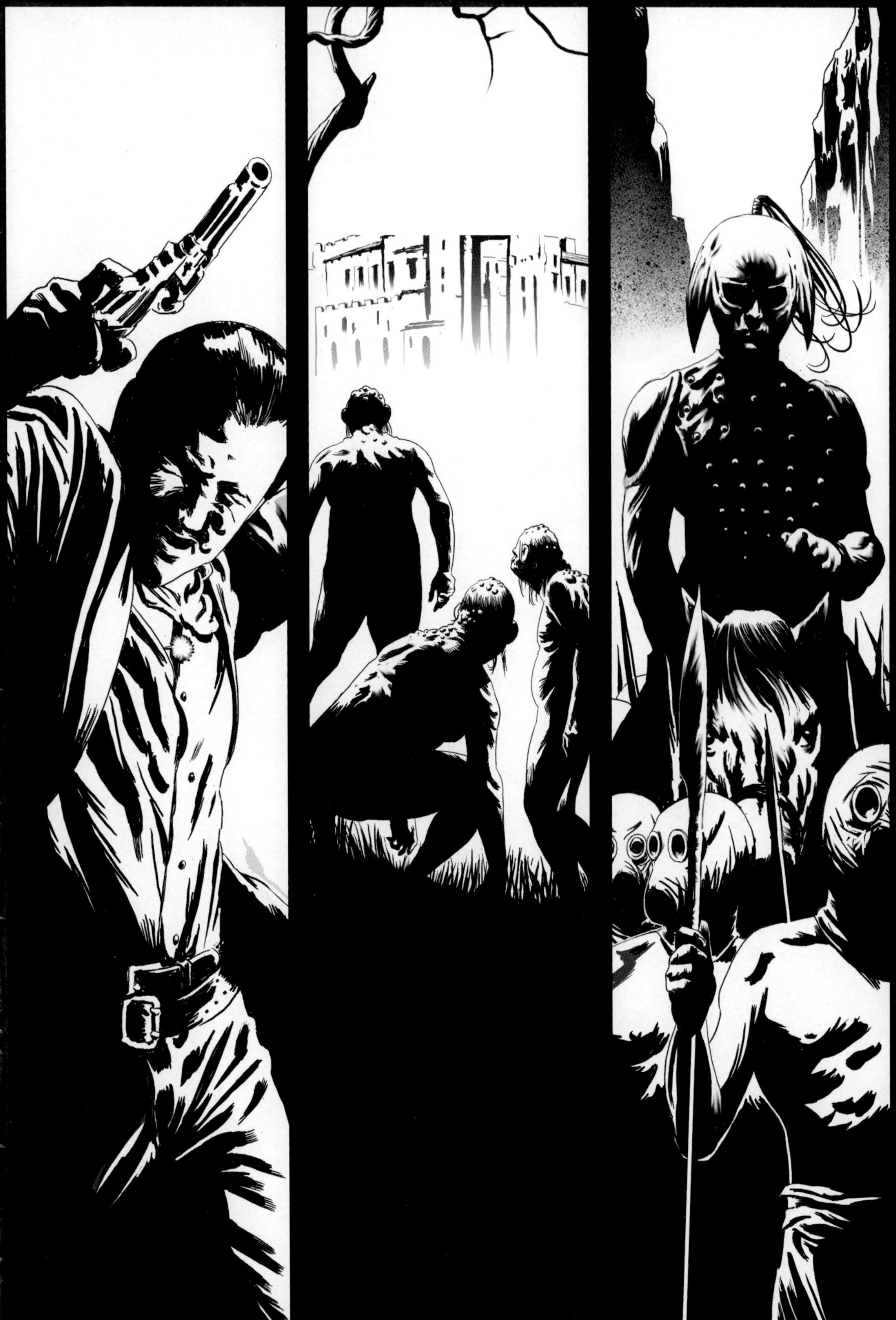

Dark Tower: Fall of Gilead #4 Variant Cover by David Lafuente

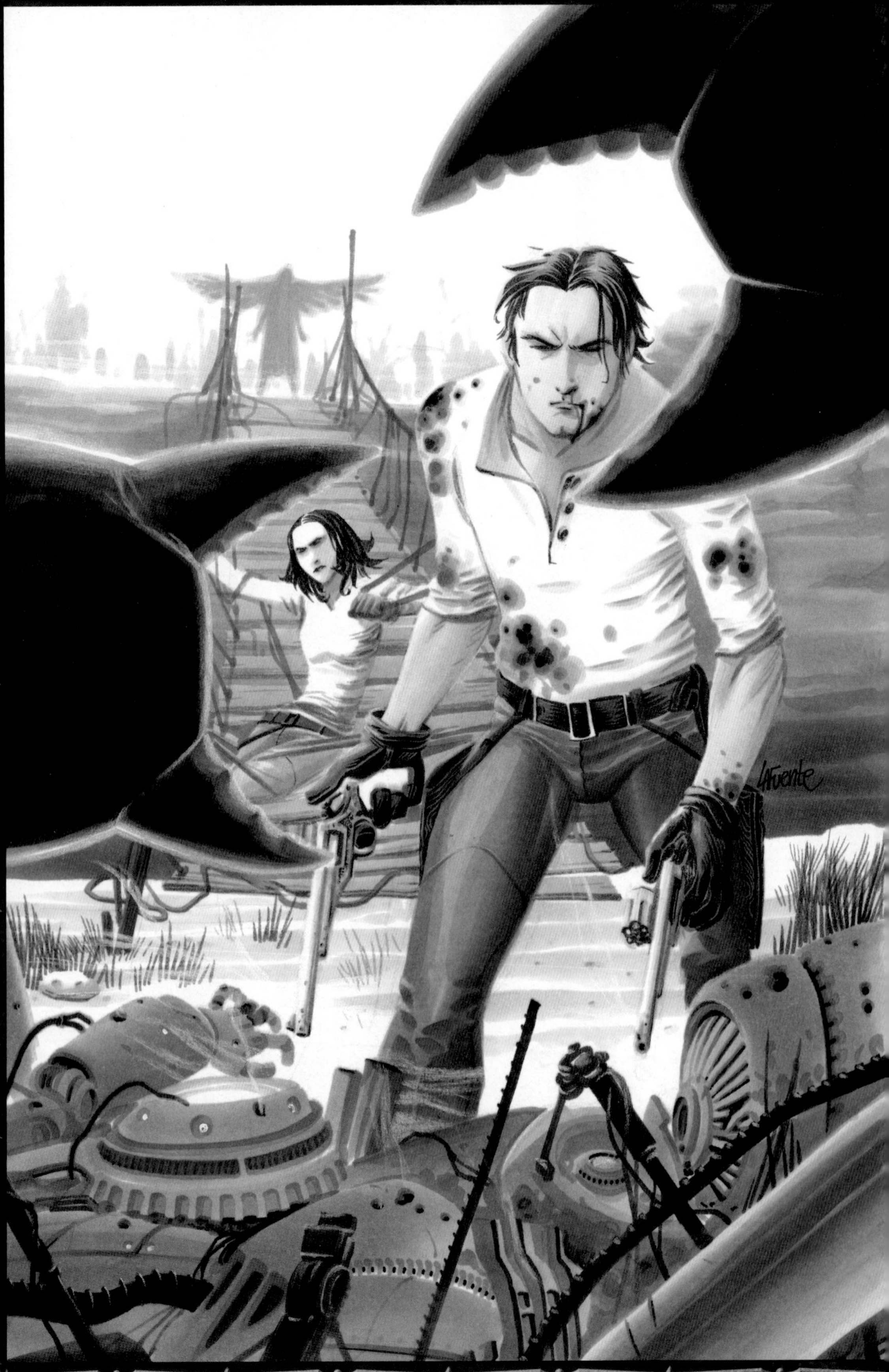
LAFUENTE

Dark Tower: Fall of Gilead **#5** Variant Cover by Rafa Sandoval

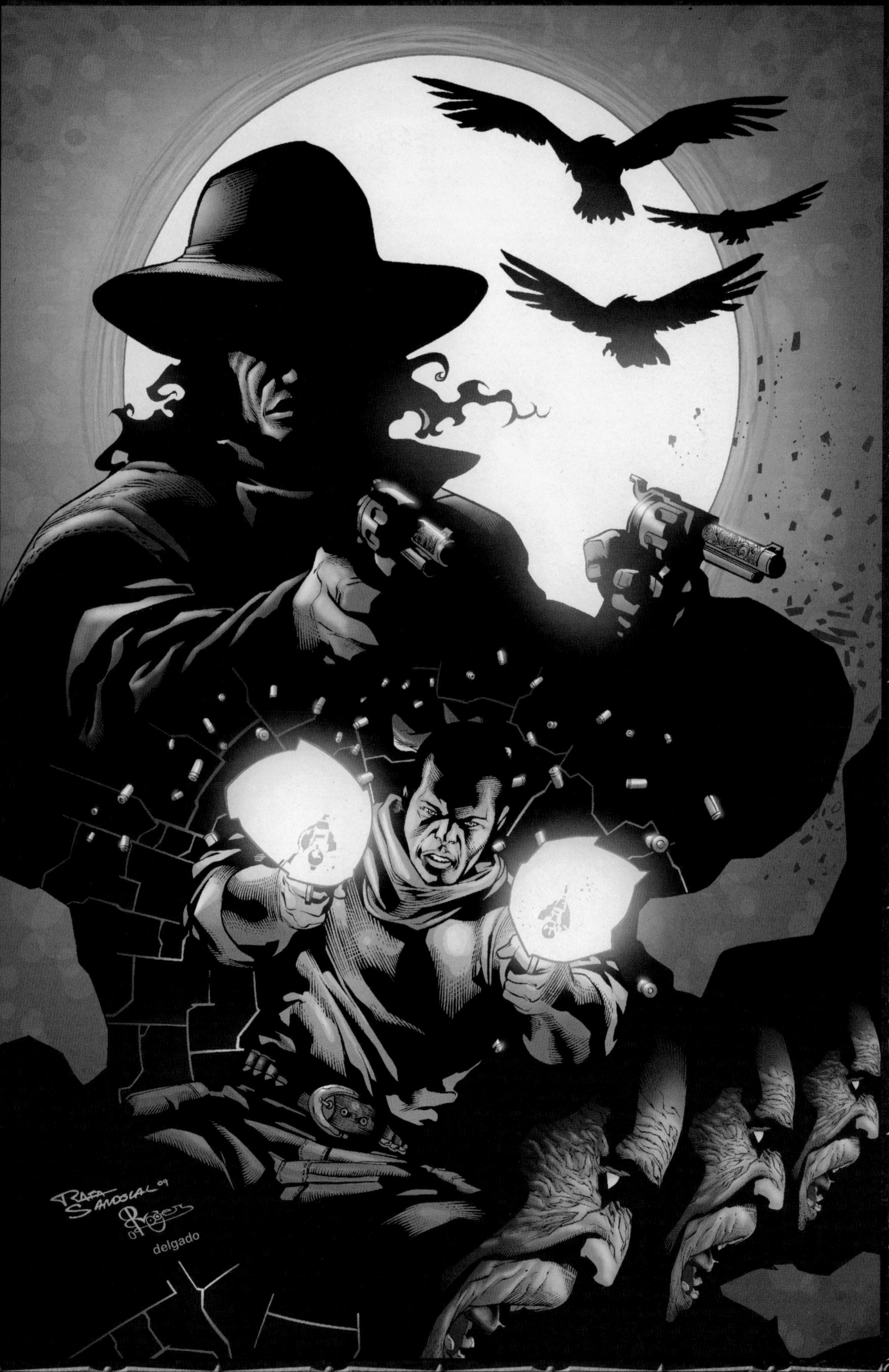
RAFA SANDOVAL 09
delgado

Dark Tower: Fall of Gilead #5 Cover by Richard Isanove

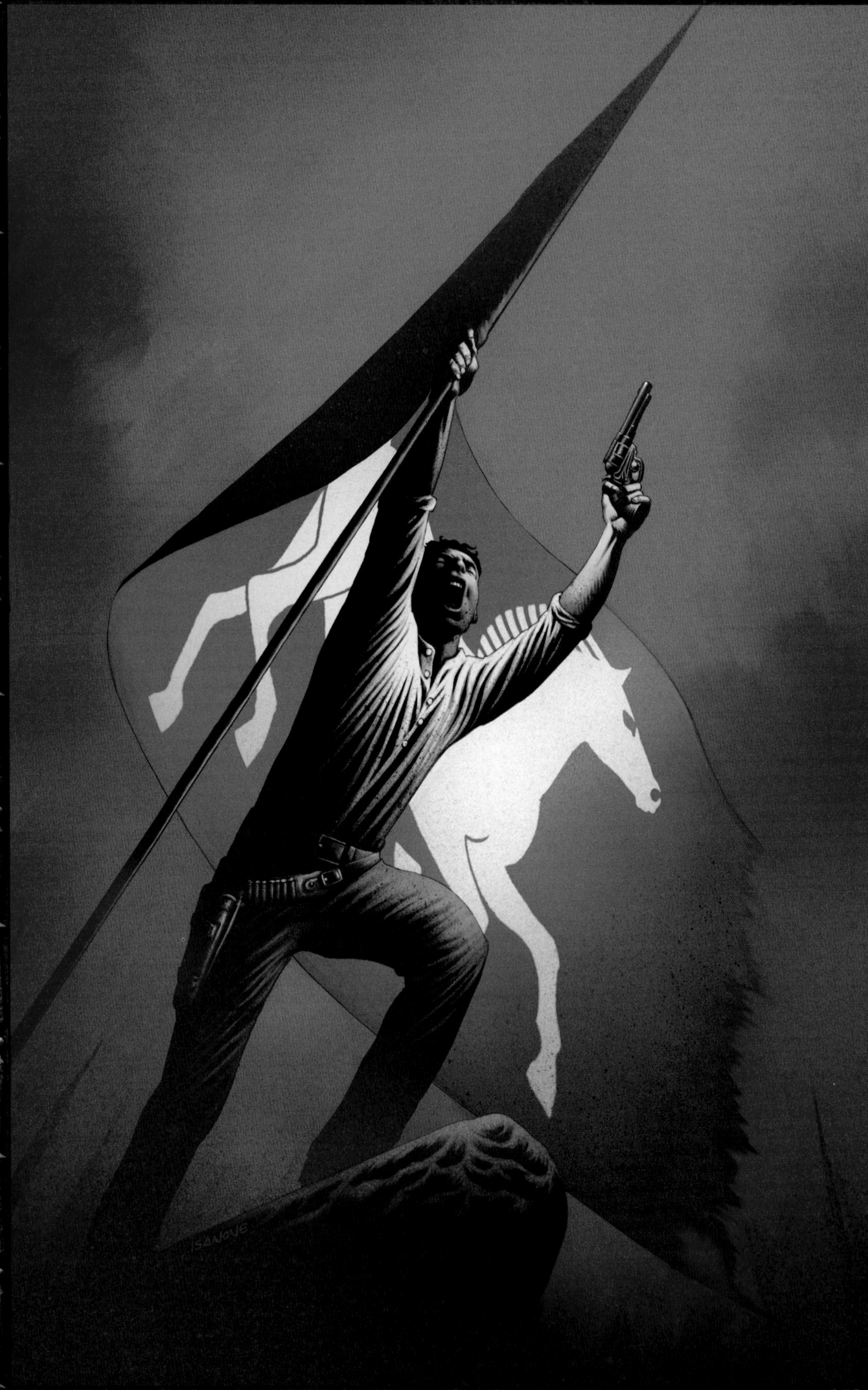
ISANOVE

Dark Tower: Fall of Gilead **#5** Sketch Variant Cover by Richard Isanove

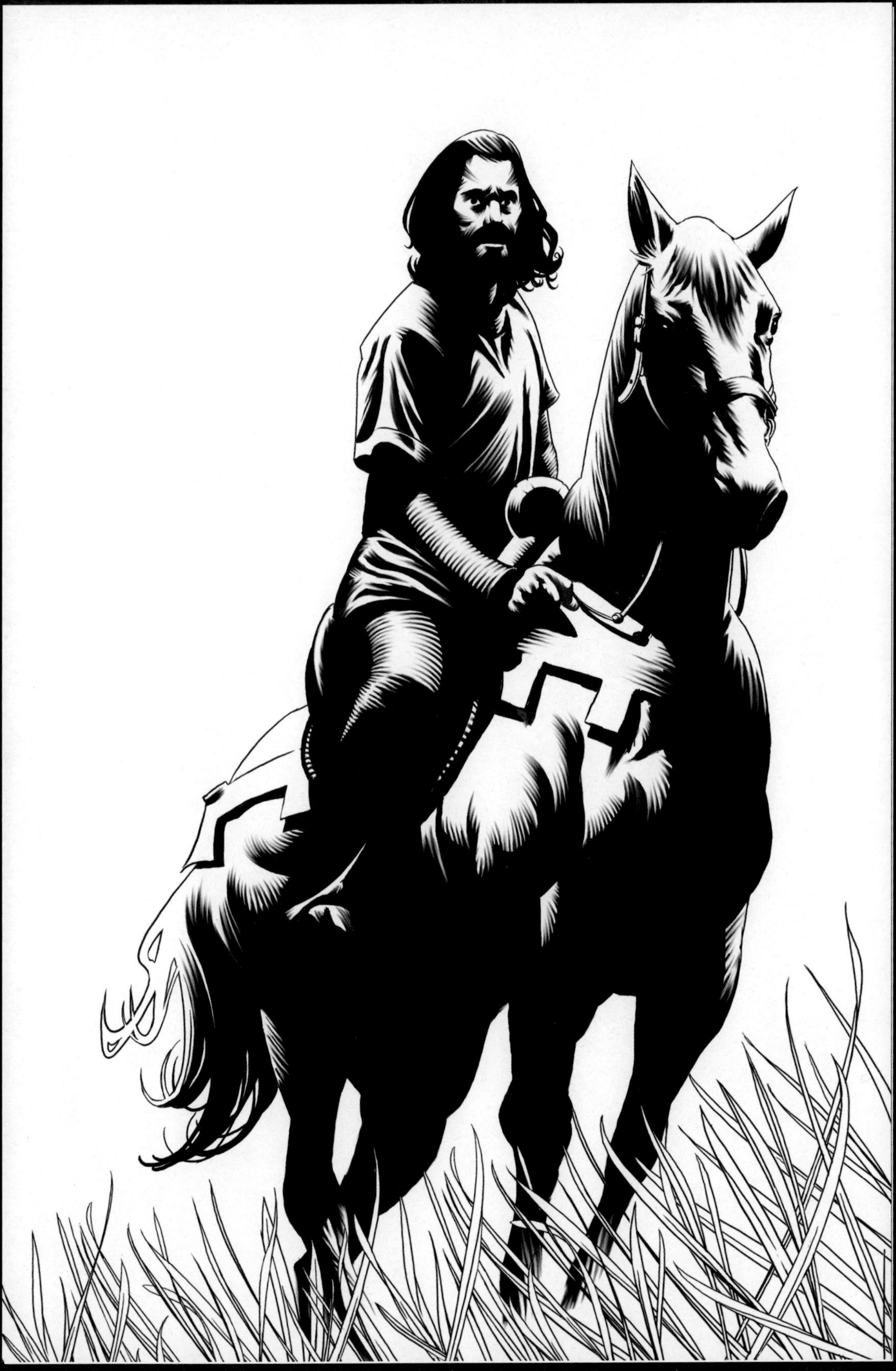

Dark Tower: Fall of Gilead #6 Cover by Richard Isanove

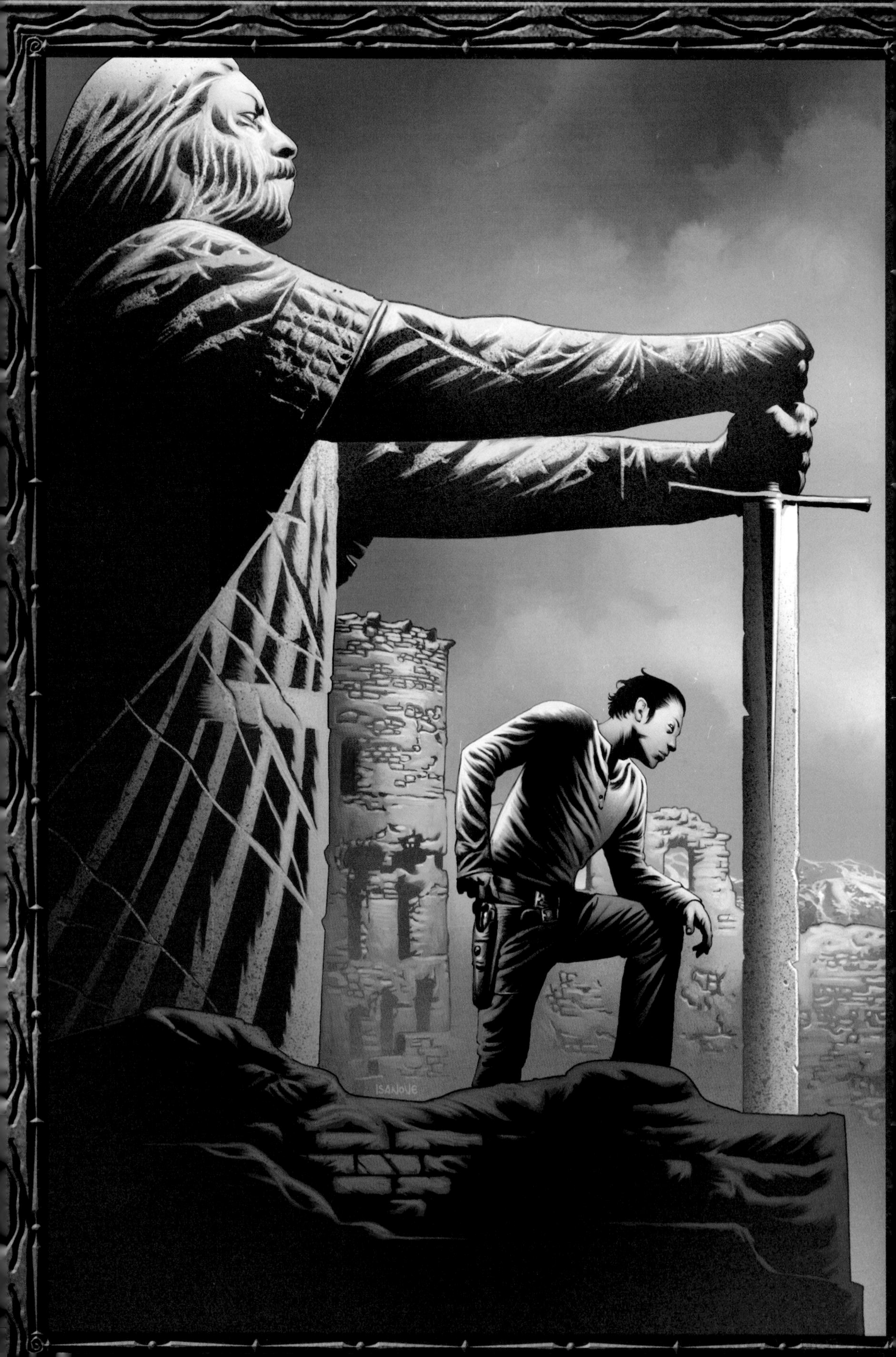

Dark Tower: Fall of Gilead #6 Sketch Variant Cover by Richard Isanove

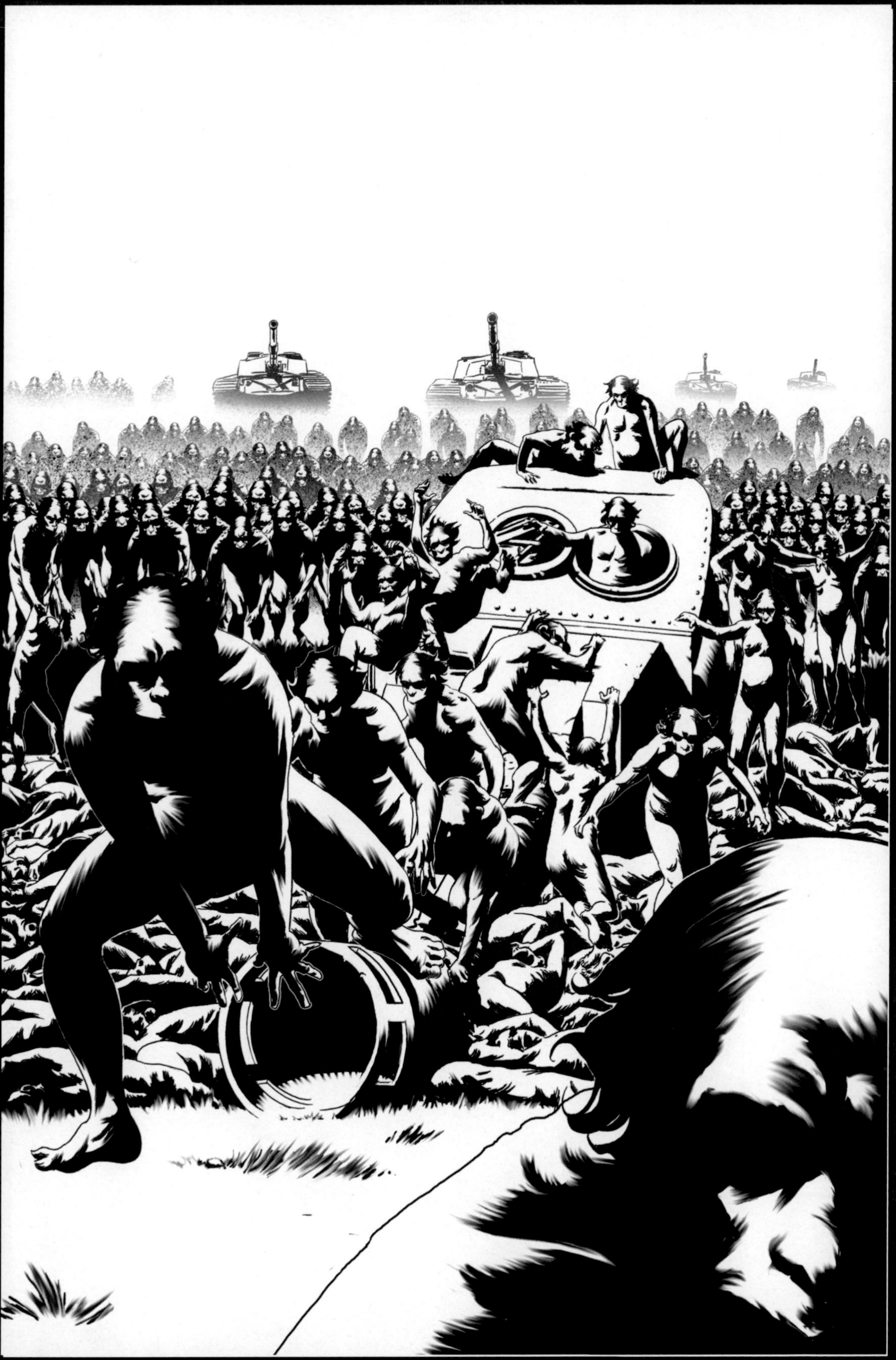

Dark Tower: Fall of Gilead #6 **Variant Cover by Tom Raney**

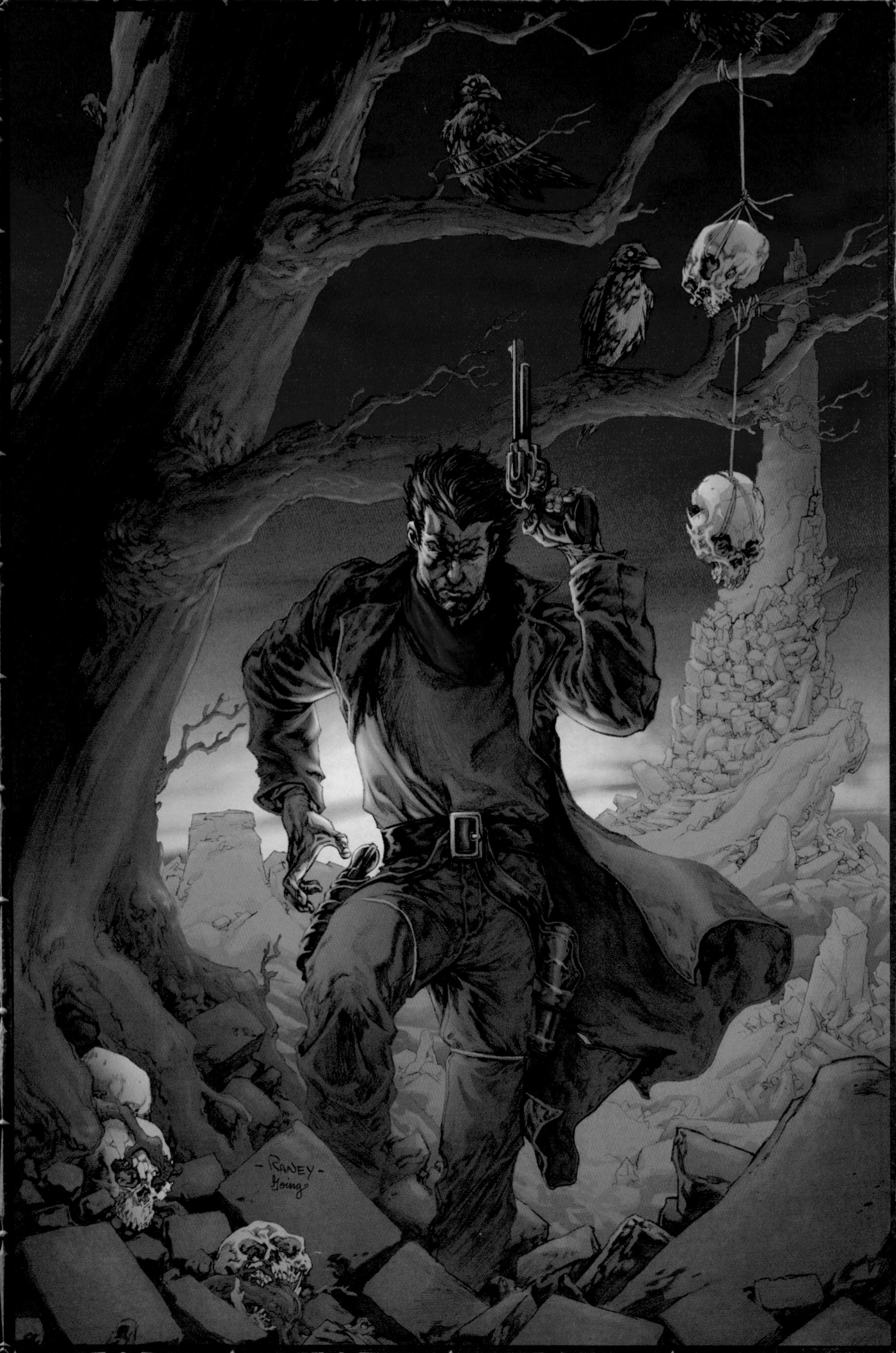
RANEY